Battling Resistance to Antibiotics and Pesticides

An Economic Approach

Edited by
Ramanan Laxminarayan

Resources for the Future
Washington, DC

Printed in the United States of America

An RFF Press book
Published by Resources for the Future
1616 P Street, NW, Washington, DC 20036–1400
www.rff.org

Library of Congress Cataloging-in-Publication Data

Battling resistance to antibiotics and pesticides : an economic approach / Ramanan Laxminarayan, editor.
    p. ; cm.
  Includes index.
    ISBN 1-891853-51-1 (hardcover : alk. paper)
1. Drug resistance in microorganisms. 2. Pesticide resistance. 3. Pesticide resistance—Economic aspects.
  [DNLM: 1. Drug Resistance. 2. Antibiotics—economics. 3. Antibiotics—standards. 4. Pesticides—economics. 5. Pesticides—standards. WB 330 B336 2002]
I. Laxminarayan, Ramanan.
  QR177 .B384 2002
  616'.01—dc21   2002010243

f e d c b a

The paper in this book meets the guidelines for permanence and durability of the Committee on Production Guidelines for Book Longevity of the Council on Library Resources.

The text of this book was designed by Betsy Kulamer and typeset in Stone Serif and Stone Sans by Carol Levie. The cover was designed by Marek Antioniak.

ISBN 1–891853–51–1

About
Resources for the Future
and *RFF Press*

Resources for the Future (RFF) improves environmental and natural resource policymaking worldwide through independent social science research of the highest caliber.

Founded in 1952, RFF pioneered the application of economics as a tool to develop more effective policy about the use and conservation of natural resources. Its scholars continue to employ social science methods to analyze critical issues concerning pollution control, energy policy, land and water use, hazardous waste, climate change, biodiversity, and the environmental challenges of developing countries.

RFF Press supports the mission of RFF by publishing book-length works that present a broad range of approaches to the study of natural resources and the environment. Its authors and editors include RFF staff, researchers from the larger academic and policy communities, and journalists. Audiences for RFF publications include all of the participants in the policymaking process—scholars, the media, advocacy groups, NGOs, professionals in business and government, and the general public.

Resources for the Future

Contents

Contributors...ix

About This Book xi

Introduction: On the Economics of Resistance 1
    Ramanan Laxminarayan

PART I. ISSUES OF OPTIMAL MANAGEMENT OF RESISTANCE

1   **Dynamics of Antibiotic Use: Ecological versus Interventionist
    Strategies To Manage Resistance to Antibiotics** 17
    James E. Wilen and Siwa Msangi

2   **Using Antibiotics When Resistance Is Renewable** 42
    Robert Rowthorn and Gardner M. Brown

3   **Value of Treatment Heterogeneity for Infectious Diseases** 63
    Ramanan Laxminarayan and Martin L. Weitzman

    Commentary: To Take or Not To Take the Antibiotic? 76
    James N. Sanchirico

    Commentary: Same Infection, Same Time, Same Antibiotic? 84
    Stephen W. Salant

4   **Pest Mobility, Market Share, and the Efficacy of Refuge Requirements for
    Resistance Management** 94
    Silvia Secchi and Bruce A. Babcock

    Commentary: Need for Direct Collaboration between Economists
    and Biologists 113
    Fred Gould

PART II. THE IMPACT OF RESISTANCE

5   **The Impact of Resistance on Antibiotic Demand in Patients with Ear Infections** 119
David H. Howard and Kimberly J. Rask

Commentary: Measuring the Cost of Resistance 134
Ramanan Laxminarayan

6   **What Can We Learn from the Economics of Pesticides? Impact Assessment of Genetically Modified Plants** 137
Hermann Waibel, Jan C. Zadoks, and Gerd Fleischer

Commentary: The Role of Ecosystem Complexity in Genetically Modified Organisms 158
Karl Seeley

7   **Elements of Economic Resistance Management Strategies— Empirical Evidence from Case Studies in Germany** 161
Gerd Fleischer and Hermann Waibel

Commentary: Can We Justify Resistance Management Strategies for Conventional Pesticides? 180
Fred Gould

8   **Pesticide Resistance, the Precautionary Principle, and the Regulation of *Bt* Corn: Real Option and Rational Option Approaches to Decisionmaking** 184
Benoît Morel, R. Scott Farrow, Felicia Wu, and Elizabeth A. Casman

9   **Resistance Economics of Transgenic Crops under Uncertainty: A Real Option Approach** 214
Justus Wesseler

Commentary: Economics of Transgenic Crops and Pest Resistance: An Epidemiological Perspective 238
Christopher A. Gilligan

PART III. THE BEHAVIOR OF FIRMS

10   **An Economic Model of a Genetic Resistance Commons: Effects of Market Structure Applied to Biotechnology in Agriculture** 263
Douglas Noonan

Commentary: Does the Monopolist Care about Resistance? 288
Carolyn Fischer

11 The Interaction of Dynamic Problems and Dynamic Policies:
    Some Economics of Biotechnology 293
    Timo Goeschl and Timothy Swanson

12 Industrial Organization and Institutional Considerations in
    Agricultural Pest Resistance Management 330
    Jennifer Alix and David Zilberman

Commentary: Strategic Issues in Agricultural Pest Resistance Management 357
    R. David Simpson

Index...363

About the Editor..377

Contributors

Jennifer Alix, graduate student, Department of Agricultural and Resource Economics, University of California, Berkeley

Bruce A. Babcock, director, Center for Agricultural and Rural Development, and professor, Department of Economics, Iowa State University

Gardner M. Brown, professor, Department of Economics, University of Washington

Elizabeth A. Casman, research engineer, Department of Engineering and Public Policy Carnegie Mellon University

R. Scott Farrow, principal research economist, Department of Engineering and Public Policy, and director, Center for the Study and Improvement of Regulation, Carnegie Mellon University

Carolyn Fischer, fellow, Resources for the Future

Gerd Fleischer, Integrated Pest Management policy expert, Rural Development Department, The World Bank

Christopher A. Gilligan, professor, Department of Plant Sciences, University of Cambridge, United Kingdom

Timo Goeschl, university lecturer, Department of Land Economy, University of Cambridge, United Kingdom

Fred Gould, professor, Department of Entomology, North Carolina State University

David H. Howard, assistant professor, Rollins School of Public Health, Emory University

Ramanan Laxminarayan, fellow, Resources for the Future

Benoît Morel, senior lecturer, Department of Engineering and Public Policy, and Department of Physics, Carnegie Mellon University

Siwa Msangi, graduate student, Department of Agricultural and Resource Economics, University of California, Davis

Douglas Noonan, graduate student, Harris School of Public Policy Studies, University of Chicago

Kimberly J. Rask, professor, Rollins School of Public Health, Emory University

Robert Rowthorn, professor, Faculty of Economics and Politics, University of Cambridge, United Kingdom

Stephen W. Salant, professor, Department of Economics, University of Michigan

James N. Sanchirico, fellow, Resources for the Future

Silvia Secchi, assistant scientist, Center for Agricultural and Rural Development, Iowa State University

Martin L. Weitzman, professor, Department of Economics, Harvard University

Karl Seeley, assistant professor, Department of Economics, Hartwick College

R. David Simpson, senior fellow, Resources for the Future

Timothy Swanson, professor, Department of Economics and Faculty of Law, University College London, United Kingdom

Hermann Waibel, professor, Institute of Economics in Horticulture and Agriculture, Department of Economics, University of Hannover, Germany

Justus Wesseler, assistant professor, Environmental Economics and Natural Resources Group, Social Sciences Department, Wageningen University and Research Center, The Netherlands

James E. Wilen, professor, Department of Agricultural and Resource Economics, University of California, Davis

Felicia Wu, graduate student, Department of Engineering and Public Policy Carnegie Mellon University

Jan C. Zadoks, professor emeritus, Laboratory of Phytopathology, Wageningen University, The Netherlands

David Zilberman, professor, Department of Agricultural and Resource Economics, University of California, Berkeley

About This Book

In recent decades, efforts to control biological organisms harmful to humans and human enterprise have been constrained by the growing resistance of these organisms to the control agents. Examples of such organisms include agricultural pests and disease-causing bacteria and viruses. Organisms with characteristics that allow them to survive the effects of control agents are favored by Darwinian selection. Over time, these resistant organisms dominate organisms that are susceptible to control agents. The evolution of resistance is strongly influenced by the behavior of individuals and institutions. In the absence of suitable economic incentives, decisionmakers (such as patients, physicians, and growers) fail to take into account the negative impact of their use of antibiotics or pesticides on future social well-being. *Battling Resistance to Antibiotics and Pesticides: An Economic Approach* is a first attempt to bring together a variety of approaches to the economics of resistance. The papers assembled here represent the cutting edge of research in this emerging field of study.

The development of bacterial resistance to antibiotics is growing to be a significant challenge in medicine, as is increasing pest resistance to pesticides in agriculture. To give but one example, the prevalence of high-level penicillin resistance in *Streptococcus pneumoniae* in the United States increased 800-fold from 0.02% in 1987 to 16.5% in 1999. Over the same period, the increase in the number of pest species resistant to one or more pesticides was no less dramatic. Balanced against these dismal statistics is hope in the form of new technologies such as pest-resistant genetically modified crops and new treatments for malaria. The present time affords a unique opportunity to learn from past experience to ensure that existing and future products are used wisely.

This book demonstrates the application of economic analysis to maximize the value of antibiotics and pesticides to society. It examines earlier efforts to manage resistance, especially in the field of agriculture, and discusses incentives that influence the behavior of firms engaged in developing and producing these products. It shows how an economic approach can not only shed light on how antibiotics and pesticides could be better used but also can help structure economic and regulatory incentives to ensure that individuals and firms act in a manner that is consistent with societal objectives.

Although the chapters in this book are focused on economic analysis, the issues they deal with are relevant to a broad audience. Detailed analyses of the multiple dimensions of resistance, lessons from past attempts to manage resistance, and directions for future strategies to combat resistance are aspects of the book that will be useful to policymakers. For professionals in the medical, public health, and agricultural arenas, the book attempts to translate some of the current economic approaches to managing resistance into guidance for practitioners.[1] Economists are provided with an overview of the relevant scientific issues as well as a variety of analytical approaches to studying the economics of resistance to antibiotics and pesticides.

The chapters in this book were developed from papers originally written for a conference on the Economics of Resistance organized by Resources for the Future and held at Airlie House in Warrenton, Virginia, on April 5 and 6, 2001.[2] The conference was held to encourage the formation of a research community to address issues related to the economics of resistance. The roughly 70 conference participants included academics; social science and medical researchers; and representatives from U.S. government agencies (Food and Drug Administration [FDA], Centers for Disease Control and Prevention [CDC], Environmental Protection Agency [EPA]), nongovernmental organizations, and the health care, pharmaceutical, and agribusiness industries. A number of participants were from countries other than the United States, including Canada, the United Kingdom, Germany, the Netherlands, and Israel. The wide array of expertise forced interdisciplinary communication that contributed to the understanding of what economics can provide in terms of making better use of biological control agents such as antibiotics and pesticides and for disciplining scientific assumptions made in economic models used to study the evolution of resistance. This book reflects the dialogue between economists, medical and agricultural experts, and policymakers at the meeting.

To a reader who has managed to escape a graduate degree in economics, the chapters in this book may appear, at first glance, to be fairly technical. Because these chapters represent some of the earliest efforts in this emerging area, much emphasis has been placed on perfecting the methodology—a fact that might not be immediately apparent to a scientific or policy audience. To make these chapters accessible to a wider audience, commentaries written by natural scientists and economists supplement the chapter summaries written by the authors themselves. The next section provides an overview of how these chapters fit together and what insights they provide. These pieces, in conjunction with the introduction to the economics of resistance in the next section, attempt to inform policymakers and health and agricultural professionals of the kinds of analyses economists engage in and to indicate the kinds of answers economists might provide in future work.[3]

Overview of Chapters

Rather than divide this book between antibiotics and pesticides, the 12 chapters have been organized into three thematic parts. Part I focuses on the use of economic tools to characterize the efficient use of antibiotics and pesticides in the face of resistance. Part II deals with a broad array of issues related to the economic impact of resistance and decisionmaking under uncertainty about future resistance. Part III examines incentives faced by companies that make antibiotics and pesticides and describes how regulatory incentives might be structured for these industries. The obvious advantage of this arrangement is that it emphasizes the commonality of issues that arise in the medical and agricultural contexts and provides the reader with insights into the issue of resistance at a broader level of abstraction.

The two opening chapters of Part I by Wilen and Msangi and Rowthorn and Brown use similar approaches to extend our understanding of the optimal use of antibiotics when there is a significant fitness cost associated with bacterial resistance. In Chapter 1, Wilen and Msangi tackle the problem of optimal use of a single antibiotic and compare strategies that lower the overall transmission of infection through better infection control methods (such as frequent hand washing by nursing staff) with those that improve antibiotic use (such as treatment guidelines and switching protocols). Although epidemiological studies have shown that infection control can be remarkably efficient in controlling the emergence of drug resistance, especially in hospital settings, this aspect of resistance management has not received sufficient attention. By comparing these policies in an economic framework, Wilen and Msangi are able to describe the balance of antibiotic control and infection control that is economically efficient. The economic element in determining this balance is worth emphasizing and can be illustrated by a provocatively extreme example. A policy of assigning a single nursing staff to a single patient can be very effective in controlling resistance, but the costs of doing so would be enormous. By using an economic metric, we can compare the economic benefit of a particular resistance management policy against the costs of implementing such a policy.

Chapter 2 by Rowthorn and Brown examines how we can make the best use of two antibiotics, each of which is effective against one strain of bacteria but not against the other. At the time of treatment, the physician may be unaware of the specific bacterial strain that he or she is treating and chooses the best possible treatment, keeping in mind that a successful treatment may cure the patient but could also increase the likelihood of resistance in the future. The authors conclude that it makes sense to treat all patients with the antibiotic that is effective against the more prevalent strain, under certain conditions, even if that antibiotic is relatively more expensive. Although one may not necessarily encounter the problem of two drugs used to treat two mutually exclusive diseases in a clinical setting, the model developed here offers a framework and provides a point of departure for more realistic variations of the problem.

Chapter 3 by Laxminarayan and Weitzman deals with the issue of treatment homogeneity when resistance is a problem. This chapter uses a fairly simple approach to show that when resistance arises as a consequence of antibiotic use, it may be shortsighted to use a single antibiotic on all patients just because that antibiotic appears to be the most cost-effective option. Indeed, it may be optimal, from society's point of view, to use different drugs on different, but observationally identical, patients and include among this menu of drugs some that may not be cost-effective from the individual patient's perspective. This result has important consequences for how one approaches antibiotic or antimalarial treatment.

In Chapter 4, Secchi and Babcock deal with the issue of optimal refuge strategies for pests when pests are mobile. A brief introduction to this topic may be helpful here. Recent improvements in agricultural technology have included the adoption of genetically modified *Bt* crops that code for the production of a protein produced in nature by the bacterium *Bacillus thuringiensis* (*Bt*). The *Bt* protein has been found to be an extremely effective pesticide while being relatively ecologically benign. Since 1998, EPA has required that all farmers growing *Bt* crops plant a certain proportion of their fields with non-*Bt* crops to delay the emergence of resistance. The underlying theory is that the non-*Bt* crops would provide a refuge for pests susceptible to *Bt*, which could then mate with the *Bt*-resistant pests that would inevitably arise from exposure of pests to *Bt* toxin. The resulting organism, it is argued, would be susceptible to *Bt* and would help reduce the likelihood that a fully resistant *Bt*-resistant pest would evolve. Current refuge requirements are made on the basis of fairly rigid assumptions about the degree of market penetration of *Bt* crops and of mobility of pests. When market penetration is assumed to be less than complete and pests are assumed to be mobile, then there is potential for non-*Bt* fields to operate as natural refuges for *Bt*-susceptible pests. Secchi and Babcock use a model of evolution of pest resistance to show that high pest mobility and low market penetration can be substitutes in managing pest resistance. When rigid assumptions such as 100% market penetration are relaxed, they find that the optimal level of refuge on *Bt* fields will be considerably smaller than the 20% refuge that is currently mandated. These conclusions are important considering the possibility that more stringent refuge requirements may result in lower compliance with refuge requirements.

Part II begins with a chapter by Howard and Rask that takes on a challenging issue in the economics of resistance—measuring the economic costs of resistance. Using data on antibiotics used to treat ear infections from the National Ambulatory Medical Care Survey from 1980 to 1998, the authors estimate the increase in the cost of antibiotic treatment attributable to increases in bacterial resistance. Although their approach is hampered by a lack of data on resistance, their analysis (which uses time as a proxy for increasing resistance) offers some insight into the order of magnitude of costs of resistance. Between 1997 and 1998, increases in drug resistance are estimated to have raised the cost of treating ear infections by about 20% ($216 million).

Chapter 6 by Waibel, Zadoks, and Fleischer shows how lessons learned from past experience with pesticides can help guide current and future regulation on *Bt* crops. They provide an overview of various methodological issues related to empirically assessing the impact of pesticides on agricultural production. Further, they argue that evaluations of *Bt* technology that take into account the resistance-related costs associated with this technology as well as recognize the alternative pest control options available to farmers are important to ensure that the benefits of this technology are not overestimated.

In Chapter 7, Fleischer and Waibel evaluate the economic impact of pest resistance to pesticides using two case studies from Germany. In the first study, they examine whether pest control costs have been increasing as a consequence of pest resistance, taking into account technological improvements in pesticides. Specifically, they identify an economic cost to pest resistance by looking at trends in consumption of pesticides relative to other chemicals on farm inputs. In the second study, they examine the private and social costs of weed resistance to atrazine. The share of maize is positively correlated with the use of atrazine. Therefore, fields that have high shares of maize reflect an implicit willingness on the part of farmers to sacrifice atrazine effectiveness in the future for greater short-term profits. Atrazine was banned in 1991, partly because of its environmental impact of polluting groundwater sources. Because farmers who used atrazine more intensively before the ban were also likely to have achieved greater profits in the short run, the ban resulted in a negative impact of these farmers' decisions on others who had been more conservative with their use of herbicides.

The methodological hurdles faced by these analyses are similar in some respects to those in the earlier chapter by Howard and Rask, illustrating the xvi • About This Book

significant advantages in contemplating analytical methods to study the economic impact of resistance. This chapter also illustrates the problem of externalities that are pervasive in the use of any pest control technology. For instance, organic farmers have used *Bt* foliar sprays for many years because *Bt* spray is one of the few pest control technologies considered to be nonchemical. With the embedding of *Bt* toxin in new crops, the widespread adoption of *Bt* crops threatens the effectiveness of foliar sprays via the development of resistance. Although conventional farmers may be able to switch to other control methods when resistance evolves, the negative impact of their adoption on organic farmers may be more long term.

Chapter 8 by Morel, Farrow, Wu, and Casman, and Chapter 9 by Wesseler address the problem of uncertainty regarding pest resistance when deciding whether to adopt genetically modified crops such as *Bt* crops described earlier. The likelihood that pests will become resistant to these new crops seems inevitable, although there is significant uncertainty about how soon this will happen. For this reason, if there is a significant risk that pests will quickly become resistant to these new crops, then farmers will want to see greater improvements in yield with the *Bt* crop (compared with the conventional, non-*Bt* crop) if they are to be convinced to switch to the new technology. The greater the risk of pest resistance, or of other ecological problems, the greater the improvement in *Bt* crop yield will have to be. Both of these chapters use the approach of real option value theory, an economic technique used to assess decisions made under uncertainty. Simply put, the option value is the economic value of delaying a decision pending the arrival of better information. Both chapters use this approach to estimate the hurdle rate or the minimum yield improvement afforded by the *Bt* crop to make the risk of adopting this technology worth it to the farmer.

Part III deals with incentives faced by producers of antibiotics and pesticides. Chapter 10 by Noonan takes on the important question of how incentives faced by monopolist producers influence the optimal size of refuges to mitigate pest resistance to genetically modified *Bt* crops. Individual farmers would not choose to adopt these strategies on their own, because the costs in terms of reduced profits clearly outweigh the individual benefit associated with lower pest resistance in the future. Therefore, EPA has mandated that refuge areas be grown with non-*Bt* crop so that the likelihood of emergence of pest resistance is minimized. Using a theoretical model, Noonan shows that monopolistic seed producers may have a greater incentive for ensuring that growers are scrupulous in planting refuges than would be the case if there was a competitive supply of genetically modified *Bt* seeds. Furthermore, this incentive may be large enough to ensure an even greater level of effort on refuges than is socially optimal. In other words, one would expect to see refuges being grown even if EPA did not mandate them. This result has important implications for public policy because it indicates that seed companies' incentives may imply that EPA regulations on growing refuge areas are unnecessary. Empirical evidence in support of this argument would make a stronger case for revisiting EPA's efforts in this area.

In Chapter 11, Goeschl and Swanson address the question of the usefulness of the patent system for encouraging the development of new antibiotics and pesticides when resistance is a recurring problem. They compare the resistance problem with running on a treadmill just to stay in the same place. Industry can either slow down the pace of the treadmill by selling less of their product, or run faster by rapidly coming up with new products to replace older products made obsolete by resistance. In making this decision, firms must keep in mind two considerations: their product could be made obsolete by resistance and their product could be made obsolete by a new product introduced by a competitor firm. The standard patent length of 17 years may not give firms sufficient incentive to care about resistance. This chapter points to the need for recognizing the shortcomings of the patent system in giving firms a greater incentive to care about resistance and the need to look in other directions to solve this problem.

Chapter 12 by Alix and Zilberman provides a striking contrast to other chapters in this book. It challenges the notion that resistance is a consequence of the overapplication of pesticides. Alix and Zilberman review the complex incentives that motivate growers and pesticide firms to show that underapplication of pesticides might be just as problematic (by not killing sufficient numbers of pests) as overapplication that could lead to increasing resistance. Overapplication may not be a problem when the pesticide industry is invested in the efficacy of its products, and this in turn depends on how strong its property rights are. The authors favor a holistic view of pesticide manufacture and use. Further, they point out that economic agents such as agricultural extension consultants and pesticide advisors have an incentive to encourage optimal pesticide use even if individual growers lack these incentives. Finally, they emphasize the need for more empirical studies on the multiple institutional and other factors that influence pesticide choice and use on the farm and the role of these influences in building pest resistance.

Final Thoughts

The application of economics to policy design involves two stages. In the first stage, economic principles can present the best-case scenario and advise us on what kind of policy will get us to that benchmark outcome. For instance, a simple policy rule in the case of antibiotics may be that we should use a variety of antibiotics in proportions determined by economic costs and the probability that bacteria will acquire resistance to each drug (see Chapter 3).

Although such an "optimal" policy may not necessarily be attainable in the real world, it helps us assess other second-best policies against the benchmark of a first-best policy.

In the second stage, we use our understanding of incentives and behavior to specify how individual agents such as physicians or farmers could be induced to follow the optimal policies outlined in the first stage or at least influence behavior such that the outcome is as close to that achieved by the first-best policy as possible. The challenge of translating the economic prescriptions into a form that is useful to policymakers is daunting. However, by not taking this important step, attempts to understand the problem of resistance will fall short of achieving an impact on policy. This book is far more successful at describing the first stage than the second. Much work remains to be done on designing incentives to ensure that antibiotics and pesticides are used optimally.

At the time of writing this, the economics of resistance is an emerging field of research, and a number of the chapters in this volume are still in the process of development. We believe that publishing these preliminary ideas will be helpful in extending the study of the economics of resistance. Recent concerns about bioterrorism and re-emerging infections such as tuberculosis remind us of the need to give more serious thought to our arsenal of antibiotics—managing those that we have efficiently and developing new ones. We hope this volume, even if it does not readily provide complete answers to such questions, provokes ideas to pursue in this growing and topical field.

Acknowledgements

My foremost debt is to the contributors without whose support and patience with multiple rounds of review, this book would have not been possible. I am grateful to Paul Portney for having both the generosity and foresight to support this endeavor, Mike Toman for his strong and unwavering support of (most of) my crazy ideas at RFF, and Susan Doyle for her remarkable job taking care of the logistics of the RFF Conference on the Economics of Resistance. I have had (and continue to have) the benefit of outstanding and truly supportive colleagues at RFF. David Simpson, Carolyn Fischer, Jim Sanchirico, Ray Kopp, Don Reisman and Rebecca Henderson, Emily Aronow, Barb Jemelkova, Kay Murphy, and Pauline Wiggins deserve particular mention in connection with this project.

The volume has also been helped by comments provided by the participants at the RFF Conference. Many reviewers contributed their time and effort to help shape these chapters with their insights and experience and helped a set of conference proceedings reach its present polished form. I would also like to thank David Bell, William Blaine, Eric Van Dusen, Gérard Gaudet and

Marc Lipsitch for helping make this book possible. I acknowledge financial support from the Agency for Health Care Research and Quality and the National Center for Infectious Disease at the Centers for Disease Control and Prevention for their sponsorship of the workshop on the Economics of Antimicrobial Resistance.

Preetha, Tejas, the Rajaramans and the other Laxminarayan (my mother) continue to anchor my life with their love and light. For this I am most grateful.

RAMANAN LAXMINARAYAN
WASHINGTON, DC

Notes

1. Note that economic intuition is only provided as guidance and cannot be substituted for actual trials to test the medical or agricultural suitability of the proposed strategies. However, even at the level of abstraction adopted by the chapters in this book, it is possible to deliver some broad insights into the resistance problem, which will then have to be tested and operationalized by practitioners.

2. The chapters have undergone substantial revision since the meeting.

3. There is a common misconception outside the economics profession that economics is largely about measuring costs (and sometimes benefits). Although this is certainly part of what economists do, these are merely stops on the way to the final destination, which is to design policies and incentives that influence human behavior. In doing this, economics offers powerful analytical tools and formal approaches to study incentives faced by individuals and ways of aligning these incentives with those of society at large.

Introduction

On the Economics of Resistance

Ramanan Laxminarayan

Some of the most amazing technological achievements of the past century have involved successful human control of biological organisms. The introduction of antibiotics in the early 1940s helped bring about dramatic declines in mortality from infectious diseases and has been widely acclaimed as one of the most important advances in the history of medicine. In the field of agriculture, the use of pesticides, insecticides, and herbicides helped bring about vast increases in food supply in both developed and developing countries. However, ever since these products were introduced, our continued capacity to use them effectively has been challenged by the ability of bacteria and pests to adapt, evolve, and escape the effect of these products. Clearly economic and behavioral factors play an important role in encouraging the rapid growth of resistance. However, our understanding of these factors lags far behind scientific understanding of the problem. The purpose of this introductory essay is to illustrate where economics might be useful in understanding and developing policy responses to the problem of resistance and to provide some insight based both on the existing literature and my own thoughts on the economics of resistance.

Problems of resistance that arise as a consequence of human-induced evolution are not restricted to antibiotics and pesticides alone. Insects can develop resistance to insecticides, malarial parasites to antimalarials, and weeds to herbicides. The common mechanism in all these instances is that selection pressure placed by the use of control agents provides a comparative advantage to the small fraction of organisms naturally resistant to the agents.

Over time, Darwinian selection favors the resistant organisms over those that are susceptible to the effect of the agent and renders the control agent ineffective. From a behavioral perspective, the underlying reason in all these instances is that individual actors such as patients, physicians, and farmers may not have the incentive to take into account the negative impact of their use of antibiotics, pesticides, and other control agents on the future effectiveness of these products for everyone else. Firms may have limited interest in the effectiveness of their products, and their goals of maximizing profits may not necessarily be consistent with societal goals of making the best use of these products.

What Role Can Economics Play?

First and foremost, economics can help provide an estimate of the economic costs and benefits of antibiotic or pesticide use and the magnitude of the impact of resistance. However, the usefulness of economics in studying resistance goes far beyond this function. Economics can play an important role both in understanding the evolution of resistance and in developing policy responses to the problem. Broadly speaking, society's battle against resistance takes place on two fronts. First, we need to manage our existing arsenal of drugs and antibiotics carefully to maximize the value derived from their use. Second, we need to develop (or encourage the development of) new drugs and pesticides to replace old products that resistance has rendered ineffective. These two strategies are intricately linked. Our efforts to better manage resistance to existing products could reduce the returns to investment in new products. So, paradoxically, the evolution of resistance may create a demand for new products that leads to greater research investment. Conversely, the greater availability of new products may increase the variety of products that we have available, and this may help us make better use of existing products (see Chapter 3).

Economics has a long history with both the optimal management of natural resources, such as oil, trees, and fisheries, and the optimal design of incentives to influence the behavior of individuals and corporate entities. Considering antibiotic or pest effectiveness as a societal resource could help devise strategies to use antibiotics and pesticides in a manner that benefits society. Economists could help design regulatory and other incentives to encourage firms to come up with new products to replace antibiotics and pesticides that are no longer effective, as well as to take resistance into account when deciding on strategies to market existing products. The existing literature and ideas for the role that economics can play in addressing the challenges of resistance are described in the sections that follow.

How Big Is the Problem?

We live in a world in which problems tend to get prioritized in order of decreasing economic significance, or so economists would like to believe. Although the enormity of the resistance problem may be self-evident to those in the medical and agricultural communities who deal with it on a daily basis, assessing the economic impact is a necessary first step to bringing the problem to the attention of policymakers and stakeholders. There has been some work in this direction, although much remains to be done.

In the medical context, economic costs associated with antibiotic resistance can be attributed to at least three factors. First, resistant infections are more expensive to treat; patients infected with resistant bacteria require longer hospitalization and face higher treatment costs than patients infected with drug-susceptible strains. Second, the risk of mortality is greater for resistant infections, and this imposes a cost on society. Finally, the cost of introducing new antibiotics to replace old ineffective ones is increasing and involves the commitment of resources that could be deployed to other public health research projects, such as developing new drugs for AIDS or cancer (Reed et al. 2001).

Resistance costs are rarely considered even in economic evaluations of antibiotic treatment alternatives because the uncertainty of the impact of current antibiotic use on future resistance diminishes the importance of resistance costs (Coast et al. 1996). Although uncertainty regarding the actual cost of resistance is considerable, some projections show that, even with conservative estimates, the cost of antibiotic resistance is high enough to influence cost–benefit decisions made at the individual prescription level (Reed et al. 2001). Therefore, it appears that the cost of antibiotic resistance may be high enough to warrant inclusion in cost-effectiveness analyses of antibiotic treatments.

The annual figure quoted most often for the economic impact of resistance in the United States ranges from $350 million to $35 billion (at 1989 dollar rates, Phelps 1989). These estimates assume 150 million prescriptions are generated each year and vary depending on, among other factors, the rate at which resistance grows with respect to increasing antibiotic use, and the probability that a patient will die following infection with a resistant pathogen (Phelps 1989). A more recent study that measured the deadweight loss associated with the loss of antibiotic effectiveness related to outpatient prescriptions in the United States to be $378 million and as high as $18.6 billion (Elbasha 1999). A report by the Office of Technology Assessment (OTA) to the U.S. Congress estimated the annual cost associated with antibiotic resistance in hospitals, attributable to five classes of hospital-acquired infections from six different antibiotic-resistant bacteria, to be at least $1.3 billion (at 1992 dollar rates) (OTA 1995). The Centers for Disease Control and Prevention estimated that the cost of all hospital-acquired infections, including both antibiotic-resistant and antibiotic-susceptible strains in their figures was $4.5 billion (OTA 1995). The lack of time series data on both antimicrobial use and bacterial resistance has made it difficult to estimate the dose–response relationship between antimicrobial use and resistance, further complicating an assessment of the economic costs of resistance.

On the pesticide front, according to the Insecticide Resistance Action Committee, an industry-funded group, insecticide resistance increases the cost of pest control by nearly $40 million each year (IRAC 2002). This estimate does not include the secondary environmental damages associated with increased pesticide use. One specific example of crop losses associated with pest resistance is resistance to the Colorado potato beetle (*Leptinotarso decemlineata*), which cost potato producers in Michigan $16 million in crop losses in 1991.

How Can We Make the Best Use of Existing Antibiotics and Pesticides?

Considering the effectiveness of antibiotics (or pesticides) as a natural resource that is much the same as a stock of fish or a forest can help us explore ways of making better use of this resource. The concept of pest susceptibility to pesticides as a natural resource was first introduced 30 years ago (Carlson and Castle 1972). Since then, there has been sporadic interest in applying the tools of economics to understanding how these agents might be better used given that resistance is a likely consequence of using them (Hueth and Regev 1974; Comins 1977a,b; Brown and Layton 1996; Laxminarayan and Brown 2001). Although the literature on pest resistance dates back to the 1970s, interest in antibiotic resistance is more recent. Interest in determining the kinds of strategies that would maximize the value from current antibiotics and pesticides has been accompanied by discussions of how economic incentives could be used to induce individuals who use these products to make better use of antibiotics and pesticides.

In the antibiotics context, Brown and Layton described a dynamic model of antibiotic use in which consumers and farmers both use antibiotics while ignoring the impact of their use on the other group (1996). This results in a greater use of antibiotics by both groups of users. Laxminarayan and Brown used a framework based on an epidemiological model of infection in which antibiotic effectiveness is treated as a nonrenewable resource (2001). In the model presented, bacterial resistance (the converse of effectiveness) develops as a result of selective pressure on nonresistant strains caused by antibiotic use. Their paper shows that the optimal proportion and timing of the use of available antibiotics can be derived as a function of the rates at which bacterial resistance to each antibiotic evolves and on pharmaceutical costs of each antibiotic.

In the agricultural economics literature, the Hueth and Regev model shows pest susceptibility to pesticides as a stock of nonrenewable natural resource that is privately costless to use in the short run but extremely costly for society to replace in the long run when new pesticides are required (Hueth and Regev 1974). Adopting this approach of treating susceptibility as an exhaustible resource in a study on the optimal management of pest resistance, Comins found that the cost of resistance is analytically equivalent to an increase in the cost of the pesticide (Comins 1977a,b, 1979).

More recently, attention has turned to the optimal management of resistance to newly introduced *Bt* (*Bacillus thuringiensis*) crops, which are genetically modified to produce a protein highly toxic to many insect pests. Because the *Bt* toxin is constantly present, unlike chemical pesticides, the strategy of managing resistance by optimally timing application of pesticides is no longer possible with the new technology. Setting aside refuge areas in which susceptible pests can survive has been proposed to reduce the selection pressure placed on them in the areas where the *Bt* crop is grown. A number of papers have been written on approaches to determining the optimal size of these refugia (Hurley et al. 1999; Hyde et al. 1999; Livingston et al. 2000; Laxminarayan and Simpson 2002).

From an economist's perspective, control of harmful biological organisms using control agents (e.g., antibiotics, antivirals, fungicides) is quite unlike other technologies in that it has two side-effects, neither of which is considered by individuals who use these agents and who act in their own self interest. In the case of pesticide use, a farmer who uses pesticides effectively will kill pests, including some that could otherwise migrate to other fields. However, the individual farmer has no incentive to recognize this positive side-effect of his or her use of pesticides. On the negative side, the use of pesticides engenders greater resistance in the future. This effect, too, is not fully taken into consideration by any individual farmer unless effects are entirely local. If one were to think about this in the context of using antibiotics to treat bacterial infections or using insecticides to kill insects, the ubiquity of this incentive problem described here becomes apparent. Depending on whether the value of the positive impact of pest reduction is greater than or less than the negative impact of future resistance, the individual farmer may use pesticides to a greater or lesser extent than would be best from a societal perspective. Public economics has a long history in dealing with externality problems, and the insights gained could offer solutions to confronting the behavioral issues regarding resistance.

In addition to our need to understand the influence of human behavior on the evolution of resistance, there are three other reasons for looking at economic outcomes in addition to biological outcomes when dealing with resistance. First, for any given resistance management strategy, economics enables us to evaluate tradeoffs between the benefits of using the product today and the future costs of resistance. One might choose to simply minimize the probability that resistance will arise; however, minimizing resistance, by itself, is a meaningless objective and can be accomplished by not using antibiotics or pesticides at all. We use these products only because they provide a benefit in terms of killing bacteria or pests. Therefore, if a particular resistance management strategy is very effective at reducing resistance but increases the number of pests, it may not necessarily be the best strategy to adopt. Moreover, the benefits and costs of using antibiotics or pesticides occur at different points in time, and economics provides a framework for making intertemporal comparisons of outcomes.

We can illustrate the importance of economics in studying the intertemporal trade-off involved in resistance management in the context of hospital infections. The overall objective of hospital infection control committees which are charged with the well-being of all patients in the hospital both in the present and in the future, is to ensure that patients recover soon and that bacterial resistance is minimized. Given that the committee's objective is to balance between treatment outcomes in the present against the possibility of future resistance, economic analysis plays a useful role in providing a metric for comparing present and future benefits and costs of antibiotic treatment.

A second, related benefit of the economic way of thinking is that it provides a consistent framework for evaluating different strategies to manage resistance, including those that do not involve changes in how we use antibiotics. For instance, simple procedures such as frequent hand washing by nursing staff could help reduce the prevalence of resistant infections in hospitals (Austin et al. 1999). However, without knowing the cost of implementing a strict hand-washing program, this strategy cannot be compared with one of restricting the use of antibiotics in the hospital.

The third benefit of introducing economic analysis is that it can alter conclusions reached by purely epidemiological models, as well as enrich their applicability to the real world where economic costs play an important role. For instance, Bonhoeffer and colleagues showed that given two identical antibiotics, a strategy of using the two drugs on equal fractions of the patient population would be superior to one in which at any given time only one drug is used on all patients and the two drugs are periodically cycled (1997). Using economic models in conjunction with mathematical disease models, it is possible to demonstrate that their conclusion rests on the assumption that both the levels of resistance to the two antibiotics as well antibiotic treatment costs are identical (Laxminarayan and Brown 2001). This may not be the case in reality. There are similar examples in the agricultural context of combining economic and biological models that illustrate the value of a multidisciplinary perspective on resistance management strategies (Munro 1997).

Although economic analysis is helpful in many ways, its usefulness rests critically on our understanding of the evolutionary processes that drive resistance. Collaborative efforts between natural and social scientists are likely to make tangible contributions to the policy process.

How Can We Encourage the Development of New Antibiotics and Pesticides?

To date, there is very little research on how the innovation of new antibiotics and pesticides may be affected by the problem of resistance. Existing work has either explored how resistance affects incentives to innovate or how market structure can influence how firms choose to develop and sell antibiotics and pesticides. Economic research has shown that research expenditures by a pharmaceutical firm will increase in response to increasing resistance to its existing portfolio of antibiotics (Kile 1989). Furthermore, this response depends on whether the current drug is made by this firm or by a rival because resistance to the rival firm's drug can only increase the value of this firm's existing portfolio.

Theoretical models have been used to illustrate the common-property problem associated with antibiotics. Tisdell used a simple, two-period model in which the number of antibiotic doses administered in the first period influences treatment effectiveness in the second period (1982). In a policy solution reminiscent of the sole-owner fishery model, Tisdell proposed either regulating first-period antibiotic consumption or granting a monopoly to sellers of antibiotics to ensure they consider the intertemporal depletion of effectiveness. Setting patent breadth optimally has been suggested as a way of solving this common-property problem and encouraging firms to take resistance into consideration (Laxminarayan 1999). Finally, other researchers have hypothesized that a competitive market for antibiotics will not be able to produce a variety of antibiotics that is optimal from the standpoint of managing drug resistance and that special incentives may be needed to encourage firms to develop new antibiotics (Ellison and Hellerstein 1999).

In spite of our best efforts to manage resistance, antibiotics and pesticides that are currently in use will inevitably be less effective in the future. Economics can help in designing incentives to encourage research and development of new products. Policymaking efforts to design such incentives to encourage innovation should be guided by two criteria. First, policies to encourage the development of new antibiotics (or pesticides) must necessarily be consistent with other policies that influence how firms choose to price and sell their products. Although we want firms to come up with new products, we also want to increase (or at the very least not decrease) their incentives to care about product effectiveness. Second, the fundamental policy objective is not just to increase incentives for firms to introduce *any* new antibiotics (or pesticides) but to specifically develop new products that are significantly different from existing ones in their mechanisms of action. This minimizes the common-property problem that arises when different firms make products with linked modes of action and, consequently, no single firm has sufficient incentive to care about declining product effectiveness. If we think of product effectiveness as a resource, like oil for instance, an optimal policy would be one that encourages drug firms to search for new "wells" of effectiveness against bacteria, rather than to drill new "wells" to extract existing reserves in competition with other producers. Given this latter criterion, standard policy solutions such as research investment tax credits and longer patent length may not necessarily solve the problem.

Increasing patent length often has been suggested as a way of encouraging innovation by increasing the return from investment (OTA 1995). In the case of products like antibiotics and pesticides in which the rate of product obsolescence is influenced by how firms price their products, increasing patent length has the additional benefit of increasing the stake that firms have in the effectiveness of their products. However, the length of their patents limits the extent to which firms have an incentive to care about the effectiveness of their products. Pharmaceutical (and pesticide) firms may have fewer reasons to care about the effectiveness of their drugs after patent expiration and are therefore likely to extract drug effectiveness at a rate greater than is socially optimal. This occurs in much the same way as a logger who has a fixed-term concession on a forest will try to cut down as many trees as possible before his concession expires, and it is a socially undesirable outcome.

Extending patent length would give pharmaceutical companies a greater incentive to care about the effectiveness of their product over a longer time horizon. Therefore, one would expect that they would be less aggressive in marketing their products in the interests of preserving their product's effectiveness and encourage careful use of their products. However, all else being equal, extending patent length is likely to increase the number of "me-too" drugs that are close substitutes of existing antibiotics and that draw on existing stocks of effectiveness (see Chapter 11, for instance). This would encourage a greater degree of competition between firms for the same stock of effectiveness and, consequently, too fast a rate of effectiveness exhaustion. This incentive mechanism is not specifically targeted at our objective of encouraging the development of new drugs with innovative modes of action that could be effective against organisms resistant to existing products. Therefore, increasing patent length (or even providing research investment tax credits, for that matter) may not be sufficient to promote the development of new classes of antibiotics.

Other policy options that have received attention in the antibiotics context include mechanisms to exchange patent length extensions for use restrictions. The OTA report on antibiotic resistance suggests that an arrangement could be worked out between the Food and Drug Administration (FDA), the Patent Office, and the pharmaceutical firm to increase the patent length while limiting the number of uses for which the antibiotic may be used. However, extensive analyses of off-label drug use have shown that antibiotics are not necessarily prescribed for only the conditions for which they received FDA approval (Christopher 1993). Therefore, such an agreement may not necessarily work without some way of enforcing restrictions on antibiotic use. These problems are likely to arise in the pesticide arena as well.

Discouraging the practice of treatment homogeneity—whereby a single antibiotic or a few antibiotics (or pesticides) are widely used while newer products are kept on the sidelines for use only for resistant infections—could influence new product development. Great emphasis is often placed on the most cost-effective antibiotic or pesticides, and new products are often kept on the sidelines as backups if the currently used product fails. On the one hand, these policies ensure a large market of resistant infections for the backup drug once the frontline drug fails. On the other hand, they may discourage manufacturers who may be unwilling to take a risk based on the current frontline product failing and would therefore be unwilling to develop a new drug. Policies that encourage product homogeneity should, therefore, be sensitive to their effect on producer incentives.

A final issue is the relative importance of innovation compared with measures to manage resistance to existing antibiotics and pesticides. Clearly, measures need to be taken on both fronts, but we need to have some assessment of the relative importance of these two avenues to addressing the resistance problem. Recent evidence suggests that new antibiotics may have much shorter life spans compared with drugs introduced a few decades ago. This may indicate significant cross-resistance between old and new products. For instance, estimates of the resistance-related costs of withdrawing organophosphates from apple farming might be too low if there had been significant cross-resistance between the old and new pesticides (Munro 1997). Finally, the costs of introducing new pesticides have increased dramatically with each generation of pesticide (Hammock and Sonderlund 1986). This is believed to be true in the case of antibiotics as well and is especially worrisome because it highlights the importance of not relying on the arrival of technological fixes to solve the problem of rising resistance.

To the extent that these problems are widespread, we can rely much less on being saved by innovation and will have to devote greater effort to conserving our existing drugs. However, the arrival of *Bt* crops that have little or no cross-resistance with older pesticides such as pyrethroids has indicated that in some instances, it may be worthwhile to anticipate a technological fix.

Directions for Further Research

The economics of resistance is in its initial stages of formation. Although this book covers a wide swath of questions, much more work is needed to respond to the growing challenges posed by increasing resistance that threatens to roll back advances made against infectious diseases and agricultural pests. A number of research issues discussed in this section are specific to antibiotics or pesticides, and so they are discussed in this order.

Antibiotics

This book makes some headway in discussing the kinds of strategies that would maximize the economic value from antibiotics. However, much remains to be done in understanding the incentives faced by patients, physicians, and hospital administrators and in designing economic incentives to ensure that antibiotics are used in accordance with a best policy. A related issue is how we might be able to discourage inappropriate use of antibiotics short of actually reviewing and second-guessing medical decisions. From a physician's perspective, there are few incentives to care about the impact of resistance and many incentives to ensure the contemporary individual patient's well-being. The high cost of liability insurance reinforces the Hippocratic oath to do the best for the patient. These factors may further induce physicians to err on the side of prescribing antibiotics when they are unnecessary and prescribing stronger, more broad-spectrum antibiotics than may be necessary. Addressing the problem of resistance may require that this fundamental contradiction between perceived patient well-being and societal well-being be resolved.

Although the public has increasingly expressed concern about the emergence of antibiotic-resistant bacteria (Barden et al. 1998), patients in general have few incentives to care about the resistance externality. Insurance shields many patients from being directly responsible for the cost of medical care, further distorting the true cost of antibiotic treatment from the patient's perspective. A large, randomized study showed that people who received free medical care used 85% more antibiotics than those required to pay for at least some portion of their medical care (Foxman et al. 1987). Incentives for better use of antibiotics may have to be strongly linked with how patients pay for antibiotics and may call for changes to insurance reimbursement for antibiotics. More research is needed to understand these linkages.

Another area in which public policy could be illuminated by more economic analysis is what often has been characterized as inappropriate use of antibiotics for farm animal feed. The science of how the use of antibiotics for growth promotion in animals results in resistant infections in humans is still in development, and there is disagreement on the relative importance of this causal factor when compared to inappropriate use of antibiotics in humans. Regardless, the need for public policy is evident. For instance, there has been a great deal of controversy surrounding FDA approval of fluoroquinolones, an antibiotic used in humans that is also approved for use in animals. In recent months, FDA has withdrawn permission for this drug to be marketed for animal use, a move that was opposed by Bayer, one of the two manufacturers of this drug. FDA's case was made on the basis of a risk analysis that showed that fluoroquinolone use in animals posed an increased risk of fluoroquinolone-resistant infections of *Campylobacter pylori*. However, the more fundamental question is why firms choose to sell antibiotics as growth promoters when such use could potentially harm the demand for the human version of these antibiotics. One possible avenue for research is to understand how factors such as the patent scope given to antibiotics, and differences in the FDA approval processes for using antibiotics in animals as growth promoters and in humans as therapeutic agents could influence incentives for pharmaceutical firms with respect to antibiotic resistance.

Pesticides

Current interest in resistance in the agricultural context has arisen with the adoption of genetically modified crops. Genetically modified corn, cotton, and soybeans that express the *Bt* protein have been widely adopted in U.S. agriculture. Unlike when other pesticides are used, EPA has formulated specific rules for growers to ensure that resistance to *Bt* does not arise. Research on economic incentives can improve current policies in at least two directions. The current strategy of using mandatory refuge areas that are monitored and enforced by seed companies may suffer from several drawbacks. Substantial monitoring and enforcement costs may need to be taken into account. Growers may follow only the letter of the law and grow refuge areas only in poor quality land where they will be much less effective. Also, individual growers may cheat and not observe the mandated refuge requirements. Finally, the extent of refuge needed may depend on concentration of other *Bt* fields in the close proximity (see Chapter 4). So, for instance, it may be more important to ensure that a cotton farmer in Louisiana follows the refuge requirement than a cotton farmer in China, where cotton fields are interspersed with other crops.

The challenge, therefore, is to design suitable incentive mechanisms that encourage each farmer to invest in more socially desirable refuge strategies. A number of different incentive mechanisms may offer alternatives to the current mandatory refuge principle. For instance, a "resistance user fee" on genetically modified seeds could be levied to force growers to bear the social cost associated with pest resistance to these crops. This user fee could be calibrated to the density of *Bt* crop in the local area and could be used to set up common refuge areas or be used to pay some farmers to grow only non-*Bt* crop. Another strategy may be to subsidize seed mixtures that contain both genetically modified and non–genetically modified varieties. The mixed seed strategy is believed to be particularly feasible in the case of the pink bollworm, in which larval movement is minimal (Tabashnik 1994). A third mechanism that could be considered in this research is the concept of tradable refuge permits. Under this framework, growers who focus on non-*Bt* crops would receive refuge permits that could then be bought by growers of *Bt* crops instead of growing their own refuge areas. This approach is similar to the concept of tradable pollution permits in the environmental economics literature, and can be applied in areas of monoculture. A fourth mechanism would allow growers to pool their non-*Bt* refuge areas or jointly pay a single farmer to grow only non-*Bt* crop as long as it satisfies biological requirements for spatial proximity to the *Bt* crop.

In pursuing these avenues of research, multidisciplinary efforts have a far greater potential to yield answers than those efforts undertaken by natural or social scientists working entirely within their own domains.

References

Austin, D.J., M.J. Bonten, R.A. Weinstein, S. Slaughter, and R.M. Anderson. 1999. Vancomycin-Resistant Enterococci in Intensive-Care Hospital Settings: Transmission Dynamics, Persistence, and the Impact of Infection Control Programs. *Proceedings of the National Academy of Sciences of the USA* 96(12): 6908–13.

Barden, L.S., S.F. Dowell, B. Schwartz, and C. Lackey. 1998. Current Attitudes Regarding Use of Antimicrobial Agents: Results from Physicians' and Parents' Focus Group Discussions. *Clinical Pediatrics* 37: 665–72.

Bonhoeffer, S., M. Lipsitch, and B.R. Levin. 1997. Evaluating Treatment Protocols to Prevent Antibiotic Resistance. *Proceedings of the National Academy of Sciences of the USA* 94(22): 12106–11.

Brown, G., and D.F. Layton. 1996. Resistance Economics: Social Cost and the Evolution of Antibiotic Resistance. *Environment and Development Economics* 1(3): 349–55.

Carlson, G., and E.N. Castle. 1972. Economics of Pest Control. In *Control Strategies for the Future*. Washington, DC: National Academy of Sciences, 79–99.

Christopher, W.L. 1993. Off-Label Drug Prescription: Filling the Regulatory Vacuum. *Food and Drug Law Journal* 48: 247–62.

Coast, J., R.D. Smith, and M.R. Millar. 1996. Superbugs: Should Antimicrobial Resistance Be Included as a Cost in Economic Valuation? *Health Economics* 5: 217–26.

Comins, H.N. 1977a. The Development of Insecticide Resistance in the Presence of Migration. *Journal of Theoretical Biology* 64: 177–97.

———. 1977b. The Management of Pesticide Resistance. *Journal of Theoretical Biology* 65: 399–420.

———. 1979. Analytic Methods for Management of Pesticide Resistance. *Journal of Theoretical Biology* 77: 171–88.

Elbasha, E. 1999. Deadweight Loss of Bacterial Resistance Due to Overtreatment. Unpublished report for the Centers for Disease Control and Prevention, Atlanta, GA.

Ellison, S.F., and J. Hellerstein. 1999. The Economics of Antibiotics: An Exploratory Study. In *Measuring the Prices of Medical Treatment*, edited by J.E. Triplett. Washington, DC: Brookings Institution.

Foxman, B., R. Burciaga Valdez, K.N. Lohr, G.A. Goldberg, J.P. Newhouse, and R.H. Brook. 1987. The Effect of Cost Sharing on the Use of Antibiotics in Ambulatory Care: Results from a Population-Based Randomized Controlled Trial. *Journal of Chronic Diseases* 40: 429–37.

Hammock, B.D., and D.M. Sonderlund. 1986. Chemical Strategies for Resistance Management. In *Pesticide Resistance: Strategies and Tactics for Management*, edited by N.R. Council. Washington, DC: National Academy Press.

Hueth, D., and U. Regev. 1974. Optimal Agricultural Pest Management with Increasing Pest Resistance. *American Journal of Agricultural Economics* 56: 543–53.

Hurley, T.M., S. Secchi, B.A. Babcock, and R. Hellmich. 1999. Managing the Risk of European Corn Borer Resistance to Transgenic Corn: An Assessment of Refuge Recommendations. Ames, IA: CARD, Iowa State University, 36.

Hyde, J., M.A. Martin, P.V. Preckel, C.L. Dobbins, and C.R. Edwards. 1999. *The Economics of Refuge Design for* Bt *Corn*. American Agricultural Economics Association Meeting, Nashville, TN.

IRAC (Insecticide Resistance Action Committee). 2002. www.plantprotection.org/irac (accessed February 15, 2002).

Kile, J.D. 1989. Research and Development in the Pharmaceutical Industry: The Impact of Drug Resistance. Doctoral dissertation. Madison, WI: University of Wisconsin.

Laxminarayan, R. 1999. Economics of Antibiotic Resistance. Doctoral dissertation. Seattle, WA: University of Washington.

Laxminarayan, R., and G.M. Brown. 2001. Economics of Antibiotic Resistance: A Theory of Optimal Use. *Journal of Environmental Economics and Management* 42(2): 183–206.

Laxminarayan, R., and R.D. Simpson. 2002. Refuge Strategies for Managing Pest Resistance in Transgenic Agriculture. *Environmental and Resource Economics* 22: 521–36.

Livingston, M.J., G.A. Carlson, and P.L. Fackler. 2000. Bt *Cotton Refuge Policy*. American Agricultural Economics Association Meeting, Tampa Bay.

Munro, A. 1997. Economics and Biological Evolution. *Environmental and Resource Economics* 9: 429–9.

OTA (Office of Technology Assessment). 1995. *Impact of Antibiotic-Resistant Bacteria: A Report to the U.S. Congress*. Government Printing Office. Washington, DC: OTA.

Phelps, C.E. 1989. Bug/Drug Resistance: Sometimes Less Is More. *Medical Care* 27(2): 194–203.

Reed, S., S. Sullivan, and R. Laxminarayan. 2001. Socioeconomic Issues Related to Antibiotic Use. In *Appropriate Antibiotic Use*, edited by D.E. Low. London: The Royal Society of Medicine Press, 41–6.

Tabashnik, B.E. 1994. Delaying Insect Adaptation to Transgenic Plants: Seed Mixtures and Refugia Reconsidered. *Proceedings of the Royal Society of London, Series B* 255: 7–12.

Tisdell, C. 1982. Exploitation of Techniques that Decline in Effectiveness. *Public Finance* 37: 428–37.

PART I

Issues of Optimal Management of Resistance

Chapter 1

Dynamics of Antibiotic Use

Ecological versus Interventionist Strategies To Manage Resistance to Antibiotics

James E. Wilen and Siwa Msangi

This chapter explores some economic and epidemiological implications of alternative disease treatment strategies in an institutional setting such as a hospital or clinic. We modify and generalize the integrated economic/epidemiological model first introduced by Laxminarayan and Brown (2001). Laxminarayan and Brown adapted an epidemiological multicompartment model of treatment and infection from Bonhoeffer and others (1997), a characterization based, in turn, on early twentieth-century population models of disease transmission and infection. Laxminarayan and Brown added an economic objective function that incorporates explicit assessment of the present value of the costs and benefits of accelerated disease reduction caused by treatment. Laxminarayan and Brown derived important qualitative conclusions about how to optimally treat a diseased population, showing how treatment and the corresponding buildup of antibiotic resistance are similar to the fundamental economic problems of optimally exploiting a nonrenewable resource. As Laxminarayan and Brown argued, in a closed system, the population of individuals responsive to or susceptible to antibiotic treatment can be thought of as a resource with positive economic value. Treatment yields a stream of benefits associated with accelerated recovery of the diseased population, but at the same time, antibiotic resistance as a result of treatment leads to a "draw down" of the stock of susceptibility. The optimal treatment decision thus must account for the dynamic trade-off associated with immediate disease reduction gains and long-term future resistance buildup costs.

Our chapter generalizes the Laxminarayan and Brown paper in an important way by including the possibility that there are fitness costs associated with genes that allow a disease to be resistant to antibiotic treatment. Laxminarayan and Brown ignored fitness costs to highlight the analogy with the nonrenewable resource problem. We show that fitness costs affect the optimal treatment regime in two major ways. First, with fitness costs it is possible that the optimal long-run treatment regime involves steady state strategies that hold resistant and susceptible populations in a symbiotic balance, more like a multispecies renewable resource problem than a nonrenewable problem. Second, with fitness costs, it is also possible that ecological (nonantibiotic) strategies that encourage susceptible bacteria to outcompete resistant bacteria are economically preferable to interventionist strategies involving aggressive antibiotic treatment. In the appendix, we solve the general problem explicitly, characterizing long-term steady states and approach paths in terms of fundamental parameters. Our chapter explains the results using modified phase diagrams that characterize the results qualitatively. We also compare the two broad kinds of treatment strategies, categorized as interventionist and ecological, with a numerical model.

This chapter examines some of the economic implications of antibiotic use within a human population and illustrates the implications of relative fitness among different disease vectors on drug resistance in the population. As emphasized throughout this book, the issue of antibiotic resistance is clearly one of the more important contemporary world health issues. Over the past few years, physicians and health care practitioners have come face to face with several virulent strains of drug-resistant diseases. To name just a few, penicillin-resistant gonorrhea; vancomycin-resistant *Staphylococcus aureus*; and the bacterial species *Enterococcus faecalis, Mycobacterium tuberculosis,* and *Pseudomonas aeruginosa,* are all just beginning to evade the reach of the current stockpile of antibiotics. These new resistant bacteria represent a clear and present danger to many in developing and developed countries alike. Much acquired antibiotic resistance has come about as a result of misuse by both physicians and self-medicating individuals, which has induced natural selection pressure favoring the survival of resistant genes within viral and bacterial species. The consequent gradual buildup of drug resistance in the population has put increasing pressure on researchers to develop new treatment agents to keep quickly mutating pathogens in check. Many observers have suggested that the large, front-loaded costs of drug innovation and the long approval lags have slowed this process, however, and knowledgeable insiders suggest that no new "miracle" drugs are on the horizon with wide effectiveness to attack these new resistant strains of disease.

Clearly, policy decisions affecting the supply side of the problem will be critical to the future of disease control because research and development at the pharmaceutical level depend on patent laws, intellectual property rights, and tax and subsidy policies. At the same time, physicians and hospitals are beginning to practice new notions of drug-use management aimed at reducing the buildup of resistance via demand side management. In this chapter, we extend the important optimal antibiotic use work by Laxminarayan and Brown (2001) to include cases in which bacterial populations can be managed when fitness costs are associated with resistance. The Laxminarayan and Brown paper poses a purposefully stark problem in which antibiotic use irreversibly degrades the stock of drug susceptibility. This framework in their modeling structure relies on the assumption that no fitness cost is associated with bacteria that is resistant to an antibiotic drug. In this chapter, we introduce fitness costs, leading to a system in which antibiotic effectiveness can be managed to a steady state. In our setting, antibiotic effectiveness can be regarded as a "renewable" rather than "nonrenewable" resource, opening up opportunities for interesting resistance management trade-offs, including possibilities of management without using antibiotics. We contrast two different regimes. We first discuss the basic epidemiological dynamics under a no-treatment policy, which we refer to as an "ecological" policy. By ecological policy, we mean a noninterventionist policy that allows a disease to progress in a manner dictated by the natural interaction among bacteria exhibiting interspecific and intraspecific competition. We then explore the treatment or "interventionist" regime for which the disease progresses in a manner dictated by interspecific and intraspecific competition that is aided and altered by antibiotic drug treatment. Finally, we compare the outcomes of interventionist and treatment regimes. This comparison is then extended with a discussion of a broader range of nondrug treatment regimes as mechanisms for managing the problem of antibiotic resistance.

Literature Review

Most of the literature that currently exists on the subject of antibiotic resistance is largely within the biological and medical science literature. Optimal human drug use has been addressed within an economic context by only a handful of economists. Among the most notable papers that have dealt with the economic considerations surrounding biological resistance have been those of Hueth and Regev (1974), Brown and Layton (1996) and, most recently, Laxminarayan and Brown (2001).

The Hueth and Regev paper was one of the first papers to examine the economics of resistance buildup. Hueth and Regev examined the problem of pest resistance within an agricultural context and handled the pest management problem in a very general, analytical framework using optimal control theory. They considered the optimal timing of pesticide application over a growing season to maximize crop profits net of pest costs and subject to biological equations of motion for crop growth and susceptibility. They concluded that the gradual depletion of resistance should be anticipated and accounted for as part of an optimal decision and that the timing of pesticide application is important.

The Brown and Layton paper examined both agricultural and human drug use in a very general analytical framework, giving more attention to the private versus public aspect of the problem. By juxtaposing the dynamic optimization problem of the social planner with the myopic and static optimization problem of the private antibiotic user, they showed that the private user treats too much compared with the social optimum of the dynamic optimizer. They also addressed the intergenerational issues that arise with increased resistance over time and discussed the issue of how many people should be treated and who should be treated first. These general discussions give a good overview of the important issues surrounding the socially optimal use of drugs in treating a population and suggest useful directions for further work. At the same time, the paper lacks some of the specificity that can be derived from more explicit epidemiological and economic formulations.

The Laxminarayan and Brown (2001) paper is among the first to recast an epidemiological model of antibiotic-resistant disease within an economic framework that considers the economic costs and benefits of treatment. The result is a series of analytical and simulation results that are sometimes in concert with, and sometimes at variance with, traditional analysis based exclusively on epidemiological modeling. The model we present takes the Laxminarayan and Brown work as a point of departure (using their notation where possible) and generalizes it in several nontrivial directions. The most important generalization is the incorporation of the possibility that resistant diseases incur a fitness cost associated with their ability to be unaffected by antibiotic treatment. As it turns out, this is a critically important feature of optimal antibiotic treatment models, and whether fitness costs are included affects the qualitative nature of the solution in surprising ways. Our second contribution is to focus on the comparison of "interventionist" strategies involving antibiotic drug use and "ecological" strategies involving control of bacterial populations without drugs.

The epidemiological model we use as a foundation for our analysis is, as in the Laxminarayan and Brown (2001) analysis, the model of infection and acquired resistance discussed in Bonhoeffer and others (1997). The Bonhoeffer model is a "multicompartment" model of treatment and infection. Because it uses a pure epidemiological model of disease, the Bonhoeffer paper does not optimize with an economic objective function but instead simulates the number of uninfected individuals over a given time horizon under different treatments. In assessing the efficacy of various policies, Bonhoeffer and others did not explicitly assign costs to either treatment actions or illness, and they ignored any role for discounting over the planning period. Laxminarayan and Brown analyzed the antibiotic treatment problem as a dynamic economic optimization problem with explicit treatment benefits, treatment costs, and discounting. Importantly, the Laxminarayan and Brown assumption of zero fitness costs leads to a characterization of the problem for which, for emphasis, the "stock of antibiotic effectiveness" is a depletable or nonrenewable resource unequivocally reduced with antibiotic use. In the model we develop, we relax this assumption to examine situations in which the stock of effectiveness is at least potentially renewable.

Epidemiological Model

The model we use follows directly from the compartment model presented by Bonhoeffer and others (1997) for a single treatment regime, which is based, in turn, on the population models of disease transmission and infection dynamics that date back to Kermack and McKendrick (1927), Soper (1929), and earlier still to Ross (1911). The malaria epidemic model of Ross and the antibiotic treatment model of Kermack and McKendrick both make use of the interaction between infected members of the population and those who are uninfected (or susceptible)—hence the name "SIS" (susceptible $\rightarrow$ infected $\rightarrow$ susceptible).

The essentials are captured in the schematic in Figure 1-1, in which we have a given entry rate E into the population of uninfected individuals, as well as an associated death rate n. The increase in the population of those infected with the drug-sensitive strain of virus or bacteria I_w is controlled by (a) the rate of transmission β and the interaction between those who are uninfected and those who are already infected, as well as (b) the natural recovery or clearance rate of the drug-sensitive strain of infection $r_w I_w$, in addition to any additional recovery provided by treatment, $f r_f (1 - s) I_w$. The rate of change of the population infected with the drug-resistant strain I_r is controlled only by the transmission/interaction effect and the natural recovery $r_r I_r$. In addition, there are death rates (m) associated with the infected population, which incorporate natural as well as disease-related effects and cross-over effects from the drug-sensitive to the resistant population caused by drug-induced acquisition of resistance $f s r_f I_w$ where s is the fraction of those treated who acquire resistance. The treatment variable f represents the fraction of the population treated with the drug and, as such, is bounded between 0 and 1. A special feature of this kind of model is that treatment is assumed to be nonselective. Thus it is assumed that infected individuals can be identified to receive treatment without knowing whether a specific individual harbors the resistance bacteria or the susceptible bacteria. The technical implication of this assumption is that one cannot control the two infected populations separately; instead, they are jointly controlled in a manner that reflects their relative abundance. Treatment control in this model essentially increases the remission rate of the individual infected with susceptible bacteria. The r_f

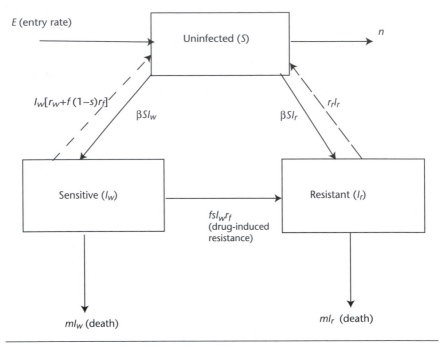

FIGURE 1-1. Schematic of Single Drug Treatment Regime

parameter represents the *additional* remission rate of bacterial infection over and above the natural recovery rate. While somewhat stylized, this model captures the essentials of infection dynamics within a population and lends itself quite easily to analysis, both numerically and analytically.

The dynamic equations of motion for the compartment model are as follows:

$$\dot{S} = E - nS - \beta S(I_w + I_r) + r_w I_w + r_r I_r + f(1-s)I_w r_f$$
$$\dot{I}_w = (\beta S - m - r_w - f r_f)I_w \qquad (1)$$
$$\dot{I}_r = (\beta S - m - r_r)I_r + f s I_w r_f$$

We follow Laxminarayan and Brown (2001) in simplifying this model by assuming that we are dealing with a closed population such as a hospital or regional clinic in an isolated area. These assumptions are embodied by assuming $E = m = n = 0$. Dealing with a closed population allows other conveniences, including the ability to normalize the whole population so that $S + I = 1$ and the ability to normalize the population of individuals infected with the susceptible bacteria strain as a fraction of the total population of infected individuals. As Laxminarayan and Brown showed, it is then possible to reduce the state variables of interest in the model to just two: the total population of infected individuals $I(t)$ and the fraction of the infected population susceptible to antibiotics $w(t)$. Because acquired resistance acts only to modify the drug-induced mortality of susceptible bacteria, it does not affect the qualitative conclusions; hence we set $S = 0$ also. These normalizations and the resultant modified state equations are as follows:

$$S + I = 1, \quad I = I_w + I_r, \quad w = \frac{I_w}{I}$$

$$\dot{I} = \left(\beta S - r_r + (r_r - r_w)w - w r_f f \right) I = \left(\beta - r_r + w[\Delta r - r_f f] \right) I - \beta I^2 \qquad (2)$$

$$\dot{w} = w\left[(1 - w)(\Delta r - f r_f) \right]$$

where the quantity $\Delta r \equiv r_r - r_w$ is referred to in the literature as the "fitness cost" of the resistant strain. This is not an economic cost but rather a biological cost to the resistant strain that is reflected in increased mortality in the absence of treatment, which arises from the possession of genes that allow it to survive under drug treatment. In other words, a positive fitness cost means that the resistant strain of bacteria or virus has an advantage that allows it to survive in the presence of the drug. But that advantage comes at a survival cost $r_r > r_w$ in the sense that the drug-sensitive strain will dominate the combined disease ecology in the absence of treatment. This can be illustrated in the phase diagrams that follow (see Figures 1-2, 1-3, and 1-4).

First we describe the phase space of this dynamical system under extreme controls, that is, control strategies with either $f = 0$ or $f = 1$. A phase diagram plots the trajectories of the two differential equations that describe the evolution of the stock of infected individuals and the proportion of receptive individuals. Generally the system will evolve from some arbitrary initial state to an equilibrium, at which point both stocks have reached their long-term steady state levels. In the absence of treatment ($f = 0$), we obtain the phase diagram in Figure 1-2, which shows the trajectories of both the stock of infected individuals and the stock of individuals receptive to antibiotic treatment.

Note that in the absence of treatment, the equilibrium is such that there is a background level of infection equal to $[(\beta - r_w)/\beta]$ and the mix of bacteria is such that all are treatable by the antibiotic ($w = 1$). Consider an infection "event" in which there is an introduction of individuals infected with a resistant bacterial strain. This is shown by the trajectory beginning with an infection level higher than the original equilibrium and a population mix of only partially receptive bacteria $w < 1$. In this case, if no treatment is initiated, the interaction between the two bacterial populations will allow the bacteria receptive to drug treatment to outcompete the drug-resistant strain, and w will rise.

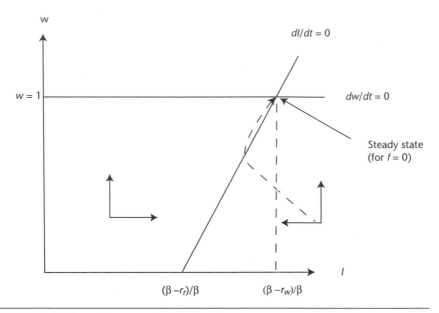

FIGURE 1-2. Phase Space under No Treatment

At the same time, because the entire bacteria population is larger than its natural equilibrium, there will be an excess of mortality and the overall population will fall. This is shown in Figure 1-2 by the trajectory that rises in w and falls and then rises in I toward the steady state. We call this outcome the outcome associated with an "ecological" strategy because it relies on natural interaction and competition between the two populations of bacteria strains to bring the system back into equilibrium. For this equilibrium outcome (that in which the resistant strain is eliminated) to occur, it is necessary for antibiotic-resistant bacteria to incur a fitness cost. The fitness cost actually operates as a reduced relative survival rate and is necessary to eventually eliminate the resistant bacteria from the system when the no-treatment option is used.

In contrast, the phase diagram for the case with full treatment ($f = 1$) is given in Figure 1-3. Again, this diagram depicts the joint evolution of the two-equation system that describes the population of infected individuals and the receptive population. We call the full treatment strategy the "interventionist" strategy, and, as can be seen, after an infection event perturbation, a lower level of steady state infection equal to $(\beta - r_r)/\beta$ is achieved, but at the cost of converting the disease population to one consisting of only resistant bacteria so that w is driven to zero. This different equilibrium occurs because treatment over the full horizon eliminates the receptive bacteria and allows the resistant bacteria to fully outcompete them in the transition to equilibrium.

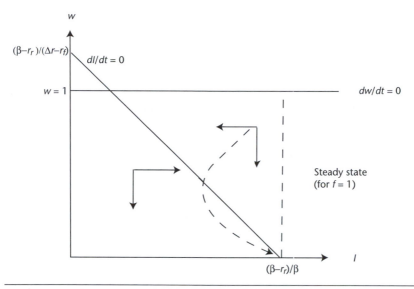

FIGURE 1-3. Phase Space under Full Treatment

As the phase diagram analysis in Figures 1-2 and 1-3 indicates, two qualitatively different equilibria are possible after an infection event perturbation under the use of extreme controls over the horizon. One, associated with what we call an ecological strategy, allows the populations of bacteria to compete in an interspecific and intraspecific manner until a (relatively) high infection level equilibrium is reached. The other, associated with an interventionist strategy, involves driving the overall infection level to a lower level but with a new disease population of antibiotic-resistant bacteria. This is the case emphasized by Laxminarayan and Brown (2001), in which the policy reduces the depletable stock of resistance to zero. Importantly, in the more general model with fitness costs, there is an economic choice to be made about which regime (ecological or interventionist) to pursue. If we consider the simplest example and assume that the treatment costs of the ecological regime are zero, then there is a cutoff treatment cost in the interventionist case that will make that strategy inferior to following the ecological strategy. In the next section, we discuss the nature of the optimal interventionist strategy further. We show that the optimal policy is not actually one in which the optimal decision is to treat at a maximum rate over the whole horizon (as depicted on the phase diagram in Figure 1-4) but one that involves a mixed strategy of maximum rates and intermediate rates of treatment. Solving the optimal treatment decision over the horizon of the interventionist case is a necessary precursor to comparing the outcomes from using the ecological or interventionist strategies.

The Economic Model

The model we use here is in the same spirit as that presented in Laxminarayan and Brown (2001), but we have generalized it to account for fitness cost. In addition, we modified the objective function to minimize the discounted sum of treatment costs and damage costs resulting from illness. Additional details and definitions are in the chapter appendix. The dynamic treatment model can be stated as follows:

$$\min_{0 \le f(t) \le 1} \int_0^\infty \left[d_I I(t) + c_f I(t)[f(t)] \right] e^{-\rho t} dt$$

$$s.t. \quad \dot{I}(t) = \left(\beta - r_r + w(t) \left[\Delta r - r_f f(t) \right] \right) I(t) - \beta (I(t))^2, \quad I(0) = I_0 \quad (3)$$

$$\dot{w}(t) = w(t) \left[(1 - w(t))(\Delta r - r_f f(t)) \right], \quad w(0) = w_0$$

The costs d_I and c_f are those of infection level in the population and treatment, respectively, while ρ is the discount rate. So now we can write out the corresponding current value Hamiltonian as

$$\mathcal{H}(\bullet) = d_I I(t) + c_f[f(t)]I(t) + \lambda(t) \left[\left(\beta - r_r + w(t)(\Delta r - r_f f(t)) \right) I(t) - \beta(I(t))^2 \right]$$
$$+ \mu(t) \left[w(t) \left\{ (1 - w(t))(\Delta r - r_f f(t)) \right\} \right] \quad (4)$$

which is minimized in each period with an appropriate choice of the optimal treatment rate f^*. There are two shadow prices, $\lambda(t)$ and $\mu(t)$, corresponding respectively to the population of infecteds $I(t)$ and the proportion susceptible $w(t)$. As is convention, t measures continuous time, later suppressed for notational convenience. Because this problem is linear in controls, we need to isolate the switching function, which is as follows:

$$\sigma(t) = \left[c_f I - \lambda(t) w(t) I(t) r_f - \mu(t)(1 - w(t)) w(t) r_f \right] \quad (5)$$

This is the coefficient on the treatment control, and the Pontryagin optimality conditions state that

$$f^* = 0 \text{ as } \sigma(t) > 0$$
$$f^* = \hat{f} \text{ as } \sigma(t) > 0 \quad (6)$$
$$f^* = 1 \text{ as } \sigma(t) < 0$$

When the switching function is negative, a maximum control that treats the whole population of infected individuals is used to minimize the Hamiltonian; when the switching function is positive, no control is warranted. These controls correspond to treatment regimes that treat the entire population with the drug ($f^* = 1$), or that treat no one ($f^* = 0$), or that treat some possibly time-varying fraction ($f^* = \hat{f}(t)$). When the switching function is zero, a so-called singular control is indicated. The complete solution to a linear control problem such as this generally involves a "synthesized" control that consists of segments of extreme controls, followed by segments of singular controls. In the appendix, we solve for the singular control $f^* = \hat{f}$ and then show how the synthesized control combines extreme and singular control regimes.

For the problem we consider in this chapter, we presume that a closed population has experienced an infection event such that the initial level of total infection is at or above the natural equilibrium and there has been some introduction of resistant bacterial infections. These kinds of events are depicted as perturbations in the phase diagrams in Figures 1-2 and 1-3. For these kinds of circumstances, there are two possibilities; each is associated with versions of the control regimes discussed earlier. One possibility is that the optimal control policy is a zero control or ecological strategy throughout. The other possibility is that an interventionist strategy is optimal. This will generally involve an initial period in which the entire infected population is treated with an extreme control $f^* = 1$ for a period, followed by a switch to a singular control $f^* = \hat{f}$ for the remaining time in the horizon.

As we show in the appendix, for the interventionist strategy, the singular control involves tracking an optimal level of the population of drug-susceptible bacteria by adjusting the control continuously as the total infection level and fraction susceptible change over time. We show that the following equation describes the optimal singular treatment level $\hat{f}$.

$$r_f[\hat{f} - f_\infty] = -\{\phi_1[I_\infty(w - w_\infty)] + \phi_2[wI_\infty - w_\infty I] + \phi_3[w_\infty(I_\infty - I)]\} \tag{7}$$

The optimal treatment level along the singular path is greater than the long-run steady state value of the treatment level f_∞ by an amount related to the differences between the long-run steady state values of the infection level I_∞ and the fraction susceptible w_∞ and the current values (I and w) of those state variables. The differences inside the brackets of the three right-hand terms of this accelerator formulation are generally positive, and the coefficients ϕ_i are generally negative; hence the treatment level is at least its steady state value plus an amount over the singular path.

The long-run steady state values for f_∞ and w_∞ are shown in the appendix to be

$$f_\infty = \frac{r_r - r_w}{r_f} \tag{8}$$

for the optimal long-run treatment rate and

$$w_\infty = \frac{(\beta + \rho - r_r)c_f}{d_I r_f + \Delta r_f c_f} \tag{9}$$

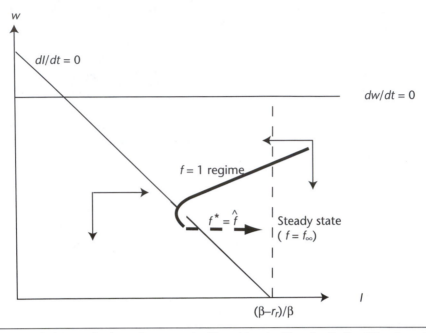

FIGURE 1-4. Pseudophase Space under Transition to Singular Path of Treatment

for the long-run fraction of the infected population that remains responsive to drug treatment. The synthesized optimal trajectory is shown in the pseudophase diagram in Figure 1-4.

The solution begins with a phase in which it is optimal to treat the entire population of infected individuals, including those infected with resistant bacteria with an extreme control of $f^* = 1$. But the cost of reducing the infection level in the aggregate is to change the proportion of bacteria that are susceptible or resistant to future treatment. This kind of outcome occurs in this model, of course, precisely because it is assumed that it is not possible to test individuals to determine whether they are infected with susceptible bacteria, and, therefore, a nonselective control is necessary. This assumption is likely to hold with current diagnostic technology because susceptibility can generally only be determined by culturing bacteria samples, and that takes time. In the future, more rapid identification techniques may be used, and that would change the nature of the whole trade-off between infection treatment and the depletion of the stock of susceptibility. In the case under examination here, control with an extreme control drives the susceptible population down and reduces the total level of infection in the system until the trajectory crosses the isocline. At that point, presuming that the extreme control is still in use, the fraction susceptible continues to fall, and the total infection level begins to rise. The total infection level rises eventually, even with sustained treatment, because with continued antibiotic treatment, the resistant bacteria eventually come to dominate the bacterial ecology, and total infection increases.

At some switch point that is optimally determined, the extreme control is converted into a singular control involving only partial treatment of the population so that $f^* = \hat{f}(t)$. When this occurs, the treatment rate is varied continuously according to the proportional adjustment in Equation 7. During the singular control period, the total infection level begins to rise, eventually reaching the steady state, asymptotically. In a similar manner, the population fraction susceptible and the fraction of the total population treated asymptote to their isocline steady state values given earlier. Note that the isoclines in the treatment phase diagram and the associated directions of motion actually only hold with the extreme control in use. When the singular control is in operation, technically speaking, the differential equation system becomes nonautonomous, and a nonautonomous system cannot be represented in a phase diagram. At the same time, we can still plot the qualitative trajectory of the singular solution in terms of the motion implied for the w and I state variables, and this is why we refer to Figure 1-4 as a pseudophase diagram.

Several qualitative characteristics of the above system are worth highlighting. First, in contrast to the Laxminarayan and Brown (2001) nonrenewable formulation that assumes no fitness cost, in this case, there is a long-run steady state in which the stock of antibiotic resistance can be considered renewable. This steady state is maintained by a fractional treatment policy that keeps the susceptible and resistant bacteria in a delicate equilibrium. This equilibrium is achieved by adjusting the treatment rate so that the sum of the natural rate of decrease of susceptible organisms augmented by extra mortality associated with partial treatment just balances the higher mortality of the resistant bacteria. Second, the control path is achieved by an interesting synthesized control consisting of extreme and singular controls. The singular control is not constant as it is in the typical renewable resource model, but instead it is chosen so that the population of susceptible bacteria "tracks" the desired path in transition to an equilibrium. This time-varying singular path is a characteristic of nonautonomous linear control problems; here the equation for the stock of infected individuals is nonautonomous because it contains $w(t)$, which itself is an explicit function of time. Third, the synthesized control may involve treatment even beyond the point at which the minimum level of infection has been reached. This at first seems counterintuitive: what is gained by continuing to pay treatment costs after the infection level has been driven to its lowest level? The answer is that it pays to continue treating because the resulting future trajectory of total infection lies below the path that would otherwise exist if, for example, treatment stopped at the level of minimum infection.

A Numerical Comparison: Renewable versus Nonrenewable Cases

To check these results and to perform comparative dynamics experiments, we developed a discretized form of this problem that can be solved with dynamic programming methods. We can optimize this problem by using the Bellman Equation, which can be written as

$$\min_{0 \le f_t \le 1} V(I_t) = d_I I_t + c_f I_t[f_t] + \delta V(I_{t+1})$$

s.t.

$$I_{t+1} - I_t = \left(\beta - r_r + w_t\left[\Delta r - r_f f_t\right]\right)I_t - \beta(I_t)^2, \ I_{t=0} = I_0$$

$$w_{t+1} - w_t = w_t\left[(1 - w_t)(\Delta r - r_f f_t)\right], \ w_{t=0} = w_0$$

(10)

where the function $V(I_{t+1})$ gives the carryover cost from one period to the next of the residual infection level, which we also seek to minimize and discount with the factor $\delta = 1/(1 + \rho)$. The optimal solution of the Bellman Equation in each period is equivalent to the optimal solution of the continuous time control problem for the corresponding periods, by Bellman's Principle of Optimal-

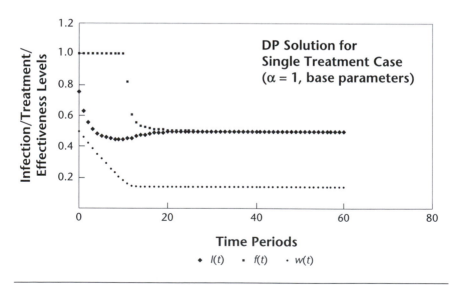

FIGURE 1-5. Behavior along Optimal Path with Fitness Cost

ity. We iterate to find a polynomial approximation to the value function $V(I_{t+1})$ and then use it to solve the Bellman Equation forward for each period. We employed a Chebychev polynomial approximation algorithm to solve for the value function, which was easily implementable in the General Algebraic Modeling System software package. A good discussion of approximation methods is given by Kenneth Judd in his book on numerical methods (1998).

Now we present the results of the dynamic programming model for single drug use, in the absence of induced resistance effects ($s = 0$) and death rate ($n = 0$). From the graph of the solution, using parameter values of $\beta = 0.6$, $r_r = 0.3$, $r_w = 0.15$, $r_f = 0.3$, we see that for the linear objective function, we ultimately approach a singular steady state, where $f_\infty = 0.5$, and the infection level asymptotes to a level of $I_\infty = 0.5$, while that of effectiveness remains at $w_\infty = 0.14$. Given a fitness cost of $\Delta r = 0.15$, f_∞ is being set in the steady state at a level where $(\Delta r - fr_f) = 0$ to hold the two bacterial populations in balance. In the steady state, the equation of motion for $w(t)$ becomes stationary and the differential equation for I satisfies

$$\dot{I} = \left[\beta - r_r + \underbrace{w\left(\Delta r - fr_f\right)}_{=0} \right] I - \beta I^2 = 0 \text{ so that } I = \frac{\beta - r_r}{\beta} = 0.5$$

as shown in Figure 1-5.

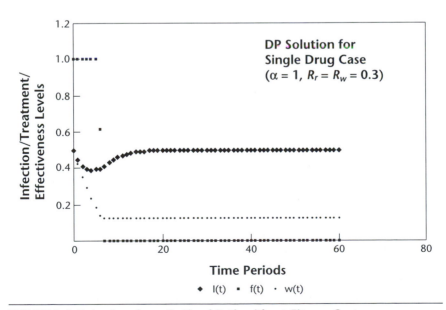

FIGURE 1-6. Behavior along Optimal Path without Fitness Cost

To contrast, we also solved for the dynamically optimal path for the case under which it is assumed that there are no fitness costs. In this case, the system is controlled at the extremes of the constraint set, without a singular path, in typical "bang-bang" fashion (see Figure 1-6).

Optimal Interventionist versus Ecological Control Regimes

The qualitative results derived from our combined economic and epidemiological model are in interesting contrast to those typically derived from pure epidemiological models. The differences, of course, emerge mainly out of the framework that poses the treatment problem as an economic optimization problem expressed in terms of costs and benefits and a discount rate. In epidemiology, most modeling is done without an explicit optimization framework, often to understand important mechanisms and the implications of various parameters and rate constants. At the same time, pure epidemiological models are used to support normative conclusions about the best course of action from among alternatives, usually without much explicit discussion of the metric of comparison. It is common, for example, to conclude that a certain treatment regime is best because it reduces incidence of disease the most among alternatives. In pure epidemiological approaches, outcomes are not monetized or discounted, nor are costs included in a manner that leads to computation of net benefits or easy comparison of different treatment regimes that involve different paths of treatment and recovery.

How do our normative conclusions derived from an integrated economic/epidemiological model differ from what might be concluded without the economics? To answer that, we first need to characterize the policy prescription that epidemiologists might adhere to when faced with the question, how should we treat when treatment results in resistance? An answer that was put forth nearly 100 years ago by Ehrlich was "frapper fort et frapper vite," which translated from the French means "hit 'em hard and hit 'em fast" (Ehrlich 1913). This sounds, of course, very much like the first stage of an optimal linear policy in which the population is hit with an extreme control. The economic results differ in that we have an answer about when to stop treating, and it is not when all of the disease has been eliminated. Instead, the economically optimal policy accounts for diminishing returns to further treatment brought on by the fact that the treatment policy itself changes the balance of susceptible/resistant bacteria to such a degree that further treatment does not yield net benefits. Interestingly, the optimal policy does continue the "hit 'em hard" treatment even when the total infection level is increasing because of the dominance of resistant bacteria, but it eventually leads into a singular control that brings the whole system into a steady state with a residual level of equilibrium infection. The economic policy backs off from Ehrlich's maxim because the economic policy accounts for costs and discounts future reductions in disease incidence. Discounting plays a role here in that reductions in disease incidence expected to occur in the far distant future are discounted and eventually deemed not worth the current expenses of control. These differences in modeling strategies raise age-old but still relevant questions about whether it is morally defensible to monetize health benefits, discount future health payoffs, or use frameworks that force consideration of interpersonal and intergenerational trade-offs.

Finally, another important question raised with the addition of an economic framework is the policy issue of choice between two control regimes. In principle, in response to any infection event, the full economic decision problem involves selecting the regime that minimizes the sum of discounted treatment and illness damage costs. We saw earlier that the optimal interventionist strategy involves a combination of extreme and singular controls, eventually asymptoting to some equilibrium level of treatment, total infection, and fraction susceptible. Let the discounted value of that fully optimal control strategy be designated as $J_{interventionist}$ and let the corresponding value of

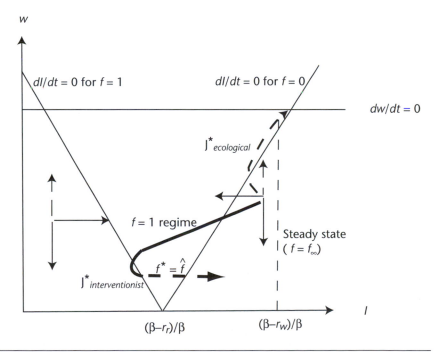

FIGURE 1-7. Hybrid Phase Space under Two Treatment Regimes

the discounted control costs for the (no-treatment) alternative be $J_{ecological}$. Then the true social economic problem is one of finding

$$J^* = \min[J_{interventionist}, J_{ecological}] \tag{11}$$

This is depicted in the phase diagram in Figure 1-7.

In this "hybrid" phase diagram, the dynamic forces depend on whether an ecological or interventionist strategy is being followed. If an ecological strategy is being pursued, the solid and light dotted lines depict initial northwest motion and then northeast motion toward the natural equilibrium at $w = 1$ and $I_\infty = (\beta - r_w)/\beta$. If an interventionist strategy is being pursued, the solid and heavy dashed lines show the trajectory motion toward the long-run equilibrium of $w = w_\infty$ and $I_\infty = (\beta - r_r)/\beta$. Using the interventionist strategy, the motion is, as discussed earlier, a synthesized control that initially moves the system southwest and then finally southeast to the equilibrium.

To verify that there is indeed an economic choice to be made between regimes, we examined this comparison between the two different regimes numerically with our base case optimization model by solving various optimization problems that differ only by the treatment cost parameter c_f. The parameters assumed in the base case run include treatment costs of $1.50 and damages of $20. As the treatment cost is increased, the solution for the interventionist strategy involves different synthesized approach paths to different long-run equilibria. Increasing c_f does not change the long-run infection level of $I_\infty = (\beta - r_r)/\beta$, but the long-run value of w_∞ rises. In addition, the present value of the discounted treatment and damage costs rise, eventually approaching the level associated with the ecological strategy. As it turns out, if the treatment cost is increased above about $13.50, it becomes optimal to abandon the interventionist strategy and to adopt the ecological strategy. At this cutoff value, the cost of treating infection with an interventionist strategy that reduces the infection damages faster does not warrant the expenditures, and it is less costly to treat the infection event with an ecological solution. This kind of comparison would not generally arise out of a pure epidemiological model because the ecological solution would be inferior under most simple noneconomic metrics of comparison.

Conclusion

The technical part of this chapter generalizes previous economic analyses of the antibiotic resistance problem by addressing the case in which disease resistance carries a fitness cost. This has important qualitative implications for economically optimal antibiotic use strategies. The first is that it allows treatment to follow a policy that treats the stock of antibiotic effectiveness as a renewable resource in contrast to the nonrenewable treatment examined by Laxminarayan and Brown (2001). The optimal treatment policy in our case is a synthesized control involving extreme and singular controls. The singular control is a nonautonomous control that causes the stock of antibiotic effectiveness to track a moving target optimal stock of effectiveness. In the long run, a balance is achieved in which the bacterial population of both resistant and susceptible bacteria is held in a delicate equilibrium by cautious partial treatment of the combined populations with a nonselective policy. The second important feature of the model presented here is that it incorporates the possibility of benign strategies that rely only on the interplay between resistant and susceptible bacteria. We refer to these as ecological strategies, but they operate by allowing the natural advantage enjoyed by susceptible bacteria to help them outcompete resistant bacteria. This is in contrast to interventionist strategies that give the resistant bacteria an ecological advantage by reducing the effective competition of susceptible bacteria. We have depicted the ecological option in the simplest fashion, as a no-treatment strategy with no costs relative to the treatment strategy.

In fact, it is probably more realistic to consider ecological strategies that also can alter key system parameters, such as the interaction rate β, at a cost. For example, suppose that there is a baseline interaction rate $\beta_{interventionist}$ associated with the interventionist regime involving aggressive treatment with antibiotics but business as usual in terms of other aspects of infection control in the hospital or other institutional setting. Suppose also that the interaction rate for the ecological strategy $\beta_{ecological}$ can be reduced at a cost $C(\beta_{interventionist} - \beta_{ecological})$ with costs convex in the reduction from the baseline. Then the regime choice problem in Equation 11 becomes

$$J^* = \min[J_{interventionist}, \min_{\beta_{ecological}} \{J_{ecological} - C(\beta_{interventionist} - \beta_{ecological}\}] \qquad (12)$$

In this slightly more general problem, a subproblem is solved first, namely the amount of costs incurred to select an optimal interaction rate that minimizes total infection, treatment, and interaction reduction costs. This is of some practical importance because it is, in fact, possible to change some of the parameters of the problem that we have been considering immutable, at a cost. For example, Austin and others (1999) report results of a hospital study that tested hand washing and staff cohorting as means of reducing vancomycin-resistant enterococci transmission. Although no costs of the interaction reduction strategy are reported by Austin and others, prevalence rates were reduced by half. This evidence suggests that the full-blown antibiotic treatment optimization problem probably should be considered as one of choice between interventionist or ecological regimes but with each optimized by other system strategies in addition to the fundamental choices of treatment rates. In an important sense, this is the value of bringing economics to important epidemiological policy problems; it illuminates important choices and trade-offs and shows how they are affected by both the epidemiological mechanisms and the economic costs and benefits of potential actions.

References

Austin, D. J., M. J. Bonten, R. A. Weinstein, S. Slaughter, and R. M. Anderson. 1999. Vancomycin-Resistant Enterococci in Intensive-Care Hospital Settings: Transmission Dynamics, Persistence, and the Impact of Infection Control Programs. *Proceedings of the National Academy of Sciences of the USA* 96: 6908–13.

Bonhoeffer, S., M. Lipsitch, and B.R. Levin. 1997. Evaluating Treatment Protocols to Prevent Antibiotic Resistance. *Proceedings of the National Academy of Sciences of the USA* 94(22): 12106–11.

Brown, G., and D.F. Layton. 1996. Resistance Economics: Social Cost and the Evolution of Antibiotic Resistance. *Environmental and Development Economics* 1(3):349–55.

Ehrlich, Paul. 1913. Chemotherapeutics: Scientific Principles, Methods, and Results. *Lancet* ii: 445, cited in Levin, B., M. Lipsitch, and S. Bonhoeffer. 1999. Population Biology, Evolution, and Infectious Disease: Convergence and Synthesis. *Science* 283: 806–9.

Hueth, D., and U. Regev. 1974. Optimal Agricultural Pest Management with Increasing Pest Resistance. *American Journal of Agricultural Economics* 56: 543–53.

Judd, Kenneth L. 1998. *Numerical Methods in Economics*. Cambridge, MA: MIT Press.

Kermack, W.O., and A.G. McKendrick. 1927. A Contribution to the Mathematical Theory of Epidemics. *Proceedings of the Royal Society of London. Series A, Containing Papers of a Mathematical and Physical Character* 115(772): 700–21.

Laxminarayan, R., and G. Brown. 2001. Economics of Antibiotic Resistance: A Theory of Optimal Use. *Journal of Environmental Economics and Management* 42(2): 183–206.

Ross, R. 1911. *The Prevention of Malaria*, Second Edition. London: Murray.

Soper, H.E. 1929. Interpretation of Periodicity in Disease-Prevalence. *Journal of the Royal Statistical Society* 92: 34–73.

Appendix

We solve the linear control problem presented in the text body in this appendix. Recall that the current valued Hamiltonian can be written as follows:

$$\mathcal{H}(\bullet) = d_I I(t) + c_f \big[f(t) \big] I(t) + \lambda(t) \Big[\big(\beta - r_r + w(t) \big(\Delta r - r_f f(t) \big) \big) I(t) - \beta \big(I(t) \big)^2 \Big]$$
$$+ \mu(t) \Big[w(t) \big\{ \big(1 - w(t) \big) \big(\Delta r - r_f f(t) \big) \big\} \Big]$$

(A1)

Recall it is assumed that the objective is to *minimize* this expression representing the discounted sum of treatment and infection damage costs. Both treatment and damage costs are assumed to be linear, the former linear in the treatment rate and the latter linear in the stock of infected individuals. The treatment rate lies within the unit interval, and the current valued shadow prices represent the marginal contributions to the treatment program costs of the stock of infected individuals and the proportion susceptible to antibiotics. We would thus expect $\lambda(t)$ to be positive and $\mu(t)$ to be negative.

Solving linear control problems begins by noting that the control variable enters the Hamiltonian in a manner multiplied by a coefficient, which we call the switching function. The switching function $\sigma(t)$ can be written as

$$\sigma(t) = \left[c_f I - \lambda(t)w(t)I(t)r_f - \mu(t)(1-w(t))w(t)r_f\right] \tag{A2}$$

so that the Hamiltonian can be rewritten as

$$
\begin{aligned}
\mathcal{H}(\bullet) = d_I I(t) + \lambda(t)&\left[(\beta - r_r + w(t)\Delta r)I(t) - \beta(I(t))^2\right] \\
&+ \mu(t)\left[w(t)\{(1-w(t))\Delta r\}\right] \\
&+ f(t)\left[c_f I - \lambda(t)w(t)I(t)r_f - \mu(t)(1-w(t))w(t)r_f\right]
\end{aligned}
\tag{A3}
$$

Now, to minimize the Hamiltonian in all periods, the optimal treatment rate control f^* must be chosen so that

$$
\begin{aligned}
f^* &= 0 \text{ as } \sigma(t) > 0 \\
f^* &= \hat{f} \text{ as } \sigma(t) = 0 \\
f^* &= 1 \text{ as } \sigma(t) < 0
\end{aligned}
\tag{A4}
$$

In other words, when the switching function is positive, it pays to set the control at its smallest possible value to minimize the Hamiltonian. When the switching function is negative, it pays to set the control at its largest value. When it is zero, the control is a singular value that remains to be determined.

Solving for the singular value involves investigating conditions that must hold when the switching function in Equation A2 is identically zero for some finite interval. If the switching function is zero, then its derivative $\dot{\sigma}(t)$ must also be zero on the interval. Differentiating the switching function in Equation A2 gives us

$$
\begin{aligned}
\dot{\sigma}(t) = &\frac{[-\dot{\lambda}Iw - \lambda\dot{I}w - \lambda I\dot{w}]}{[\lambda Iw]}(\lambda Iwr_f) \\
&+ \frac{[-\dot{\mu}w(1-w) - \mu\dot{w}(1-w) + \mu w\dot{w}]}{\mu w}(\mu wr_f) + c_f\dot{I} = 0
\end{aligned}
\tag{A5}
$$

We also know from the Pontryagin conditions that the adjoint variables must satisfy

$$\dot{\lambda} = \rho\lambda - \{d_I + \lambda[\beta(1-I) + w[\Delta r - r_f f] - r_r]\} + \lambda\beta I - c_f f \tag{A6}$$

and

$$\dot{\mu} = \rho\mu - \{\lambda I[\Delta r - r_f f] - \mu w[\Delta r - r_f f] + \mu(1-w)[\Delta r - r_f f]\} \tag{A7}$$

Substituting these and the state equations for $\dot{w}$ and $\dot{I}$ into the expression for the rate of change of the switching function in Equation A5 we have

$$\dot{\sigma}(t) = -\left[\frac{\dot{\lambda}}{\lambda} + \frac{\dot{I}}{I}\right](\lambda I w r_f) + \left(\frac{\dot{w}}{w}\right)\left[-\lambda I w r_f + \mu w^2 r_f\right]$$
$$-\left[\frac{\dot{\mu}}{\mu} + \frac{\dot{w}}{w}\right](1-w)\mu w r_f + c_f \dot{I} = 0 \tag{A8}$$

But from Equations A6 and A7, it can be shown that

$$\left[\frac{\dot{\lambda}}{\lambda} + \frac{\dot{I}}{I}\right] = (\rho + \beta I) - \left[\frac{d_I + c_f}{\lambda}\right] \quad \text{and} \quad \left[\frac{\dot{\mu}}{\mu} + \frac{\dot{w}}{w}\right] = \rho - \left[\Delta r - r_f\right]\left[\frac{\lambda I}{\mu} - w\right]$$

Substituting these into the expression in A8 gives us

$$\dot{\sigma}(t) = \left\{-(\rho + \beta I) - \left[\frac{d_I + c_f f}{\lambda}\right]\right\}(\lambda I w r_f) + \left(\frac{\dot{w}}{w}\right)\left[\mu w r_f - c_f I\right]$$
$$-\left\{\rho - \left[\Delta r - r_f f\right]\left[\frac{\lambda I}{\mu} - w\right]\right\}(1-w)\mu w r_f + c_f \dot{I} = 0 \tag{A9}$$

Expanding this gives us

$$\dot{\sigma}(t) = -\rho\left[\lambda I w r_f + (1-w)\mu w r_f\right] + \left(d_I + c_f f\right)I w r_f - \beta I^2 \lambda w r_f$$
$$+ (1-w)\left[\Delta r - r_f f\right]\left[\mu w r_f - c_f I + w r_f \lambda I - w^2 \mu r_f\right] + c_f \dot{I} = 0 \tag{A10}$$

Using Expression A2 for the switching function, it can be shown that the terms inside the first bracket in Equation A10 equal $c_f I$. Moreover, substituting terms from the switching equation definition in Equation A2 into terms multiplying $(1 - w)[\Delta r - r_f f]$ in the second line cancels them out, leaving

$$\dot{\sigma}(t) = -\rho c_f I + d_I I w r_f - \beta I^2 \lambda w r_f + c_f f I w r_f + c_f \dot{I} = 0 \tag{A11}$$

Dividing by I and then inserting the state equation for $\dot{I}/I$ gives

$$\dot{\sigma}(t) = -\rho c_f + d_I w r_f - \beta I \lambda w r_f + c_f \beta (1 - I) - c_f r_r + c_f w \Delta r = 0 \tag{A12}$$

Because the switching function is zero along the singular interval, its first derivative is also zero and hence Equation A12 must hold. But a constant switching function also implies that the second derivative is zero, and hence we can differentiate the above expression again to get

$$\frac{d}{dt}\left[\dot{\sigma}(t)\right] = \left[d_I r_f \dot{w} - \beta r_f \lambda w I\right]\left[\frac{\dot{I}}{I} + \frac{\dot{w}}{w} + \frac{\dot{\lambda}}{\lambda}\right] - \beta c_f \dot{I} + c_f \dot{w} \Delta r = 0 \tag{A13}$$

Collecting and rearranging terms, we have

$$\frac{d}{dt}[\dot{\sigma}] = \frac{\dot{w}}{w}\left[d_I r_f w - \beta r_f \lambda w I + c_f \Delta r w\right] - \frac{\dot{I}}{I}\left[\beta r_f w \lambda I + c_f \beta I\right] - \frac{\dot{\lambda}}{\lambda}\left[\beta r_f I w \lambda\right] = 0 \tag{A14}$$

Substituting terms in Equation A12 into the first term in brackets to eliminate the shadow price and collecting terms leaves us with

$$\frac{d}{dt}[\dot{\sigma}] = \left[\frac{\dot{w}}{w}\right]\left\{\rho c_f - c_f \beta (1 - I) + c_f r_r\right\} - \left[\frac{\dot{I}}{I}\right](c_f \beta I) - \left[\frac{\dot{I}}{I} + \frac{\dot{\lambda}}{\lambda}\right](\beta r_f I w \lambda) = 0 \tag{A15}$$

Substituting instate and costate equations for the log derivatives and canceling and collecting terms gives us

$$\frac{d}{dt}[\dot{\sigma}] = \left[\frac{\dot{w}}{w}\right]\left\{\rho c_f - c_f \beta (1 - I) + c_f r_r\right\} - \left[\frac{\dot{I}}{I}\right](\rho c_f + 2\beta I c_f)$$
$$+ \rho^2 c_f - \rho d_I w r_f - \rho c_f w r_f f + \rho \beta I c_f = 0 \tag{A16}$$

This equation must be satisfied along the singular path. Once the state equations for $\dot{w}$ and $\dot{I}$ are inserted into Equation A16, the result is an equation describing the singular control $\hat{f}$ for the treatment rate as a function of the two state variables. The singular path thus derived is a nonautonomous path because the optimal treatment rate $\hat{f}(t)$ varies over time to make the two state variables "track" their optimal singular path values. This will be seen when the log derivatives of the two costate equations are substituted in, leaving an equation describing the optimal singular control as a feedback function of the two state variables. Before solving the full solution for the singular control at any point in time along the singular path, consider first the singular control at the long-run equilibrium steady state. Inspecting Equation A16 shows that when the system ultimately reaches its equilibrium, both log derivatives vanish, and the remaining part of Equation A16 describes conditions in equilibrium. In particular, we can solve for the long-run equilibrium values of the control and state variables f_∞, I_∞, w_∞ using

$$\rho^2 c_f - \rho d_I w_\infty r_f - \rho c_f w_\infty r_f f_\infty + \rho \beta I_\infty c_f = 0 \tag{A17}$$

which can be rearranged to solve for the long-run equilibrium value of the singular control, namely

$$f_\infty = \frac{\beta + \rho - r_r}{r_f w_\infty} - \frac{d_I}{c_f} \tag{A18}$$

Because $r_f f_\infty = \Delta r$ also, we can substitute and rearrange to solve for

$$w_\infty = \frac{(\beta + \rho - r_r)c_f}{d_I r_f + \Delta r \, c_f} \tag{A19}$$

Now we are ready to describe the full solution to the singular control at any point along the singular path, including the long-run steady state equilibrium. To do this, we substitute the state equations into Equation A16 and collect and rearrange terms to get

$$\frac{d}{dt}[\dot\sigma] = \left(\Delta r - r_f f\right)\left\{(1 - w)\left[c_f\left(\rho - \beta(1 - I) + r_r\right)\right] - w c_f\left(\rho + 2\beta I\right)\right\}$$
$$- c_f(\rho + 2\beta I)\left[\beta(1 - I) - r_r\right] + r_f w \beta I d_I + r_f \beta w I c_f f \tag{A20}$$
$$- (\rho + \beta I)\left(-\rho c_f + d_I w r_f\right) - \rho c_f w r_f f - \beta I c_f w r_f f = 0$$

By adding and subtracting $\rho c_f w \Delta r$, we can collect terms involving $(\Delta r - r_f f)$ to get

$$\left(\Delta r - r_f f\right)\left\{(1 - w)\left[c_f\left(\rho - \beta(1 - I) + r_r\right)\right] - w c_f(\rho + 2\beta I) + \rho w c_f\right\}$$
$$- c_f(\rho + 2\beta I)\left[\beta(1 - I) - r_r\right] + \beta I \rho c_f + \rho^2 c_f - \rho w\left[c_f \Delta r + d_I r_f\right] = 0 \tag{A21}$$

Making appropriate substitutions for combinations of parameters that describe equilibrium values for various state and control variables in Equations A18 and A19, we can then write the full solution for the singular control as

$$r_f(f_\infty - \hat{f}) = \frac{\rho\left\{\rho\left[\dfrac{w - w_\infty}{w_\infty}\right] + \beta I\left[\left(\dfrac{w}{w_\infty}\right) - \left(\dfrac{I}{I_\infty}\right)\right]\right\} + \beta(I_\infty - I)[\rho + 2\beta I]}{(1 - w)\left[\rho - \beta(I_\infty - I)\right] - 2w\beta I} \tag{A22}$$

What is the intuition behind this expression for the singular control? Note that in the long-run equilibrium in which all variables are stationary, we know that the total level of infected individuals will equilibrate at $I_\infty = (\beta - r_r)/\beta$. In addition, the equilibrium value of the treatment rate must be such that $r_f f_\infty = r_r - r_w$. This treatment rate ensures that the extra mortality to the susceptible bacteria caused by the equilibrium treatment rate just brings into balance the susceptible mortality rate after treatment with the higher mortality rate of resistant bacteria caused by the fitness cost. Finally, there is a long-run equilibrium value given for the proportion of susceptible bacteria w_∞. Using these definitions in the singular solution, the solution for the optimal treatment rate can be seen to be a type of mixed accelerator. That is, the difference between the current optimal treatment rate and its long-run equilibrium value is related to the difference between the current fraction of susceptible bacteria and its long-run value $(w - w_\infty)$ and the difference between the current and long-run values of the total infection level $(I - I_\infty)$.

$$r_f\left(\hat{f} - f_\infty\right) = -\left\{\phi_1\left[I_\infty(w - w_\infty)\right] + \phi_2\left[wI_\infty - w_\infty I\right] + \phi_3\left[w_\infty(I_\infty - I)\right]\right\} \qquad \text{(A23)}$$

In this accelerator representation, each accelerator coefficient is a function of the current state variables so that $\phi_i = \phi_i(w,I)$ in which the specific functions are determined by Equation A22. The adjustment toward the long run in which the treatment rate holds the stock of total infections and susceptible infections constant is seen as one in which the gaps between current and long-run values of the state variables gradually converge.

In summary, the optimal interventionist treatment profile associated with this single drug problem is generally one in which the entire population is treated for a period, followed by a period using a time-varying singular control that takes the system to a long-run equilibrium. As we showed in the body of this chapter, this usually means overshooting the level at which the total population of infected individuals is minimized. In principle, we can determine the switch point at which treatment changes from an extreme control (in which $f = 1$) to one using the singular control.

Chapter 2

Using Antibiotics When Resistance Is Renewable

Robert Rowthorn and Gardner M. Brown

When an antibiotic is "correctly" prescribed to treat an infection, it can have two effects. In the present, it cures the patient. But used across many patients, the practice allows the selection of more resistant organisms, thus reducing the future effectiveness of the drug not only against the strain that causes the illness under treatment but also against other organisms that could otherwise be controlled by the drug. If we do not account for this intertemporal dynamic, we cannot make socially optimal decisions about which antibiotics to use and how much of each to prescribe. This is particularly true when the evolution of resistance is fast paced. One way to address the problem is by simulation: different treatment strategies are specified, and outcomes are ranked according to some criterion. However, because so many options are possible, it is easy to miss some excellent, even optimum, outcomes. In this chapter, the optimal use of antibiotics is analyzed with mathematical methods developed to study other dynamic natural resource allocation problems, such as groundwater or forest resources. In the model applied here, two antibiotics are available to treat two strains of infections. Each drug is effective for only one strain. Only one drug is used per patient at a time in this model, and the doctors do not know which strain a patient has. Each cure has the same benefit. Infection and treatment dynamics follow the basic SIS (susceptible → infected → susceptible) model. The rate at which healthy people are infected by a given strain is governed by a common transmission coefficient. The rate at which sick people are cured in the absence of treatment is governed by a spontaneous recovery rate for each strain and the fraction treated. Except for the fraction of the population treated and the level of infection in the steady state (when those infected balance those cured), all other interesting results depend on both economic and epidemiological parameters. The fraction of the infected population treated by each antibiotic in the steady state varies inversely with the rate of spontaneous recovery.

About two decades after Fleming discovered the mold from which penicillin is produced, the drug was introduced into clinical practice (Garrett 1994). Since that time, tens of thousands of antibiotic products have been developed to successfully treat diseases that previously had fateful consequences. In the United States alone at least 150 million courses of antibiotics are prescribed annually (McCaig and Hughes 1995). Annual production in the United States exceeds 50 million pounds, 40% of which is destined for animal use (Levy 1998). The success of antibiotics in treating diseases engendered so much optimism that it was easy to conclude, as many did, that the conquest of all infectious diseases was imminent (Garrett 1994).[1] Such optimism has to be leavened with a downside to antibiotic use.

When antibiotics annihilate drug-susceptible strains, a fertile environment is left for the drug-resistant strains to flourish. Conceptually then, the effectiveness of antibiotics (or drug resistance) is a natural resource reduced by use, often quite quickly. Massad and others (1993), citing other literature, stated that the introduction of sulfonamide in the treatment of gonorrhea led to most new cases caused by sulfonamide-resistant gonococci six years later. More spectacularly, the effectiveness of penicillin in treating staphylococci-causing infections was less then 50% after two years of extensive clinical use of the drug (Bryson and Szybalski 1955).

A technical negative externality, multiple drug resistance, is caused by repeated use of antibiotics. Although multiple drug resistance is more prevalent in nosocomial (hospital-acquired) strains (McGowan 1983; Massad et al. 1993), drug-resistant community strains, illustrated by the recent rise in tuberculosis cases in the United States, are of great concern to disease control specialists. It is particularly disturbing that one study found more than one-half of the patients were infected with a strain resistant to one drug and about one-third were infected with a strain resistant to more than one drug. The incidence of multiple-drug resistance has more than doubled since that time (Institute of Medicine 1992). Multiple-drug resistance arising from drug use has at least two drawbacks. In the case of tuberculosis, the disease is extremely contagious, which enhances the rate of infection. More generally, multiple-drug resistance induced by drug use can lead to treatment costs of $150,000 per patient, an order of magnitude higher than traditional treatment costs (Institute of Medicine 1992).

Although it is widely recognized that antibiotic use causes increased resistance, the epidemiologists and biologists in the research community have not responded by building optimization models. Instead, simulations are conducted on alternative-use patterns. An excellent illustration is the research by

Bonhoeffer and others (1997). Their study used three treatment protocols. In the first protocol, both drugs were given to each infected individual; in the second protocol, two equal proportions of those infected were treated by two candidate drugs; and in the third protocol, all patients were given a single drug at any given time with periodic cycling between two drugs. Because these are very restrictive options, it is unlikely that an optimum treatment option will be discovered, except fortuitously. Moreover, unlike economists, epidemiologists attribute the same value to a successful treatment today as they do to a successful treatment 20 years from now. Thus an optimum treatment strategy derived from an economic formulation of the problem necessarily differs from an epidemiological formulation in which the discount rate is assumed to be zero.

Economists in general, and natural resource economists in particular, have been slow to recognize that gaining a better understanding of optimal antibiotic use is of enormous social importance and that our canonical models provide us with substantial comparative advantage in tackling the problem. Brown and Layton (1996) looked briefly at the trade-off between antibiotic use in humans and animals. Laxminarayan (1999) tackles patent breadth for antibiotics and has an empirical chapter on forecasting resistance. Laxminarayan and Brown (2001) treat antibiotic effectiveness as a nonrenewable resource. In the following analysis, we take the natural next step and study the pattern of optimal use of two antibiotics when effectiveness (resistance) is a renewable resource.

Antibiotics Model

The model set out in this chapter considers a very simple case. There are two strains of infection, and there are two treatments, each of which is effective against only one of the strains and is totally ineffective against the other.[2] Infected individuals have a spontaneous recovery rate even if they are not treated; however, their recovery rate is increased if they receive appropriate treatment. Individuals can only be infected by one strain at a time, and the probability of infection by a particular strain is the same for all healthy members of the population regardless of their past medical history. Infection is not fatal, and the population is constant.

The policy problem is to find an optimal balance between the costs and benefits of treatment, taking into account how current treatment decisions will affect the effectiveness of future treatment options. In this calculation, the definition of costs is fairly obvious. They are simply the normal costs associated with medical treatment, in particular, the cost of drugs. Regarding benefits, from a public standpoint, what matters is the health of the population in general. We assume that the overall health of the population is the benefit that is weighed against cost in choosing the optimum treatment strategy.

The optimum strategy depends on the information available to the authorities and also the economic, legal, and political constraints under which they operate. We assume that the public authorities have the following information. They know all the basic parameters of the model, such as the efficacy of treatment and rates of spontaneous recovery and transmission of infection. From periodic sampling, they also know the prevalence of each strain of infection in the population as a whole, and they know who is sick. However, for reasons of time or expense, it is impractical to test each sick individual to ascertain which strain of infection is involved. Thus, treatment cannot be tailored to the needs of specific individuals. If only a fraction of the sick individuals receive a particular treatment, there will be some patients for whom this treatment is wasted because they will receive a drug for which their strain of infection is resistant. Also, there will be others who could benefit from this treatment but do not receive it. One possibility is to administer a cocktail of both treatments to all patients. This maximizes the possibility of cure, but may be prohibitively expensive. Such difficulties are inevitable given the lack of information.

Mathematical Formulation

Infections and treatments are indexed by the subscript $i = 1, 2$. Each treatment is only effective against one strain of infection. Patients who are infected with strain i and receive treatment j ($\neq i$), or who are not treated at all, recover spontaneously at a rate r_i, which denotes the fitness cost of the bacteria. If they receive the effective treatment i, their recovery rate is equal to $r_i + \alpha_i$. The average recovery rate for such patients is a weighted sum of these two rates. It is equal to $(1 - f_i)r_i + f_i(r_i + \alpha_i)$, where f_i is the proportion of patients receiving treatment i. Let I_i denote the number of individuals infected with strain i and let $I = I_1 + I_2$. If the total population is fixed at N, the number of healthy individuals is equal to $N - I$. We ignore births and immigration. In standard fashion, we assume that the number of healthy individuals who become infected with strain i per unit of time is equal to $\beta_i(N - I)I_i$. This is the appropriate expression if infected individuals are randomly distributed among the healthy population and transmit their infection via proximity. The dynamics of infection and treatment specified reflect the research of Kermack and McKendrick (1927) and are summarized by the following differential equations:

$$\dot{I}_1 = \beta_1(N - I)I_1 - (r_1 + f_1\alpha_1)I_1$$
$$\dot{I}_2 = \beta_2(N - I)I_2 - (r_2 + f_2\alpha_2)I_2$$

Suppose that the social value of being healthy is p and that the cost of treatment i is equal to c_i. In each case, the units are money per individual per unit of time. The flow rates of aggregate benefits and aggregate costs are equal to $p(N - I)$ and $(c_1 f_1 + c_2 f_2)I$, respectively. Thus, the net flow of benefits per unit of time is equal to $p(N - I) - (c_1 f_1 + c_2 f_2)I$. The economic objective is to maximize the present value of net benefits formed by the following integral, subject to initial conditions, appropriate constraints, and the preceding differential equations:

$$J = \int_0^\infty e^{-\rho t} \left[p(N - I) - (c_1 f_1 + c_2 f_2) dt \right]$$

where ρ is the social discount rate. Note that this integral may not converge if ρ is zero.

Some Simplifications

To simplify the analysis, we normalize by assuming that $N = 1$. We also make the following substantive assumptions. The two treatments are equally effective against the appropriate infection ($\alpha_1 = \alpha_2 = \alpha$), and the two strains are equally contagious ($\beta_1 = \beta_2 = \beta$). Finally, all patients receive exactly one kind of treatment ($f_1 + f_2 = 1$). Hence we can write $f_1 = f$ and $f_2 = (1 - f)$, and thus any allowable treatment strategy can be fully described by specifying the trajectory of the single control variable f. With these additional assumptions, the optimization problem is to find the time path of f that maximizes the integral

$$J = \int_0^\infty e^{-\rho t} (p - AI) dt \tag{1}$$

subject to

$$\dot{I}_1 = [\beta(1 - I) - r_1 - \alpha f] I_1 \tag{2a}$$

$$\dot{I}_2 = [\beta(1 - I) - r_2 - \alpha(1 - f)] I_2 \tag{2b}$$

$I_1(0), I_2(0)$ are given and
$A = p + c_1 f + c_2(1 - f)$
$I = I_1 + I_2$
$0 < I_1, I_2 < I$
$I < 1$
$0 \leq f \leq 1$
$0 < c_1, c_2, p, r_1, r_2, \rho, \alpha, \beta$

Steady State
Let I^*, f^* be such that

$$\beta[I - I^*] - r_1 - \alpha f^* = 0 \tag{3a}$$

$$\beta[I - I^*] - r_2 - \alpha(1 - f^*) = 0 \tag{3b}$$

Then
$$f^* = \frac{\alpha + (r_2 - r_1)}{2\alpha} \tag{4}$$
$$I^* = 1 - \frac{r_1 + r_2 + \alpha}{2\beta}$$

This solution is independent of economic parameters. If the steady state involves the use of both antibiotics, and not everyone is infected, then $0 < f^*$, $I^* < 1$. This will be the case if and only if

$$\alpha > |r_1 - r_2| \tag{5}$$
$$\beta > \frac{r_1 + r_2 + \alpha}{2}$$

These inequalities imply that the rate of infection exceeds the fitness cost

$$\beta > r_1, r_2 \tag{6}$$

If this were not true, then the spontaneous rates of recovery of at least one strain would exceed the rate of infection, and ultimately this strain would be naturally eliminated without treatment. We can write Equations 2a and 2b as follows:

$$\dot{I}_1 = [-\beta(I - I^*) - \alpha(f - f^*)]I_1 \tag{7a}$$

$$\dot{I}_2 = [-\beta(I - I^*) + \alpha(f - f^*)]I_2 \tag{7b}$$

Because $I = I_1 + I_2$, it follows that

$$\dot{I}_1 = -\beta(I - I^*)I + \alpha(f - f^*)(I_2 - I_1) \tag{8}$$

Also,

$$\frac{\dot{I}_2}{I_2} - \frac{\dot{I}_1}{I_1} = 2\alpha(f - f^*) \tag{9}$$

Thus I_2/I_1 is constant if $f = f^*$. If $I = I^*$ and $f = f^*$, , then both I_1 and I_2 remain constant.

Hamiltonian Conditions

The current value Hamiltonian formed from Equations 1, 7a, and 7b is

$$\mathcal{H} = p - AI + m_1[-\beta(I - I^*) - \alpha(f - f^*)]I_1 + m_2[-\beta(I - I^*) + \alpha(f - f^*)]I_2 \tag{10}$$

The variable A is an analytical substitution, defined earlier as $p + c_1 f + c_2(1 - f)$. An economic interpretation of this variable is provided later in the chapter; m_1 and m_2 are the costate variables (shadow prices). Because $\partial A/\partial f = c_1 - c_2$, it follows that

$$\frac{\partial \mathcal{H}}{\partial f} = -(c_1 - c_2)I + \alpha[m_2 I_2 - m_1 I_1] \tag{11}$$

Thus, for an optimum

$$f \begin{Bmatrix} = 0 \\ \in [0,1] \\ = 1 \end{Bmatrix} \text{as } -(c_1 - c_2)I + \alpha[m_2 I_2 - m_1 I_1] \begin{Bmatrix} < \\ = \\ > \end{Bmatrix} 0 \tag{12}$$

Before setting down the costate equations for the Hamiltonian Equation 10, let us first consider the economic interpretation of Equation 12.

As in other renewable resource problems, the costate variable m_i can be interpreted as a shadow price. This variable indicates the marginal benefit to society of increasing the stock of infection i. Because infection is harmful, the shadow price is negative, and $-m_i$ is the amount society is willing to pay for treatment that reduces the stock of infection i by one unit. In the present model, there are two different infections to consider. As can be seen from Equations 7a and 7b, a change Δf in the share of patients treated by drug 1 causes the number of people infected by strains 1 and 2 to change by $-\alpha I_1 \Delta f$ and $+ \alpha I_2 \Delta f$, respectively. The social value of these changes is equal to $m_1(-\alpha I_1 \Delta f)$ and $m_2(\alpha I_2 \Delta f)$. Their combined value is $\alpha(m_2 I_2 - m_1 I_1) \Delta f$. The total cost of achieving such an outcome is $(c_1 - c_2)I \Delta f$. When both antibiotics are used, so that variation in either direction is possible, the marginal cost of switching drugs must be exactly equal to the social benefit. Thus,

$$(c_1 - c_2)I = \alpha[m_2 I_2 - m_1 I_1] \tag{13}$$

This is merely the condition for an interior solution as given in Equation 12.

If the marginal cost of switching treatments is different from the social value of the resulting change in infection stocks, then only one of the drugs should be used. For example, if the cost of switching to antibiotic 1 is less than the associated gain in social value, then this drug should be used exclusively. This occurs when $(c_1 - c_2)I < \alpha[m_2 I_2 - m_1 I_1]$ as specified in Equation 12. In this case, $f = 1$, which implies that $f_1 = 1$ and $f_2 = 0$.

The costate equations of the current value Hamiltonian for $i = 1$ and 2 are

$$\dot{m}_1 = \rho m_1 + A + m_1[\beta(I - I^*) + \alpha(f - f^*)] + \beta[m_1 I_1 + m_2 I_2] \tag{14a}$$

$$\dot{m}_2 = \rho m_2 + A + m_2[\beta(I - I^*) - \alpha(f - f^*)] + \beta[m_1 I_1 + m_2 I_2] \tag{14b}$$

These are derived by recognizing that $\partial I / \partial I_i = 1$ because $I = I_1 + I_2$.

Using Equations 2a and 2b, and recalling the definition of A, Equations 14a and 14b can be written as follows

$$\rho m_1 = -p - [c_1 f + c_2(1 - f)] + \dot{m}_1 + [m_1 \partial I_1 / \partial I_1 + m_2 \partial I_2 / \partial I_1] \tag{15a}$$

$$\rho m_2 = -p - [c_1 f + c_2(1 - f)] + \dot{m}_2 + [m_1 \partial I_1 / \partial I_2 + m_2 \partial I_2 / \partial I_2] \tag{15b}$$

To interpret these equations, let us take Equation 15a as an example. Similar observations apply to Equation 15b. Consider an exogenous increase of 1 unit in I_1. The (negative) shadow price of this strain of infection is m_1, so in financial terms, the additional infection is equivalent to a negative windfall equal to m_1 units of money. At an interest rate of ρ, this windfall would generate a negative income stream equal to ρm_1 per period. Thus, the left-hand side of Equation 15a represents the opportunity cost of additional infection. The other side of the equation brings together the various consequences of this event. All items are measured at their marginal valuations on the optimum path. The two initial terms evaluate the impacts of additional infection on current levels of sickness and medical treatment. Both terms are negative because extra sickness and medical treatment are social costs. The remaining terms are forward looking. They indicate how an increase in I_1 affects the future shadow price of this strain of infection ("capital appreciation") and the growth rates of infection in general.

There is another economic interpretation of the costate equations. Rewriting Equation 14a as

$$\rho = \frac{\dot{m}_1}{m_1} - \frac{A}{m_1} + VMP(I_1)$$

(where VMP is the value of the marginal product) illustrates the arbitrage principle governing the use of a natural resource. At all times, the rate of return on rival assets (ρ) should equal the marginal rate of return on investment in managing each infection. That rate has three components. The first term on the right-hand side is the rate of price appreciation or depreciation of the asset. The second term, $-A/m_1$, is the marginal generalized stock externality. It captures how the value of the objective function, the net benefits of being healthy, changes if I_1 changes. The last term captures the "own" real marginal rate of return on the stock of infection because

$$VMP(I_1) = \frac{\partial \dot{I}_1}{\partial I_1} + \frac{m_2}{m_1} \frac{\partial \dot{I}_2}{\partial I_1}$$

Thus, Equation 15a has an intuitive meaning. Along the optimum path, the opportunity cost of infection is equal to the actual flow of present and future costs and benefits.

Interior Solution

Suppose there is an optimum path along which $0 < f < 1$ for an open segment. Let $A^* = p + c_1 f^* + c_2 (1 - f^*)$. In the appendix we derive the following equations:

$$2m_1 I_1 = \frac{+(c_2 - c_1)I}{\alpha} - \frac{1}{\beta}\left[A^* - \frac{(c_2 - c_1)I[\rho + \beta(I - I^*)]}{\alpha(I_2 - I_1)}\right] \tag{16a}$$

$$2m_2 I_2 = \frac{-(c_2 - c_1)I}{\alpha} - \frac{1}{\beta}\left[A^* - \frac{(c_2 - c_1)I[\rho + \beta(I - I^*)]}{\alpha(I_2 - I_1)}\right] \tag{16b}$$

$$
\begin{aligned}
2\alpha[f - f^*]&\left[\beta(I_2 - I_1)^2 I - 2I_1 I_2(\rho + \beta(I - I^*))\right] \\
&= \frac{-\alpha\rho A^* [I_2 - I_1]^2}{(c_2 - c_1)} + [I_2 - I_1]I[\rho + \beta(I - I^*)][\rho + \beta I] \\
&\quad + \beta^2[I_2 - I_1](I - I^*)I^2
\end{aligned}
\tag{17}
$$

Using Equation 17 to eliminate $f - f^*$ from Equations 7a and 7b, we get a pair of differential equations of the form

$$
\begin{aligned}
\dot{I}_1 &= F_1(I_1, I_2) \\
\dot{I}_2 &= F_2(I_1, I_2)
\end{aligned}
\tag{18}
$$

This system has a fixed point at $P = (I^*_1, I^*_2)$, where

$$
\begin{aligned}
I^*_1 &= \frac{1}{2}\left[1 - \frac{(\rho + \beta I^*)(c_2 - c_1)}{\alpha A^*}\right]I^* \\
I^*_2 &= \frac{1}{2}\left[1 + \frac{(\rho + \beta I^*)(c_2 - c_1)}{\alpha A^*}\right]I^*
\end{aligned}
\tag{19}
$$

Because $A^* > 0$, these equations imply that $I^*_2 \gtrless I^*_1$ as $c_2 \gtrless c_1$.

In the steady state, the level of infection is highest for the strain that is most expensive to treat. The more expensive it is to mitigate, the more of a bad thing people are willing to put up with. The exact steady state level of infection for each strain depends on the relative costs of treatment, the benefit of a cure, and the discount rate—the rate we are willing to trade off the value of a cure today against the ensuing cost of increased resistance in the future. If each antibiotic is the same, then half the infected population will be treated by each antibiotic, and the infection level is then the same for each strain. When the antibiotics are different in cost, the fraction of the population greater than half treated by the cheapest drug is scaled up by the cost difference between the two antibiotics and the discount rate and scaled down by the cost of infection. The corresponding values for the costate variables are m_1^* and m_2^*, which are both equal to $m^* = -A^*/(\rho + \beta I^*)$. In the steady state, the amount society is willing to pay to reduce the level of infection of each strain is the same. It varies directly with the discount rate and the rate of infection and inversely with the cost of infection. In an "autonomous" problem of the present type, any fixed point is either unstable or is a saddle point.[3] By linearizing the above equations around p, it can be shown that, for small values of ρ, this point is an unstable focus (see appendix). Hence any minor displacement from the steady state leads to an outward spiral. Simulations indicate that the resulting spiral may eventually approach a limit cycle. They also suggest that p is a saddle point for larger values of ρ.

Note that the system of differential Equations 18 also has a fixed point at $(I^*/2, I^*/2)$. However, as can be seen in Equations 16a and 16b, the associated shadow prices are infinite, and remaining at this point cannot be optimal.

The Singular Path

The system of differential equations discussed earlier determines a family of curves in (I_1, I_2) space. Suppose that $p = (I_1^*, I_2^*)$ is a saddle point. In this case, there is a unique curve that passes through the steady state (I_1^*, I_2^*) and along which the direction of movement is toward this steady state. This curve is the singular path. The shape of the curve when $c_2 > c_1$ is shown in Figure 2-1. Convergence toward the steady state is asymptotic. In the course of time, the pace of change slows down, but the steady state is never actually reached. Along the singular path, f is chosen according to Equation 17, and the shadow prices m_1 and m_2 are given by Equations 16a and 16b. They converge to a common value m^*.

Optimum Solution

Determining the optimum solution in the present model is not straightforward. There are two main problems. The first is to find a solution that satisfies the Hamiltonian conditions. This is especially difficult when ρ is small, because some of the optimum paths may then contain spirals and even a limit cycle. The second problem arises because our Hamiltonian is not concave in the state variables, and the standard sufficiency theorems of Mangasarian or Arrow and Kurz do not apply. Thus, even if we can find a solution satisfying the necessary Hamiltonian conditions, this may not guarantee that the solution is optimal. There may be other solutions that also satisfy these conditions.[4]

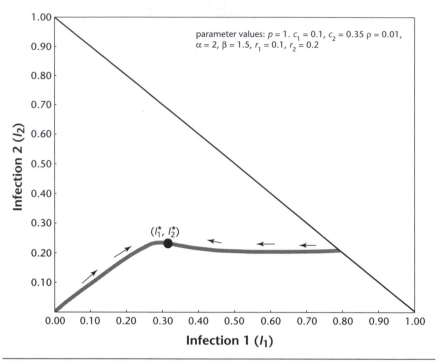

FIGURE 2-1. The Singular Path

Despite considerable effort, these difficulties so far have prevented us from finding a definitive answer to the optimization problem. Simulations indicate that over a variety of parameter values, $p = (I_1^*, I_2^*)$ is an optimal point. If the system happens to be at this point, it is optimal to remain there by keeping f equal to f^*. If the system is not at this point, optimal behavior depends on the size of ρ relative to other parameters. When ρ is small, the system is highly nonlinear, and we have no clear intuition about the nature of the optimum solution.

The situation is much simpler when ρ is large enough to ensure that p is a saddlepoint. In this case, there is a singular path that converges to the fixed point, and we propose the following solution to the optimization problem. For points already on the singular path, we choose f according to Equation 17, which takes us along this path toward the steady state. For other points, we choose the value of f which leads as quickly as possible to the singular path. If (I_1, I_2) lies above the singular path, we take $f = 0$, thereby ensuring that all patients receive the treatment that is effective against infection 2. This causes I_2 to fall rapidly until we eventually hit the singular path. If (I_1, I_2) lies below the singular path, we take $f = 1$, thereby ensuring that all patients receive the treatment that is effective against infection 1. This causes I_2 to fall rapidly until once again we hit the singular path. In either case, having reached the singular path, we stay on it and converge toward the steady state. This is illustrated in Figure 2-2.

In the steady state, relative treatment levels naturally depend on relative spontaneous recovery rates. To maintain constant relative infection rates for each strain, the fraction of patients treated with drug 1 must be as follows:

$$f^* = \frac{\alpha + (r_2 - r_1)}{2\alpha} \tag{4}$$

Thus, other things being equal, the greater the spontaneous recovery rate of a particular strain is, the smaller the fraction of patients treated with the drug effective against this strain is. In the steady state, drug therapy is therefore concentrated on strains that have the lowest rate of spontaneous recovery.

No matter what the initial starting point, we have a rule to determine which trajectory to follow. This trajectory takes us as rapidly as possible to the singular path, and when this path is reached, we remain on it to converge asymptotically to the steady state. Choosing the appropriate initial values for the shadow prices m_1 and m_2, we find that all of the necessary conditions for

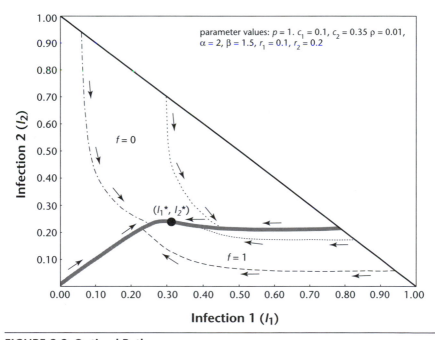

FIGURE 2-2. Optimal Paths

an optimum are satisfied. In the present case, these necessary conditions may not be sufficient for an optimum because the Hamiltonian is not concave in the state variables. It is theoretically possible, although unlikely, that our proposed solution is not optimal. Very many simulations, not reported here, suggest that our solution is in fact optimal.

Conclusion

Starting from an arbitrary position, suppose the optimum treatment strategy is followed. The resulting path converges to the long-run steady state when the treatments are used in proportions f^* and $1 - f^*$, which are independent of the costs of treatment, c_1 and c_2, but depend only on the spontaneous recovery rates, r_1 and r_2, and the effectiveness of treatment α. The steady state stock of infection is higher, not surprisingly, for the strain with the highest marginal treatment cost. However, the negative shadow prices (m_1 and m_2) are the same for each stock of infection. This is because we assume that the benefits of cure and the contagion parameters (β_1 and β_2) are the same for each strain of infection. For points on the singular path during the transition to the steady state, the optimum treatment proportions depend on both economic and epidemiological parameters. For other points, the optimum strategy is to reach the singular solution as fast as possible by setting $f = 0$ or 1, as required. The resulting path is conventionally known as the most rapid approach path. Inspection of the current value Hamiltonian (Equation 10) warns us of this case because it is linear in the control variable f.

The solution to the optimization problem was substantially simplified by assuming that every infected person received some form of treatment. This may be unrealistic. Tens of millions of people in the United States today have no health insurance, and some fraction of them will go untreated if infected. We also assumed that, apart from a uniform discount factor, good health is valued uniformly across individuals. If this assumption is modified, the optimum solution may be such that some people are denied treatment today to treat those willing or able to pay more tomorrow. Our analysis assumed that patients are not given antibiotic cocktails made up of more than one drug. This assumption may rule out strategies that are superior to those examined here. Finally, both drugs were assumed to be available at any time, thus precluding consideration of optimal cycling.

References

Benhabib, J., and K. Nishimura. 1979. The Hopf Bifurcation and the Existence and Stability of Closed Orbits in Multisector Models of Optimal Economic Growth. *Journal of Economic Theory* 27: 421–44.

Bonhoeffer, S., M. Lipsitch, and B. Levin. 1997. Evaluating Treatment Protocols to Prevent Antibiotic Resistance. *Proceedings of the National Academy of Sciences of the USA* 94: 12106–11.

Brown, G., and D.F. Layton. 1996. Resistance Economics: Social Cost and the Evolution of Antibiotic Resistance. *Environment and Development Economics* 1(3): 349–55.

Bryson, V., and W. Szybalski. 1955. Microbial Drug Resistance. *Advanced Genetics* 7: 1–46.

Garrett, L. 1994. *The Coming Plague: Newly Emerging Diseases in a World Out of Balance.* New York: Penguin Books.

Institute of Medicine. 1992. *Emerging Infections: Microbial Threats to Health in the United States.* Washington, DC: National Academy Press.

Kermack, W.O., and A.G. McKendrick. 1927. A Contribution to the Mathematical Theory of Epidemics. *Proceedings of the Royal Society of London. Series A, Containing Papers of a Mathematical and Physical Character* 115(772): 700–21.

Laxminarayan, R. 1999. Economics of Antibiotic Resistance. Doctoral dissertation. Seattle, WA: University of Washington.

Laxminarayan, R., and G.M. Brown. 2001. Economics of Antibiotic Resistance: A Theory of Optimal Use. *Journal of Environmental Economics and Management* 42(2): 183–206.

Leonard, D., and N. Van Long. 1992. *Optimal Control Theory and Static Optimization in Economics.* Cambridge, U.K.: Cambridge University Press.

Levy, S.B. 1998. The Challenge of Antibiotic Resistance. *Scientific American* 278(3): 46–53.

Massad, E., S. Lundberg, and H.M. Yang. 1993. Modeling and Simulating the Evolution of Resistance against Antibiotics. *International Journal of Biomedical Computing* 33: 65–81.

McCaig, L.F., and J. M. Hughes. 1995. Trends in Antimicrobial Drug Prescribing Among Office-Based Physicians in the United States. *Journal of the American Medical Association* 273(3): 214–19.

McGowan, J.E., Jr. 1983. Antimicrobial Resistance in Hospital Organisms and Its Relation to Antibiotic Use. *Reviews of Infectious Diseases* 5(6): 1033–48.

Ryder, H.E., Jr., and G.M. Heal. 1973. Optimal Growth with Intertemporally Dependent Preferences. *Review of Economic Studies* 40: 1–31.

Skiba, A.K. 1978. Optimal Growth with a Convex–Concave Production Function. *Econometrica* 46(3): 527–39.

Tepper, B.S. 1969. Microbial Resistance to Drugs. In *Biology of Population: The Biological Basis of Public Health,* edited by B.K. Sladen and F.B. Bang. New York: American Elsevier Publishing Co.

Appendix

Equations 14a and 14b can be written as follows:

$$\dot{m}_1 = \rho m_1 + A - m_1 \frac{\dot{I}_1}{I_1} + \beta(m_1 I_1 + m_2 I_2)$$

$$\dot{m}_2 = \rho m_2 + A - m_2 \frac{\dot{I}_2}{I_2} + \beta(m_1 I_1 + m_2 I_2)$$

(A1)

Because $d(m_i I_i)/dt = \dot{m}_i I_i + m_i \dot{I}_i$, the equations for Equation A1 can be written

$$\frac{d(m_1 I_1)}{dt} = \left[\rho m_1 + A + \beta(m_1 I_1 + m_2 I_2)\right] I_1$$

$$\frac{d(m_2 I_2)}{dt} = \left[\rho m_2 + A + \beta(m_1 I_1 + m_2 I_2)\right] I_2$$

(A2)

Subtracting yields

$$\frac{d(m_2 I_2 - m_1 I_1)}{dt} = \rho(m_2 I_2 - m_1 I_1) + \left[A + \beta(m_1 I_1 + m_2 I_2)\right](I_2 - I_1)$$

(A3)

Interior Solutions

Consider a path for which the switching equality in Equation 12 holds continuously. Within this segment,

$$m_2 I_2 - m_1 I_1 = -\frac{(c_2 - c_1)I}{\alpha}$$

(A4a)

Because this equality holds throughout the segment, we can differentiate to obtain

$$\frac{d(m_2 I_2 - m_1 I_1)}{dt} = \frac{-(c_2 - c_1)\dot{I}}{\alpha}$$

Using Equation 8, it follows from Equation A1 to Equation A3 that

$$-\frac{\rho(c_2 - c_1)I}{\alpha} + \left[A + \beta(m_1 I_1 + m_2 I_2)\right](I_2 - I_1)$$

$$= -\left(\frac{c_2 - c_1}{\alpha}\right)\left[-\beta(I - I^*)I + \alpha(f - f^*)(I_2 - I_1)\right]$$

(A4b)

Define

$$A^* = p + c_1 f^* + c_2(1 - f^*)$$

Then $A + (c_2 - c_1)(f - f^*) = A^*$, and we can write Equation A4b as follows

$$\frac{-\rho(c_2 - c_1)I}{\alpha} + A^*(I_2 - I_1) + \beta(m_1 I_1 + m_2 I_2)(I_2 - I_1) - \frac{(c_2 - c_1)}{\alpha}\beta(I - I^*)I = 0$$

Thus

$$m_1 I_1 + m_2 I_2 = -\frac{1}{\beta}\left(A^* - \frac{(c_2 - c_1)I[\rho + \beta(I - I^*)]}{\alpha(I_2 - I_1)}\right)$$

(A5)

From Equations A4 and A5 we obtain

$$2m_1I_1 = \frac{+(c_2-c_1)I}{\alpha} - \frac{1}{\beta}\left(A^* - \frac{(c_2-c_1)I[\rho+\beta(I-I^*)]}{\alpha(I_2-I_1)}\right)$$

$$2m_2I_2 = \frac{-(c_2-c_1)I}{\alpha} - \frac{1}{\beta}\left(A^* - \frac{(c_2-c_1)I[\rho+\beta(I-I^*)]}{\alpha(I_2-I_1)}\right)$$

(A6)

From Equation A5, noting that $I = I_1 + I_2$ and $\dot{I} = \dot{I}_1 + \dot{I}_2$, it follows that

$$\frac{\alpha\beta}{(c_2-c_1)}(I_2-I_1)^2\frac{d(m_1I_1+m_2I_2)}{dt}$$

$$= (I_2-I_1)^2\frac{d}{dt}\left(\frac{[\rho+\beta(I-I^*)]I}{(I_2-I_1)}\right)$$

$$= (I_2-I_1)\left[\rho+\beta(I-I^*)+\beta I\right]\dot{I} - [\rho+\beta(I-I^*)]I[\dot{I}_2-\dot{I}_1]$$ (A7)

$$= [\rho+\beta(I-I^*)]\left((I_2-I_1)\dot{I} - I[\dot{I}_2-\dot{I}_1]\right) + \beta I(I_2-I_1)\dot{I}$$

$$= [\rho+\beta(I-I^*)](2I_2\dot{I}_1 - 2I_1\dot{I}_2) + \beta I(I_2-I_1)\dot{I}$$

$$= -2[\rho+\beta(I-I^*)]I_1I_2\left(\frac{\dot{I}_2}{I_2}-\frac{\dot{I}_1}{I_1}\right) + \beta I(I_2-I_1)\dot{I}$$

This can be written as follows

$$\frac{\alpha\beta}{(c_2-c_1)}(I_2-I_1)^2\frac{d(m_1I_1+m_2I_2)}{dt}$$

$$= -4\alpha[\rho+\beta(I-I^*)]I_1I_2[(f-f^*)+\beta I(I_2-I_1)] - \beta(I-I^*)I + \alpha(f-f^*)(I_2-I_1)$$

$$= \alpha[f-f^*]\left[\beta(I_2-I_1)^2I - 4I_1I_2[\rho+\beta(I-I^*)]\right] - \beta^2(I_2-I_1)(I-I^*)I^2$$

(A8)

Noting that $I = I_1 + I_2$ and using Equations A2 and A5, it can be shown that

$$\frac{d(m_1I_1+m_2I_2)}{dt} = (\rho+\beta I)(m_1I_1+m_2I_2) + AI$$

$$= -\frac{\rho A^*}{\beta} + (A-A^*)I$$

$$+ \frac{(\rho+\beta I)(c_2-c_1)I[\rho+\beta(I-I^*)]}{\alpha\beta(I_2-I_1)}$$ (A9)

$$= -\frac{\rho A^*}{\beta} - (c_2-c_1)(f-f^*)I$$

$$+ \frac{(\rho+\beta I)(c_2-c_1)I[\rho+\beta(I-I^*)]}{\alpha\beta(I_2-I_1)}$$

From Equations A5 and A9 it follows that

$$\alpha(f - f^*)\Big(\beta(I_2 - I_1)^2 I - 4I_1I_2\big[\rho + \beta(I - I^*)\big]\Big) - \beta^2(I_2 - I_1)(I - I^*)I^2$$
$$= \frac{-\alpha\beta}{c_2 - c_1}(I_2 - I_1)^2\left[\frac{\rho A^*}{\beta} + (c_2 - c_1)(f - f^*)I\right]$$
$$+ (I_2 - I_1)I\big[\rho + \beta(I - I^*)\big](\rho + \beta I)$$

which can be written as

$$2\alpha(f - f^*)\Big(\beta(I_2 - I_1)^2 I - 2I_1I_2\big[\rho + \beta(I - I^*)\big]\Big)$$
$$= \frac{-\alpha\rho A^*(I_2 - I_1)^2}{(c_2 - c_1)} + (I_2 - I_1)I\big[\rho + \beta(I - I^*)\big](\rho + \beta I) + \beta^2(I_2 - I_1)(I - I^*)I^2 \tag{A10}$$

Because $I = I_1 + I_2$, this determines f as a function of I_1 and I_2.

Determination of I_1^* and I_2^*

Suppose $f = f^*$ and $I = I^*$. Equation A10 is then satisfied if either

$$I_1 = I_2 = I^*/2$$

or

$$-\frac{\alpha\rho A^*(I_2 - I_1)}{c_2 - c_1} + \rho I^*(\rho + \beta I^*) = 0 \tag{A11}$$

The point $I_1 = I_2 = I^*/2$ cannot be a stationary solution to the optimization problem because the associated shadow prices m_1 and m_2 are infinite (see Equation A6). From Equation A10,

$$I_2 - I_1 = \frac{(\rho + \beta I^*)(c_2 - c_1)I^*}{\alpha A^*}$$

Because $I_1 + I_2 = I^*$, it follows that $I_1 = I_1^*$ and $I_2 = I_2^*$ where

$$I_1^* = \frac{1}{2}\left[1 - \frac{(\rho + \beta I^*)(c_2 - c_1)}{\alpha A^*}\right]I^*$$
$$I_2^* = \frac{1}{2}\left[1 + \frac{(\rho + \beta I^*)(c_2 - c_1)}{\alpha A^*}\right]I^* \tag{A12}$$

Because $A^* > 0$, it follows that $I_2^* > I_1^*$ when $c_2 > c_1$.

Linear Approximation

Let

$$g = f - f^*$$
$$z_1 = I_1 - I_1^*$$
$$z_2 = I_2 - I_2^*$$
$$z = I - I^*$$

(A13)

Then

$$I = z + I^*$$
$$I_2 - I_1 = (z_2 - z_1) + \left(I_2^* - I_1^*\right)$$

(A14)

From Equations 7a and 7b in the text

$$\frac{dz_1}{dt} = (-\beta z - \alpha g)\left(I_1^* + z_1\right)$$

(A15a)

$$\frac{dz_2}{dt} = (-\beta z + \alpha g)\left(I_2^* + z_2\right)$$

(A15b)

To investigate the behavior of (I_1, I_2) around (I_1^*, I_2^*), we investigate the behavior of (z_1, z_2) around $(0, 0)$. To this end, we express the right-hand side of the above equations as linear functions of z_1 and z_2, ignoring higher-order terms.

Let us first consider Equation A10. Using Equations A13 and A14 and equating first-order terms, we obtain

$$2\alpha g\left(\beta\left(I_2^* - I_1^*\right)^2 I^* - 2\rho I_1^* I_2^*\right)$$

$$= -\frac{2\alpha\rho A^*\left(z_2 - z_1\right)\left(I_2^* - I_1^*\right)}{c_2 - c_1}$$
$$+ (z_2 - z_1)I^*\rho(\rho + \beta I^*)$$
$$+ \left(I_2^* - I_1^*\right)z\rho(\rho + \beta I^*)$$
$$+ \left(I_2^* - I_1^*\right)I^*\beta z(\rho + \beta I^*)$$
$$+ \left(I_2^* - I_1^*\right)I^*\rho\beta z + \beta^2\left(I_2^* - I_1^*\right)z I^{*2}$$

(A16)

$$= (z_2 - z_1)\rho\left(\frac{-2\alpha A^*\left(I_2^* - I_1^*\right)}{(c_2 - c_1)} + I^*(\rho + \beta I^*)\right) + z\left(I_2^* - I_1^*\right)(\rho + \beta I^*)(\rho + 2\beta I^*)$$

$$= -(z_2 - z_1)\rho(\rho + \beta I^*)I^* + z\left(I_2^* - I_1^*\right)(\rho + \beta I^*)(\rho + 2\beta I^*)$$

Using Equation A16 we can eliminate g from Equations A15a and A15b. Let

$$J = 2\left(\beta\left(I_2^* - I_1^*\right)^2 I^* - 2\rho I_1^* I_2^*\right)$$

$$K = \frac{-\rho(\rho + \beta I^*)I^*}{J}$$

$$L = \frac{\left(I_2^* - I_1^*\right)(\rho + \beta I^*)(\rho + 2\beta I^*)}{J}$$

Then Equation A16 can be written as

$$\alpha g = K(z_2 - z_1) + Lz \tag{A17}$$

Hence, linearizing Equation A15a, we obtain

$$\begin{aligned}
\frac{dz_1}{dt} &= \left[-\beta z - K(z_2 - z_1) - Lz\right]I_1^* \\
&= \left[-(L + \beta)z - K(z_2 - z_1)\right]I_1^* \\
&= \left[-(L + \beta)(z_1 + z_2) - K(z_2 - z_1)\right]I_1^* \\
&= \left[\left[(K - L) - \beta\right]z_1 - \left[(K + L) + \beta\right]z_2\right]I_1^*
\end{aligned} \tag{A18a}$$

Likewise, from Equation A15b, we obtain

$$\begin{aligned}
\frac{dz_2}{dt} &= \left[-\beta z + K(z_2 - z_1) + Lz\right]I_2^* \\
&= \left[(L - \beta)z + K(z_2 - z_1)\right]I_2^* \\
&= \left[(L - \beta)(z_1 + z_2) + K(z_2 - z_1)\right]I_2^* \\
&= \left[-\left[(K - L) + \beta\right]z_1 + \left[(K + L) - \beta\right]z_2\right]I_2^*
\end{aligned} \tag{A18b}$$

In matrix notation

$$\begin{bmatrix} \dfrac{dz_1}{dt} \\ \dfrac{dz_2}{dt} \end{bmatrix} = D\begin{bmatrix} z_1 \\ z_2 \end{bmatrix}$$

where

$$D = \begin{bmatrix} \left[(K - L) - \beta\right]I_1^* & -\left[(K + L) + \beta\right]I_1^* \\ -\left[(K - L) + \beta\right]I_2^* & \left[(K + L) - \beta\right]I_2^* \end{bmatrix}$$

Note that

$$|D| = -4\beta K I_1^* I_2^*$$

$$TrD = L\left(I_2^* - I_1^*\right) + (K - \beta)I^* \tag{A19}$$

The eigen values of D satisfy the characteristic equation

$$\lambda^2 - \lambda trD + |D| = 0$$

Hence the roots λ_1 and λ_2 are given by

$$\lambda_i = \frac{trD \pm \sqrt{(trD)^2 - 4|D|}}{2}$$

From Equation A19, it follows that

$$\begin{aligned}
JtrD &= \left(I_2^* - I_1^*\right)JL + I^* JK - \beta I^* J \\
&= \left(I_2^* - I_1^*\right)^2 (\rho + \beta I^*)(\rho + 2\beta I^*) \\
&\quad - \rho I^{*2}(\rho + \beta I^*) \\
&\quad - 2\beta I^* \left[\beta\left(I_2^* - I_1^*\right)^2 I^* - 2\rho I_1^* I_2^*\right] \\
&= \left(I_2^* - I_1^*\right)^2 \left[\rho^2 + 3\beta\rho I^*\right] - \rho I^* \left[\rho I^* + \beta\left(I_2^* - I_1^*\right)^2\right] \\
&= \rho^2 \left[\left(I_2^* - I_1^*\right)^2 - I^{*2}\right] + 2\beta\rho\left(I_2^* - I_1^*\right)^2 I^* \\
&= -4 I_1^* I_2^* \rho^2 + 2\beta\rho\left(I_2^* - I_1^*\right)^2 I^* \\
&= 2\rho\left[\beta\left(I_2^* - I_1^*\right)^2 I^* - 2\rho I_1^* I_2^*\right] \\
&= \rho J
\end{aligned}$$

Thus

$$trD = \rho > 0 \qquad\qquad\qquad\qquad\text{(A20)}$$

For small ρ, it is clear from Equation A12 that $J > 0$, and hence $K < 0$, and $|D| > 0$. Moreover, $(trD)^2$ is of order ρ^2 and $|D|$ is of order ρ. Thus, for small ρ, the discriminant $(trD)^2 - 4|D|$ is approximately equal to $-4|D|$ and is therefore negative. This implies that the roots λ_1 and λ_2 are complex conjugates of the form $\theta + \phi i$ and $\theta - \phi i$ where $2\theta = tr\, D = \rho > 0$. Thus, in the vicinity of (I_1^*, I_2^*), every path is an explosive spiral. The smallest displacement from this steady state will generate a spiral motion outward.

Notes

1. Often optimism about the healing power of antibiotics is misguided. Physicians routinely prescribe antibiotics for situations in which antibiotics cannot be effective. Levy reports circumstances when more than 80% of the physicians sampled had prescribed antibiotics "against their better judgment." One-third of the annual outpatient prescriptions for antibiotics are believed to be unnecessary (Levy 1998).

2. Drugs are, in general, differentially effective against different types of infection. One drug may be quite effective against certain types of infections but ineffective against other infections. We consider a highly simplified case in which there only two drugs and two variants of a certain infection. Each drug is effective against one variant but totally ineffective against the other variant. This assumption simplifies the exposition without sacrificing anything fundamental. Our analysis can be easily modified to cover the more realistic case in which each drug is to some extent effective against both variants of the infection.

3. See Leonard and Van Long (1992, 294–5).

4. These difficulties are illustrated in Skiba (1978), who presents a model in which there are many different solutions that satisfy the Hamiltonian conditions and in which an optimal path may be a spiral. Ryder and Heal (1973) and Benhabib and Nishimura (1979) present models in which optimal paths may have a limit cycle.

Chapter 3

Value of Treatment Heterogeneity for Infectious Diseases

Ramanan Laxminarayan and Martin L. Weitzman

Treatment homogeneity is valued in the medical profession. Uniform treatment guidelines are often used to ensure that all physicians prescribe a safe, efficacious, and cost-effective drug in treating a medical condition. However, such a policy may be undesirable when drug resistance is endogenous. In the case of infectious diseases, selection pressure imposed by the use of any single drug (antibiotic, antiviral, or antimalarial) sooner or later leads to the evolution of resistance (by bacteria, viruses, or parasites) to that drug. In this chapter, we show that a "mixed strategy" of multiple drug use is generally desirable and analytically characterize the conditions under which this strategy is optimal.

From an economist's perspective, the treatment of infectious diseases is fundamentally different from the treatment of noninfectious conditions such as arthritis, cardiovascular disease, or cancer. Unlike the case of noninfectious or chronic diseases, two social externalities—one positive and the other negative—inherently characterize the treatment of infectious diseases. Take the case of antibiotics (although the situation can be generalized to antivirals and antimalarials as well). On the one hand, antibiotic treatment cures the patient, thereby preventing the disease from being transmitted to other individuals. On the other hand, drug treatment selects in favor of harmful mutations or organisms that are resistant to the drug, increasing the likelihood that the drug will be less effective in the future. Because the individual patient fails to take into account either of these externalities when deciding to seek treatment, a Pigovian tax or subsidy of treatment could in principle correct for externality (depending on whether its impact on overall social welfare is negative or positive).[1]

The externality problem implicit in the decision on whether to seek treatment for infectious diseases has been well documented in earlier work (Philipson 2000). In this chapter, we extend this literature to look at externalities arising from the *choice* of drug treatment once the decision to treat has been made. The degree of homogeneity in the choice of drug treatments for infectious diseases is remarkable. For instance, in 1997, nearly 60 percent of all cases of acute ear infections (a common condition in young children) in the United States were treated with amoxicillin. In fact, amoxicillin accounted for 35 percent of *all* antibiotics used by physicians, and the five most commonly used antibiotics used accounted for 72% of *all* antibiotics used by physicians in this country. This degree of homogeneity has been witnessed even in the developing world. In most African countries, chloroquine was the most commonly used drug to treat malaria for many years. In fact, in some malaria-endemic countries, it was even mixed in with common salt to ensure widespread and uniform malarial prophylaxis.

There are reasons why uniformity of treatment is frequently encountered. In many developing countries, all drug procurement is centralized and controlled by the government. Therefore, the government determines which drugs should be even allowed into the country, thereby influencing the choice of treatment. In developed countries such as the United States, clinical treatment guidelines for community-level infections are typically issued by national public health bodies, such as the American Association of Pediatrics and the Centers for Disease Control and Prevention. In addition, individual hospitals both set and follow treatment guidelines on the basis of the advice of the hospital's infection-control committee. The choice of drug treatment is, all other things being equal, often made on the basis of the principle known as cost-effectiveness (Weinstein and Fineberg 1980). In simple terms, the drug with the smallest ratio of treatment cost to effectiveness is the drug of first choice for *all* patients. In addition, individual patients acting in their own self-interest tend to prefer the most cost-effective drug option.

There are good reasons why such homogeneity is actively promoted among the medical profession. Clinical guidelines and national treatment policy recommendations provide guidance to individual physicians on which drugs are to be used for first-line treatment, which drugs are to be used for second-line treatment should the first-line treatment fail, and which drugs are to be used in case of complications. By specifying treatment in the form of simple uniform decision rules, national policies are particularly useful in ensuring safe and accurate medical treatment while relieving the physician of some of the burden of medical decisionmaking.[2] Following uniform guidelines reduces the liability associated with medical error for physicians.

However, as this chapter demonstrates, significant disadvantages may be associated with promoting a single drug as the first-line treatment for a given condition.

The starting point of this chapter is the observation that, to the extent that most patients in a region or country are treated with the same drug for a given infectious disease, the use of a single drug places "excessively" high selection pressure on organisms that are susceptible to that particular drug and increases the likelihood that a resistant strain will evolve and proliferate. As resistance to the recommended first-line drug builds up, that drug is replaced by an alternative that is used until resistance to this second drug also increases, and so on in succession. The main message of this chapter is that the optimal solution may therefore be to use not just a *single* drug throughout the population as first-line agent, but to prescribe a variety of drugs, randomized over patients, to ensure inordinate selection pressure is not placed on any single drug or class of drugs.

This chapter also indirectly addresses the question of whether more expensive, highly effective drugs should be kept on the sidelines for use in the event of serious, resistant infections or whether they should be deployed alongside less effective agents on the frontlines against infectious diseases. The benefit of having an effective drug available as backup should all else fail cannot be disregarded, nor should the more effective drug's ability to relieve selection pressure on the first-line drug be ignored (when the effective drug is also used).[3] What, then, is the optimal solution? The answer, as it often happens, lies somewhere between the black and the white—it may be to use more effective drugs in both roles.

The problem is not defining the extent to which the more effective drug should be used but rather describing a standard policy based on guidelines for first-line treatment in this situation. As the simple model of this chapter will show, it is generally more desirable to use less expensive agents on a greater fraction of patients and more expensive agents on a smaller fraction—right from the beginning—all else being equal. In this sense, the concept of uniform guidelines may be fundamentally flawed in the presence of endogenously generated resistance. Of course, it is difficult to specify these "mixed-policy" fractions in the form of a standard, uniform, guidelines-based policy. For instance, in a geographically isolated area, it may be optimal for the single family practitioner serving these areas to prescribe a wide array of antibiotics (only in cases in which they are required, of course) so that selection pressure on no single antibiotic is allowed to build up. Clearly, there are practical difficulties of doing so. The single most important difficulty is that it makes sense from the individual physician's perspective to do what everyone else in the country is doing and to prescribe the most commonly used antibiotic. Herein lies the intrinsic externality issue related to drug prescribing. Physicians have an incentive to prescribe in concordance with the rest of the medical community in the interest of, if nothing else, reducing their liability in malpractice claims. Of course patients are put at ease with a single, unified decisive choice. But such concordance increases the selective pressure on the drug of common choice. Guidelines that pick out a single drug for such targeted, nationwide use may therefore be exacerbating selection pressure on that single drug to a degree that is socially undesirable.

The emphasis placed on using a single drug may occur even in the absence of uniform treatment guidelines. Decentralized decisionmakers (i.e., individual physicians or patients) may not take into account the risk involved in prescribing a single drug repeatedly for a common condition such as an ear infection. The individual physician's encouragement of the development of resistant organisms globally whenever he or she decides to use that drug represents a negative externality. This externality remains uncorrected because the individual physician bears only a negligible fraction of the total burden of resistance that he or she may be placing on others with every treatment decision.

The problem of excessive selection pressure arising from the use of a single drug occurs not only in countries where physicians are the primary source of treatments but also in countries where the disease is home treated, as is the case with malaria in Africa. Here too, patients would prefer to be treated with the most cost-effective drug available to them. However, from a societal perspective, it may be optimal to use other drugs that are not cost-effective from the individual patient's perspective. The question then is how patients might be persuaded to use these other drugs even if it is not in their self-interest to do so.

One might argue that the logical extension of the strategy to treat different patients with different drugs is to treat individual patients with more than one drug. Such a strategy is already standard practice for the treatment of human immunodeficiency virus and tuberculosis. In each of these cases, the underlying principle is that the probability of a multigenic resistance in a microbe is much lower than the probability of a genetic mutation conferring resistance to one drug. Using two drugs ensures that each drug exercises a protective effect over the other. However, with the argument used for drug combinations, resistance to a drug is *exogenous*. The reasoning we follow in developing the argument for using a wider variety of drugs as first-line agents runs along similar lines, as do our policy prescriptions, except that in our case, drug resistance develops *endogenously* as an evolutionary reaction to excessive usage. The solution to the problem of endogenously growing drug resistance then may be to extend the combination treatment concept to a community level. Further, routinely using two antibiotics on a single patient may be undesirable for medical reasons.[4] The alternative is to treat different patients suffering from the same infectious disease with different drugs, a prescription that is difficult to implement using a guidelines-based policy. In any event, this chapter concentrates on this case—of treating different patients with the same infectious disease with different drugs—in the context of endogenously induced disease.

We fully recognize that to simplify the complex task of medical decision-making to fit into the boundaries of theoretical economic analysis is to issue an open invitation for criticism. The constraints imposed by the degree of abstraction in developing the arguments in this chapter—or the specific applicability of the results—cannot be overstated. This chapter addresses only problems associated with guidelines that recommend one kind of drug per patient as first-line therapy and does not refer to guidelines that promote judicious drug use, safe doses, overall safety, and so forth. We are not suggesting the use of combinations of drugs on individual patients but rather a strategy of treating different patients with different drugs. This principle, known as antibiotic heterogeneity, is beginning to enter the set of options being considered by medical professionals. However, it runs fundamentally counter to the long-held belief in the medical profession of the existence of a "best treatment" for a disease and the deeply felt need for uniformity in drug treatment.

Guidelines that promote uniformity in the choice of drug for treating infectious diseases may be inherently self-defeating because using the greatest variety of drugs decreases the likelihood that microbes will acquire and maintain resistance to any single class of drugs. The single most important message of this chapter is that, from a societal perspective, it may even be desirable to treat some patients with more expensive drugs even while it is individually suboptimal to do so. The precise fraction of patients that should be treated with these more effective drugs can be determined using fairly straightforward criteria, which we demonstrate in the sections that follow.

Model of Endogenous Resistance

This section presents our "core model" of endogenously generated resistance to drug therapies. It goes without saying that such a model must of necessity be formulated at a very high level of abstraction. Nevertheless, as will become clear, it is little short of amazing how much analytical insight emerges from even such a simple formulation.

Let there be available m possible drug therapies (indexed $i = 1,2,\ldots,m$), each of which may be used to counter some particular disease. For analytical simplicity, we imagine that everyone in the population is treated with exactly one complete treatment dose of one of the drugs. Critical to our analysis are the ideas that we are allowing a "mixed strategy" of different drugs to be used on different people and that the model should tell us when this strategy is optimal rather than excluding it a priori. Let x_i represent the fraction of the population treated with drug i, where

$$\sum_{i=1}^{m} x_i = 1 \tag{1}$$

and

$$0 \le x_i \le 1 \tag{2}$$

Let the cost (inclusive of c non-drug treatment costs) of drug i (per unit of population) be given by

$$c_i > 0 \tag{3}$$

Resistance to drug i by the underlying pathogen is assumed to be a Poisson process with intensity parameter

$$\theta_i > 0 \tag{4}$$

where θ_i is a (very small-valued) parameter representing the probability that resistance to drug i will develop endogenously (presumably by mutation) in the pathogen in any one person treated by that drug. (Here we refer to *endogenously acquired* resistance, which develops spontaneously by Poisson mutation in the pathogen in a patients being treated using the drug, as opposed to *epidemic* resistance by the pathogen, which results from infection by a drug-resistant pathogen from another person treated by that same drug.)

When a fraction x_i are treated by drug i, the probability that a resistant strain emerges is (to a first-order approximation)

$$\theta_i x_i \tag{5}$$

If such a resistant strain emerges, it will put at risk of epidemic resistance all x_i people treated by drug i. Let the social loss *per person* of being placed "at risk" by resistance developing in the drug by which they are being treated be denoted

$$L > 0 \tag{6}$$

Then, combining Equations 5 with 6, the expected social loss *per person* of being put "at risk" by drug i is

$$L[\theta_i x_i] \tag{7}$$

whereas the *total* expected social loss from being put "at risk" by being exposed to pathogens that are resistant to drug i is

$$[L x_i][\theta_i x_i] \tag{8}$$

In other words, we assume that it takes time to change these treatment fractions and that individuals who continue to be treated with drug i after a resistant strain has emerged are at risk for treatment failure.

Let

$$N_i \equiv \frac{1}{\theta_i} \tag{9}$$

be the average number of people that can be expected to use drug i before resistance sets in. Then the total expected social loss Expression 8 can be rewritten as

$$\frac{Lx_i^2}{N_i} \tag{10}$$

The *optimal drug combination problem* in this model is one of minimizing

$$\sum_{i=1}^{m}\left[c_i x_i + \frac{L}{N_i} x_i^2\right] \tag{11}$$

subject to

$$\sum_{i=1}^{m} x_i = 1 \tag{12}$$

and

$$0 \leq x_i \leq 1 \tag{13}$$

Characterizing the Optimal Drug Combination

The effectiveness of all drugs is assumed to be identical. Without loss of generality, suppose the drugs are arrayed from least to most expensive, so that

$$c_1 \leq c_2 \leq \ldots \leq c_n \tag{14}$$

It is quite obvious that it will never be optimal to use (to prescribe positive amounts of) a *more* expensive drug while not using (prescribe zero amount of) a *less* expensive drug. To see beyond this what is the form of an optimal policy, and what it depends on, let us begin by analyzing in full detail the situation for *two* drugs ($m = 2$).

There are two possible solutions—an interior solution and a corner solution of the form $x_1 = 1$, $x_2 = 0$. The latter corresponds to the necessary and sufficient first-order corner condition

$$c_2 \geq c_1 + \frac{2L}{N_1} \tag{15}$$

From Equation 15, we may say that a "mixed" interior solution using both drugs is optimal if and only if the following condition is met:

$$(c_2 - c_1)N_1 \leq 2L \tag{16}$$

What is the intuition behind Condition 16? The precise economic condition under which it is optimal to include drug 2 in our menu is that the increase in cost associated with treating with the more expensive drug in place of the cheaper drug is less than or equal to the expected benefit from using two drugs in place of one. The term on the right-hand side, $2L/N_1$, represents the marginal expected social cost per person associated with treating another patient with drug 1. As long as the increased treatment cost of using drug 2 in place of drug 1 is less than the expected increase in cost associated with endogenously generated resistance if drug 1 were to be used, it makes economic sense to use drug 2.

Next, consider the more general case in which m is an arbitrary positive integer (larger than two). The first-order condition for a fully interior solution is the existence of a positive multiplier λ, which is dual to Equation 12, that satisfies for positive x_i the conditions

$$c_i + \frac{2Lx_i}{N_i} = \lambda \tag{17}$$

The multiplier λ can therefore be interpreted as the "user cost" of any drug being used in the menu. Therefore, for any drug i that is being used, the total user cost equals the sum of the treatment cost c_i and the resistance cost $(2x_i/N_i)L$, in which the resistance cost equals the marginal probability of inducing a resistant infection with another treatment multiplied by L, the associated social cost of inducing resistance in the population. Although the treatment costs of drugs in our optimal menu can vary greatly, their user cost is identical. In other words, if two drugs are included in our optimal menu and one costs less than the other, then the resistance cost of the cheaper drug must exceed that of the more expensive drug so that the user cost of the two drugs is identical. The resistance cost of a drug is, of course, a function of the fraction of the population being treated with that drug, and a high treatment fraction implies a larger resistance cost.

The astute reader may have guessed where we are headed. The optimal decision rule is to use the lowest cost drug(s) first, as standard economic intuition would dictate. What is not so standard, however, is the form in which these costs arise. In addition to the treatment cost that the individual patient faces, there is an additional cost associated with the increased probability of drug resistance associated with each use of the drug. This resistance cost is endogenously determined by the fraction of the infected population that is administered the drug in question. Therefore, the optimal menu design is such that the sum of treatment and resistance costs of *all* drugs on the menu is identical, thus ensuring that some drugs may find their way into this menu even if they are not the least expensive from a treatment cost perspective. Making use of Equation 17, Condition 12 can be rewritten as

$$\lambda = \frac{\sum_{k=1}^{m} c_k N_k}{\sum_{k=1}^{m} N_k} + \frac{2L}{\sum_{k=1}^{m} N_k} \tag{18}$$

The next step is to determine the optimal user cost for a given set of drugs that are available to the social planner (not just those that will be included on the menu). The optimal user cost can be expressed as the sum of the resistance probability weighted *average* cost of *all* available drugs and the expected marginal cost of treatment failure associated with any single treatment when *all* available drugs are being used.

Combining Equations 18 and 17, the "interiorness" condition $x_i > 0$ is equivalent to the condition $c_i \le \lambda$, or equivalently,

$$x_i = (\lambda - c_i) \frac{N_i}{L} \tag{19}$$

which is the appropriate generalization of Equation 16. From an economic perspective, it is optimal to include any drug i in the menu of the drugs so long as the cost of the drug is less than or equal to the benchmark user cost λ. It is now intuitively clear what is an easy-to-apply myopic algorithm for determining optimal drug use. Suppose by induction it is known that an optimal solution includes a positive use of all drugs j where $j < i$ for some i. The next question to ask is whether it is additionally optimal to use drug i at a positive level. The answer is "yes" if and only if

$$\sum_{j<i} (c_i - c_j) N_j < 2L \tag{20}$$

By repeatedly asking the induction question in the form of Equation 20, it is possible to build up an optimal solution inductively by using a simple recursive algorithm based on the easily interpretable economic Equation 20.

We can rewrite the "interiorness" Equation 20 as follows:

$$c_i \le \frac{\sum c_j N_j}{\sum N_j} + \frac{2L}{\sum N_j} \tag{21}$$

Equation 21 means that drug i will be used as long as the marginal cost of using this drug is less than the weighted average cost of all drugs that are already in use. The weights are expected life span, measured in number of treatments before resistance evolves, plus the average cost of treatment failure associated with each additional treatment.

Let us assume that the second term on the right-hand side of Equation 21 is small. Even so, we could still want to use more than one drug, which is quite unlike the standard cost-effectiveness criterion in which drugs are used strictly in the order of lowest to highest cost, and only one drug is used at any given time. When this second term is large, then we may want to use drugs whose marginal cost *exceeds* the average cost of all drugs weighted by their expected life spans. Note, however, that we would *never* want to use a more costly drug j while excluding a cheaper drug k, even if

$$N_j > N_k \tag{22}$$

In other words, the value of N_i by itself does not determine whether a drug will be included in an optimal program. However, N_i does determine the fraction of patients who should be treated with drug i, as is demonstrated by rewriting Equation 17 as

$$x_i = (\lambda - c_i)\frac{N_i}{L} \tag{23}$$

From Equations 17 and 18, for any two drugs j and k being used in positive amounts, we can write

$$\frac{x_j}{x_k} = \frac{(2L + \Sigma c_i N_i - c_j \Sigma N_i) N_j}{(2L + \Sigma c_i N_i - c_k \Sigma N_i) N_k} \tag{24}$$

We have already noted that the parameter N_i does not ever invert the order in which a drug i is included in the overall drug menu. However, from Equation 24, the average useful lifetime parameters $\{N_i\}$ could result in a relatively less cost-effective drug being used on a larger fraction of patients, such that $x_k > x_j$ even while $c_k > c_j$, so long as N_j is sufficiently larger than N_k.

Referring back to Expression 14, if one were to follow the traditional medical cost-effectiveness criterion, one would first use only drug 1, then later switch to drug 2 when resistance evolved to drug 1, and so on. However, moving sequentially in strict order of increasing cost-effectiveness ratios and treating all patients with the same drug at the same time can be myopically ineffective whenever account is taken of the inescapable fact that immunity is endogenous—as we have just shown. In fact, it is not even optimal to use the most cost-effective drug on the largest number of patients. When resistance evolves endogenously, a parameter representing the average number of patients who must be treated before resistance appears determines (along with drug costs) the optimal intensity of drug usage.

Discussion

The externality problem associated with the treatment of infectious diseases—one that is related to a treatment's dual properties of reducing contagion and limiting drug resistance—has a reduced-form structure that is extremely familiar to any economist. Externalities are a common problem, whether they are related to highway congestion or air pollution, and copious economics papers have dealt with these issues. Always, a negative externality calls for using less of the privately optimal good and more of the privately more expensive alternatives. What is unusual about drug resistance is that this problem has not been widely recognized as a social externality—possibly of enormous consequence. Following this line of thinking, we arrived at simple criteria for choosing an optimal antibiotic policy, which contrasts sharply with the conclusion of the standard conventional health economists' individualistic cost-effectiveness analysis.

Under the standard cost-effectiveness approach, the economic criteria most commonly used in offering an economic perspective on the optimal choice of first-line treatment is that the drug with the lowest ratio of cost to effectiveness is selected as the primary or first-line drug. When this criterion is followed, it ignores the possibly large negative externality of overusing a particular drug. A large number of papers in the medical literature use the private-cost approach to determine the "optimal" treatment for a communicable disease. But the very nature of a communicable disease means there is a potentially large externality associated with drug treatments. The standard medical approach fails to recognize the externality problem associated with the uniform use of a single drug. The externality here is similar to the one encountered in agriculture in which all farmers decide to grow a single "optimal" crop, thereby encouraging the evolution of pests that can wipe out the entire monoculture. Although in the agricultural context, the solution is to grow different varieties dispersed spatially, in the medical context, the true optimal solution is analogously to use a "mixed" variety of drugs in fractions that are proportional to their individual cost-effectiveness.

There are many instances in which we could move from a policy of a nationally recommended treatment to a policy in which local doctors have more control over the drug prescribed. So the recommended policy change is from one of active promotion of treatment heterogeneity to a more decentralized approach to decisionmaking. Such a strategy would raise much concern over the lack of a "national strategy" to combat a disease such as malaria even if such a coordinated strategy would hasten the day when the prescribed guideline treatment would become ineffective.

Without a doubt, there may be practical problems with using a variety of drugs at the health care setting for a single infectious condition. For instance, a physician may have to explain to individual patients why they are getting different drugs. The specific treatment given by different doctors will differ depending on their (different) assessments of probability weights. This is potentially problematic because patients typically look to doctors to resolve uncertainty by prescribing the "single best" treatment.

Herein lies the dilemma. We have boxed ourselves into a particular way of reasoning that there is a "best" treatment for an ailment, one that is attributable to the fact that we are not used to having any externalities in medicine. The single best treatment approach works well for noninfectious conditions but breaks down badly for infectious diseases, in which significant negative externalities are likely to be present in the form of endogenously generated drug resistance. Once we become aware of the nature of this particular externality as one that requires the physician to also consider society's best interests, while determining what is in the best interest of the patient, then an optimal strategy may well involve a mixture of less expensive and more-expensive drug therapies.

Drug resistance is endogenous. The current strategy has been to wait for resistance to evolve before being surprised each time it appears, as if it were an ad hoc problem requiring some quick fix. Economists can contribute to the formulation of strategies that would internalize the cost of endogenously generated resistance into the process of treatment decisionmaking. This chapter tries to take a first step in such a direction.

References

Philipson, T. 2000. Economic Epidemiology. In *Handbook of Health Economics*, edited by A.J. Culyer and J.P. Newhouse. New York: Elsevier, 1762–99.
Weinstein, M.C., and H.V. Fineberg. 1980. *Clinical Decision Analysis*. Philadelphia, PA: W.B. Saunders Company.

Notes

1. It is useful to contrast *appropriate* drug treatment (or treatment for a bacterial infection that is likely to be cured faster because of that treatment) with *inappropriate* drug treatment (which does not cure the patient any faster than if that treatment were not used). An example of appropriate drug treatment is the use of antibiotics to cure bacterial infections; an example of inappropriate drug treatment is prescribing antibiotics for viral infections. Appropriate drug treatment benefits both the individual patient and society, whereas inappropriate drug treatment benefits neither the patient nor society. Although inappropriate drug treatment is a significant factor in the growing resistance of microbes to drugs, this chapter focuses exclusively on optimal policies related to appropriate drug treatment. In practice, appropriate drug treatment often is linked to a guidelines-type policy under which physicians are expected to adhere uniformly to a predetermined sequence of drugs to be used for treatment.

2. National policies are especially useful in countries in which the primary health care provider is typically a health care worker with limited training. In countries in which government-run public health facilities are the primary sources of drugs, national policies determine which drugs are available at different levels of the health care system. For instance, a second-line drug may only be available at a hospital and not at a primary care clinic.

3. An important argument against keeping newer, more effective drugs on the sidelines as backups is that such a policy tends to lower the incentive for drug firms to develop new drugs that may not be used extensively during the life of their patent protection.

4. These medical reasons may include undesirable side-effects from using two drugs, more complicated dosage regimens, and economic costs.

Commentary

To Take or Not To Take the Antibiotic?

James N. Sanchirico

I must admit that when I got sick in the past, my only thoughts were on how to get better and how to get better sooner. And if that included taking antibiotics, then that is what I did. After reading Chapters 1 and 2, what before was almost an instinctive decision has now become more complicated and involves not just my private benefits and costs, but also society's.

What are the private benefit and costs? If prescribed appropriately, antibiotics will treat my infection and in many cases get me back on my feet sooner. Antibiotics also reduce the risks that the infection will lead to more serious health problems in the future. According to WebMD (http://www.webmd.com), antibiotics are the treatment of choice for streptococcal strains, and if left untreated, strep throat can lead to rheumatic fever (mostly in children) or inflammation of the kidneys. As far as the costs, there is the cost of purchasing the antibiotics and the opportunity costs that include time spent on doctor visits and increased susceptibility to other infections while taking the antibiotic.

What are the social benefits and costs? A reassuring fact is that treating my infection with an antibiotic is also good for society. By taking an antibiotic, for instance, I can be slowing down, eliminating, or both, the spread of an infection in my community.[1] Unfortunately, every time I decide to use antibiotics, I am increasing the probability that a particular bacterial strain will become resistant to the antibiotic. In other words, my decision to use the antibiotic today has a cost in terms of reduced effectiveness that is borne in the future by both current and future generations.[2] What is also unsettling is that because resistance can spread from one bacterium to another (cross-resistance), it is possible that each use of one antibiotic can lead to more than one bacterium becoming resistant.

What are the implications of the private and social benefits and costs on the level of antibiotic use? If individuals only weigh the private benefits and costs when deciding to use antibiotics, then their consumption will be less than what is optimal for society. In other words, I would not be taking into account that antibiotics will reduce the spread of infection in the community. However, antibiotic use could exceed some socially optimal level if the costs of reduced effectiveness are not taken into account.[3] Many argue that the overprescription of antibiotics in cases in which they are inappropriate, such as viral infections, is evidence that individuals (both those who are ill and those who prescribe the treatment) are not taking into account the social costs associated with antibiotic use.

How should society balance the positive and negative trade-offs associated with treating bacterial infections with antibiotics? And on what economic and epidemiological factors should such an optimal policy be based? These are the questions that both chapters address using stylized models that capture conditions likely to exist in a remote hospital. The chapters assume that a social planner (e.g., hospital administrator) is given the task of determining the optimal strategy to treat bacterial infection(s) over time by taking into account both the positive and negative externalities of antibiotic use.

Both chapters frame the problem using a related and well-developed literature on the exploitation of renewable (e.g., fish, trees) natural resources. They also extend the Laxminarayan and Brown (2001) analysis on the economics of antibiotic resistance by taking into account the case in which there is a nonzero fitness cost of resistance. The fitness cost of resistance is the evolutionary disadvantage placed on resistant strains relative to susceptible strains in the absence of antibiotics. The chapters differ in the number of antibiotics available for use and the number of bacterial strains: Wilen and Msangi (Chapter 1) and Brown and Rowthorn (Chapter 2) illustrate the socially optimal treatment for the case with one and two drugs, respectively.

While the underlying economic, epidemiological, and institutional assumptions of the analyses are not likely to hold in practice, the stylized models do highlight the economic and public health intertemporal trade-offs associated with using antibiotics. The chapters also illustrate the insights that economic analysis can bring to the public health debate on antibiotic use.

Disease Ecology

The chapters are based on the SIS (susceptible → infected → susceptible) model of infection and treatment attributed to Kermack and McKendrick (1927). The model with and without treatment is illustrated in the Wilen and

Msangi chapter using phase diagrams to describe the different dynamic trajectories. Because some people might not be familiar with phase diagrams or completely clear on how resistance develops over time, I will elaborate further on the disease ecology as modeled in these chapters.[4]

To frame the discussion, I will use a form of Equation 1 found in Wilen and Msangi's discussion (Chapter 1) (notation and variable definitions follow directly). Applying all of the same assumptions and substituting in $S = 1 - I$ and $I = I_w + I_r$, I get

$$\frac{dI_w}{dt} = \beta(1 - I_w)I_w - r_w I_w - \beta I_w I_r - r_f I_w f \tag{1}$$

$$\frac{dI_r}{dt} = \beta(1 - I_r)I_r - r_r I_r - \beta I_w I_r \tag{2}$$

Note that this system of equations is also the special case of the Rowthorn and Brown model with $f_2 = 0$. These differential equations represent the instantaneous rate of change of resistant and susceptible bacterial strains. In other words, the equations provide structure to explain how the levels of these bacteria change from one period to the next. For example, if each strain is independent of the other, the first term [$\beta(1 - I_i)I_i$ with $i = w, r$] indicates that it would grow to a population of 1 in the long run (steady state, which is defined where $dI_i/dt = 0$). If we include the second term, which is the natural mortality rate of the two strains, then the populations would grow to $1 - r_i/\beta$. This is the point at which growth is directly offset by deaths and the population level remains stable over time.

The disease ecology is such that the resistant and susceptible bacterial strains are not independent, and, in fact, they compete against one another. This competition is represented by the third term, $\beta I_w I_r$. The competition is essentially the battle of the weakest, because the strain that dies off the fastest loses. For instance, if the natural mortality rate of the resistant strain (r_r) is greater than the susceptible strain (r_w), then in the long run without treatment ($f = 0$), the only strain that would persevere is the susceptible one. In other words, if we do not use antibiotics, then the resistant strain would go extinct. The "do-nothing" strategy is what Wilen and Msangi have called the ecological strategy. The difference between the natural mortality rates is called fitness cost ($\Delta r = r_r - r_w$), which as Wilen and Msangi discuss, is solely a biological cost.

What happens to the disease ecology when we use antibiotics ($f > 0$)? Operationally, this means that the fourth term in Equation 1 is positive ($r_f I_w f$). The consequence of this is that it shifts the relative advantage from the susceptible strain to the resistant strain as it increases the mortality rate of the susceptible strain. All else being equal, the lower the level of the susceptible strain in existence, the less competition the resistant strain has. Therefore, the more we treat with antibiotics, the easier we are making it for the resistant bacteria to survive. As the level of the resistant strain increases, for example, from treating all individuals ($f = 1$), the more resistance builds and the less effective the antibiotic becomes.[5] In the limit, therefore, all infected people would be taking the antibiotic, but it would be having no effect on the infection. This story is found in Wilen and Msangi's Figure 1-3.

The Case of One Antibiotic and One Infection

As mentioned previously, Wilen and Msangi considered the case in which there is only one antibiotic. The social planner is assumed to choose the optimal time path of treatment such that discounted present value of costs (damage and treatment) is minimized. With one antibiotic, the planner can either decide to use it (interventionist strategy) or not use it (ecological strategy) in any given period.

In this setting, the optimal strategy is to treat the entire population initially and then at some point begin to treat only a fraction of the population. Over time, the fraction treated decreases, which maintains the effectiveness of the antibiotic longer. Eventually, the fraction of the population treated approaches the long-run solution in which the level of effectiveness and infection remain constant. This solution is depicted in Wilen and Msangi's Figure 1-4. While the long-run level of infection is independent of economic parameters, the optimal level of effectiveness depends on the costs of treatment. In particular, one treats less when costs are higher. Therefore, the higher the cost of treatment, the higher the level of effectiveness (and lower levels of resistance) in the long run, everything else being equal.

Wilen and Msangi provide a nice discussion on how their formulation of the model and their results differ from those used in epidemiology to study different antibiotic treatment strategies (Bonhoeffer et al. 1997). For example, the authors find that the strategy of treating the entire population initially (illustrated numerically in their Figure 1-5) is consistent with the "hit 'em hard and hit 'em fast" rule of thumb. According to the authors, their optimal strategy differs from the rule of thumb because it stops treating the entire population before the disease is eliminated.

Why is there a difference between the economic and epidemiological strategies? As the authors mention, the economic policy takes into account both the costs today to treat and the increasing costs associated with future treatment because continuing to treat at high levels builds up resistance. So how will a public health official know when to stop treating with the antibiotic? This is a difficult question, and one that I believe is not satisfactorily addressed in their analysis. I suspect that the omission is due to the fact that there is no simple analog to the epidemiological rule of thumb to help guide the decision. In fact, the time to stop treatment depends not just on the particular disease ecology, initial levels of infection, costs of treatment, and the discount rate but also on relative levels and interplay among these factors.[6]

The Case of Two Antibiotics and Two Strains

Rowthorn and Brown generalized the Wilen and Msangi model to the case with two antibiotics and two types of infection. The generalization, however, comes at the cost of increasing complexity, the implications of which are well detailed in the chapter. Two simplifying assumptions are that each antibiotic is only effective against one type of infection and that all infected individuals are treated with only one antibiotic.[7] By making these assumptions, the authors have ruled out the ecologist strategy of Wilen and Msangi as well as the possibility of treating with an antibiotic cocktail. The authors also assume that doctors do not have enough information on which type of infection the patient has (it is either not feasible or too costly to test the patients) to determine which antibiotic will be effective. Therefore, some fraction of those using an antibiotic will not get better. If they do get better, it is not because they are taking the antibiotic. The social planner is assumed to know the level of each infection in the closed population.

Unlike the Wilen and Msangi formulation whose objective function is to minimize costs, the objective function of the Rowthorn and Brown model is to maximize the discounted present value of net benefits. Net benefits are defined as the social value of being healthy times the number of healthy individuals less the costs of treating infections with both antibiotics. Qualitatively, the objectives are the same.[8] Having said that, there are subtle important differences between the two frameworks. For example, the Wilen and Msangi optimal solution is essentially a cost-effective strategy, which does not necessarily include valuing public health. The approach by Rowthorn and Brown assumes that there is some constant social value of being healthy across individuals in the closed population and across generations. Whether such a value exists and can be measured and whether it is morally defensible is unclear. In the end, both modeling frameworks are not immune to embedding judgments on these issues and both raise important questions on how society might want to think about valuing public health today and in the future.

The Rowthorn and Brown model has two state equations (two levels of infection) and two controls (two antibiotic treatment rates), which are reduced to one with the assumption that all infected individuals are treated ($f_1 = 1 - f_2$). It is possible that each strain of infection has its own transmission rate, natural mortality, mortality induced by treatment, and so forth. Allowing for all this heterogeneity in the model, however, makes it difficult to disentangle what is caused by what. In the end, the authors assume most of this heterogeneity away and focus on economic differences in the treatment costs of the two antibiotics.

They find that the relative levels of infection in the long run depend on the cost of treatment (c_i), benefit of a cure (p), discount rate (ρ), natural mortality rates (r_i), effectiveness of the treatments (α), and contagion rate of the diseases (β).

The fraction treated with each antibiotic depends only on the disease ecology (fitness cost and effectiveness of the treatments). Everything else being equal, the infection with the highest cost of treatment is most prevalent in the long run. The authors' interpretation of this result is that people are more tolerant of a bad thing the more expensive it is to mitigate. This result is consistent with Wilen and Msangi, who found that the higher the cost of treatment, the higher the level of effectiveness.

What are the qualitative characteristics of the optimal use of antibiotics over time? Like the Wilen and Msangi chapter, there is no closed form dynamic solution implying that the authors must use numerical methods to solve for possible optimal solutions. Rowthorn and Brown found that the planner initially should use exclusively the antibiotic that is effective against the strain that is most prevalent. However, if this antibiotic is also the more expensive one, then it is not clear that this remains the optimal strategy. Of course, it would never make sense to employ the more expensive antibiotic if the other type of infection was more prevalent (the planner would be simply throwing money and antibiotics away). At some point, it becomes advantageous to employ both antibiotics simultaneously, but as the authors mention, it is not clear how the parameters affect this switching time.

Discussion

These chapters have raised some important economic and epidemiological issues associated with antibiotic resistance. The two chapters employ optimal control frameworks as the means to understand how a social planner might balance the social and private benefits and costs over time. The balance is found when the (marginal) returns to treating one more individual today are equal to the (marginal) costs of increased resistance borne in the future.

More important than the particular results, which are based on assumptions that are not likely to apply to many settings, are the different policy implications that come out of models that take into account both economic and epidemiological factors. For example, the costs of treatment affect not only the amount of population treated in any period but also the development of resistance over time. To natural resource economists, the difference is not surprising because there is a long history of analyses combining biological and economic factors that derive different conclusions than those derived only from biological models. In the current public health debate, however, it appears that these types of models and strategies are not being considered and as such, the qualitative nature of the findings are probably more surprising to that audience.

Although each chapter sets out to characterize the optimal use of antibiotics, while taking into account resistance costs, neither addresses how these control strategies might be implemented. For example, in non-hospital settings, how can policymakers provide the correct signals such that private individuals and those who prescribe the antibiotics do what is in the best interest of society? And how does the current health care system impede or facilitate the ability of policymakers in such an endeavor? Nor do the chapters explain how the resistant strain comes to be (e.g., is it because patients do not complete their full course of antibiotics?). Finally, both chapters take the stock of antibiotics as fixed, but there are critical feedbacks between the demand for antibiotics and the supply of new antibiotics, which might mitigate or delay the development of resistance in our current stock.

References

Anderson, R.M., and R.M. May. 1991. *Infectious Diseases of Humans: Dynamics and Control.* Oxford, U.K.: Oxford University Press.

Bonhoeffer, S., M. Lipsitch, and B.R. Levin. 1997. Evaluating Treatment Protocols to Prevent Antibiotic Resistance. *Proceedings of the National Academy of Sciences of the USA* 94(22): 12106–11.

The Economist. 2001. The Line of Least Resistance. May 5, 71–2.

Ellison, S.F., and J.K. Hellerstein. 1999. The Economics of Antibiotics: An Exploratory Study. In *Measuring the Prices of Medical Treatments,* edited by J.E. Triplett. Washington, DC: Brookings Institution, 118–43.

Laxminarayan, R., and G.M. Brown. 2001. Economics of Antibiotic Resistance: A Theory of Optimal Use. *Journal of Environmental Economics and Management,* 42(2): 183–206.

Kermack, W.O., and A.G. McKendrick. 1927. A Contribution to the Mathematical Theory of Epidemics. *Proceedings of the Royal Society of London. Series A, Containing Papers of a Mathematical and Physical Character* 115(772): 700–21.

Notes

1. This is what economists call a positive externality. An externality exists when the welfare of one individual depends not only on his or her actions but also on the actions of other individuals who are out of his or her control. Other (positive externalities) benefits include both a reduction in the probability that the infection will lead to further

medical complications requiring more costly treatments and a potential reduction in the number of days out of work.

2. This is what economists call a negative externality.

3. See Ellison and Hellerstein (1999) for the potential implications of these benefits and costs on the price of antibiotics and incentives for research and development of new antibiotics.

4. See Anderson and May (1991), Bonhoeffer et al. (1997), and *The Economist* (2001) for more information on disease ecology and how resistance develops.

5. The disease ecology models used in both chapters do not take into account cross-resistance.

6. The discount rate reflects a social rate of time preference where a positive discount rate implies that future benefit and costs associated with treatment are valued less by the social planner than those incurred today, all else being equal. A zero discount rate corresponds to the case in which all benefits and costs are weighed equally, irrespective of when they occur.

7. The assumptions regarding the disease ecology are essentially the same in both chapters.

8. To illustrate this, first rewrite the total social value of being healthy as $pN - pI$ and note that because the population size is exogenous, it does not affect the marginal decision rules found in the necessary and sufficient conditions for an optimal solution. The only factor that affects the optimal solution is $-pI$, which is the reduction in the total value of health (pN) caused by infection in the society. In other words, it is the cost to society associated with the level of infection, which is $d_I I$ in the Wilen and Msangi chapter.

Commentary

Same Infection, Same Time, Same Antibiotic?

Stephen W. Salant

Rowthorn and Brown (Chapter 2) and Laxminarayan and Weitzman (Chapter 3) characterize the socially optimal way to treat one kind of bacterial infection in a population when multiple antibiotics are available. The first of these formulations is static, whereas the second is dynamic. In both formulations, choosing the antibiotic best suited for each patient in isolation is not socially optimal because such a policy disregards the effects such a choice imposes on third parties. When the third-party effects of such choices are taken fully into account, it often turns out—for different reasons in the two formulations—to be optimal to treat the same type of infection in different individuals at the same time with different antibiotics.

Neither chapter considers the practical difficulties of implementing such a policy. One of these antibiotics will typically be less costly for the individual patient than the other if priced at marginal cost. There is no discussion of how patients can be induced or compelled to take the antibiotic that is not the best treatment for their illness for the sake of anonymous third parties. Nor is there any discussion of how insurance coverage and market power distort from marginal costs the prices that presumably strongly influence antibiotic choices in decentralized settings. The exclusive focus of both chapters is on the socially optimal policy—not its implementation.

The Static Analysis of Laxminarayan and Weitzman

Laxminarayan and Weitzman have provided us with a short, thought-provoking analysis on the optimal way to treat a single kind of bacterial infection afflicting a group of patients when several antibiotics exist, each of which could cure a patient at a different cost. According to the authors, current medical practice involves treating patients uniformly with the same antibiotic—the cheapest available after full account is taken of the bacteria's susceptibility to each drug. If increasing resistance to this first-line antibiotic subsequently renders a second-line antibiotic the least expensive option, the recommendation is then revised, and the second-line treatment is used uniformly on all untreated patients. This policy leads to the use of several antibiotics, with each used to such an extent that the cost per cure is equalized. This so-called "uniform treatment policy" may *seem* the sensible way to cure the group at least aggregate cost. But Laxminarayan and Weitzman explain why it is not and what policy is best within their stylized formulation.

To understand Laxminarayan and Weitzman's critique of current practice and their proposed alternative, familiarity with the highway congestion analogy underlying their analysis is helpful. The model of highway congestion appeared in the first edition of Pigou's *Economics of Welfare* (1920, 194). For Laxminarayan and Weitzman's analogy to work, each vehicle must be assumed to transport a single motorist. Suppose a group of motorists (the counterpart of the patients) desires to get from a common origin (the infected state) to a common destination (the cured state) by any of a set of routes (antibiotic treatments) connecting these two points. Suppose that the time required to get to the destination depends on the route taken (just as the cost per cure depends on the antibiotic) because of variations in "exogenous" factors such as the length and the number of lanes of each route (the counterpart to the inherent attributes of each antibiotic) as well as in such "endogenous" factors as additional minutes of delay caused by congestion (the counterpart of the additional cost per cure caused by induced resistance). Does the policy of (a) directing all motorists to the fastest route (the least-cost antibiotic)—taking full account of the current level of congestion on each route—and (b) changing that recommendation if another route becomes the fastest—minimize aggregate hours spent en route to the destination? Such a policy will result in the motorists being allocated among the various routes in such a way that the travel time on every route is equalized.

The highway analogy exposes the logical flaw in the "uniform treatment" policy. Under that policy, full account is taken of the current delays caused by the congestion along each route. But *no account* is taken of the fact that the policy being considered will affect the congestion and hence the delays on each route. Failure to take these consequences into account constitutes the flaw in the uniform treatment policy—whether applied to highway congestion or to antibiotic resistance.

Granted, the delay imposed by one additional motorist on the first-line route may *seem* inconsequential—say, 0.01 minutes (0.6 seconds) per motorist. But if 10,000 other motorists are on that same route, the delay imposed on everyone adds up: the resulting *aggregate* increase in travel time would in that case be $(0.01)(10,000) = 100$ minutes (1 hour and 40 minutes)! Consequently, as long as the fastest second-line route takes fewer than 100 minutes longer than the congested first-line route, aggregate travel time could be reduced by requiring the additional motorist to use the fastest *untraveled* route. Suppose that in the absence of any congestion on the other routes, the best of them takes 60 minutes longer than the first-line route when it is congested with 10,000 cars. Then 40 minutes in aggregate travel time is saved by directing that additional motorist to the slower route. Note the tradeoff: one motorist has to spend an extra hour in his or her car on the second-line route so that each of 10,000 motorists avoids a 0.6-second delay that would be caused if he or she instead took the first-line route. Indeed, a *further* reduction in aggregate travel time could have been achieved if some of these 10,000 motorists had been assigned to the second-line route.

The optimal solution characterized by Laxminarayan and Weitzman takes this line of argument to its logical conclusion and applies it not to highway congestion but instead to antibiotic resistance. Without loss of generality, label the cheapest antibiotic in the absence of any induced resistance "antibiotic 1," the next cheapest "antibiotic 2," and so forth. In their solution, a designated number of patients are treated with antibiotic 1, a different number are treated with antibiotic 2, and so forth in such a way that (a) every patient is treated (and cured) using *some* antibiotic and (b) no reassignment of one or more patient(s) to different antibiotics would reduce the aggregate cost of curing everyone. A more formal comparison of the two policies is presented in the appendix to this commentary.

The optimal solution has several striking characteristics. If some antibiotics that could cure the disease are not used because of their cost, there will be a "boundary" antibiotic k such that every antibiotic 1, 2, ..., k is used to some extent, and none of the remaining antibiotics are used at all. The range of antibiotics used will be *at least as wide* as in the uniform treatment policy. Thus, if the optimal solution would use antibiotics 1, ..., k, the uniform policy would use 1, ..., j where $j \leq k$. How readily the given bacteria develop resistance to each of the *unused* antibiotics has no effect on the optimal solution. But their susceptibility to the k antibiotics that *are* used *does* influence the number of patients assigned to each of these antibiotics. The simplest case occurs when the k antibiotics are *equally* susceptible to resistance—that is, when adding a given number of patients to *any* of the k used antibiotics raises its cost per cure because of the induced resistance by the same amount per additional patient. In that case, the optimal solution involves putting more people on antibiotic 1 than on antibiotic 2, more on antibiotic 2 than on antibiotic 3, and so forth.

But the optimal solution has one troubling characteristic that we caught a glimpse of in the numerical example—it creates arbitrary distinctions among identical people and treats them differently. Just as everyone traveling on the first-line route in the optimal solution gets to the common destination faster than everyone traveling on the second-line route, so everyone treated using antibiotic i incurs a smaller cost to be cured than everyone treated with antibiotic $i + 1$ (where $i + 1 \leq k$). Some people might find the proposed solution inequitable. But equity aside, it poses two practical difficulties.

First, patients using a more expensive antibiotic when others in the same situation are being cured at less expense with a different antibiotic are apt to *demand* that their physicians prescribe the cheaper drug for them. If the physicians refuse, the patients may threaten to sue or to switch doctors. It is not clear to me that physicians currently unwilling to rein in parents demanding antibiotics for their children's viral ear infections can be relied on to enforce the arbitrary discrimination inherent in the cost-minimizing policy.

But assume every physician in a given hospital or a given state acquired the necessary backbone to do exactly what the optimal policy calls for—to prescribe for some subgroup of patients who would have received the first-line drug, the second-line drug instead. As a result, resistance to the second-line drug would increase and achieving a cure with it would become more costly than with the first-line drug. Even if patients within the jurisdiction of a given hospital or state could be coerced to settle for the second-line drug despite its higher cost, patients merely visiting the jurisdiction who might otherwise have taken the second-line drug would now strictly prefer the first-line drug as less costly. In theory, for every patient we force to take the second-line drug instead of the first-line drug, there will be one patient we cannot force who will switch from the second-line drug to the first-line drug. This offsetting behavior stops only when there remain no patients outside our jurisdiction on the second-line drug. Only then will our proposed reform have any effect on the aggregate costs of treating the patients under our control. In short, for the policy to have beneficial effects, a sufficient portion of the patients with the infection has to be under our control.

The Dynamic Analysis of Rowthorn and Brown

Whereas the Laxminarayan and Weitzman chapter is based on the economist's static model of highway congestion from Pigou (1920), Rowthorn-Brown's chapter is based on the epidemiologist's dynamic model of infection from Kermack and McKendrick (1927). In their formulation, there are two antibiotics and two strains of the infection. As a simplification, antibiotic 1 is assumed to have no effect on strain 2, and antibiotic 2 is assumed to be similarly ineffective against strain 1. Against strain i ($i = 1, 2$), one course of antibiotic i succeeds in the fraction a_i of the cases. Let c_i denote the cost of a 14-day course of antibiotic i. Suppose it is known that I_1 people have strain 1 and I_2 people have strain 2, but it is too costly to identify the strain infecting any given patient. Let I denote the aggregate number of people infected with the two strains: $I = I_1 + I_2$. Hence, the probability that a person will be cured if he or she takes antibiotic i for 14 days is the product of (a) the probability that he or she has strain i (I_i/I) and (b) the probability that the antibiotic will be successful, given that the person has strain i. If a person places monetary value P on being cured, then he or she will strictly prefer antibiotic 1 if $(P)(a_1)(I_1/I) - c_1 > (P)(a_2)(I_2/I) - c_2$ and will weakly prefer antibiotic 2 otherwise. Notice that this decision rule takes no account of the contagion rates of the two strains or the number of healthy people who might potentially become infected. Such information is irrelevant to the choice of what is the best treatment for any given individual patient, but it is obviously central to how he or she should be treated if the goal is instead to promote the welfare of the society as a whole. Rowthorn and Brown never discuss this decision rule, but it seems pertinent to mention as the counterpart to Laxminarayan and Weitzman's uniform treatment policy. Both policies take into account current levels of resistance, but neither takes into account the consequences for third parties of an individual's choice of antibiotic.

The third parties affected in Rowthorn and Brown's formulation are not, as with Laxminarayan and Weitzman, other individuals suffering from the same disease at the same time (the other motorists currently on the same roadway). For the most part, the third parties will be those infected in the future by either the individual who is now being treated or by those he or she infects. The core of the Rowthorn–Brown's model is a pair of differential equations describing the evolution in continuous time of the number of people infected with the two strains (the two "state variables"), given the fraction of infected people treated with each antibiotic over time (the two "control variables") and exogenous parameters describing rates of contagion, the size of the entire population, and so forth. To simplify their theoretical analysis, the authors excluded from consideration control strategies in which (a) some infected patients receive neither antibiotic or (b) some receive both antibiotics at once. This reduces the number of control variables to one: the fraction of infected patients treated with antibiotic 1 (the fraction using antibiotic 2 can then be inferred as the complement).

Given this descriptive core model, the authors use Pontryagin's maximum principle to deduce a set of first-order conditions that must necessarily hold if the discounted integral of the excess of benefits over costs is maximized. Analysis of the problem turns out to be tricky for a variety of reasons well documented in the chapter. The phase portrait used to describe the optimal solution highlights the evolution of the two state variables but, to those unfamiliar with such diagrams, probably obscures the optimal time path of the control variable(s). Depending on the number of people infected by the two strains initially, it is socially optimal to prescribe the same antibiotic for everyone during a finite time interval and then to begin using the other antibiotic on some fraction of the infected patients.

Whether such a model is formulated in continuous or in discrete time is largely a matter of taste. I have a minor preference for a discrete-time formulation because it is easier to explain to nonspecialists and to simulate. It may be helpful, therefore, to reformulate the dynamic system in discrete time such that each period consists of 14 days, the length of one course of an antibiotic. The core of the model would then be a pair of difference equations.

As a newcomer to the area of antibiotic resistance, I do not know what progress has been made since 1927 in numerically implementing the discrete-time counterpart to the Kermack–McKendrick model. But I can well imagine that some distinguished economists are very knowledgeable about the empirical implementation of this model (at least for some infections and some sets of antibiotics), just as others are well informed about dynamic optimization. One problem is getting practitioners from different disciplines to communicate effectively. I would think an accessible, user-friendly simulation model that could be manipulated online or in an electronic worksheet would facilitate such communication. One constrained optimization package (Solver) is standard equipment in most Microsoft Excel versions[1] and greatly enhanced versions can seamlessly replace the standard package within Excel at reasonable prices (http://www.frontsys.com/). Rowthorn and Brown emphasized that the dynamic problem they analyzed resembles those that arise in resource economics. How dynamic resource problems of approximately the same complexity as Rowthorn and Brown's can be solved and presented to nonspecialists using Excel's Solver is well-illustrated throughout Jon Conrad's 1999 undergraduate textbook, *Resource Economics*. But whether it be a canned program like Solver or one specially tailored to the problem, such a user-friendly tool that permits calculation of the optimal program online or on one's personal computer would facilitate dialogue between the scientists and social scientists. The scientists have a comparative advantage in choosing the appropriate dynamic system and calibrating it empirically. They may conclude that the Kermack–McKendrick dynamic system should reflect uncertainty or should be otherwise modified. The social scientists, in turn, have a comparative advantage in numerically solving the dynamic optimization problem specified by the scientists, ascertaining that the optimum has been properly identified[2] and using dynamic optimization theory (a) to explain the intuition for the optimal strategy and (b) to illuminate its sensitivity to perturbations in the specification.

Besides the promotion of dialogue and collaboration, such simulation exercises can make two other important contributions. First, they eliminate the need to exclude a priori strategies, which, for some sets of parameters of interest, may include the actual optimum. For example, as simplifications, Rowthorn and Brown excluded strategies in which some patients receive both antibiotics simultaneously or some patients receive neither drug. The simulation should be flexible enough to include *all* possible strategies.[3]

There is a final and decisive reason for considering such simulation models. The socially optimal policy worked out in each chapter differs from current practice. This tells us only that *some* improvement is possible. But it tells us nothing whatsoever about the *magnitude* of the potential improvement. Clearly, there is no point in abandoning current practice to achieve a minuscule improvement. A carefully calibrated simulation can clarify whether improvements of significant magnitude are achievable. If they are, it may nonetheless be possible to capture much of that potential gain using a strategy simpler than the fully optimal one—say, in Rowthorn and Brown's case, by using the best of the simpler strategies in which everyone is treated at any given time with the same drug. A calibrated simulation can clarify this issue as well.

References

Conrad, J. *Resource Economics*. 1999. Cambridge, U.K.: Cambridge University Press.

Kermack, W., and A.G. McKendrick. 1927. A Contribution to the Mathematical Theory of Epidemics. *Proceedings of the Royal Society of London. Series A, Containing Papers of a Mathematical and Physical Character* 115(772): 700–21.

Myerson, R. 1981. Optimal Auction Design. *Mathematics of Operations Research* 6: 58–73.

Pigou, A.C. 1920. *Economics of Welfare*. London: Macmillan.

Appendix to the Laxminarayan and Weitzman Model

Suppose there are $\bar{w}$ infected individuals and m antibiotics that can be used to treat them. In the absence of resistance, antibiotic i ($i = 1, \dots, m$) can cure someone at cost C_i. Index the antibiotics so that $C_i < C_{i+1}$. If Y_i individuals are assigned drug i, the cost increases by $s_i Y_i$ because of the induced resistance. Hence, the aggregate cost of treating Y_i individuals with antibiotic i is $Y_i(C_i + s_i Y_i)$. Define average cost (AC_i)(the cost per person treated with antibiotic i) as

$$AC_i(Y_i) = \frac{Y_i(C_i + s_i Y_i)}{Y_i} = C_i + s_i Y_i$$

Define marginal cost (MC_i) (the increase in the aggregate cost of treating patients with antibiotic i when an additional person is given drug i) as

$$MC_i(Y_i) = \frac{d}{dY_i} Y_i(C_i + s_i Y) + C_i + 2 s_i Y_i$$

Let the superscript u denote the uniform treatment policy and the superscript o denote the optimal policy. Then the following conditions uniquely define the number of patients taking each antibiotic under the two policies (as well as j, k, λ, and γ):

Under the uniform treatment policy

$$\sum_i Y_i^u = \overline{w} \tag{1}$$

$$Y_i^u > 0 \quad \text{and} \quad AC_i\left(Y_i^u\right) = \gamma \quad \text{for} \quad i = 1,\dots,j \tag{2}$$

$$Y_i^u = 0 \quad \text{and} \quad AC_i(0) \geq \gamma \quad \text{for} \quad i = j+1,\dots,m \tag{3}$$

Under the optimal policy

$$\sum_i Y_i^o = \overline{w} \tag{4}$$

$$Y_i^o > 0 \quad \text{and} \quad MC_i\left(Y_i^o\right) = \lambda \quad \text{for} \quad i = 1,\dots,k \tag{5}$$

$$Y_i^o = 0 \quad \text{and} \quad MC_i(0) \geq \lambda \quad \text{for} \quad i = k+1,\dots,m \tag{6}$$

Because $MC_i(Y_i) > AC_i(Y_i)$ for $Y_i > 0$, $\lambda > \gamma$. A solution in which $j = k = 2$ is illustrated in Figure A-1 (for simplicity, drawn with $s_1 = s_2$). In the uniform treatment policy, the *average cost* per patient is equalized (at γ, the height of the lower horizontal line in the figure). The horizontal components of the intersection of that line with AC_1 and AC_2 indicate the number of patients assigned drug 1 (Y_1^u) and drug 2 (Y_2^u), respectively, under the uniform treatment policy.

Similarly, in the optimal policy, the *marginal cost* of adding another patient to either antibiotic is equalized (at λ, the height of the higher horizontal line). The horizontal components of the intersection of that line with MC_1 and MC_2 indicate the number of patients assigned drug 1 (Y_1^o) and drug 2 (Y_2^o), respectively under the optimal policy. As drawn, λ (and hence γ) pass beneath C_3 (and hence beneath $C_4,\dots,C_n$); hence, $j = k = 2$. It is possible, however, to devise cases in which the optimal policy uses a broader assortment of antibiotics ($j < k$). As the graph reflects, if the optimal policy replaces the uniform treatment policy, some of the patients who would have taken drug 1 are given drug 2, because this causes increased resistance to drug 2 and reduced resistance to drug 1, $AC_1(Y_1^o) < AC_2(Y_2^o)$ under the optimal policy.

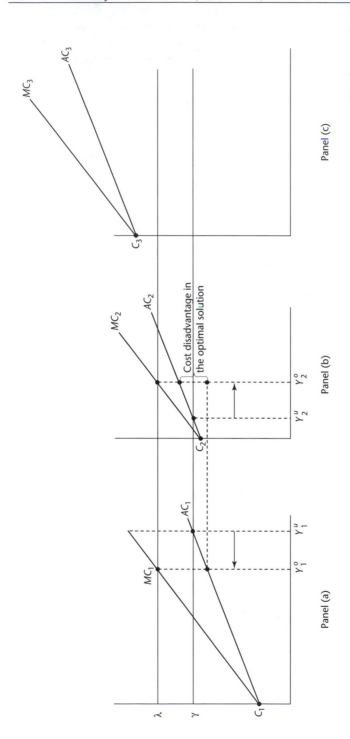

FIGURE A-1. Average and Marginal Costs under Uniform and Optimal Treatment Policies

Notes

1. Look under Tools and click on Add-Ins to load Solver. If the Solver package is not available under Add-Ins, load it from the program disks or consult with your system administrator.

2. When using Solver on dynamic problems, for example, I always include a column to verify that the strategy the program locates as optimal satisfies the necessary conditions for a maximum in every period.

3. Many unexpected solutions in optimization or equilibrium problems have been identified during a computerized simulation. My own work on losses from horizontal mergers (an equilibrium problem) and on the social and private advantages of creating asymmetries in two-stage games (an optimization problem) grew out of computerized simulations. The example in Myerson (1981) of a seller facing buyers of unknown but correlated types who, by cleverly exploiting the correlation between them, can always extract their *entire* surplus was also first identified by a computer simulation. In all of these examples, the surprising result would have been missed if the computer-assisted search was artificially restricted to the class the researcher thought a priori would contain the solution.

Chapter 4

Pest Mobility, Market Share, and the Efficacy of Refuge Requirements for Resistance Management

Silvia Secchi and Bruce A. Babcock

Bt crops, the first generation of agricultural biotechnology, have been widely adopted in the United States. There are concerns about the possible development of resistance to *Bt* by the targeted pests; therefore, the U.S. Environmental Protection Agency has mandated the use of refuges. Refuges are portions of the field in which non-*Bt* seed is planted. This practice allows the interbreeding of pests and slows resistance.

The current policy is based on the assumption that the market share of *Bt* crops is 100%. However, if market penetration is lower, pest mobility can substantially alter the efficacy of refuges. When pests are mobile, untreated fields serve as "natural refuge" because pests from untreated fields can move to treated fields. The importance of natural refuges depends on pest mobility and market penetration. High mobility and low market penetration increase substitution possibilities between mandatory and natural refuges because the pests—and their genetic makeup—behave like a common property resource among farmers and there are high levels of externalities.

We focus on the impact of market penetration and pest mobility on resistance buildup to improve the effectiveness of the current policy and to identify the level of market penetration at which natural refuges become ineffective. We use a simulation model to mimic the behavior of profit-maximizing farmers on nine adjacent *Bt* and non-*Bt* corn fields for 15 years. Farmers planting the non-*Bt* corn use economic thresholds to decide whether to apply a non-*Bt* pesticide. A random element is introduced to mimic the real variability of the pest population from year to year. The mobility of the pest is parameterized by the percentage of the pest population on a field that moves to neighboring fields.

We find that farmers using traditional hybrids have a higher pest population, which is highly susceptible to *Bt*. The negative externality produced by the net influx of these pests into the *Bt* fields is small, and it is more than offset by the positive impact that the susceptible pests have on delaying resistance buildup. Furthermore, the number of pests moving into the non-*Bt* fields is low and does not cause significant damage.

We also find that resistance does not spread from the *Bt* to the non-*Bt* fields, and that lack of complete market penetration significantly reduces the buildup of resistance on *Bt* fields unless mobility is very low. This suggests that the current policy is only optimal if market penetration is complete or mobility is close to zero.

The use of agricultural biotechnologies has been increasing dramatically in the United States since the mid-1990s. Among the most successful crops are *Bt* plant-pesticides, which are engineered to express the *Bacillus thuringiensis* (*Bt*) δ-endotoxins and target the European corn borer (ECB). *Bt* pesticides have long been used in spray form by organic and integrated pest management farmers, and their effectiveness and safety are well established. The U.S. Environmental Protection Agency (EPA) requires farmers who want to grow *Bt* corn and cotton to follow resistance management plans to slow resistance to the *Bt* toxins because organic farmers and environmental groups are concerned about the possible development of resistance to *Bt* by the targeted pests. Moreover, EPA is interested in resistance issues because of the provisions of the Federal Insecticide, Fungicide, and Rodenticide Act and the Food Quality Protection Act. Because of these acts, the agency is reassessing the environmental and human health impacts of pesticides that have long been on the market, such as the organophosphates. Some of these older products may be withdrawn from the market, and EPA is concerned about the long-term viability of alternative, more environmentally friendly products such as the *Bt* crops (see for instance EPA 1998a).

Specifically, the EPA resistance management plan consists of a combination of mandatory refuges and high doses. Refuges are portions of the field in which non-*Bt* seed is sown and *Bt* insecticides are not sprayed to allow the interbreeding of pests susceptible to *Bt* with resistant pests. This interbreeding slows resistance buildup. Refuges are coupled with high doses of the toxin expressed by the plants throughout the season and in all the plant tissues so only the few resistant pests survive on *Bt* crops.

The use of untreated areas as refuges for susceptible pests is not a novel idea. It has been analyzed by entomologists at the theoretical level (Georghiou and Taylor 1977; Caprio 1998), and it has been advocated in practice as a strategy to slow the resistance to acaricides used to control the two-spotted spider mite in pear orchards (Croft and Dunley 1993), imidacloprid applied to suppress the Colorado potato beetle in potatoes (Dively et al. 1998), and foliar applications of *Bt* used to control the diamondback moth in cabbage cultivations (Perez et al. 1997). The genetic underpinning of the high-dose refuge strategy is that the resistance to the pesticide follows the Hardy-Weinberg principle (Hartl and Clark 1989). This means that resistance is given by a single, non-sex linked gene with two alleles, so that the pest population is composed of homozygote-susceptible (SS), heterozygote (RS), and homozygote-resistant (RR) individuals. The majority of the pest population is susceptible to the pesticide because the resistance gene R is rare and recessive. Therefore, most pests are SS type. In addition, pesticides also control RS-type pests. Because the *Bt* crops are high dose, all but the RR-type pests, and possibly a small minority of the RS-type pests, are killed. The refuge works in slowing resistance because the small number of resistant survivors from the *Bt* fields mate with the (mostly SS type) pests from the refuge, so that the offspring is SR type.

EPA's current refuge requirements for *Bt* crops are based on the assumption that the market share of the *Bt* seed is 100%. This is equivalent to assuming pest mobility does not cause pest management externalities. In general, though, pest management externalities occur because farmers who do not control a particular pest will have higher pest populations than those who do. The movement of these pests from the fields of noncontrolling farmers into the fields of controlling farmers creates two externalities. A negative externality is created because damaging pests travel from uncontrolled fields to controlled fields, causing damage on the controlled fields. However, this movement also creates a positive externality with respect to resistance management because those pests that move will be more susceptible to the control practice. The time dimension is very important to both these types of externalities. The effects of differential pest pressure may be felt within a growing season or generation of pests[1] if the pests cause damage after they move. But, perhaps more importantly, these effects take place from one generation or growing season to the next. In addition, the externalities caused by differential resistance frequencies are inherently dynamic because the spread of resistance takes place from one generation to the next.

If all farmers use the same pest control practices and in all other ways are identical, then the external costs and benefits of pests moving from field A to field B are offset by the costs and benefits of pests that move from field B to field A. That is, 100% market penetration implies that no externalities are present, and the analysis of optimal resistance management strategies can proceed under this assumption (see for example Hurley et al. 1999). Pest mobility can substantially alter the efficacy of using refuge as a resistance management strategy when market penetration of the resistance-inducing control strategy is less than 100%. When pests are mobile, untreated fields can serve as "natural refuge" because pests from untreated fields can move to treated fields. The ability of natural refuge to substitute for regulatory refuge depends on both pest mobility and market penetration. High mobility and low market penetration clearly should increase substitution possibilities. But it is not certain if natural refuge can serve as a substitute if market penetration is say, 50%, and pest mobility is small.

EPA implicitly acknowledges that pest mobility is a crucial component of the *Bt* resistance question because the very rationale of EPA's regulatory effort is based on the possibility that, because of pest mobility, resistance may spread, making the *Bt* used as a spray in organic farming ineffective (EPA 1998a). The same population biology processes behind the in-field refuge strategy apply to the field-to-field case. EPA and entomologists, in fact, refer to fields planted with non-*Bt* hybrids as unstructured or market-driven refuge (see for instance EPA 1998b).

Figures 4-1 and 4-2 show the level of *Bt* corn market penetration in 1999 by county for the United States. Clearly, market penetration is quite variable across regions, ranging from less than 10% to more than 50% of the corn acreage. This variability suggests the need to analyze in more detail the importance of market penetration in the development of resistance. On the one hand, the penetration of the *Bt* technology could remain limited, and the presence of unstructured refuge might be enough to guarantee that resistance never becomes a concern. This is a distinct possibility, given the Japanese and European position on genetically modified organisms (GMOs): a European or Japanese ban on GMO imports would have a dramatic impact on the adoption of *Bt* crops in the United States. On the other hand, the benefits of *Bt* corn could prompt rapid, widespread adoption. In the analysis that follows, we do not specify the forces driving market penetration. Besides the behavior of export markets, other factors that have the potential to influence the planting decisions of farmers are Farm Bill provisions, the relative pricing of the *Bt* seed, and the role of bundling.[2] Moreover, planting decisions always depend on the local characteristics of the farm system, such as the history of corn borer infestations. Our analysis focuses on the impact of market penetration on resistance and the role of pest mobility in determining the size of the externalities to improve the effectiveness of resistance management policy. In particular, identification of the threshold market penetration for which the unstructured refuge becomes ineffective could prompt regulatory authorities to monitor refuge compliance more closely or to increase the level of refuge recommended in a region.

The issues considered in this chapter are likely to become more central to policymakers because the industry is developing new genetically modified crops that will be active against both the corn rootworm and the ECB and because interest is growing in developing resistance management plans for current pesticides so as to extend their life.

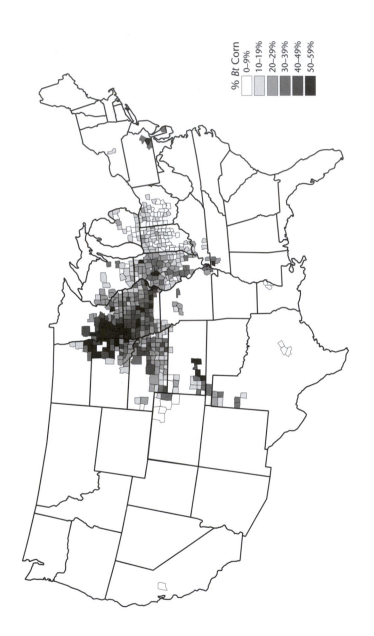

FIGURE 4-1. U.S. Distribution of *Bt* Corn

Notes: The figure represents the percentage of total corn acreage planted to *Bt* corn hybrids in counties in which more than 50,000 acres of corn were planted. *Source*: *Bt* corn industry sales data compiled by FSI, Inc. 1999.

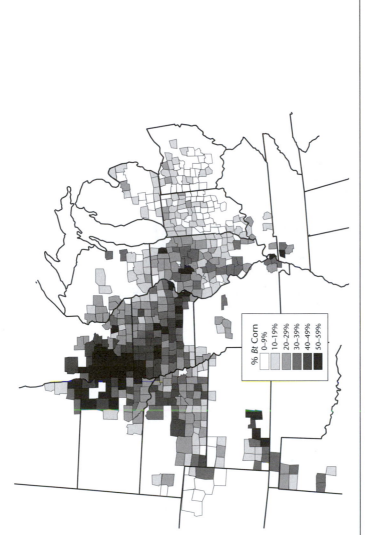

FIGURE 4-2. Distribution of *Bt* Corn—Central Corn Belt

Notes: The figure represents the percentage of total corn acreage planted with *Bt* corn hybrids in Central Corn Belt counties in which more than 50,000 total acres of corn were planted. *Source*: *Bt* corn industry sales data compiled by FSI, Inc. 1999.

To study the effects of pest mobility and incomplete market penetration on pest resistance, we developed a dynamic farm production model and used simulation results to analyze the interplay between the externalities created by pest mobility and the management of resistance at different levels of market penetration and pest mobility. Our analysis focuses on *Bt* corn and the ECB. Our objective was to determine the effect of pest mobility on the buildup of resistance. A recent study suggested that ECB mobility is higher than previously assumed (Showers et al. 2000), but given the insufficient amount of evidence, the following model analyzes the problem at various levels of pest mobility. We applied the model to the case of corn production and used a grid of nine fields that can be sown with the *Bt* seed or with a traditional corn hybrid. The model was developed along the methodological lines of Lazarus and Dixon (1984) and Hurley and others (forthcoming). Lazarus and Dixon used a nonlinear programming model to combine both common-property resource issues with explicit genetics for the corn rootworm, whereas Hurley and others examined the economic value of mechanisms to slow resistance buildup for *Bt* crops. Our analysis also followed a line of research begun in the 1970s (Taylor and Hadley 1975; Hueth and Regev 1974; Regev et al. 1976, 1983) that treats susceptibility to a pesticide as a nonrenewable resource. We built on these studies by maintaining the key assumption that susceptibility is nonrenewable. This means that no fitness costs are associated with resistance: resistant pests have the same reproductive potential and survival capacity as susceptible ones.

Our Model

Our model builds on Hurley and others (forthcoming). It is based on pest population dynamics that allow the direct measurement of resistance development following the Hardy-Weinberg principle described in the introduction. The only difference from the genetics of the pest population in the Hurley and others model is that a random element is introduced to mimic the real variability of the pest population from year to year. ECB populations are highly variable, and it is difficult to accurately predict corn borer pressure from the previous year's pest population size. Also, adding a stochastic element prevents a collapse in the ECB population in the field without suddenly increasing the population size beyond reason. Deterministic models tend to exhibit such a long-term collapse of the pest population, a phenomenon that most observers think is unrealistic.

Each year, the initial pest population size on the non-*Bt* fields is drawn from a uniform random distribution. The stochastic shock does not affect the genetic makeup of the pest population because it represents environmental conditions such as weather and amount of rainfall. The random number is the same for all the fields considered, reflecting the fact that atmospheric conditions are likely to be similar across adjacent fields. On the *Bt* fields, the size of the initial population equals survivors from the previous year plus a fraction of the same population shock that affects the non-*Bt* fields. Scaling down the shock increases the realism of the simulation results in two ways. First, simulated ECB populations on the *Bt* fields tend to be smaller than those in the non-*Bt* fields. This allows resistance to *Bt* to actually occur.[3] Second, farmers treating with traditional sprays on the non-*Bt* fields will be unable to drive the pest populations to extinction because of the larger population shocks.

The pest population analyzed has two generations per year (bivoltine), but the model is generalizable to univoltine or multivoltine populations. More generally, this framework is easily applicable to all pests that exhibit some degree of mobility, ranging from insects to weeds and fungi, and to crops that suffer damage from a common pest population.[4]

The model is based on nine corn fields, some of which—always the same[5]—are planted with *Bt* corn. Following Onstad and Guse (1999) and Mason and others (1996), the damage function of the ECB is linear, but differentiated, across generations. First-generation ECBs cause more damage to corn because they attack it at an earlier stage of development when the plant stalk can withstand less damage. The farmer planting the non-*Bt* corn has the choice of applying a non-*Bt* based pesticide for both the first- and second-generation pests. The cost of applying the chemical input is fixed, and the pesticide has a maximum efficacy bound that is set at various levels ranging from 70% to 90%. The reason for analyzing various levels of efficacy is that the level of efficacy of the sprayed pesticide determines the effective size of the unstructured refuge: for a given level of market penetration, the higher the efficacy of the spray, the lower the effective level of unstructured refuge. Also, the effectiveness of sprays has been increasing in the recent past, so that at this time, efficacy can reach 90% in optimal conditions (Hellmich 1998). The decision to spray is based on economic thresholds described in Mason and others (1996); the thresholds depend on the level of damage of the pest, the costs of spraying, and, of course, the effectiveness of the pesticide. As we noted earlier, the pest population modeled is in the high range because this is mostly the case in locations where significant acreage of *Bt* corn is planted.

Bt farmers plant corn and refuge, which is left unsprayed. The refuge size considered is 20% of the field, which is consistent with current EPA regulation. Following Hurley and others (forthcoming), this proportion of the field is constant throughout the time horizon. The yearly profit per acre for the *Bt* farmer is given by

$$(1-\theta)\left\{pY\left[1-\left(E_{G1}N_{G1}+E_{G2}N_{G2}\right)\right]-\beta\right\}+\theta pY\left[1-\left(E_{G1}N_{G1}+E_{G2}N_{G2}\right)\right]-C \qquad (1)$$

where[6]

θ = proportion of refuge, here 20%
p = real corn price per bushel at 1992 prices, $2.35
Y = pest-free average yield, 130 bushels per acre
N_{G1} and N_{G2} = number of pests per plant, first and second generations
E_{G1} and E_{G2} = damage per pest per plant, E_{G1} = 0.05 and E_{G2} = 0.024
C = costs of production net of the spraying price, $185 per acre
β = Bt premium, $10 per acre

We assume there are no price or yield differentials between the Bt corn and the hybrid planted in the refuge. Because the damage function is linear, and mating is random, we can rewrite Equation 1 as

$$pY\left[1-\left(E_{G1}N_{G1}+E_{G2}N_{G2}\right)\right]-C-\left(1-\theta\right)\beta \tag{2}$$

The non-Bt farmer maximizes

$$pY\left[1-E_{G1}N_{G1}\left(1-\alpha S_1\right)-E_{G2}N_{G2}\left(1-\alpha S_2\right)\right]-C-\chi\left(S_1+S_2\right)$$
$$\text{s.t. } \alpha \in \left[0.7, 0.8, 0.9\right] \text{ and } S_1, S_2 \in \{0,1\} \tag{3}$$

where

χ = cost of the spray application, $14 per acre
S_1 = non-Bt spray application for first-generation ECB
S_2 = non-Bt spray application for second-generation ECB
α = maximum efficacy of the non-Bt spray

The sizes of the initial pest population in the Bt and non-Bt fields in each season are calibrated to ensure that spraying occurs regularly in the non-Bt fields throughout the 15 years considered and that the pest population in the Bt fields can reach the small size necessary for resistance to develop in the absence of mobility but does not collapse and can increase again once resistance is established. The initial pest population in the non-Bt fields each year is given by

$$N_{G1}(t) = \varepsilon$$

and

$$\varepsilon \sim U[0, 0.1] \tag{4}$$

The initial pest population in the *Bt* fields each year is given by the surviving second-generation pests, S_{G2}, plus the stochastic element e scaled by a factor ϕ

$$N_{G1}(t) = S_{G2}(t-1) + \phi e$$

$$\phi = 0.000001$$

and

$$\varepsilon \sim U[0, 0.1] \tag{5}$$

The presence of the previous year's survivors in the determination of the initial pest population for the next season guarantees that the pest population numbers in the *Bt* fields can increase once resistance is established. The shock, common to *Bt* and non-*Bt* fields, guarantees that the population does not collapse, whereas the scaling factor ϕ ensures that, at first, the pest population numbers decrease enough for resistance to develop.

The intraseason population dynamics, that is, the relationship between first and second generation, are the same as in Hurley and others (forthcoming) and is detailed in Onstad and Guse (1999). The approach is based on density-dependent survival of the corn borers. This simulates the fact that competition causes a reduction in survival as the density of corn borers increases so that the growth function of the pests follows a logistic curve.

Equations 1 and 3 incorporate the effects of the population dynamics and the impact of changes in the pest's genetic makeup. Changes in N_{G1} and N_{G2} can be the direct result of changes in the pest population's size or, indirectly, can be caused by variations in the genetic frequency of resistant pests. As resistance increases, there is a decrease in the effectiveness of the *Bt* toxins so that more pests survive and damage the crop. Because our focus is resistance to *Bt*, we will assume that resistance to the spray pesticides used by the farmers planting conventional hybrids does not develop. This would be the case, for instance, if farmers rotated pesticides with different modes of action. The rate of interest used for calculating the net present value of production is 4%. As noted earlier, the time horizon used is 15 years, which is a conservative estimate of the time in which backstop technologies will become available.

The mobility of the pest is parameterized by the percentage of the pest population on a field that moves to neighboring fields and then breeds with the local population. Here we use three levels of pest mobility: 1 pest per 10,000, 1 pest per 100,000, or 1 pest per 1,000,000 will leave the field. Note that such low mobility will tend to give conservative results in terms of resistance development (simulated resistance levels will likely be overstated) because low mobility will limit the influx of susceptible pests into the *Bt* fields.

This form of effective pest mobility is de facto a reduced form embodying two kinds of variables: the first is the pest mobility proper, as determined by biological and environmental factors, and the second is the farm size. The larger the field, the less likely pests are to create an externality by migrating from one farm to the next, as they tend to live and mate within the perimeter of the field. Consistent with field evidence, only first-generation ECBs are modeled as moving outside the field.[7]

We assume that pests will move only to adjacent fields. We also assume that the grid of nine fields examined is representative of a larger production region that follows the same production practices as those described in this grid. More specifically, this entails that the production characteristics of the nine fields examined are mirrored in the neighboring nine field groups. An example is given in Figure 4-3, in which the gray area in the center is the field actually analyzed in the simulations.

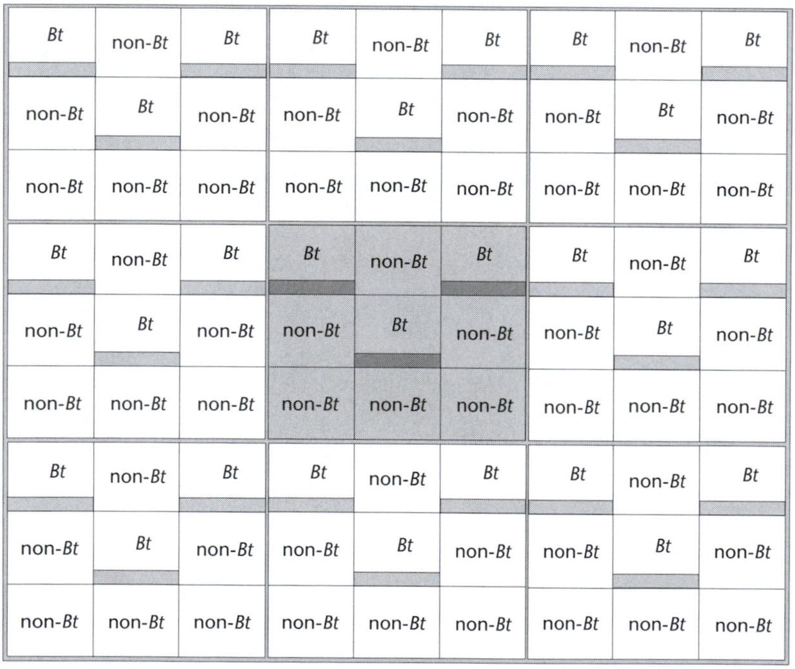

Bt	non-*Bt*	*Bt*	*Bt*	non-*Bt*	*Bt*	*Bt*	non-*Bt*	*Bt*
non-*Bt*	*Bt*	non-*Bt*	non-*Bt*	*Bt*	non-*Bt*	non-*Bt*	*Bt*	non-*Bt*
non-*Bt*	non-*Bt*	non-*Bt*	non-*Bt*	non-*Bt*	non-*Bt*	non-*Bt*	non-*Bt*	non-*Bt*
Bt	non-*Bt*	*Bt*	*Bt*	non-*Bt*	*Bt*	*Bt*	non-*Bt*	*Bt*
non-*Bt*	*Bt*	non-*Bt*	non-*Bt*	*Bt*	non-*Bt*	non-*Bt*	*Bt*	non-*Bt*
non-*Bt*	non-*Bt*	non-*Bt*	non-*Bt*	non-*Bt*	non-*Bt*	non-*Bt*	non-*Bt*	non-*Bt*
Bt	non-*Bt*	*Bt*	*Bt*	non-*Bt*	*Bt*	*Bt*	non-*Bt*	*Bt*
non-*Bt*	*Bt*	non-*Bt*	non-*Bt*	*Bt*	non-*Bt*	non-*Bt*	*Bt*	non-*Bt*
non-*Bt*	non-*Bt*	non-*Bt*	non-*Bt*	non-*Bt*	non-*Bt*	non-*Bt*	non-*Bt*	non-*Bt*

FIGURE 4-3. Example of the Spatial Grid Used in the Model

Note: The darker areas in the *Bt* fields represent refuges.

This formulation has the advantage that the positioning of fields in the grid becomes irrelevant, and the only variable that affects results is how many *Bt* fields there are in the grid, which allows us to concentrate on market penetration. The model is programmed in Matlab's simulation environment, Simulink. Each 15-year scenario is replicated 100 times. It is important to note that the cost of pesticide application per acre for the non-*Bt* fields represents only the direct cost. It does not include the time that the farmer spends scouting for pests to determine the pest population levels. Therefore, the results presented in the next section will generally underestimate the benefits of *Bt* corn.

Results

Results for the baseline case of zero mobility correspond to the zero and full-market penetration cases. If all farmers plant non-*Bt* hybrids, no resistance to *Bt* will occur and profits will be determined by the efficacy of the sprayed pesticides and the modalities of their applications. If, however, all farmers plant *Bt* corn, the evolution of resistance will follow the same path as if only one farmer were planting *Bt*, acting in an isolated environment.

In the baseline case of no pest mobility, the net present value per acre of planting *Bt* corn for 15 years is $1,300.85. There is little variability in the returns across the simulation runs because *Bt* toxins are extremely effective in killing ECB, and the population does not have time to recover in the 15-year time horizon considered. The average proportion of final frequency of resistance alleles is 0.76, with a standard deviation of 0.29. Therefore, on average, at the end of the 15-year time horizon, resistance alleles account for 76% of the total, implying that resistance does indeed occur with zero mobility and 20% refuge. This result is consistent with previous findings (see, for example, Hurley et al. forthcoming). As for the farmers planting a non-*Bt* hybrid, their profits will depend on the effectiveness of the pesticide they have at their disposal and on the pest population dynamics. Table 4-1 shows how profits increase as the pesticide efficacy goes up. For any given pesticide efficacy, profits are always higher for the lower pest population because the population causes less damage and requires fewer pesticide applications.

TABLE 4-1. Average Net Present Value of Non-*Bt* Profits per Acre with Zero Mobility

Pesticide efficacy (percentage of pest population killed)	Dollars
70	$1,122.80 (27.96)
80	$1,161.62 (24.04)
90	$1,213.72 (13.37)

Note: Standard deviations across simulation runs are in parentheses.

The effect of an increase in pesticide efficacy is twofold. First, the number of applications to control first-generation corn borers increases because the cost of application is the same but its productivity is higher. Second, the number of pesticide applications to control second-generation corn borers goes down as the first application's level of control increases.

Table 4-2 reports the average numbers of times that spraying occurs for first- and second-generation borers in the 15-year time frame. For instance, a farmer who has at his or her disposal a pesticide with an 80% efficacy will spray on average 7.6 years out of 15 for first-generation borers and 9.2 years out of 15 for second-generation borers. The results reported in Table 4-2 illustrate that the average pest populations used in the simulations were set at a high level. This choice is motivated by two considerations. First, *Bt* adoption rates are likely to be higher where corn borer pressure is intense because the technology is more valuable to farmers. If the farmer had not adopted *Bt*, he or she would have had to spray very frequently, therefore returns would have been substantially lower. Second, in terms of the development of resistance, lower pest populations are not likely to exhibit a substantially different behavior because the pest population will be lower in both the *Bt* and non-*Bt* fields.

The introduction of mobility has little effect on the profits of the *Bt* farmers. The reason for this is that the corn borers moving into the *Bt* field from the non-*Bt* fields tend to be susceptible to the *Bt* toxin so the pests are killed off and are not able to cause any damage. Thus the size of the negative externality caused by the pests not killed on the *Bt* fields is nearly zero.

Similarly, for the non-*Bt* farmers, profits are unaffected by changes in the level of market penetration for all levels of mobility considered. Returns depend only on the efficacy of the pesticides that farmers have at their disposal. The reason resides in the much lower pest population densities that are found in the *Bt* fields, the relatively low levels of mobility considered in the simulations, and the fact that the spray pesticides have a mode of action different from *Bt* so they can easily kill the few resistant pests moving out of the *Bt* fields. Thus the size of the negative externality caused by surviving pests moving from *Bt* fields to non-*Bt* fields is also nearly zero.

TABLE 4-2. Average Number of Pesticide Applications for the Non-*Bt* Farmers

Pesticide efficacy (percentage of pest population killed)	First-generation	Second-generation
70	6.7 (1.9)	12.5 (1.3)
80	7.6 (1.8)	9.2 (1.8)
90	8.6 (1.8)	4.5 (1.8)

Note: Standard deviations across simulation runs are in parentheses.

As for resistance, with 20% refuge in the *Bt* fields, there are no changes to the genetic makeup of the pest population in the non-*Bt* fields. This indicates that the spread of foci of resistance outside the *Bt* fields might become a concern only for very high levels of market penetration and low compliance to the refuge recommendations. This does not imply that no resistance will develop in the *Bt* fields. As we will see next, this is not generally the case. It does however mean that resistance is probably going to be contained in the *Bt* fields because very few resistant corn borers will move out of the field. The small number that move to the non-*Bt* areas will either mate with susceptible insects or be killed by the applications of spray pesticides. This suggests that the size of the negative externality caused by movement of resistant ECB from *Bt* fields to non-*Bt* fields is also small.

In the *Bt* fields, resistance could very well develop depending on the level of market penetration, the efficacy of the pesticide used in the non-*Bt* areas, and the level of mobility and of pest population pressures. Specifically, lower levels of mobility cause more resistance to develop because of the isolation of resistant pests. Figure 4-4 shows that resistance is not an issue for pest mobility levels greater than 1 in 100,000 pests moving out of a field. Higher levels of mobility introduce enough susceptible pests into the *Bt* fields to dilute the resistance genes. That is, when mobility is high, natural refuge caused by incomplete market penetration of the technology is extremely effective in limiting the buildup of resistance on *Bt* fields. This suggests that the optimal level of regulatory refuge could be substantially lower when market penetration is low than when it is high.

Resistance on *Bt* fields could become a concern if mobility is very low and market penetration is high. As Figure 4-4 illustrates, for very low mobility, the final frequency of resistance would be higher than 0.1 for market penetration levels greater than 60%. It is important to note that neither market penetration nor pesticide efficacy play a role in the development of resistance for the higher levels of mobility: the absolute number of pests leaving the non-*Bt* fields is always high enough to guarantee that resistance does not take hold.

The proportion of resistant alleles stays low irrespective of the level of market penetration and pesticide efficacy for the highest levels of mobility. Even more interestingly, standard deviations are very low, and the final frequency of resistance is well below 0.01 in all the simulation runs. Things are not substantially different if mobility decreases to 0.001%, with two exceptions. Standard deviations increase for the highest level of market penetration, and there is a positive, if low, probability that the final frequency of resistance might be high. If pesticide efficacy is 70%, the probability that the final frequency of resistance exceeds 0.1 is 0.0025.

Both pesticide efficacy and market penetration play a role in the lowest level of mobility analyzed here. Figure 4-4 indicates that, if the *Bt* technology

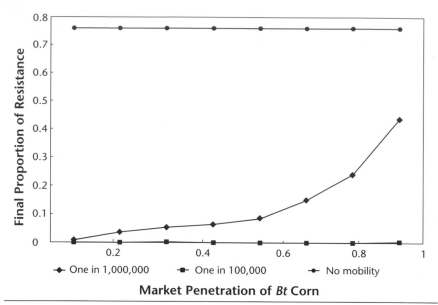

FIGURE 4-4. Average Final Proportion of Resistant Alleles in the *Bt* Fields with 70% Efficacy in the Non-*Bt* Fields

is used in half of the fields or so, resistance will increase substantially. Variances are very high as well, and they tend to increase as market penetration increases. Also, at this very low level of mobility, lower pesticide efficacy will marginally increase the development of resistance, at low levels of market penetration, above the levels shown in Figure 4-4. The reason is that the lower efficacy of the pesticide will bring about higher numbers of susceptible corn borers moving into the *Bt* fields. As they mate with resistant corn borers, the number of heterozygotes increases.

As discussed earlier, these results are much less worrisome than they might appear at first sight when we take into account that the very small population size will ensure that the resistance is not transmitted to the non-*Bt* fields. The few resistant pests escaping from the *Bt* fields will either mate with susceptible pests or be killed off by the pesticides used by the non-*Bt* farmers, which have a mode of action different from *Bt*. This underscores the importance of the assumption we made that the farmers planting traditional hybrids do not use a *Bt*-based spray. If the non-*Bt* areas were sprayed with a *Bt*-based pesticide, resistance might well spread from the transgenic planted fields.

Conclusion

In general, in the case of *Bt* corn, the net outcome of the presence of external-ities discussed in the introduction is clear. Farmers using traditional hybrids have a higher pest population that is highly susceptible to *Bt*. The negative externality produced by the net influx of these pests into the *Bt* fields is small. And it is more than offset by the positive impact that the susceptible pests have on delaying resistance buildup. Furthermore, the number of pests mov-ing into the non-*Bt* fields is very low and does not cause significant damage.

The simulation results indicate some parameter levels at which the spread of resistance might become a concern. First, the results are fairly robust—resistance does not spread from the *Bt* to the non-*Bt* fields, at least in the 15-year time horizon considered here. This is an important result because it sug-gests that even if foci of resistance develop, they will be contained by the higher population pressure in adjacent fields: the high dose concept does indeed work. Second, for the two higher levels of mobility considered—which are still very conservative in terms of how many corn borers will move from field to field—the *Bt* fields themselves do not become significantly resistant.

In addition, for the levels of mobility considered, lack of complete market penetration of *Bt* corn significantly reduces the buildup of resistance on *Bt* fields. This suggests that the optimal level of refuge on *Bt* fields is likely consid-erably lower than the 20% level set by current regulations. This suggests that the 20% refuge is probably only optimal if market penetration is complete or mobility is zero—which are exactly the scenarios considered by previous analy-ses that were consulted when EPA decided on the 20% refuge level.

To put the mobility parameters into perspective, let us consider some of the results of the Showers and others (2000) paper mentioned in the introduc-tion. According to the U.S. Department of Agriculture (USDA 1999), the aver-age farm size in the United States in 1997 was 436 acres or 1.744 square kilo-meters. If we simplistically assume that the farms are square, they will have a side of about 1,321 meters. Showers and others in 1986 released 283,436 adult corn borers at the beginning of the growing season.[8] They set up traps at 200, 800, and 3,200 meters from the release site. At the 3,200-meter distance, they retrieved 35 corn borers, or 0.012% of the insects that had been released. Of course, caution is necessary in the use of these data. For instance, the Showers experiment set up the traps to retrieve the corn borers in habitats different from corn: in the specific case mentioned here, they were three combinations of brome, alfalfa, giant foxtail, and a creek. Showers reports that habitat was a significant factor in determining the number of corn borers retrieved. This indicates that corn-from-corn movements might have different characteristics from the ones Showers and others reported in 2000. The direction of flight also seems to be significant, and this suggests that the dispersal might not be eous as the simulations have assumed. Despite these caveats, the Showers results indicate that the levels of mobility used in the s discussed earlier are likely to be lower than they actually are.

rket penetration plays a role at the lowest level of mobility. In such a ario, having more than 50% of the fields planted with Bt corn might be problematic. In general, the results on the frequency of resistance in the Bt fields are highly dependent on the level of pest mobility. This points out the importance of collecting more information on the characteristics of the movement of the ECB. The simulations presented here suggest other questions for future research. First, the grid size could be increased to analyze whether scale plays a role in the spread of resistance. In particular, in all the cases presented here, the Bt fields were contiguous to at least one non-Bt field. A finer grid could allow the exploration of the case of a less-than-complete market penetration with Bt fields being completely surrounded by Bt fields. Second, if mobility is very low, the assumption of random mating is likely to become less representative of the behavior of the pest population: the number of corn borers in the Bt fields is very low, so it might happen that the resistant borers surviving in the Bt portion of the fields will tend to mate among themselves, as will the susceptible borers living in the refuge. Therefore, the possibility of nonrandom mating in the Bt fields should be taken into account, and its impact on resistance development should be examined. Third, the simulations suggest that compliance to the refuge recommendations might be critical to the preservation of susceptibility. The introduction of a compliance function could increase the significance of the model's results. Also, more work is needed on the determinants of market penetration. In particular, the role of export markets behavior and historical corn borer infestations in determining planting decisions needs to be further investigated. These issues seem to have been the main influences behind the recent trends of Bt corn acreage (USDA 2001).

Finally, the results also suggest that, under certain circumstances, tradable refuges might be used to compensate farmers planting traditional hybrids for the positive externality they provide to farmers planting Bt crops.[9] So far, EPA has focused on in-field refuges, which, as we noted earlier, might be problematic from the standpoint of compliance. Tradable refuges might be a superior policy if pest mobility is high and market penetration is low.

References

Caprio, M.A. 1998. Evaluating Resistance Management Strategies for Multiple Toxins in the Presence of External Refuges. *Journal of Economic Entomology* 91(5): 1021–31.

Croft, B.A., and J.E. Dunley. 1993. Habitat Patterns and Pesticide Resistance. In *Evolution of Insect Pests: Patterns of Variation*, edited by K.C. Kim and R.A. McPheron. New York: John Wiley and Sons.

Dively, G.P., P.A. Follett, J.J. Linduska, and G.K. Roderick. 1998. Use of Imid Treated Row Mixtures for Colorado Potato Beetle (Coleoptera: Chrysomelid agement. *Journal of Economic Entomology* 91(2): 376–87.

Georghiou, G.P., and C.E. Taylor. 1977. Operational Influences in the Evolution of Insecticide Resistance. *Journal of Economic Entomology* 70(3): 319–23.

Hartl, D.L., and A.G. Clark. 1989. *Principles of Population Genetics*, Second Edition. Sunderland, MA: Sinauer Associates.

Hellmich, R.L. 1998. Personal communication with the authors, December 8.

Hueth, D., and U. Regev. 1974. Optimal Agricultural Pest Management with Increasing Pest Resistance. *American Journal of Agricultural Economics* 56: 543–51.

Hurley, T.M., B.A. Babcock, and R.L. Hellmich. Forthcoming. Biotechnology and Pest Resistance: An Economic Assessment of Refuges. *Journal of Agricultural and Resource Economics*.

Hurley, T.M., S. Secchi, B.A. Babcock, and R.L. Hellmich. 1999. *Managing the Risk of European Corn Borer Resistance to Transgenic Corn: An Assessment of Refuge Recommendations*. Staff Report 99-SR88. Ames, IA: Center for Agricultural and Rural Development, Iowa State University.

Lazarus, W.F., and B.L. Dixon. 1984. Agricultural Pests as Common Property: Control of the Corn Rootworm. *American Journal of Agricultural Economics* 66: 456–65.

Mason, C.E., M.E. Rice, D.D. Calvin, J.W. Van Duyn, W.B. Showers, W.D. Hutchinson, J.F. Witkowski, R.A. Higgins, D.A. Onstad, and G.P. Dively. 1996. *European Corn Borer Ecology and Management*. North Central Regional Extension, Publication No. 327. Ames, IA: Iowa State University.

Onstad, D.W., and C.A. Guse. 1999. *Economic Analysis of Transgenic Maize and Nontransgenic Refuges for Managing European Corn Borer (Lepidoptera: Pyralidae)*. Unpublished report. Champaign, IL: Center for Economic Entomology, Illinois Natural History Survey.

Peck, S.L., F. Gould, and S.P. Ellner. 1999. Spread of Resistance in Spatially Extended Regions of Transgenic Cotton: Implications for Management of *Heliothis virescens* (Lepidoptera: Noctuidae). *Journal of Economic Entomology* 92(1): 1–16.

Perez, C.J., A.M. Shelton, and R.T. Roush. 1997. Managing Diamondback Moth (Lepidoptera: Plutellidae) Resistance to Foliar Applications of *Bacillus thuringiensis*: Testing Strategies in Field Cages. *Journal of Economic Entomology* 90(6): 1462–70.

Regev, U., A.P. Gutierrez, and G. Feder. 1976. Pests as a Common Property Resource: A Case Study of Alfalfa Weevil Control. *American Journal of Agricultural Economics* 58: 186–97.

Regev, U., H. Shalit, and A.P. Gutierrez. 1983. On the Optimal Allocation of Pesticides with Increasing Resistance: The Case of the Alfalfa Weevil. *Journal of Environmental Economics and Management* 10: 86–100.

Showers, W.B., R.L. Hellmich, M.E. Derrick-Robinson, and W.H. Hendrix III. 2000. *Aggregation and Dispersal Behavior of Marked and Released European Corn Borer (Lepidoptera: Crambidae) Adults*. Unpublished report. Ames, IA: Corn Insects and Crop Genetics Research Unit, USDA-ARS and Department of Entomology, Iowa Agriculture and Home Economics Experiment Station, Iowa State University.

Taylor, C.R., and J.C. Hadley. 1975. Insecticide Resistance and the Evaluation of Control Strategies for an Insect Population. *The Canadian Entomologist* 107: 237–42.

USDA (U.S. Department of Agriculture). 1999. Farms and Land in Farms—Final Estimates 1993–1997. Statistical Bulletin N. 955. <http://usda.mannlib.cornell.edu/usda/reports/general/sb/b9550199.pdf> (accessed August 25, 2000).

————. Economic Research Service. 2001. Agricultural Biotechnology: Adoption of Biotechnology and Its Production Impacts. Briefing Room. <http://www.ers.usda.gov/ Briefing/Biotechnology/chapter1.htm> (accessed November 15, 2001).

U.S. EPA (Environmental Protection Agency). 1998a. *The Environmental Protection Agency's White Paper on* Bt *Plant-Pesticide Resistance Management.* Washington, DC: U.S. EPA.

————. 1998b. Pesticide Fact Sheet August 17. <http://www.epa.gov/fedrgstr/EPA-PEST/1998/August/Day-17/attri.htm> (accessed October 30, 1999).

Notes

1. Some pests, such as the European corn borer, can have one to four generations in each growing season.

2. Bundling would occur, for example, if the seed producers sold a superior seed only in a *Bt* form. Farmers wanting to take advantage of such a product would have no choice but to plant a *Bt* crop.

3. It is essential that populations decline to fairly small numbers for resistance to become prevalent because the initial frequency of the resistance gene is very low to start with. As the pest population size declines, susceptible pests (and their genes) will all be killed by the pesticide. This natural selection pressure allows the resistant pests to take over.

4. For instance, the model could be applied to corn and cotton, which are both ECB hosts.

5. This appears to be a nontrivial question when analyzing resistance development (see Peck et al. 1999).

6. For the specific values see Mason and others (1996,) Onstad and Guse (1999), and Hurley and others (forthcoming).

7. The reason for this appears to be that second-generation pests have less of an incentive to leave their corn field, because the corn is at a later development stage and provides a better habitat.

8. Showers and others (2000) also released—and recaptured—corn borers further into the growing season. However, the number of corn borers retrieved at a distance greater than one kilometer was always lower in the second release, indicating that corn borers tend to move further away at the beginning of the season.

9. We are grateful to David Simpson for pointing this out to us.

Commentary

Need for Direct Collaboration between Economists and Biologists

Fred Gould

Chapter 4 by Secchi and Babcock reinforces the need for interdisciplinary interaction in solving agricultural problems. As a biologist, I assume that the economic assumptions of Secchi and Babcock are appropriate and concentrate on the ecological and agricultural assumptions of their model. In this regard, two major assumptions about insects and farmers in their chapter stand out as problematic. The assumption of zero or very low levels of movement of corn borers among cornfields contrasts with the view of entomologists. The assumption that farmers will plant *Bt* corn in the same fields year after year and plant non-*Bt* corn in the same fields year after year is especially unlikely if movement of the European corn borer is even three orders of magnitude higher than assumed by Secchi and Babcock. The reasoning here is relatively straightforward. Before a farmer ever plants *Bt* corn, let us assume there are 1,000 corn borers per acre in all fields. If the farmer plants non-*Bt* corn in field A during year 1, on average, the density of corn borers from that field that will infest it in year 2 is about 1,000 per acre (assuming that regional pest densities are not in a long-term phase of increase or decline). If field B is planted with high-dose *Bt* corn in year 1, the number of corn borers from that field that are expected to infest it in year 2 is fewer than 1 per acre because of the high efficacy of the toxin. If 1 out of every 100 corn borers from field A moves to field B, there will be about 990 corn borers per acre in field A and fewer than 11 per acre in field B. In North Carolina, and I assume in Iowa too, a farmer faced with this situation would most likely decide to rotate corn varieties in year 2, planting *Bt* corn in field A where there were lots of corn borers, and planting non-*Bt* corn in field B where there were very few pests.

The assumption of the model that the farmer does not rotate fields between *Bt* and non-*Bt* seems incorrect, but the real question is whether this incorrect assumption has any consequences on the rate of resistance evolution. Secchi and Babcock indicate they are aware that Peck and others (1999) have published results indicating that this issue of rotation "appears to be non-trivial," so the logic in not addressing the issue is not clear. Furthermore, the insect modeled by Peck and others has a much higher rate of interfield movement than assumed by Secchi and Babcock for corn borers, and that difference minimizes the impact on resistance development of choosing not to rotate fields. Gould (1986) modeled Hessian fly adaptation to conventionally bred, insecticidal wheat cultivars. This insect has mobility more comparable to the mobility of corn borers than the system modeled by Peck and others. In the Hessian fly work, I assumed either 1% interfield movement or 10% interfield insect movement and a high initial resistance frequency of 0.1 or 0.2. I ran the model with and without rotation of fields between the planting of wheat that was toxic and nontoxic to Hessian fly. The simulations that included field rotation resulted in rapid evolution of Hessian fly strains with tolerance of the toxic wheat. When fields were not rotated and initial gene frequency was 0.1, the rate of increase in resistance frequency was rapid for the first few generations in the toxic crop, but then the resistance frequency in the toxic crop declined and almost stabilized at a low, nonproblematic frequency (because of recessiveness). At lower initial gene frequencies, the stabilized frequency is expected to be even lower.

The difference in outcome related to farmer behavior was dramatic, and the resistance dynamics in the nonrotation simulations were nonlinear. It is, therefore, useful to at least present a simplified description of the population and genetic dynamics in the nonrotated case. In the first year, the toxic and nontoxic fields start with identical Hessian fly density. After the first year, the insect density in the toxic fields diminishes because approximately 96% of the susceptible Hessian flies are killed. By the second year, the frequency of resistant insects in the toxic fields increases dramatically, but there are not enough of them to cause significant damage. In the nontoxic wheat field, the population size of susceptible insects increases steadily. By the third year, the density of Hessian flies in the nontoxic wheat is more than 100 times higher than in the toxic wheat field, so movement of 10% of the insects from the nontoxic to the toxic wheat can just about swamp out the few resistant insects in the toxic crop. This lowers the overall frequency of resistant insects and begins a long selection phase in which the resistance frequency increases at an almost imperceptible rate. The agronomic problem with this approach is that the fields that are always planted to Hessian fly-susceptible wheat are expected to develop very high densities of the pests, and that could cause major yield loss.

For the European corn borer, it is generally assumed that the *Bt* resistance gene frequency (Andow et al. 2000) is much lower than assumed in the Hessian fly model (about 0.001 or 0.0001). With low rates of interfield movement of adult corn borers and without rotation, the interplay of population dynamics and population genetics is expected to stymie pest adaptation. If Secchi and Babcock changed the assumptions in their model such that corn farmers plant *Bt* corn in the fields expected to have high densities, they would get a different output.

Before any future work is done on *Bt*/non-*Bt* rotation, the rates used for interfield movement of corn borers should be reassessed because this too could have a major impact on the model output. While we will never have perfect knowledge of the rates of movement, we already know that the movement is more than zero. Farmers know that when a field previously planted with *Bt* corn is planted with non-*Bt* corn in the following year, the infestations are much higher than would be expected if only offspring from corn borers that developed in that field in the past year were infesting the newly planted field.

Secchi and Babcock justify their use of very low rates of interfield movement on the basis of results of an unpublished report by Showers and others (2000). They cite this study as capturing only 0.012% of the artificially released corn borer adults at 3,200 meters from the release site. This number is presented as an absolute parameter, as if 99.998% of the insects moved less than this distance. I do not have access to the cited publication. However, if this research was conducted like other insect release, recapture studies, only a small fraction of the released insects is ever recovered. Therefore, it is not appropriate to use calculations based on the number of insects released. Furthermore, as the distance from the point of release increases, the sampling devices become effective over a smaller and smaller percentage of the area where the insects could be moving (i.e., as the trap distance from the point of release increases, the circumference of the circular area where insects could be increases proportionately as 6.28 times the distance. Therefore, the capture rate also must be adjusted for the fraction of the area at a distance of 3,200 meters that was sampled (Southwood 1978).

The statement that direct interdisciplinary interactions are needed to address most real-world problems has been repeated thousands of times, so there is certainly nothing new in stating it one more time. However, the Secchi and Babcock work serves as a reminder of the importance of this comment. Without direct input from biologists, economists may make naïve assumptions. Had biologists written this paper, the result may have been no more useful because the economic aspects would probably have been naïve. If both biologists and economists had an equal voice in developing this model, it would have been much more useful.

References

Andow, D.A., D.M. Olson, R.L. Hellmich, D.N. Alstad, and W.D. Hutchison. 2000. Frequency of Resistance to *Bacillus thuringiensis* Toxin Cry1Ab in an Iowa Population of European Corn Borer (Lepidoptera: Crambidae). *Journal of Economic Entomology* 93: 26–30.

Gould, F. 1986. Simulation Models for Predicting Durability of Insect-Resistant Germ Plasm: Hessian Fly (Diptera: Cecidomyiidae)-Resistant Winter Wheat. *Environmental Entomology* 15: 11–23.

Peck, S., F. Gould, and S.P. Ellner. 1999. Spread of Resistance in Spatially Extended Regions of Transgenic Cotton: Implications for Management of *Heliothis virescens* (Lepidoptera: Noctuidae). *Journal of Economic Entomology* 92: 1–16.

Showers, W.B., R.L. Hellmich, M.E., and W.H. Hendrix III. 2000. *Aggregation and Dispersal Behavior of Marked and Released European Corn Borer (Lepidoptera: Crambidae) Adults*. Unpublished report. Ames, IA: Corn Insects and Crop Genetics Research Unit, USDA-ARS and Department of Entomology, Iowa Agriculture and Home Economics Experiment Station, Iowa State University.

Southwood, T.R.E. 1978. *Ecological Methods*, Second Edition. London: Chapman & Hall.

PART II

The Impact of Resistance

Chapter 5

The Impact of Resistance on Antibiotic Demand in Patients with Ear Infections

David H. Howard and Kimberly J. Rask

It is widely recognized that patterns of antimicrobial use affect prevailing rates of resistance. Less often noted is that, in some cases, resistance will affect prescribing patterns. The first relationship is driven by the biological process of natural selection, the second is driven by physicians' rational behavioral responses to a changing environment. When presented with a patient, a physician must estimate for every available antibiotic the probability that the patient's infection will be cured by the drug. These probabilities will depend on a number of factors, one of which is the rate of resistance to each antibiotic prevailing in the surrounding community. The higher the rate of resistance to a particular antibiotic is, the lower the ex ante probability that it will be effective. All else being equal, the physician will choose the antibiotic associated with the highest probability of cure. Resistance affects physicians' drug choice via these probabilities; once the rate of resistance to a particular antibiotic reaches a critical level, physicians will cease to use it, instead prescribing its closest substitute. The purpose of this chapter is to measure empirically the impact of resistance on physicians' drug choice. Documenting the relationship between resistance and drug choice is important because the drugs to which many pathogens have developed resistance are typically the least expensive antibiotics. Therefore, increasing levels of resistance will increase drug spending.

The data used to estimate the relationship come from a physician office visit-level survey spanning the period 1980 to 1998. They consist of 6,928 observations on patients younger than 18 years of age with a diagnosis of otitis media who received a prescription for 1 of 18 antibiotics.

We use a conditional logit model to estimate market shares for each drug as a function of drug attributes such as price. We combine these attributes with a time trend variable and interpret these time–attribute interactions as measuring the impact of resistance levels (which are not observed) on physicians' drug choice. Using these results, we simulate what market shares would have been in 1997 and 1998 had resistance levels remained at 1990 levels by restricting the time–attribute coefficients to zero. By multiplying the market share for each drug by its price and then summing over drugs, we estimate what total spending would have been. Comparing this figure with actual spending, we conclude that resistance, by inducing physicians to switch to more expensive antibiotics, increased annual antibiotic spending for initial otitis media visits by about 20% in 1997 and 1998. Although this figure is only a very rough approximation, it shows that when measuring the burden of antimicrobial resistance, it is important to consider the impact of resistance on drug choice and spending.

Over the last 20 years, use of and spending on new antibiotics has increased. This trend is of interest to policymakers for several reasons. First, antibiotics, one of the most frequently prescribed drug classes in the outpatient setting, are a natural target for cost-cutting efforts. The cost difference between new and old antibiotics is substantial, and there is concern that physicians and patients are not sufficiently price sensitive (Berman et al. 1997; Foxman et al. 1987; Reed et al. 2002). Second, and more importantly, the use of newer, more powerful antibiotics is both a cause and consequence of increasing antimicrobial resistance. The use of an antibiotic kills off only bacteria susceptible to the antibiotic, leaving resistant bacteria in its wake. New broad-spectrum antibiotics, which tend to be effective against many different bacterial species, may contribute to the more rapid development of resistance. At the same time, the use of new antibiotics may be a consequence of resistance if their adoption is motivated by physicians' belief that old antibiotics will not be effective.

In this chapter, we estimate a discrete choice model of physicians' antibiotic choice for children with ear infections. Our data were taken from an office-visit level survey and span the period 1980 to 1998, which allowed us to observe how prescribing trends have changed over time. We chose to look at ear infection, or otitis media, because it is one of the most common reasons apart from regular checkups for physician office visits by children. Resistance to antibiotics among the microorganisms that cause ear infections in children has increased in the last decade. In *Streptococcus pneumoniae*, which causes up to 50% of ear infections, penicillin resistance was found in fewer than 10% of isolates in 1988 but more than 50% of isolates in 1998 (Jacobs 2000).

Previous economic research on antimicrobial resistance has highlighted the negative externality associated with antibiotic use, decreased future antibiotic effectiveness (Ellison and Hellerstein 1999; Brown and Layton 1996), and derived optimal-use policies analogous to optimal extraction policies for a natural resource (Goeschl and Swanson 2000; Laxminarayan 2001; Laxminarayan and Weitzman [Chapter 3]; Wilen and Msangi [Chapter 1]). Laxminarayan shows, for example, that periodically removing an antibiotic from use, a policy known as "cycling," is optimal only under a restrictive set of assumptions about hospitals' costs. Goeschl and Swanson and Laxminarayan and Weitzman show that generally it is optimal to use a number of different antibiotics simultaneously, with the use of a particular antibiotic determined by its effectiveness and price (see Laxminarayan and Weitzman, Chapter 3). We view our study as complementary to these efforts. As long as we have included policy-relevant variables, the estimates presented here can be used to design programs to achieve the antibiotic use levels recommended by theory.

An unresolved question in the economic and medical literature on resistance, and one of interest to policymakers, is what is the economic impact of resistance? Much of the literature discusses the cost in terms of adverse events (see, for example, Coast et al. 1996), and patient death because of resistance in hospitals, though rare, has been documented at a number of institutions. In outpatient settings, organisms remain susceptible to at least a few antibiotics (although they may eventually become resistant), and severe complications caused by unresolved ear infection are infrequent.[1] The prevailing resistance levels in a community may influence physicians' choices of initial antibiotic therapy and hence costs. Resistance induces a shift toward newer antibiotics, the incremental cost of which may be attributed to resistance after controlling for their more favorable dosing and side-effect profiles.[2] Figure 5-1 shows that per-prescription spending on antibiotics used to treat ear infections in children grew from $13 to more than $20 (in 1996 dollars) between 1980 and 1998.

We use demand estimates to simulate how much of the growth in the use of new antibiotics was caused by increases in resistance.

Our study adds to and builds on the growing body of literature on pharmaceutical demand and markets. A number of studies have investigated the impact of price, advertising, and past use on physicians' choice of antibiotic (Berndt et al. 1995; Ellison et al. 1997; Rizzo 1999). The Ellison and others study is most relevant to ours because it focuses on a specific class of antibiotic, cephalosporins. Our study differs from theirs in that we define the market by indication rather than antibiotic class. We also observe individual characteristics, which allows us to estimate the impact of physician specialty on price sensitivity.

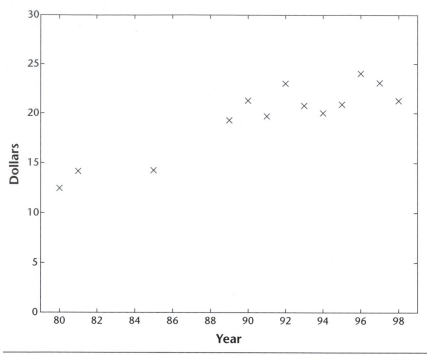

FIGURE 5-1. Average Spending per Prescription

Choice Model

The decisionmaker in our choice model is the physician. We do not dwell on the divergence between physicians' incentives and patients' utility here, but it is worth mentioning that antibiotic prescribing and physician visit time may be substitutes in production. Thus, reimbursement arrangements will influence physicians' choice between writing an antibiotic prescription and watchfully waiting. In addition, should physicians decide to prescribe, their choice of antibiotic from among the available drugs will be affected by reimbursement arrangements (i.e., the more powerful the antibiotic, the lower the probability that the patient will require a follow-up visit). We plan to examine these issues in future work.

We estimate a mixed multinomial logit model of product choice. Write the utility V of physician i from antibiotic j as

$$V_{ij} = \gamma R_{ij} + \alpha' p_{ij} + \beta' x_{ij} + \varepsilon_{ij} \tag{1}$$

where γ represents the coefficient on the resistance term, α and β represent the coefficients on the other independent variables, $R \in [0,1]$ is the physician's expectation that the infection is resistant to drug j, p_{ij} is the price of drug j interacted with individual characteristics (including the date on which the individual is making the choice), x_{ij} are drug attributes other than price interacted with individual characteristics, and ε_{ij} is an identically independently distributed error term. Note that the prevailing level of resistance varies by place and time, so R is subscripted by i. Let y_{ij} be an dummy variable indicating if drug j was chosen by individual i identically independently distributed.

$$y_{ij} = 1 \text{ if } V_{ij} = \max\left\{V_1^i, ..., V_{iJ}\right\} \tag{2}$$

where
$$R_j' = \left[R_{1j}, ..., R_{Nj}\right]$$
$$p_j' = \left[p_{1j}, ..., p_{Nj}\right]$$
$$x_j' = \left[x_{1j}, ..., x_{Nj}\right]$$
$$\theta = \{\gamma, \alpha, \beta\} \text{ and is the vector of coefficients of independent variables}$$

The demand D for drug j is
$$D(R_j, p_j, x_j; \theta) = \sum_i w_{ij} y_{ij} \tag{3}$$

where w_i is a sample weight. The impact of resistance on drug treatment costs is

$$\sum_j \left[p_j D(R_j, p_j, x_j; \theta) - p_j D(0, p_j, x_j; \theta)\right] \tag{4}$$

Here, the first term in the brackets is actual demand, and the second term is what drug spending would be if resistance levels were 0 for all demanders.

Empirical Model

We want to estimate Equation 4. We observe $D(R_j, p_j, x_j; \theta)$, which is simply the empirical demand for each drug, but we do not observe $D(0, p_j, x_j; \theta)$. To calculate what demand for each drug would be in the absence of resistance, we estimate a discrete choice model of antibiotic demand. Because we assume that utility is linear in parameters, we ignore the marginal impact of resistance on utility γ because it is multiplied by 0 and drops out of Expression 1 when calculating $D(0, p_j, x_j; \theta)$. We cannot simply ignore the impact of resistance on physicians' drug choice, however, because doing so would impart bias to the coefficients on the remaining, observable product attributes. Our admittedly crude approach to this problem is to take advantage of the fact that resistance was not widespread during the early period covered by our data; surveillance records indicate that resistance among the pathogens causing ear infections was fairly low and stable before 1990, after which it began to rise steadily. We combine product attributes p_j and x_j with dummy variables equal to zero for drugs prescribed before 1990 and equal to the number of years after 1990 for drugs prescribed after 1990. For example, the price–time interaction term for a prescription issued in 199X is $p_j \times \max\{199X - 1990,0\}$. Assuming that physicians' underlying preferences have not changed over time, the coefficients on these variables will equal the bias on the product attribute coefficients caused by the omission of resistance, and the uninteracted coefficients will represent physicians' "true" preferences for various product attributes.

To estimate $D(0, p_j, x_j; \theta)$ we first estimate Equation 1 and then compute Equations 2 and 3 for the post-1996 portion of the data, restricting the coefficients on the time-attribute interactions to be zero. Thus we obtain an estimate of what demand for various antibiotics would have been in years 1997 and 1998 in the absence of increased resistance, controlling for the superior observable attributes of the newer, more expensive drugs. Using these demand estimates to compute Equation 4, we measure the marginal cost of increases in resistance after 1980, ignoring the cost of resistance that developed prior to that time.

The actions of drug companies with respect to price levels and new product introductions depend on prevailing resistance levels, and the formula in Equation 4 may misstate the true impact of resistance. At one extreme, the introduction of new antibiotics may be motivated by resistance to older agents. If this is the case, then Equation 4 significantly understates the impact of resistance on costs. At the other extreme, all of the new products currently on the market would have been introduced in the absence of resistance, but their prices would be lower because the older antibiotics would be better substitutes. If this is the case, then the formula overstates the costs of resistance.[3] Wishing to err on the conservative side, we computed Equation 4 for the years 1997 and 1998 using 1990 prices or, for drugs introduced after 1990, their prices during their first year on the market. We assumed (conservatively) that all subsequent price increases were caused by increases in resistance rather than other factors.

We estimate Equation 1 using a random-parameters multinomial logit model (see Brownstone and Train 1999), which assumes that the taste parameters are randomly distributed in the population. Unlike a conventional conditional logit model, the random-parameters specification relaxes the independence of irrelevant alternatives property, but, unlike a multinomial probit model, it does not entail estimation of an unrestricted variance–covariance matrix either. Let μ^r be the rth random draw from a distribution and write the taste parameter on attribute k as a function of this draw $\beta_k^r = b_k + s_k \mu_k^r$. Then utility for individual i and product j (now including price in x_{ij}) is

$$V_{ij}^r = b'x_{ij} + \sum_k s_k \mu_{rk}^r x_{kij} + \varepsilon_{ij} \tag{5}$$

The b_k's are mean coefficients, and the s_k's are spread coefficients. If we assume that the e_{ij}'s follow an extreme value distribution, then, after algebraic manipulation (see Maddala 1983, 60–1), the simulated probability that individual i chooses drug j, SP_{ij}, can be written as

$$SP_{ij} = \frac{1}{R} \sum_r \frac{\exp(V_{ij})}{\sum_j \exp(V_{ij})} \qquad (6)$$

and the log-likelihood is

$$LL(\theta) = \sum_i \sum_j y_{ij} \log SP_{ij} \qquad (7)$$

We estimate the model using a simulated maximum likelihood routine (McFadden and Train 2000).[4]

The Data

Our main data source was the National Ambulatory Medical Care Survey (NAMCS). For selected years before 1989 and every year between 1989 and 1998, the National Center for Health Statistics drew a sample of office-based physicians from the master files of the American Medical Association and the American Osteopathic Association. Selected physicians were asked to record information on a subsample of office visits occurring during a randomly chosen week (different physicians were assigned different weeks, so data were recorded throughout the year). Some questions were not asked in all years, making it impossible to include some potentially interesting patient characteristics, but at the very least, respondents recorded information on patient diagnoses, patient demographics, basic physician characteristics, and drugs prescribed.

From the NAMCS for 1980, 1981, 1985, and 1989 to 1998, we selected as our initial sample all patients younger than 18 years of age with a diagnosis of otitis media, as long as that diagnosis was listed before any mention of a diagnosis for a respiratory problem (NAMCS allows physicians to record up to three diagnoses). This last step was taken so we could be reasonably certain that any antibiotic received was for otitis media rather than another problem.

From the medical literature, we compiled a list of medications commonly prescribed for otitis media. We then narrowed the sample by selecting only patients who received one of the 18 drugs from this list for which at least 25 patients in the sample had received prescriptions. The 18 drugs account for more than 99% of all antibiotic prescriptions in the sample. Approximately 30% of otitis media patients do not receive an antibiotic. This percentage has remained constant over time, and we omitted these individuals from our analysis.

Information on drug characteristics other than price was taken from an antibiotic guide (Gilbert et al. 2000). The variable "price" measures the total cost to the insurer and patient of a prescription. We calculated mean cost per prescription from the 1996 Medical Expenditure Panel Survey (MEPS) household component.[5] We constructed a price index for each drug using per-pill prices reported in Gilbert and others and the *Red Book* (Medical Economics Data 1981; 1985). Using the price index, we inflated or discounted the cost for each drug (from MEPS) to the appropriate year. These data and the NAMCS data were combined to form a dataset containing individual- and choice-specific attributes. Variables are summarized in Table 5-1.

The drug attribute called "broad spectrum" deserves a brief explanation. Three bacterial species cause otitis media: *S. pneumoniae*, *Hemophilus influenzae*, and *Moraxhella catarrhalis*. *S. pneumoniae* is by far the most common, accounting for up to 50% of otitis media cases. A narrow-spectrum antibiotic, as we have defined it, is active against only *S. pneumoniae* (in its nonresistant form). A broad-spectrum antibiotic, by contrast, can kill all three bacterial species (in their nonresistant forms). Widespread administration of a broad-spectrum antibiotic leads to resistance in *H. influenzae* and *M. catarrhalis*,[6] whereas administration of a narrow-spectrum antibiotic does not affect the evolutionary path of these species.

In addition to dummy variables indicating each drug's class, we included in all models a dummy variable equal to one if the drug is amoxicillin. More

Table 5-1. Variable Descriptions (sample size 6,928)

Variable	Mean	Description
Drug characteristics		
Price	16.46	Price of regimen
Doses	28.57	Doses per regimen
GI upset	5.73	Rate of gastrointestinal upset (1–16)
Rash	0.80	Equals 1 if rash is a frequent side-effect
Broad spectrum	0.46	Equals 1 if antibiotic is active against *M. catarrhalis*
Amoxicillin	0.54	Equals 1 if the drug is amoxicillin
Penicillin	0.58	Equals 1 if the drug is a member of the penicillin class
Cephalosporin	0.19	Equals 1 if the drug is a member of the cephalosporin class
Interaction terms		
Infant	0.40	Patient is less than two years of age
Specialist	0.13	Physician is an otolaryngologist or other specialist
No. meds	1.52	Number of medications prescribed at the visit
Year	2.06	Number of years after 1990

than 40% of the patients in our sample received a prescription for amoxicillin, and we found that including an amoxicillin dummy greatly increased the predictive power of the model. Amoxicillin is the standard "first-line" therapy recommend by treatment guidelines (see, for example, Gilbert et al. 2000), and these may exert an independent effect on physicians' antibiotic choices that is being captured by the coefficient on this variable.

Our data have a number of limitations. There is a great deal of drug price dispersion, and we did not observe if the prescription was filled with a generic or branded version. Thus, the prices we assigned to each drug may misstate actual costs faced by individuals. We also did not observe quantity prescribed. Although regimens are fairly standardized, one response to antibiotic resistance has been to increase dosages to treat bacteria with intermediate-level resistance. In other cases, physicians may decrease the duration of therapy to minimize the selective pressure on microorganisms.

We do not have data on advertising and detailing expenditures and, insofar as we know, no such data exist going back to 1980. However, even if we did have these data, it is not clear that we would want to include them. The ability to treat resistant bacteria is a strong selling point of the newer drugs and is explicitly mentioned in some print advertisements. If the claims related to resistance in drug advertisements or detailing activities motivate physicians to switch drugs, then we would want to attribute the change in behavior to resistance, not advertising or detailing.

Estimation and Results

Table 5-2 displays parameter estimates. The first column presents results from a standard conditional logit model, and the second and third columns present results from a mixed multinomial logit model.

Note that each of the drug attributes except drug class interacts with the following individual characteristics: an infant patient, a specialist physician, number of prescriptions received by the patient (a crude measure of disease severity), and year. Interacting patient characteristics with drug class indicators produced unstable estimates. We combined a number of other individual attributes with drug attributes in our initial estimates, such as region, but none were consistently significant. Some of the most interesting individual attributes, insurance source for example, were not reported in every year of the survey.

Based on the specification test outlined in Theorem 2 of McFadden and Train (2000), we rejected the hypothesis that conditional and mixed multinomial models are equivalent. Thus, we based our simulations on the mixed multinomial estimates. The econometric literature provides little guidance regarding which or how many of the coefficients in the mixed logit should be

TABLE 5-2. Conditional and Mixed Logit Results

	Conditional logit		Mixed logit			
	b	SE	b	SE	S	SE
Price	−0.042	(0.004)*	−0.174	(0.011)*	0.365	(0.015)*
× Infant	−0.005	(0.003)	0.011	(0.007)		
× Specialist	0.012	(0.004)*	0.046	(0.009)*		
× No. meds.	0.001	(0.002)	−0.003	(0.004)		
× Year	0.004	(0.001)*	0.015	(0.001)*		
Doses	−0.019	(0.007)*	−0.018	(0.009)	−0.059	(0.051)
× Infant	−0.001	(0.005)	−0.013	(0.006)*		
× Specialist	0.021	(0.007)*	0.016	(0.008)*		
× No. meds.	0.007	(0.004)*	0.009	(0.004)*		
× Year	−0.002	(0.001)	−0.004	(0.001)*		
GI upset	−0.113	(0.011)*	−0.122	(0.014)*		
× Infant	0.003	(0.008)	0.022	(0.009)*		
× Specialist	−0.018	(0.011)	0.003	(0.012)		
× No. meds.	0.025	(0.005)	0.016	(0.006)*		
× Year	0.001	(0.002)*	0.014	(0.002)*		
Rash	−0.739	(0.171)*	−1.038	(0.178)*		
× Infant	0.007	(0.106)	0.020	(0.110)		
× Specialist	−0.133	(0.137)	−0.175	(0.142)		
× No. meds.	−0.158	(0.068)*	−0.139	(0.071)*		
× Year	0.166	(0.021)*	0.058	(0.022)*		
Broad spectrum	0.119	(0.121)	1.281	(0.168)*		
× Infant	0.351	(0.084)*	0.224	(0.091)*		
× Specialist	0.327	(0.125)*	0.181	(0.134)		
× No. meds.	−0.067	(0.057)	−0.077	(0.061)		
× Year	−0.053	(0.018)*	−0.134	(0.019)*		
Amoxicillin	2.655	(0.070)*	2.916	(0.092)*		
Penicillin class	−0.884	(0.088)*	−0.700	(0.095)*	−0.045	(3.089)
Cephalosporin class	−0.596	(0.099)*	−0.243	(0.117)*	0.382	(2.405)
Sample size	6,928		6,928			
Log-likelihood	13,908		13,200			

* Significant at 95% level of confidence.

allowed to vary, so our choices in this matter were somewhat ad hoc. We found that, inexplicably, some combinations of random coefficients produced parameter estimates that rose without bound.[7] Taking these restrictions into account, we allowed the coefficients on price, pills per regimen, and drug class to vary. Simply allowing the coefficients on the drug class indicators to vary replicated a nested logit model. Allowing the coefficients on price and pills per regimen to vary, which further relaxed the independence of irrelevant alternatives axiom, counts for heterogeneity in the drug prices and insurance arrangements faced by patients and the work schedules of patients' parents. We assigned triangle distributions on the interval [−1,1] to the μ_k's. The model was estimated via simulated maximum likelihood using 150 Halton draws of μ_k for each k.[8]

Turning our attention now to the parameter estimates from the mixed multinomial logit model, all of the coefficients on the first six drug attributes were of the expected sign, and five were significant at the 5% level. The coefficients on the drug class indicators were also significant at conventional levels. The finding that price was negatively and significantly related to demand is interesting in and of itself. Some researchers worry that because medical expenses are covered by insurance, physicians have no incentive to consider price when prescribing drugs. Clearly this is not the case, although we found in another model in which price was interacted with insurance type (not shown) that physicians of insured patients were less sensitive to price.

All six of the attribute–year interactions were significant, and five had a different sign from their corresponding level coefficient. To understand this result, consider the coefficient on the price–year interaction, which was positive. One possible interpretation is that physicians have become less sensitive to price, an unlikely occurrence in light of the growth of managed care (see, for example, Weiner et al. 1991). Another interpretation, and the one we prefer, is that physicians' price sensitivity is unchanged or possibly even greater, but resistance has induced them to substitute toward more expensive drugs, which, because of the omission of resistance as an observed drug characteristic, was reflected as a positive coefficient on the price–year interaction. Of course other trends may affect physicians' and patients' preferences over antibiotic attributes. However, a number of these can be ruled out based on the pattern of coefficients. For example, physicians may be more likely to prescribe broad-spectrum drugs for children whose mothers work. Yet the negative coefficient on the spectrum–year interaction indicates that the increase in the number of working mothers has not had a significant impact on antibiotic prescribing trends.

Of the five spread coefficients, only the one for price is significant at the 5% level. The fact that the spread coefficient is greater than the mean coefficient implies that about 10% of the sample derives positive utility from higher prices. Although this is an unfortunate by-product of assuming that the μ_k's can take on negative values, our market share predictions (see Figure 5-2) are close enough to actual market shares that we do not believe this is a substantial liability in terms of predicting behavior.[9]

Resistance and Empiric Substitution

Before computing Equation 4, we validated the model by comparing predicted and actual market shares. Figure 5-2 displays actual market shares (the bars) and predicted market shares, $D(R_j, p_j, x_j; \hat{\theta})$, as well as the 95% confidence intervals based on 100 bootstrap runs.

A single simulation run entails (a) drawing the b_k's and s_k's from their respective distributions, (b) drawing μ'''s from triangle distributions, (c) drawing ε_{ij}'s from independent logistic distributions, (d) computing utility levels for Equation 1, and (e) computing Equation 2 and then Equation 3 to calculate market shares. Considering that we have 18 different market shares to predict, the model does a tolerably good job. The confidence intervals around the means of the predicted market shares are quite wide because of the random parameter specification. Some of the means are off by quite a bit too, but others are very close to actual market shares (for example, for trimethoprim-sulfamethoxazole).

We calculated that the average spending per prescription for antibiotics to treat new cases of otitis media during 1997 and 1998 was $18.41. Our predicted per-prescription cost is $19.20 (95% confidence interval: $17.08, $21.39). We estimated by restricting the coefficients on the year–attribute interactions to be zero that in the absence of resistance, the per-prescription cost would be only $15.05 (95% confidence interval: $13.66, $17.03).

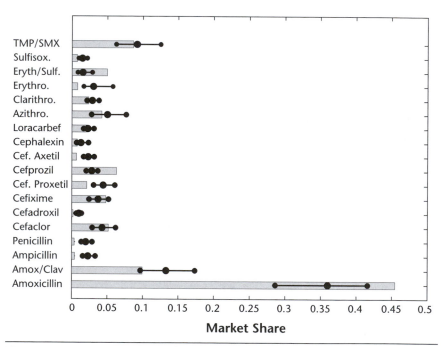

Figure 5-2. Actual and Predicted Market Share

Notes: The bars represent actual market shares. TMP/SMX = trimethoprim/sulfamethoxazole, Sulfisox. = sulfisoxazole, Eryth/Sulf. = erythromycin/sulfisoxazole, Erythro. = erythromycin, Clarithro. = clarithromycin, Azithro. = azithromycin, Cef. Axetil = cefuroxime axetil, Cef. Protexil = cefpodoxime protexil, and Amox/Clav = amoxicillin clavulanate.

Multiplying the difference between the actual per prescription cost and the simulated per-prescription cost by the total number of prescriptions for otitis media per year—about 12 million—yields an estimate of the impact of resistance on antibiotic costs: ($18.01 − $15.09) × 12,000,000 ≈ $40,000,000. Thus we concluded that resistance increases total spending on antibiotics to treat new episodes of ear infection (about $216 million) by about 20%.

Conclusion

Increasing the resistance of microorganisms to commonly prescribed antibiotics has led clinicians, biologists, and even some economists to call for policies restricting antibiotic use. However, there is not much information on the scope of the problem, especially in outpatient settings. Previous efforts to estimate the impact of resistance have focused on measuring patient morbidity and mortality. These estimates understate the cost of resistance to the extent that they fail to take account of the impact of resistance on physicians' antibiotic choices. The greater the prevalence of resistance is, the more likely physicians are to use expensive antibiotics. Based on this principle, our "back-of-the-envelope" simulations show that resistance increases antibiotic costs for ear infection by $35 million annually. This is not to say that this entire cost is a deadweight loss—resistance is a natural consequence of the selective pressures brought about by antibiotic use. Nevertheless, the size of the figure suggests that there may be large returns to efforts to slow the development of resistance.

Acknowledgements

We thank John McGowan, Ernie Berndt, seminar participants at the Economics of Resistance conference sponsored by Resources for the Future, and an anonymous reviewer for comments and helpful suggestions.

References

Berman, S., P.J. Byrns, J. Bondy, P.J. Smith, and D. Lezzotte. 1997. Otitis Media-Related Antibiotic Prescribing Patterns, Outcomes, and Expenditures in a Pediatric Medicaid Population. *Pediatrics* 100(4): 585–92.

Berndt, E.R., L.T. Bui, D.H. Reiley, and G.L. Urban. 1995. Information, Marketing, and Pricing in the U.S. Anti-Ulcer Drug Market. *American Economic Review* 85(2): 100–5.

Brown, G., and D.F. Layton. 1996. Resistance Economics: Social Cost and the Evolution of Antibiotic Resistance. *Environment and Development Economics* 1(3): 349–55.

Brownstone, D., and K. Train. 1999. Forecasting New Product Penetration with Flexible Substitution Patterns. *Journal of Econometrics* 89(1): 109–29.

Coast, J., R.D. Smith, and M.R. Millar. 1996. Superbugs: Should Antimicrobial Resistance Be Included as a Cost in Economic Evaluation? *Health Economics* 5: 217–26.

Culpepper, L., and J. Froom. 1997. Routine Antimicrobial Treatment of Acute Otitis Media: Is It Necessary? *Journal of the American Medical Association* 278(20): 1643–5.

Ellison, S.F., I. Cockburn, Z. Griliches, and J. Hausman. 1997. Characteristics of Demand for Pharmaceutical Products: An Examination of Four Cephalosporins. *RAND Journal of Economics* 28(3): 426–46.

Ellison, S.F., and J.K. Hellerstein. 1999. The Economics of Antibiotics: An Exploratory Study. In *Measuring the Prices of Medical Treatments*, edited by J.E. Triplett. Washington, DC: Brookings Institution, 118–51.

Foxman, B., R. Burciaga Valdez, K.N. Lohr, G.A. Goldberg, J.P. Newhouse, and R.H. Brook. 1987. The Effect of Cost Sharing on the Use of Antibiotics in Ambulatory Care: Results from a Population-Based Randomized Controlled Trial. *Journal of Chronic Diseases* 40: 429–37.

Gilbert, D.N., R.C. Moellering, and M.A. Sande. 2000. *The Sanford Guide to Antimicrobial Therapy*. Hyde Park, VT: Antimicrobial Therapy, Inc.

Goeschl, T., and T. Swanson. 2000. Lost Horizons: The Interaction of IPR Systems and Resistance Management. Paper presented at International Workshop on Antibiotic Resistance: Global Policies and Options. February 2000, Cambridge, MA.

Jacobs, M.R. 2000. Increasing Antibiotic Resistance among Otitis Media Pathogens and Their Susceptibility to Oral Agents Based on Pharmacodynamic Parameters. *Pediatric Infectious Disease Journal* 19(5): S47–56.

Laxminarayan, R. 2001. Bacterial Resistance and the Optimal Use of Antibiotics. Resources for the Future discussion paper 01–23. Washington, DC: Resources for the Future.

Maddala, G.S. 1983. *Limited-Dependent and Qualitative Variables in Econometrics*. Cambridge, U.K.: Cambridge University Press.

McFadden, D., and K. Train. 2000. Mixed MNL Models for Discrete Response. *Journal of Applied Econometrics* 15(5): 447–70.

Medical Economics Data, Inc. 1981. *Red Book*. Montvale, NJ: Medical Economics Data.

———. 1985. *Red Book*. Montvale, NJ: Medical Economics Data.

Philipson, T. 2000. Economic Epidemiology. In *Handbook of Health Economics*, edited by A.J. Culyer and J.P. Newhouse. New York: Elsevier, 1762–99.

Reed, S.D., R. Laxminarayan, D.J. Black, and S.D. Sullivan. 2002. Economic Issues and Antibiotic Resistance in the Community. *Annals of Pharmacotherapy* 36: 148–54.

Revelt, D., and K. Train. 1998. Mixed Logit with Repeated Choices: Households' Choices of Appliance Efficiency Level. *Review of Economics and Statistics* 80(4): 647–57.

Rizzo, J.A. 1999. Advertising and Competition in the Ethical Pharmaceutical Industry: The Case of Antihypertensive Drugs. *Journal of Law and Economics* 42(1): 89–116.

Ruud, P. 1996. *Approximation and Simulation of the Multinomial Probit Model: An Analysis of Covariance Matrix Estimation*. Unpublished report. Berkeley, CA: University of California.

Train, K. 1999. Halton Sequences for Mixed Logit. Unpublished report. Berkeley, CA: University of California.

Weiner, J.P., A. Lyles, D.M. Steinwachs, and K.C. Hall. 1991. Impact of Managed Care on Prescription Drug Use. *Health Affairs* 10: 140–54.

Notes

1. Indeed, the majority of ear infections resolve without therapy, and some researchers (although not those holding screaming infants) have questioned the benefits of antibiotic therapy in new cases (Culpepper and Froom 1997).

2. See Philipson (2000) for an excellent discussion of why traditional cost-of-illness measures understate the burden of infectious diseases.

3. Marginal revenue is negative above profit maximizing prices, so using prices above the profit maximizing prices to approximate demand levels in the absence of resistance would underestimate total revenue (and thus make the difference between revenue with resistance and estimated revenue in the absence of resistance appear greater).

4. Matlab programs for mixed multinomial logit models can be downloaded from David Howard's website (www.sph.emory.edu/~dhhowar).

5. These costs reflect transaction rather than list prices but may not take into account manufacturer rebates.

6. *H. influenzae* and *M. catarrhalis* have "innate" as opposed to "acquired" resistance to narrow-spectrum antibiotics.

7. Ruud (1996) found that models in which all coefficients were allowed to vary produced unstable parameter estimates.

8. Train (1999) found that the use of Halton draws reduced simulation error in mixed multinomial logit models.

9. To avoid this problem, Revelt and Train (1999) suggested restricting the spread coefficient on price to be zero (i.e., not allowing the price parameter to vary in the population). Based on our conversations with clinicians and our initial results, we believe it is important to allow price to vary, given that we do not include measures of patients' income or insurance coverage. Another option is to assume that the mean coefficient on price has a beta distribution. The parameters of this distribution can be difficult to identify, however.

Commentary

Measuring the Cost of Resistance

Ramanan Laxminarayan

An important empirical challenge in the economics of resistance has been the measurement of the cost of resistance. Although there is widespread agreement that resistance places an economic burden on society, nobody is quite sure how large this burden might be. Earlier efforts to quantify the social welfare losses associated with bacterial resistance to antibiotics arrived at a range that varied from $300 million to $30 billion depending on factors such as the value attributed to lost human lives (Phelps 1989). A 1999 study estimated that the deadweight loss associated with the loss of antimicrobial effectiveness associated with outpatient prescriptions in the United States was $378 million and possibly as high as $18.6 billion (Elbasha 1999).

More recent efforts to measure the cost of resistance in hospital settings have focused on measuring differences in the cost of treating resistant infections and susceptible infections (Howard et al. 2001). However, this is a difficult empirical problem confounded by the reality that sicker patients are more likely to have longer hospital stays and therefore are more likely to contract a resistant infection. Conversely, patients with resistant infections are more likely to have longer hospital stays and to be sicker. This bidirectional causality is problematic and confounds efforts to measure the increase in the cost of hospital stays attributable to a resistant infection. The increased cost of hospital stays attributable to resistant infections may be important to hospital administrators. However, the economic impact of this increase may be less important to society than the economic burden placed on health care systems of needing to periodically move to more effective and expensive antibiotics. Infections that were once treatable using penicillin, which costs pennies, now require antibiotics that cost hundreds of dollars. Without a doubt, the antibiotics in use today are more powerful and much more expensive than the older drugs used a few decades ago. Furthermore, it is certainly true that the introduction of new antibiotics has been necessitated by growing bacterial resistance to older drugs. What is not clear is precisely what proportion of the increase in the drug cost of treating infections has been caused by increasing drug resistance and what proportion is attributable to the fact that new drugs have other desirable properties, such as more convenient dosing and fewer side effects. The empirical challenges facing such an economic assessment should not be underestimated.

David Howard and Kimberly Rask review data on antibiotics used to treat ear infections from the National Ambulatory Medical Care Survey from 1980 to 1998 to estimate the increase in the cost of antibiotic treatment that is attributable to increases in bacterial resistance. Although their approach is hampered by a lack of data on resistance, their analysis (which uses a time proxy for resistance) offers some insight into the order of magnitude of costs of resistance. They find that between 1997 and 1998, increases in drug resistance raised the cost of treating ear infections by about 20% ($216 million).

Such an estimate is useful to policymakers for at least two reasons. It provides some idea of the magnitude of the resistance problem before investing resources in additional research and surveillance. Moreover, this estimate provides an upper bound on the likely resistance-related costs of using antibiotics in other uses, such as for growth promotion in animal feed. While this is not necessarily a problem with antibiotics used to treat ear infections, a similar estimate of the resistance-related costs of salmonella infections could, for instance, provide an idea of the order of magnitude of economic cost of using fluoroquinolones for growth promotion.

A few drawbacks in this analysis could be addressed in future work in this area. First, lacking an explicit measure of resistance, one is not sure if the increase is because of increases in resistance or because of improved attributes of the drug. Although the authors readily acknowledge this problem, the method they used to correct for the problem—using a time dummy—may have problems because of the strong contemporaneous correlation between other attributes and time (Nelson and Kang 1994). Second, measuring the cost of resistance by itself may have less meaning than measuring the *net* cost of antibiotic use. Antibiotic use brings both benefits (by curing infections) as well as costs (by increasing bacterial resistance). Howard and Rask's estimates look only at the cost side and offer no guidance on the magnitude of deadweight losses associated with resistance when the benefits of antibiotics are taken into consideration. Finally, there has been a large increase in the number of antibiotic prescriptions over the years. Between 1980 and 1996, the number of antibiotic doses prescribed by office-based physicians increased by

44.2%, whereas the increase between 1992 and 1996 was 12.7% (McCaig and Hughes 1995). Some proportion of this increase is also attributable to increasing resistance and needs to be considered.

What kind of analysis might one look for to correct some these problems? Admittedly, estimating the societal benefits of antibiotic use (in terms of faster recovery of patients as well as reduced probability that the infection will be transmitted to another uninfected individual) is problematic. However, it may be possible to arrive at more accurate estimates of increases in antibiotic costs attributable to increases in resistance. One way of doing this is by using data on antibiotic use and resistance from different regions. Better data on drug resistance are becoming more widely available and could be used for such an analysis. All else being equal, one would expect average cost of antibiotic treatment to be greater in areas where resistance to older drugs was relatively greater. Although such an exercise would be valuable in evaluating the cost of resistance in a community setting, a more modest effort might focus on just a hospital setting where resistance can be measured more accurately and the dynamics of infection and the evolution of resistance better understood.

References

Elbasha, E. 1999. *Deadweight Loss of Bacterial Resistance Due to Overtreatment.* Unpublished report. Atlanta, GA: Centers for Disease Control and Prevention, 1–53.

Howard, D., R. Cordell, J.E. McGown, R.M. Packard, R.D. Scott II, and S.L. Solomon, for the Workshop Group. 2001. Measuring the Economic Costs of Antimicrobial Resistance in Hospital Settings: Summary of the Centers for Disease Control and Prevention Emory Workshop. *Clinical Infectious Diseases* 33: 1573–8.

McCaig, L.F., and J.M. Hughes. 1995. Trends in Antimicrobial Drug Prescribing among Office-Based Physicians in the United States. *Journal of the American Medical Association* 273(3): 214–9.

Nelson, C., and H. Kang. 1994. Pitfalls in the Use of Time as an Explanatory Variable in Regression. *Journal of Business and Economic Statistics* 2(1): 73–82.

Phelps, C.E. 1989. Bug/Drug Resistance: Sometimes Less Is More. *Medical Care* 27(2): 194–203.

Chapter 6

What Can We Learn from the Economics of Pesticides?

Impact Assessment of Genetically Modified Plants

Hermann Waibel, Jan C. Zadoks, and Gerd Fleischer

Genetically modified plants represent a new technology widely applied for crop protection purposes (approximately 50 million hectares in 2001). The introduction of this crop protection technology is remarkably parallel to the introduction of chemical pesticides some 50 years earlier. Both technologies require intensive regulation, can produce negative externalities, and are components of integrated pest management. Therefore, the economic analysis of genetically modified organisms can draw from some methodological advances achieved through economic studies of pesticides. We review the lessons learned from the economics of chemical pesticides and investigate the extent to which these can be applied to genetically modified organisms used as crop protection agents and have actually been applied in recent economic analysis of biotechnology.

We draw the lessons from a review of the literature on the economics of pesticides use. We find three major advancements in the methodology of pesticide productivity assessments: (a) the treatment of pesticides not as directly productive inputs, such as fertilizers; (b) a better of understanding of producers' risk preferences with respect to pesticide use; and (c) the treatment of pest susceptibility as a natural resource.

We explore the extent to which these three concepts show up in the studies of the economics of genetically modified resistant varieties. Our review suggests that they are not well covered. However, the reasons for this gap are not identified in our chapter. Instead, we present an outline for a conceptual framework of how concepts that have emerged from the economics of pesticide use can be applied to genetically modified organisms. In this outline, we emphasize two aspects: the measurement of the benefits of genetically modified organisms relative to a realistic reference system and the measurement of one major externality that can be expected with the diffusion of genetically modified organisms (which is the development of pest resistance buildup). We describe the use of stochastic simulation approach as a methodology to deal with the uncertainty arising from such processes. In this context, we discuss some possibilities and problems of collecting data for conducting further economic analysis of genetically modified organisms that should also be feasible under the conditions of developing countries.

When synthetic pesticides were introduced 50 years ago, great expectations were raised. Initially there have been similar, highly optimistic statements on genetically modified organisms (GMOs) that as yet have mostly new crop protection traits. However, crop protection scientists generally have become more realistic in their expectations. Although the discussion on the risks and the economically optimal level of synthetic pesticide use has not yet come to a conclusion, GMOs have raised concerns in many parts of civil society, especially in Europe. There are obvious parallels between the introduction of pesticides and the "GMO revolution" in crop protection.

The negative externalities of pesticide use were subject to serious criticism, mainly stimulated by the publication of Rachel Carson's *Silent Spring* in 1962 and by the assessment of Pimentel and others (1986, 1993). Proponents of GMOs see these plants as the most promising way to escape the pesticide treadmill and as a necessity to overcome the world's food problem. For example, *The Economist* (1999) warned policymakers against slowing the development of GMOs in response to public panic about perceived health risks, pointing to their economic benefits for agriculture.

Scientists today may be in a better position to carefully plan the introduction of GMOs if they draw on the experience gained in crop protection from the introduction of chemical pesticides (Zadoks and Waibel 2000). Both technologies were rapidly introduced by multinational companies. Both quickly dominated the scientific debate and reached high adoption rates among farmers. Zadoks and Waibel concluded that the history of pesticides provides some warnings relevant to the future of GMOs: (a) high pesticide usage is counterproductive because fundamental agroecological principles are neglected, (b) the technology requires intensive regulation and has nonetheless many external effects that reduce its net social benefit, (c) early estimates of benefits from pesticides were overoptimistic, and (d) intensive use of pesticides made farmers dependent on them and farmers lost other important pest management options.

The lessons from the pesticide story are useful to better understand the political economy of the introduction of the GMO technology. More importantly, the theoretical and methodological insights that economists gained over the past 30 years when studying the effects of pesticides provide a baseline from which similar studies on GMOs can take off. Because scientists so far lack the procedures to fully understand the ecological and human health risks associated with GMOs, it is especially important that the benefits of this technology be thoroughly studied by applying appropriate methodological tools.

Productivity Measurement

The methodology used for the economic assessment of pesticide productivity has made important advancements over the last decades. Initially, economists treated pesticides in a conventional production function framework, that is, assuming them to be yield-increasing factors like nitrogen fertilizer. Using a Cobb–Douglas (C–D) function framework, Headley (1968) estimated the marginal productivity of aggregated pesticide use in U.S. agriculture for the period 1955 to 1963. He found the marginal value of a $1.00 expenditure for chemical pesticides to be approximately 4 US$, concluding that additional net benefits could be achieved by applying more pesticides. The figure derived in Headley's analysis has been widely cited and dominated the debate in the following decades. The productivity effects of pesticides were overestimated because neither the level of pests nor the effect of other damage control factors (e.g., agronomic practices) were considered.

Lichtenberg and Zilberman (1986) were among the first to point out the methodological problems of applying a standard production function framework to pesticides. They provided a theoretical explanation as to why production function specifications, which ignore the damage reduction characteristics of pesticides and treat them as directly yield-increasing inputs, can overestimate marginal pesticide productivity. The (a) misspecification of the production relationships, (b) the omission of pest population levels and other environmental factors, and (c) the use of pesticide expenditure as a variable instead of the total costs of abatement in previous analyses ascribes productivity effects to pesticides that in reality are caused by other factors. As a remedy, Lichtenberg and Zilberman suggested modifying the conventional (logarithmic) specification of the Cobb–Douglas production function:

$$\ln Q = \alpha + \beta \ln Z + \gamma \ln X$$

where α is a constant term, γ and β are coefficients of independent variables, and agricultural output Q is a function of Z productive inputs and X pesticide inputs. They incorporate an abatement function $G(X)$ showing the proportion of the destructive capacity of the damaging agent eliminated by the application of a level of control agent X, that is, pesticides. They showed that the marginal product (marginal effectiveness) of the damage control agent in the abatement function specification $G(X)$ declined faster than the marginal product of pesticides in the Cobb–Douglas function $(1/X)$ with a constant elasticity.

Empirical studies applying the Lichtenberg and Zilberman framework have confirmed their hypothesis. For example, Babcock and others (1992) compared the marginal product derived from a conventional Cobb–Douglas function with a damage control specification using data from North Carolina apple producers. At the average fungicide application rate, the C–D results exceeded the damage function estimate by a factor of almost 10. Including state variables in their production process model, Blackwell and Pagoulatos (1992) suggested that ignoring natural abatement factors might overestimate the marginal productivity of pesticides. Chambers and Lichtenberg (1994) applied a dual representation of the Lichtenberg and Zilberman damage control specification to an aggregate U.S. agriculture data set. They concluded that the aggregate pest damage in U.S. agriculture was lower than previous estimates suggested. Their model also hints at the important distinction between pesticides as single damage control agents and total damage abatement. The long-run price elasticity of pesticides was found to be on the order of –1.5, while the elasticity of abatement subject to the prices of all other input factors was found to be consistently less than –0.1, suggesting that the contribution of pesticides to the economic outcome of pest control is overestimated.

However, it was also shown that the choice of the functional form influences the conclusion with regard to pesticide productivity. For example, Carrasco-Tauber and Moffitt (1992) used the Lichtenberg–Zilberman framework to analyze 1987 cross-sectional data. They compared the conventional C–D function with three different specifications of the abatement function (Weibull, logistic, and exponential). The exponential form in the damage control specification showed a marginal productivity of pesticides of less than unity suggesting pesticide overuse, whereas all other functional specifications showed results similar to those found by Headley (1968). Although the exponential form is commonly used in pesticide kill functions (e.g., Regev et al. 1976), there is no theoretical basis for choosing one functional form over the other.

Overwhelmingly, however, results from applying the damage abatement function confirm not only the results of farm-level economic studies (e.g., Webster et al. 1999) but also those of numerous casual observations of pest management specialists that pesticides are more likely to be overused than underused.

Risk Reduction

Excessive pesticide use commonly is rationalized by the argument that the excess of the marginal cost over the expected value of the marginal product could be interpreted as a risk premium paid by risk-averse producers (Feder 1979; Tisdell et al. 1984; Antle 1988). Risk reduction was believed to be the farmer's main motivation in applying pesticides (Reichelderfer 1981). From a comprehensive literature review, Pannell (1991) concluded that the net effect of risk on optimal pesticide use might be minimal. He pointed out that uncertainty about some variables such as pest density and pest mortality does in fact lead to higher pesticide use under risk aversion, whereas factors like output price and yield lead to lower pesticide levels if uncertainty is considered. In his analysis of Californian cotton production, Hurd (1994) found no empirical support for the theory that pesticides reduce risk or that integrated pest management (IPM) is a risky technology. The conclusion found in the study of Saha and others (1997) that in fact pesticides may be risk increasing is supported by other studies (Horowitz and Lichtenberg 1993; Regev et al. 1997).

Contrary to the interpretation derived from the expected utility concept, these conclusions are challenged by the hypothesis provided through prospect theory (Kahneman and Tversky 1979). Both experimentally and in real-world decisionmaking, even portfolio managers in the business world tend to weigh losses substantially more than objectively commensurate gains (Kahneman and Tversky 2000). The decisionmaker's utility function, therefore, seems to differentiate between gain and loss. While decisionmakers are risk averse in a gain situation they may become risk takers in a loss situation. Hence loss-averse farmers will behave inconsistently, that is, they apply pesticides although this strategy is risk inefficient. Empirical evidence for such behavior is provided by the study of Rola and Pingali (1993) on the economics of insecticide use in Asian rice production. In their comparison of four insect control strategies, depending on the model, the expected monetary value, and the certainty equivalent of "natural control" exceeded those of farmers' insecticide use practice. In any case, certainty equivalents exceeded expected monetary values, indicating risk-taking behavior. Hence, prospect theory could provide an explanation for continuously high levels of insecticide use in Asian rice production in spite of evidence that this strategy is not economical.

Regardless of the behavioral assumptions for decisionmaking in pest management and pesticide use, earlier conclusions in economic literature that pesticides are risk-reducing inputs is subject to restrictive assumptions. Hence, there are few reasons to attribute additional benefits to pesticides because of their risk-reducing effects. Risk reduction is one of the arguments used to justify the introduction of GMOs. Thus, sound economic analysis is needed to examine the hypothesis that transgenic varieties do indeed possess risk-reducing properties that could be added to their assumed productivity-enhancing benefits. Such analysis also must include the behavioral implications for decisionmaking by small-scale farmers faced with prospects expressed in "the language of loss," which is often used by pesticide advertisements, especially in developing countries.

Interaction with Natural Resources

Decrease in productivity occurs over time as a result of biological processes known as resistance to pesticides and pest resurgence. Agricultural producers will adjust their practices to this productivity decline. For instance, pesticide demand increases with rising levels of resistance (Carlson 1977). However, the reaction of the producer to increase the rate of an input factor whose marginal productivity declines is contradictory to economic rationale when applying a conventional production function framework. Following the Lichtenberg and Zilberman (1986) framework, resistance (R) can be introduced into the abatement function:

$$G\,(X,\,R)$$

Lichtenberg and Zilberman (1986) showed that in fact the marginal effectiveness function is shifted to the left, implying a higher optimal dose compared with a situation without resistance or making the shift to a new, more effective, and probably more costly chemical product economically necessary. From the natural resource economics point of view, resistance means the loss of the biological capital, that is, pest susceptibility to the pesticide (Hueth and Regev 1974). Fleischer (1998a) has estimated the present value of the costs of resistance to the herbicide atrazine in German maize production. Taking a low discount rate to reflect the irreversibility of resistance development, the resource costs are in the range of about 4,600 DM to 6,000 DM per hectare.

The negative side-effects of the loss of beneficial organisms in particular on the ecosystem can change the marginal productivity of pesticides over time. Beneficial organisms act as natural damage control agents in the abatement function. In principle, they are available to growers as a ubiquitous common-property resource. The economic effect of a reduction in numbers of beneficial organisms or a change in their species composition is an even more complex issue than the process of pesticide resistance. Although the emergence of resistance requires adjustments in the dose level or prompts the switch to new and usually more expensive chemicals, the depletion of beneficial organisms generally leads to a dependence on chemical plant protection.

The phenomenon of path dependence was first introduced to the field of pest management by Cowan and Gunby (1996). They pointed out that self-reinforcing mechanisms, such as network externalities from adoption and increasing returns to scale, keep cropping systems on a pesticide path although more economical alternatives are available. Today's pesticide use may not only predetermine future pesticide use but also artificially stimulate the introduction of GMOs. It thus may lower the profitability of alternative strategies such as IPM in the future.

Conceptually, the effect of increasing dependence on pesticides is illustrated in Figures 6-1a and 6-1b. Figure 6-1a shows the conventional fertilizer production function with pesticide use as a discrete choice. The shift in the yield/revenue curve is the result of pesticide application. The cost of pesticides is the intercept of the fertilizer cost curve. Hence, net benefits of pesticide use equate to the difference in the revenue curve (ΔR) less pesticide (C_p) and additional fertilizer costs (ΔC_f). Higher pest pressure as a result of pesticide application in prior periods will make the revenue curves drift apart. Yields and revenues in the "without pesticide" situation drop because of higher crop loss compared with the initial starting point (Figure 6-1a) whereas agricultural yield Y_s may go up as a result of varietal improvement (Figure 6-1b). As long as the divergence of the revenue curves is larger than the increase in costs, pesticides appear to become more profitable over time.

The process comes to an end when the current cropping system becomes less profitable than an alternative, presumably less pesticide-intensive system. From a private producer's point of view, a change in the cropping system is not economical before that point is reached. By then, the resource depletion process is ongoing, and the farmer has become dependent on pesticide use. This dependency is shown as an increase in the marginal product of pesticides relative to other input factors when taking the farmer's point of view within the framework of a partial analysis. Under a resource economic framework, this additional "benefit" is actually an expression of the depletion of natural resources and thus must be interpreted as costs.

Both susceptibility of pests toward pesticides and the stock of beneficial organisms are common-property resources. Therefore, individual producers do not perceive their actions to have much influence on these resources, and, as a result, they operate within a myopic optimization framework. Consequently, an externality is produced with an "off-time nature," that is, the externality effect is felt only in the future, not in the period when it is caused. The depletion of these two resources nevertheless has implications for the assessment of pesticide productivity and consequently must be taken into account when estimating benefits. Although resistance mainly affects the factor X (i.e., pesticide use) in the damage control function, the effect of pesticides on beneficial organisms affects the potential crop damage. In other words, the cost of resistance is shown as the amount farmers spend on damage abatement. These costs would be internalized[1] if the sector is treated as

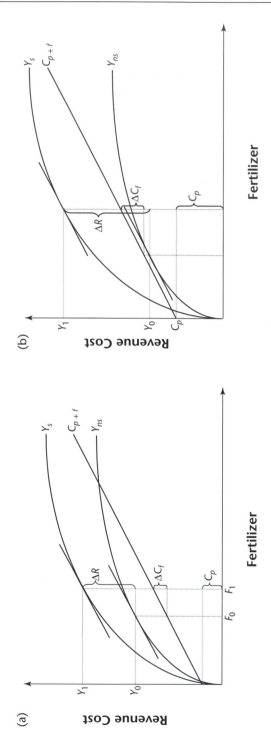

FIGURE 6-1. (a) Costs and Revenues of Pesticide Use in t_0 (b) Costs and Revenues of Pesticide Use in t_1.

one firm, ignoring spread effects caused by common access. The effect of a reduced stock of beneficial organisms is an overestimation of the benefit of pesticides because the probability of pest attack and the expected level of infestation are rising. In this context, it is no surprise that, analyzing pesticide trials from agricultural research,[2] Oerke and others (1994) found that crop losses for eight major crops have increased in relative terms over time.[3]

The nature of current GMOs with disease- and pest-resistant traits suggests that the same principles that are used in measuring pesticide productivity should be applicable to GMOs. This implies, first, that pest-resistant traits in transgenic varieties must be treated as damage control agents and not as yield-increasing inputs. After all, using *Bacillus thuringiensis* (*Bt*) genes is like making a pesticide inside the plant instead of placing it there indirectly as with systemic pesticides. Second, whether GMOs do indeed possess risk-reducing properties or are even risk increasing when compared with alternative plant protection technologies needs to be examined. The largely unknown ecological and human health implications and the growing influence of consumer reactions to policy decisions about GMOs, also in developing countries (Paarlberg 2000), lend some support to the latter hypothesis. Third, the natural resource effects of a large-scale introduction of transgenic crops must be captured in economic analysis. Ecological effects such as the development of new biotypes that overcome the resistance traits, outcrossing of genes, and intertemporal carryover effects of transgenic crop residues can result in significant damage abatement or prevention costs.

Recent Economic Studies of GMOs

Traditionally, economists have measured the impact of technological change in agriculture by using the perfect market model. The innovation, after being adopted by farmers, lowers the marginal costs of production and leads to a shift in supply. Depending on the demand elasticity of the product for which the innovation is introduced, the price of the product will decrease (Figure 6-2). The more elastic the demand is, the more the benefits go to producers as indicated by area "$ebcd - p_0aep_1$" while the welfare of consumers is increased by area p_0abp_1.

If demand is completely elastic, as is the case when the world market price of a commodity is not affected by the supply (small country case), all benefits go to producers of the commodity and the producers and distributors of the innovation. The market model needs adjustment if the supplier of the technology behaves as a monopolist. This is the case for biotechnology innovations that enjoy intellectual property protection. Here, the monopolist is able to set the price above marginal costs and as a consequence will not pass all surplus to the market. Finally, when applied to a particular technology in a

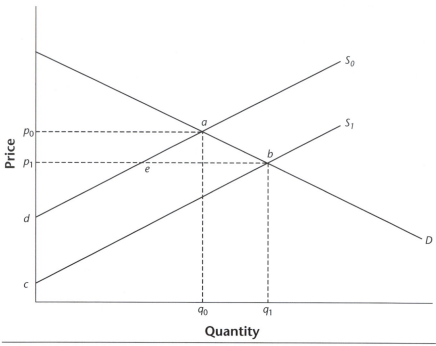

FIGURE 6-2. Economic Impact of Biotechnology Innovations

particular sector of the economy, the model shown in Figure 6-2 operates in a partial equilibrium mode, that is, other economywide effects are not included.

The limitations of the use of the market model for impact assessment of agricultural technology have been well documented (Alston et al. 1998). They include the following:

- How can we correctly estimate the percentage of research-induced reduction in production costs?
- How can we estimate the size of the industry affected by the innovation?
- How can we estimate changes in the supply of inputs induced?
- How can we estimate when benefits from adoption commence, that is, what is the time lag between the introduction of an innovation and its adoption?

In addition to these measurement problems, the market model can lead to an underestimation or overestimation of the benefits of a technology if a large proportion of the produce is not marketed or if poor infrastructure results in high transaction costs. Overestimation can occur if the technology generates negative externalities in terms of natural resource and environmental effects.

Underestimation can occur if the technology produces positive environmental and natural resource management benefits not included in the market effects.

The few economic studies of biotechnology in agriculture to date calculated the economic surplus. In estimating the supply shift that is the most crucial variable in such studies, the lessons learned from economic studies of pesticides were not always applied. Instead, modern biotechnology was treated as a "yield-increasing" and at the same time "cost-saving" technology. Most of these studies were conducted on *Bt* crops in the United States. One was conducted in China and another ex ante study on potatoes and sweet potatoes was conducted in developing countries.

In the study of Falck-Zepeda and others (2000) on *Bt* cotton in the United States, information from surveys of farmers and on-station experiments were used to "refine" econometric estimates of shifts in supply from *Bt* cotton. Although the authors recognized that there was great deal of variance in pest pressure, yields, seeding rates, and other production characteristics among producers of *Bt* corn it is not clear how their model takes account of this variation. Ultimately, elasticity of supply taken from literature data was treated as a random variable in a stochastic simulation procedure to model economic surplus.

Fernandez-Cornejo and McBride (2000) summarized the effects of genetically engineered crops on yields, pesticide use, and returns as reported in previous studies of herbicide-tolerant soybeans, corn, and cotton; *Bt* cotton; and *Bt* corn. Some of these studies used experimental data; others were based on surveys. The authors reviewed the statistical and practical problems ensuing from controlled experiments and those resulting from farm surveys as well as some solutions to overcome these problems. However, it is not clear to what extent these standards were applied to the economic studies on genetically modified crops in the United States. For example, most of the studies did not discuss the problem of defining a valid reference system (Zadoks and Waibel 2000) because neither the control plots in experiments nor farmers' current practices may qualify for this.

Carpenter and Gianessi (2001) updated their previous estimates of the benefits associated with the adoption of genetically modified crop varieties of corn, cotton, and soybeans in U.S. agriculture. They did not mention the methodological procedure of their analysis but they nevertheless drew clear-cut conclusions. "... *Bt* corn varieties allowed farmers to control the European corn borer, an insect that is difficult to control using conventional insecticides ... Prior to the introduction of *Bt* corn, few growers were spraying for the corn borer. Instead, yield losses sometimes reached 300 million bushels of corn per year. With *Bt* corn, losses from the corn borer are eliminated. The primary benefit of Bt corn varieties has been increased yields" (Carpenter and Gianessi 2001,1) Similar conclusions were drawn for herbicide-resistant varieties and *Bt* varieties of other crops. Conversely, the conclusion for insect- and virus-resistant potatoes was different. "The recent introduction of a highly effective conventional insecticide and the refusal of processors to accept genetically modified potatoes have limited the adoption of these new varieties" (Carpenter and Gianessi 2001, 2).

In China, the study of Pray and others (2001) examined the amount and distribution of benefits among different groups of farmers and between farmers, seed companies, and research institutes. The data were drawn from a single recall survey of 283 cotton farmers in two provinces of Northern China and compared adopters and nonadopters of *Bt* cotton. Among both groups, a differentiation was made between varieties. The authors found that *Bt* cotton increased farmers' income through increased yields and reduced pesticide costs, the latter generating additional health benefits. Their conclusions were based on averages, but a high variation could be observed across locations and varieties. Only 14% of the respondents belonged to the group of nonadopters.

The only ex ante study in developing countries for virus resistance of potatoes[4] until now was conducted by Quaim (2000).[5] The author concluded "handsome" internal rates of return of 60% to 77% for biotechnology investments in sweet potatoes and of 52% to 56% in potatoes. A limitation of this study is that the author ignored the recommendation in the recent agricultural economics literature (Davis and Espinoza 1998) that stochastic simulation should be used instead of sensitivity analysis to address the problem of uncertainty. Also, in view of the sparse empirical database used by the author, the validity of his ex ante analysis largely depends on the treatment of risk in the calculations of rates of return.

To sum up our coverage of recent studies of GMOs, the following methodological limitations of previous economic analyses of crop protection related to biotechnology innovations can be observed: The nature of pest- and disease-resistant varieties as damage control agents is ignored because, like in the earlier analysis of pesticides, they are not treated as damage reduction factors. Most studies assume that current pest management is ineffective in preventing crop loss mainly because either no pesticides are available or they have become ineffective as a result of pest resistance. At this point, the question of the correct reference system to be used emerges again. To compare transgenic crops with "traditional" crops first requires an optimization of the current system. In this regard, all previous studies are static. They compare a "new" technology with a "depreciated"[6] one, that is, they compare different points in the life cycle of a technology.

Furthermore, most previous studies do not account for risk, although uncertainty with transgenic crops is high in several respects. For example, price risk is high because there can be dramatic consumer reactions in response to health fears, regardless of whether these fears are based on scientific evidence or merely consumer perception. Finally, none of the studies reviewed attempted to account for negative externalities from GMOs, although some of the effects, such as the development of resistance, are expected to occur, while the extent of such events and their timing is subject to considerable uncertainty.

The recent literature on the economics of pesticides and on GMOs has provided some important lessons. Highlighting the potential overestimation of benefits and especially an underestimation of the external costs is justified when following a "precautionary principle" in conducting economic studies of new technologies. Although claims of positive externalities also have been made for pesticides (e.g., Avery 1995), and the role of GMOs as a public good in fighting hunger and poverty is often underlined in documents of development organizations, available empirical evidence of such additional benefits is sparse. Furthermore, there are serious theoretical problems with the concept of positive externalities attributable to chemical pesticides (Pearce and Tinch 1998).

A Conceptual Framework for Economic Analysis of GMOs

We propose a research-oriented concept for the economic assessment of GMOs. During the initial stage of adoption, such a normative approach is necessary to improve the estimates of future benefits and costs.

Economic assessment of public or private investments in transgenic crops requires a comparison of the sum of the expected discounted benefits with that of known and expected discounted costs. Traditionally, economists undertook such cost–benefit analysis by applying the concept of economic surplus, mostly in a partial equilibrium mode. This is appropriate as long as forward and backward linkages to other sectors of the economy are small and no externalities are to be expected from the technology. The experience gained with synthetic pesticides (Zadoks and Waibel 2000) suggests that external costs exist and may be higher than initially expected.

The proposed investment in GMOs should be assessed against other potential innovations. In the case of transgenic crops, which are designed for better pest management, technological options such as IPM and biological control might be used as reference points. Because the adoption of those techniques has been impeded by a long-term subsidy policy for synthetic pesticides (Repetto 1985, Waibel and Fleischer 1995), the net benefits of genetic modification as a new technology can be overestimated.

Benefit Assessment

To assess benefits, the impact on the productivity of the agricultural sector must be measured as accurately as possible. Market distortions, which occur in most agricultural markets in industrial countries, require an open economy framework, that is, one that values the additional production gained or the resources saved using shadow prices. Although the choice of the appropriate model to measure benefits is important, it is equally important that the model be based on carefully collected data, which must represent the actual conditions of practical farming. Therefore, data collected from experiments conducted in research stations are inappropriate, especially for genetically modified crops designed for pest control. Mostly, the conditions of research stations with continuous cropping of few crops generate higher pest pressure than found under real-world conditions. In the case of controlled experiments conducted in farmer fields, possible adjustment strategies of farmers are often ignored because treatment strategies are fixed beforehand. Thus benefits tend to be overestimated.

Data based on interviewing farmers who adopted transgenic varieties and those who did not often suffer from a selection bias called self-selection (Fernandez-Cornejo and McBride 2000). In surveys, farmers are not assigned randomly to either group (adopters and nonadopters); they make the adoption decision themselves. Therefore, adopters and nonadopters may be systematically different, hence the observed differences in productivity may not be fully attributable to the adoption decision. Although there are statistical procedures to control for self-selection, the correction depends on whether all important factors that cause a systematic difference are actually measured. This, however, often is not possible in "one-shot" surveys.

Instead of data from controlled experiments, surveys, or both, field-based, season-long observations of farm and plot-level data on the amount and the timing of inputs are needed to measure the impact of transgenic crops at the farm level. At harvest time, yields are more accurately measured by applying crop-cut sampling. Also, conclusions should not be based only on short-term technology adoption (one or even two years). In view of the variation of pest populations over time, we submit that to measure the field-level impact of transgenic crops, a period of five years is needed. This seems essential because of the following reasons. First, farmers are likely to gain experience and thus improve their performance via reduction of pesticide use, changes in seed rates, or modifications of their cropping patterns. Second, externalities that result in changes to the ecosystem will not be noticeable immediately, for example, changes in the number of beneficial insects as well as resistance buildup in target pests. Ideally, data would have to be collected before transgenic crops were adopted by the farmers. This, however, is hardly possible as, unlike a technology that is introduced by farmer training, the adoption of transgenic varieties is not known beforehand. Instead, early and recent adopters can be compared with a fixed control group of nonadopters. Based on experience from impact assessment of farmer field schools, a minimum of

30 to 50 farmers per group is sufficient (Kenmore 1996). The data on farm economic parameters must be complemented by historical information on the pest complex and a description of the ecological conditions of the area.

To avoid overestimation of the impact of a transgenic resistant variety over the conventional method of pest control, first data should be analyzed using the damage control framework; second data should be corrected for economically inefficient pesticide use (which exists as suggested by the fact that IPM can increase farm profits). The damage control framework was applied by Huang and Qiao (2000) to pesticide use in rice in China and by Ajayi (2000) to cotton in Côte d'Ivoire.

Costs of Externalities

Some of the externalities attributable to pesticide use are difficult to internalize because they only occur in the long run and because they affect common-property resources. This is typical for pesticide resistance. It happens over time, and it is the result of the actions of all farmers who apply pesticides. The combined effect of their action is the reduction of the resource "susceptibility," a typical common-property resource.

Similar effects can be expected to take place with pest resistance of a crop variety. While resistant plants may become ineffective against pests, pests may lose their susceptibility toward pesticides. Resistant varieties produced by classical breeding methods eventually may be attacked by new strains of the pest against which the resistance does not work. Such strains appear naturally by mutation and recombination of genes and may be augmented by indiscriminate pesticide use. Hundreds of such events are on record over the last 80 years for wheat, potatoes, rice, and scores of other crops. In either case, a genetic change in the pest population terminates the economic lifetime of an asset, be it the pesticide or the resistant variety. In either case, the pest population may increase and cause significant damage. The natural resource implications of the two cases could be different.

Similarly, transgenic resistance may become ineffective. Genes for *Bt* tolerance have already been found in target pest populations (Gould et al. 1997). As with classical breeding for monogenic resistance (Zadoks 1993), new (trans)genes will be kept in store. The loss of host plant resistance through the appearance of new pest genotypes and the changes in pest population can be considered as resource depletion in pest management. It is thus a cost to current and future users of pest control technology.

Measuring costs for newly introduced transgenic crops may be difficult. However, change might be observable by comparing recent adopters with early adopters as mentioned previously. Also, data from experiments may provide some indication of the time span until resistance occurs. In addition, expert opinion can be used to judge when and how rapidly resistance will develop.

Conceptually, the costs of resistance development and the benefits of preventing or delaying it are shown in Figure 6-3. Although the general shape of the curve is known, the critical parameters that need to be determined are t_{1S1} (t_{1S2}) and t_{2S1}(t_{2S2}) in Figure 6-3. Here, t_1 is the time when resistance (breakdown of resistance of varieties) starts to take place and t_2 is the point in time when the effective price of the variety has reached the costs (C_s) of a substitute technology. The areas (A and B) under the resistance curves for two alternative resistance management strategies RMS_2 and RMS_1 are the total costs of resistance.[7] The benefit of improved resistance management (RMS_1) is indicated by area A in Figure 6-3. To compare annual costs with annual benefits, these need to be discounted and converted into an annuity.

The parameters t_1, t_2, and the slopes of the resistance curves of Figure 6-3 are subject to some degree of uncertainty, that is, the experts may vary in their opinions. Hence, to calculate the costs of resistance, these assumptions need to be subjected to risk analysis using stochastic simulation approaches. Here, cumulative probability distributions of an objective variable such as net benefit are generated by applying a random generator to a set of input variables with defined range and distribution type. Figure 6-4 conceptualizes this procedure by hypothetically comparing two resistance management strategies

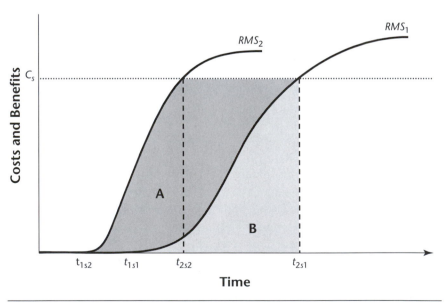

FIGURE 6-3. Costs of Resistance and Benefits of Resistance Management

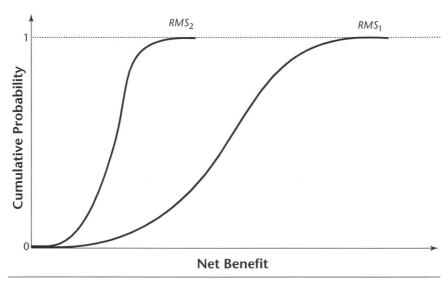

FIGURE 6-4. Stochastic Simulation of Net Benefits of Two Resistance Management Strategies

RMS_1 and RMS_2. RMS_1 in this context may refer, for example, to more restrictive requirements of refuge areas with nontransgenic crops.

Although this method will not eliminate the causes of uncertainty, it will provide a better basis for decisionmaking because measures of economic performance will be presented as what they really are, probabilistic values and not rigid numbers. Furthermore, the differences between management strategies can be presented by their degree of stochastic dominance.

Conclusion

Careful economic analysis of the GMO technology is necessary if society wants to avoid the mistakes made with the assessment of synthetic pesticides. Empirical analysis must look at the benefits as well as at the risks. Critical benefit assessment is important because there is a tendency among scientists to be overoptimistic at the beginning. Thus, an appropriate framework and a solid empirical basis are necessary. As long as the risks of GMOs are poorly understood, an overestimation of their benefits can be highly misleading.

From a methodological point of view, GMOs in crop protection should be treated in a damage control framework. Simply looking at yield can lead to the wrong conclusions. Also, care needs to be taken when defining the counterfactual. An agroecosystem "degraded" by misguided human interventions with indiscriminant pesticide use is not a suitable reference system. Therefore, to avoid comparing extreme situations, corrective adjustments must be applied to the current farming systems.

Most of the data collected or made available for the assessment of GMOs are subject to a considerable degree of uncertainty. On the cost side, however, analysts can arrive at minimum values rather than ignoring the risks of transgenic crops. Based on accepted ecological principles, effects like resistance are known to take place, but the time when they will occur is highly uncertain. The costs of resistance can be estimated initially from the interpretations of actual field conditions by independent experts and can be refined as more time-series data become available.

Sensitivity analysis with arbitrary calculations of scenarios will not provide results consistent with economic principles. Instead, it should become standard procedure of applied economic analysis to use stochastic simulation and to present results as cumulative probability distributions rather than as rigid numbers.

Acknowledgements

The authors acknowledge the assistance of Diemuth Pemsl and Imke Panschow in the preparation of this paper. We also thank Dr. Peter Kenmore (Food and Agriculture Organisation of the United Nations) and the anonymous reviewers for their very helpful comments.

References

Ajayi, O. 2000. *Pesticide Use Practices, Productivity and Farmers' Health: The Case of Cotton-Rice Systems in Côte d'Ivoire, West Africa*. Pesticide Policy Project, Publication Series Special Issue No. 3. Hannover, Germany: University of Hannover.

Alston, J.M., M.C. Marra, P.G. Pardey, and T.J. Wyatt. 1998. *Ex Pede Herculem? A Meta-Analysis of Rates of Return to Agricultural R&D*. Davis, CA: Global and Regional Program on Agricultural Research, Extension, and Education, International Food Policy Research Institute (IFPRI) and University of California Agricultural Issues Center.

Antle, J.M. 1988. *Pesticide Policy, Production Risk, and Producer Welfare: An Econometric Approach to Applied Welfare Economics*. Washington, DC: Resources for the Future.

Avery, D.T. 1995. *Saving the Planet with Pesticide and Plastics*. Indianapolis, IN: Hudson Institute.

Babcock, B., E. Lichtenberg, and D. Zilberman. 1992. Impact of Damage Control and Quality of Output: Estimating Pest Control Effectiveness. *American Journal of Agricultural Economics* 74: 163–72.

Blackwell, M., and A. Pagoulatos. 1992. The Econometrics of Damage Control—Comment. *American Journal of Agricultural Economics* 74: 1040–4.

Carlson, G.A. 1977. Long-Run Productivity of Insecticides. *American Journal of Agricultural Economics* 59: 543–8.

Carpenter, J.E., and L.P. Gianessi. 2001. *Agricultural Biotechnology: Updated Benefits Estimates.* Washington, DC: National Center for Food and Agricultural Policy.

Carrasco-Tauber, C., and L.J. Moffitt. 1992. Damage Control Econometrics—Functional Specification and Pesticide Productivity. *American Journal of Agricultural Economics* 74: 158–62.

Carson, R. 1962. *Silent Spring.* Boston: Houghton Mifflin.

Chambers, R.G., and E. Lichtenberg. 1994. Simple Econometrics of Pesticide Productivity. *American Journal of Agricultural Economics* 76(3): 407.

Cowan, R., and P. Gunby. 1996. Sprayed to Death: Path Dependence, Lock-In and Pest Control Strategies. *The Economic Journal* 106: 521–42.

Davis, G.C., and M.C. Espinoza. 1998. A Unified Approach to Sensitivity Analysis in Equilibrium Displacement Models. *American Journal of Agricultural Economics* 80: 868–79.

The Economist. 1999. Frankenstein Foods. February 20, 1999: 17

Falck-Zepeda, J.B., G. Traxler, and R.G. Nelson. 2000. Surplus Distribution from the Introduction of a Biotechnology Innovation. *American Journal of Agricultural Economics* 82: 360–9.

Feder, G. 1979. Pesticides, Information and Pest Management under Uncertainty. *American Journal of Agricultural Economics* 61: 97–103.

Fernandez-Cornejo, J., and W.D. McBride. 2000. Genetically Engineered Crops for Pest Management. US Agriculture, Farm Level Effects. AER.786. Washington DC: Economic Research Service/USDA.

Fleischer, G. 1998. *Ökonomische Ansätze in der Pflanzenschutzpolitik—Das Beispiel der Zulassungsprüfung.* Kiel, Germany: Vauk Verlag, Landwirtschaft und Umwelt, Schriften zur Umweltökonomik, 15.

Fleischer, G. 1998. *Ökonomische Bewertung in der Pflanzenschutzpolitik—Das Beispiel des Zulassungsverfahrens.* Kiel, Germany: Schriften zur Umweltökonomik, Wissenschaftsverlag Vauk.

Fleischer, G. 2000. Resource Costs of Pesticide Use in Germany—The Case of Atrazine. *Agrarwirtschaft* (Journal of the German Association of Agricultural Economists) 49 (11): 379–87.

Gould, F., A. Anderson, A. Jones, D. Sumerford, D.G. Heckel, J. Lopez, S. Micinski, R. Leonard, and M. Laster. 1997. Initial Frequency of Alleles for Resistance to *Bacillus Thuringiensis* Toxins in Field Populations of *Heliothis virescens. Proceedings of the National Academy of Sciences of the USA* 94: 3519–23.

Headley, J.C. 1968. Estimating the Productivity of Agricultural Pesticides. *American Journal of Agricultural Economics* 50: 13–23.

Horowitz, J.K., and E. Lichtenberg. 1993. Insurance, Moral Hazard and Agricultural Chemical Use. *American Journal of Agricultural Economics* 75: 926–35.

Huang, J., and F. Qiao. 2000. Farm Pesticide, Rice Production and Human Health. Paper presented at the International Consultative Workshop on Effective and Sustainable Use of Biotechnology in Integrated Pest Management in Developing Countries. November 2000, Hangzhou, P.R. China.

Hueth, D., and U. Regev. 1974. Optimal Agricultural Pest Management with Increasing Pest Resistance. *American Journal of Agricultural Economics* 56: 543–53.

Hurd, B. 1994. Yield Response and Production Risk: An Analysis of Integrated Pest Management in Cotton. *Journal of Agricultural and Resource Economics* 19(2): 313–26.

Kahneman, D., and A. Tversky. 1979. Prospect Theory: An Analysis of Decision Under Risk. *Econometrica* 47: 263–91.

———. 2000. *Choices, Values and Frames.* Cambridge, U.K.: Cambridge University Press.

Kenmore, P. 1996. Integrated Pest Management in Rice. In *Biotechnology and Integrated Pest Management,* edited by G.J. Persley. Wallingford, U.K.: CABI, 76–97.

Lichtenberg, E., and D. Zilberman. 1986. The Econometrics of Damage Control: Why Specification Matters. *American Journal of Agricultural Economics* 68: 261–73.

Oerke, E.-C., H.W. Dehne, F. Schönbeck, and A. Weber. 1994. *Crop Production and Crop Protection: Estimated Crop Losses in Major Food and Cash Crops.* Amsterdam: Elsevier.

Paarlberg, R.L. 2000. Governing the GM Crop Revolution—Policy Choices for Developing Countries. Food, Agriculture, and the Environment. Discussion paper 33. Washington, DC: International Food Policy Research Institute.

Pannell, D.J. 1991. Pest and Pesticides, Risk and Risk Aversion. *Agricultural Economics* 5: 361–83.

Pearce, R., and R. Tinch. 1998. The True Price of Pesticides. In *Bugs in the System,* edited by B. Vorley and D. Keeney. London: Earthscan.

Pimentel, D., H. Acquay, M. Biltonen, P. Rice, M. Silva, J. Nelson, V. Lipner, S. Giordano, A. Horowitz, and M. D´Amore. 1993. Assessment of Environmental and Economic Impacts of Pesticide Use. In *The Pesticide Question—Environment, Economics, and Ethics,* edited by D. Pimentel and H. Lehman. New York: Chapman & Hall, 47–84.

Pimentel, D., and L. Levitan. 1986. Pesticides: Amounts Applied and Amounts Reaching Pests. *BioScience* 36: 86–91.

Pray, C.E., D. Ma, J. Huang, and F. Qiao. 2001. Impact of *Bt* Cotton in China. *World Development* 29(5): 813–25.

Quaim, M. 2000. *Potential Impacts of Crop Biotechnology in Developing Countries.* Doctoral dissertation. Bonn, Rheinische Friedrich-Wilhelms-Universität.

Regev, U., N. Gotsch, and P. Rieder. 1997. Are Fungicides, Nitrogen and Plant Growth Regulators Risk-Reducing? Empirical Evidence from Swiss Wheat Production. *Journal of Agricultural Economics* 48(2): 167–78.

Regev, U., A.P. Gutierrez, and G. Feder. 1976. Pest as a Common Property Resource—A Case Study in Alfalfa Weevil Control. *American Journal of Agricultural Economics* 58: 186–97.

Reichelderfer, K.H. 1981. Economic Feasibility of Biological Control of Crop Pests. In *Biological Control in Crop Production,* edited by G.C. Papavizas, B.Y. Endo, D.L. Klingman, L.V. Knutson, R.D. Lumsden, and J.L. Vaughan. Montclair, NJ: Allenheld Osmun.

Repetto, R. 1985. *Paying the Price—Pesticide Subsidies in Developing Countries.* Research Report No. 2, Washington DC: World Resources Institute.

Rola, A.C., and P.L. Pingali. 1993. *Pesticides, Rice Productivity and Farmer's Health: An Economic Assessment.* Los Banos, Philippines: The International Rice Research Institute, and Washington, DC: World Resources Institute.

Saha, A., C.R. Shumway, and A. Havenner. 1997. The Economics and Econometrics of Damage Control. *American Journal of Agricultural Economics* 79(3): 773–85.

Tisdell, C.A., B.A. Auld, and K.M. Menz. 1984. On Assessing the Value of Biological Control of Weeds. *Protection Ecology* 6: 169–79.

Waibel, H., and G. Fleischer. 1995. State Intervention or Free Market Economy: Underlying Conditions for Disseminating Integrated Pest Management. Agriculture + Rural Development working paper. University of Hannover, Germany: Pesticide Policy Project.

———. 1998. *Kosten und Nutzen des chemischen Pflanzenschutzes in der Deutschen Landwirtschaft aus Gesamtwirtschaftlicher Sicht* (Social Costs and Benefits of Chemical Plant Protection in German Agriculture). Kiel, Germany: Vauk Verlag.

Waibel, H., G. Fleischer, and H. Becker. 1999. The Economic Benefits of Pesticides : A Case Study from Germany. *Agrarwirtschaft* (Journal of the German Association of Agricultural Economists), 48(6): 219–30.

Waibel, H., and S. Setboonsarng. 1993. Resource Degradation Due to Chemical Inputs in Vegetable-Based Farming Systems in Thailand. *Journal of the Asian Farming Systems Association* 2(1): 107–20.

Webster, J.P.G., R.G. Bowles, and N.T. Williams. 1999. Estimating the Economic Benefits of Alternative Pesticide Usage Scenarios: Wheat Production in the United Kingdom. *Crop Protection* 18(1991): 83–9.

Zadoks, J.C. 1993. The Partial Past. Comments on the History of Thinking about Resistance of Plants against Insects, Nematodes, Fungi, and Other Harmful Agents. In *Durability of disease resistance,* edited by T. Jacobs and J.E. Parlevliet. Dordrecht, The Netherlands: Kluwer Academic Publishers, 11–22.

Zadoks, J.C., and H. Waibel. 2000. From Chemical Pesticides to Genetically Modified Crops—History, Economics, Politics. *Netherlands Journal of Agricultural Science* 48: 125–49.

Notes

1. Of course, the resource rent of susceptibility and the loss-of-control options are not internalized.

2. Such experiments are especially suitable to show these effects because of long-term and often year-round use of pesticides.

3. The results of Oerke et al. (1994) need to be interpreted with care because most of their data came from on-station pesticide trials.

4. This study included transgenic sweet potatoes in Kenya and transgenic potatoes in Mexico.

5. Quaim (2000) also included banana tissue culture in Kenya. However, this is not relevant in the context of our topic.

6. If a pest develops resistance to a pesticide, that pesticide is comparable to an asset that has reached the terminal point of its service life. The same will eventually happen to the "new" technology, hence its present value tends to be overstated if resistance is ignored.

7. In fact, costs of resistance may be infinite if susceptibility cannot be reestablished. Hence, the costs of resistance must be expressed as an infinite annuity.

Commentary

The Role of Ecosystem Complexity in Genetically Modified Organisms

Karl Seeley

Work in the 1970s on pesticide resistance made important progress, but it included an important simplifying assumption. Pest infestations were treated as exogenous, as if the level of infestation facing a farmer in any growing season depended only on the number of pests left alive the previous year plus some random factors; all other farmer decisions were irrelevant. This approach made the analysis easier because it limited the farmer's decisions to the choice of how much pesticide to use each season. More pesticide this year meant higher yields this year and fewer pests to control next year but also more resistance in the pest population. The optimal path was driven by the relative strength of these forces.

In this context, the chapter by Waibel, Zadoks, and Fleischer (Chapter 6) is a valuable contribution to the literature; its key insight is that pest infestation is in part endogenous—it depends on many farmer decisions, such as crop rotations, and the preservation of predators that can reduce pest populations. This places their work in a more recent tradition that acknowledges a broader set of choices facing farmers in managing pest losses.

In particular, the authors compare pest resistance with ecosystem deterioration. The health of the soil (and the resulting health of the crop) and the abundance of beneficial predators play crucial roles in determining the extent of losses to pests. As with resistance, deterioration of these attributes requires increased pesticide use for the same level of control. But ecosystem decline exacts an additional cost. Pest resistance itself has no effect on the efficacy of alternative strategies (e.g., resistance to a given pesticide generally will not confer on a pest any advantage in avoiding a predatory insect), whereas the ecosystem itself is the very foundation of those alternatives. Thus if there is a link between ecosystem deterioration and use of a pesticide or a genetically engineered crop, the probable development of resistance is compounded by the increasing cost of pursuing alternatives pest-management strategies.

Charles Benbrook (1999) has neatly summed up the problem:

> Cost-effective use of pest management technology, regardless of its genesis, depends upon the degree to which it helps diversify and complicate the challenges faced by pest species within farm fields. Many technologies once heralded as major innovations have failed because of agriculture's tendency to rely on technology to simplify and homogenize systems rather than to diversify them.

In other words, the problem with genetically engineered plants is not something inherent but rather the risk of misusing them in the same way that conventional pesticides have been misused.

This raises the question of how to get the benefits of pesticides or genetically engineered plants while discouraging excessive simplification. A direct approach is Michael Gray's proposal for prescriptive use of genetically modified plants in controlling corn rootworm (2000). Much as we cannot purchase many medicines without a doctor's prescription, farmers would have to demonstrate that they had scouted the previous season and that an economic threshold for adult rootworms had been exceeded. While this presumably would limit socially unwarranted use of the new crops, it would also be expensive and almost certainly unwelcome by farmers, who are not usually looking for additional regulatory procedures.

But it does at least start the debate about complexity in agroecosystems. I make two conjectures. First, ecosystem complexity on farms is a good because it reduces pesticide use and slows the development of pest resistance.[1] Second, because both pesticide use and pest resistance are negative externalities, ecosystem complexity creates positive externalities. The economic challenge that Waibel, Zadoks, and Fleischer point to is to find instruments that encourage useful forms of complexity on farms. It is hard to reward complexity directly because it is hard to quantify the components of it that are worth fostering. We could look, however, at making simplification more costly to farmers, leading them to avoid it. The best tool for that strategy may be a tax on pesticides.

This is ironic, because genetically engineered plants are seen by many as a replacement for pesticides. If we make the chemicals more expensive, that would seem to encourage even more reliance on the new crops and thus exacerbate the misuse of the new technology that we were trying to prevent. But for the foreseeable future, the simplified ecosystems we would like to avoid will continue to depend on some pesticides, even if the new crops replace others. Therefore, a strategy that makes simplification more expensive may encourage wise use of biotech crops. As a model, the state of Iowa has had success in reducing fertilizer use without yield loss through a modest fertilizer tax. The revenues of the tax fund education on careful fertilizer use. It is worth considering a similar levy on pesticides and using the funds to support pest scouting and other measures to reduce farmers' costs of managing intricate ecosystems on their property.

References

Benbrook, C.M. 1999. World Food System Challenges and Opportunities: GMOs, Biodiversity, and Lessons from America's Heartland. Paper presented at the University of Illinois World Food and Sustainable Agriculture Program. January 1999, Urbana-Champaign, IL. http://www.biotech-info.net/IWFS.pdf (accessed March 10, 2002).

Gray, M.E. 2000. Prescriptive Use of Transgenic Hybrids for Corn Rootworms: An Ominous Cloud on the Horizon? Paper presented at the University of Illinois Crop Protection Technology Conference, January 2000, Champaign-Urbana, IL. Available at <http://www.biotech-info.net/mgray.pdf>.

Zadoks, J.C. *What Can We Learn from the Economics of Pesticides?* Presented at RFF Conference on the Economics of Resistance, April 2001, Warrenton, VA.

Note

1. Jan Zadoks pointed out that "complexity" should not be mindlessly worshiped. He used the example of barberry, which serves as an obligate host for wheat stem rust. Eliminating barberry from wheat-growing areas arguably reduces the complexity of the local ecosystem, but also reduces rust infestation in a sustainable way. Nonetheless, the simplifications prompted by over-reliance on pesticides (or possibly genetically engineered plants) seem unlikely to be of this beneficent kind.

Chapter 7

Elements of Economic Resistance Management Strategies—Empirical Evidence from Case Studies in Germany

Gerd Fleischer and Hermann Waibel

Although resistance against pest control agents is perceived as a major threat for crop protection, there is considerable uncertainty about the economic justification of resistance management strategies. This chapter adopts a resource economic point of view. Pest susceptibility toward control measures is treated as biological capital. The objective is to identify the major factors to consider when evaluating resistance management strategies. The economic theory of nonrenewable resources suggests that three variables need to be taken into account: (a) the uncertainty of decisionmakers about the parameters and the scale of the economic impact of resource depletion, (b) the direction and rate of technological change, and (c) the extent of common-property characteristics of pest susceptibility and its effects on different groups of farmers when adaptation to resistance spread is taking place.

The importance of those factors is further explored in two case studies using data from German agriculture. The first study underpins the importance of the sectorwide economic consequences of resistance. Such information is considered valuable for designing and implementing effective and efficient resistance management strategies. A log-linear regression model is used to entangle the effect of technological path dependency on pesticide use. With a note of caution, the rising trend in crop protection costs can be attributed to resource degradation, with development of resistance as one important factor. The second case study deals with the costs of weed resistance against atrazine and demonstrates the importance of the discount rate and the distributional consequences of regulatory decisions. Based on a representative set of time-series data, resource costs of atrazine use are assessed by differentiating farm plots according to their share of maize in the crop rotation. The results show that social costs of resistance development are far higher than private costs.

The chapter highlights some of the methodological difficulties in measuring the economic impact of resistance. The analysis nevertheless provides some evidence that sectorwide consequences should not be neglected. It also suggests that the sustainability and equity impacts of resistance development should be given more weight in regulatory decisionmaking about pesticides.

Trends in crop protection are increasingly a matter of concern, both for industrialized countries with considerably high intensity of chemical pesticide use and for less developed countries. Less-developed countries still have lower overall pesticide use levels but there is frequent overuse as well, especially in crops like cotton and rice. Changes in pest control strategies, such as the adoption of integrated pest management, are necessary elements of the global agenda for sustainable agricultural development (Schillhorn van Veen et al. 1997).

Appropriate pesticide resistance management strategies are part of such a strategy. The threats of resistance and the induced increased risk of pest outbreaks can put farmers on a pesticide treadmill leading them to use ever-increasing amounts and stronger pesticides to kill mutating pests with severe consequences (van den Bosch 1978). Resistance is increasingly perceived as an important constraint to effective crop protection that limits the prospects for matching the projected increase in global food demand, especially in developing countries (Yudelman et al. 1998). Therefore, resistance management is in the interest of the agricultural community (Nevill et al. 1998). Manufacturers of plant protection products have established a number of industrywide public–private committees for information exchange and to create awareness about resistance management (GCPF 2000).

There is still considerable uncertainty about the payoff of such strategies in terms of a net social benefit because of incomplete information about the potential economic consequences of inaction. Until now, few attempts have been made to obtain reliable estimates on the costs and benefits of resistance management. Results were generally not made available to decisionmakers, especially the end users of chemical pesticides. There are also concerns that available estimates about the social costs of pesticide resistance could be flawed because farmers may have internalized these costs already in their decisions about pesticide use (Pearce and Tinch 1998). Furthermore, as demonstrated by Pannell and Zilberman (2000) for weed resistance in Australia, farmers may have little incentive to adopt resistance management strategies because of existing socioeconomic constraints.

The debate on resistance management is analogous to the discussion about pesticide externalities on human health and the environment. Similarly, methodological problems have hampered the interpretation of the results of studies on the negative impacts of pesticide use. Only in recent years have economic studies become available that have contributed to a quantitative assessment of the external costs of current pesticide use levels in agriculture (Pimentel et al. 1993; Steiner et al. 1995; Waibel and Fleischer 1998b). This kind of information allows us to judge the efficiency and cost-effectiveness of regulatory approaches that address the risks for human health and the environment (Oskam et al. 1997). When external costs are taken into account, the conventionally held estimates about the net social benefits of pesticides must be adjusted (Pearce and Tinch 1998).

Similar empirical evidence about the magnitude of the private and social costs of resistance should be presented to make the case for resistance management strategies. This chapter aims to contribute to the debate by presenting methodologies for assessment, as well as some empirical evidence, by using a resource economic framework for evaluation.

The objectives of the chapter are as follows:

- to reveal the conditions under which the spread of resistance is likely to produce social costs,
- to present methodologies for assessing economic consequences of resistance, and
- to identify factors that are important for designing economically efficient resistance management strategies.

The next section explains the nature of the resistance management problem by using a resource economic framework. It reveals the conditions under which conservation of the susceptibility resource is likely to pay off. The two case studies present quantitative evidence for the costs of resistance development based on case studies in German agriculture. The results of the case studies bring us to a conclusion on decisive variables for the design of resistance management strategies.

Economic Effects of Resistance: When Does Resource Conservation Pay?

The emergence of resistance of pests, weeds, or diseases against a pest control agent is a process of the depletion of a naturally inherent resource that is the susceptibility toward the specific mode of action of the pest control agent. Pest susceptibility thus can be treated as a biological capital (Hueth and Regev 1974). Several biological factors determine resistance development: the initial frequency of resistant individuals in a pest population, the target mode of the pest control agent, the mode of inheritance, and the relative fitness of the resistant individuals (Zwerger and Walter 1994). Among the socioeconomic factors, the frequency of treatment and the size of the treated area are important parameters for resistance management strategies because those factors determine the selection pressure.

From the point of view of economic efficiency, farmers and other pesticide users would make perfectly rational decisions about optimal resource use under two conditions: (a) when perfect information on all parameters of the biological process of resistance development is available and (b) when externalities are absent, such as in the case of the spread of resistance from one farm to other economic units. Under the economic efficiency scenario, no public intervention in resistance management would be warranted because the endogenous market response to resistance would determine an efficient outcome. In this case, all relevant economic impacts of resistance development would be internalized.

At least in some cases, these assumptions do not hold. Then spread of resistance should be considered as market failure that needs to be corrected to provide an efficient outcome. To determine some criteria for the extent to which public policy intervention might be justified, we will take a closer look at the characteristics of the resistance problem and its implications for economic evaluation. This discussion will underpin the need to determine specific solutions for both the information and the externality problems.

Characteristics of the Resistance Problem Relevant to Economic Evaluation

The nature of the resource susceptibility of an individual pest as biological capital needs some clarification. We can distinguish between two forms of biological capital: the stock of susceptibility against a specific pesticide and the stock of susceptibility against the total of available options for pest control in a given cropping system and location.

Pesticide treatment eliminates susceptible individuals from the pest population of a given location. Frequent application causes a gradual shift in the genetic composition of the pest population, with a gradual increase in the share of resistant individuals. Eventually, the stock of susceptible pests is exhausted, thus rendering the pesticide ineffective. Depending on the relative fitness of the resistant individuals, this process may be reversed over time when the pesticide is no longer applied. However, in most cases of resistance, the susceptibility resource is practically depleted for the typical time horizon that is relevant in agricultural production (Rubin 1996). Therefore, in the following discussion, the susceptibility resource shall be assumed to be quasi-exhaustible because the share of susceptible individuals remains below a critical level where the ecological service provided by the susceptibility resource can become economically relevant.

Once depleted, pest susceptibility is no longer available in terms of effectiveness of a control measure. The intertemporal sum of the services provided by a given stock of an exhaustible resource is finite. If we use the standard resource economic model, optimal resource use would be determined by the total initial stock of the resource, the choke price for the resource, the social discount rate, and the optimal depletion time that is itself a function of the other parameters (Perman et al. 1996).

The economic impacts of resource depletion would be negligible if alternative pest control technologies are equally cost-effective. The choke price for the resource would not differ from the extraction costs, thus rendering the value of the resource stock zero. Farmers could deplete the resource and thereafter simply switch to other control options without suffering economic loss.

The available range of options to control a pest also must be seen as a resource. On the one hand, the availability and the price of substitutes determine the value of the resource stock threatened by depletion through resistance. On the other hand, the range of options might be limited, although in principle new options can become available through the discovery of new technologies. The choke price for the stock of control options is determined by the level of crop protection costs that render a cropping system unprofitable in a given location. A pest simply becomes uncontrollable using available technologies in a cost-effective manner. Examples for such a scenario were experienced in many parts of the world, for example, in cotton production in the United States (NAS 1975), in Latin America (Thrupp 1996), Central Asia (Yudelman et al. 1998), and China and India (Schillhorn van Veen et al. 1997).

Technological progress can postpone resource depletion because the effect is resource augmenting. The total stock of available options can be augmented by both human and physical capital. Human capital improves the management of the resource. The availability of substitute technological options is determined by the direction and rate of technological progress and its related costs.

Present trends in crop protection research and development suggest that the technological progress is driven by the strategies of a small number of large, specialized, multinational firms. High fixed costs of product development and registration create entry barriers to the market for small firms (IVA 1999). Many innovations of nonchemical options such as improved cultural control techniques cannot be appropriated by private firms, which limits their diffusion. In some areas of pest control, the rate of resistance development is currently faster than the supply of new pest control methods. This situation reduces the number of options available in the technology basket.

Moreover, technological progress is at risk of failure because there is the potential that unforeseen negative externalities occur. New technologies with unknown risks are traded against available technologies with risks that, supposedly, are fully known and regarded as manageable.

Decisionmaking in Resistance Management

The individual farmer as a user of pesticides is the final decisionmaker in resistance management. Assuming that externalities and perfect knowledge about the parameters of resistance development are absent and that farm-level decisionmakers appreciate their user costs, resistance could be perfectly internalized into farm-level decisionmaking. However, there is considerable uncertainty involved because of a lack of prior information on the parameters of the resistance development process. This refers both to the biological factors that determine the selection of resistant individuals and to the socioeconomic parameters that determine the economic importance perceived by the farmer, for example the value of substitutive technologies.

A further problem stems from the fact that most models assume a single-pest/single-pesticide relationship. Some pests develop resistance against more than one pesticide even when they have not yet been used (cross-resistance), and some pesticides provoke resistance in more than one pest species (Rubin 1996). The starting date and the path of resistance development cannot be predicted with certainty, although some researchers consider resistance development to be inevitable (Rubin 1996). Therefore, resistance development must be treated in a risk-analytic framework considering options in decision-making at the farm level.

Institutions supporting and governing the information environment and use conditions can directly and indirectly influence resistance management decisions. Neglect of resistance may induce underinvestment in the research and development of alternative options. There is a considerable time lag between the inception of research and readiness for wide adoption. This holds true for output from cutting-edge modern science as well as for adaptive research on agroecosystem management.

In a dynamic context, the expectations of the decisionmakers at both the farm and the research institution level for the parameters of future technological progress are relevant. This makes the discount rate of future costs of adaptation to resource depletion the decisive variable for determining the profitability of resistance management strategies.

The likelihood of concerted resistance management at the community or sector level depends on the magnitude of resistance spread, that is, the extent to which open access to resource use is involved. Regev and others (1976) argued that the greater the mobility of pest populations is, the greater the likelihood that farmers would view pest susceptibility as a common-property resource. Pests and diseases are more likely to be mobile across field margins than are weeds. For pests, farmers have the incentive to completely ignore the consequences of decisions that lead to resistance buildup (Carlson and Wetzstein 1993). Also, the field size is likely to play an important role in the buildup of resistance. On the one hand, larger plots tend to contain resistance within field margins. On the other hand, a structure of small plots may be useful to maintain spatial crop or diversity in varieties.

Conclusions on Determining Variables

Applying a resource economic framework shows that to determine optimal resistance management strategies, at least three variables need to be taken into account: (a) the uncertainty of decisionmakers about the parameters and scale of the economic impact of resource depletion, (b) the direction and rate of technological change, and (c) the extent of common-property characteristics of pest susceptibility and its effects on different groups of farmers when adaptation to resistance spread is required.

Case Study Evidence for Costs of Resistance

The following section presents methodological approaches for measuring the impact of the variables mentioned earlier and empirical evidence from case studies in German agriculture. The first example uses aggregated time-series data from the German farm accountancy network database. This analysis establishes an intertemporal linkage of pesticide use patterns. Growth trends in pesticides can partly be explained by prior usage, which depletes natural resources. Although the database does not allow us to identify a specific resistance variable, it can be assumed that one of the likely causes for rising sector-wide crop protection costs is the frequent appearance of resistance.

The second case study explores the costs of resistance on a specific crop. So far, weed resistance against atrazine has been the most significant case in German agriculture. The analysis shows that the economic value of the susceptibility resource depends on the discount rate. We also discuss the distributional consequences of adaptation to resistance spread.

Measuring Sectorwide Consequences of Short-Term Maximization Strategies in Crop Protection—Pesticide Use in German Agriculture

The approach used in this case study contributes to the debate about the appropriate methodological approach for pesticide productivity assessment. The starting point in this debate was the challenge posed on productivity estimates derived from the conventional Cobb–Douglas function approach by Lichtenberg and Zilberman (1986). They argued for using a damage abatement function approach. Results of productivity estimates differ widely depending on the functional form used. So far, there is no conclusive evidence of the superiority of a specific functional form. One reason for this could be the lack of information about the role that the natural resource base plays in crop protection (Waibel et al. 1999).

In the following discussion, we explore an indirect way to measure the impact of resistance. Resistance has been shown to lead to declining pesticide productivity over time (Carlson 1977). Crop loss must be prevented with an increasing amount of resources, either by increasing the dosage and frequency of a chemical or by switching to more expensive pest control measures. If resistance spreads sectorwide, pest control costs are expected to increase. Higher amounts and more expensive pesticides will be used because these inputs dominate in present crop protection strategies. Thus, we hypothesize an intertemporal linkage between expenses for pest control in prior periods and those in following crop seasons.

The overall development of crop protection costs over time becomes the main indicator for assessing the economic dimension of the resistance problem. Crop protection costs relative to other economic factors should remain constant if no resistance or other forms of resource degradation would occur, or at least if we can control for changes to relative prices of inputs and technological progress. Hence, rising pest control costs—relative to the real costs of other production factors—would indicate economic impacts of resource degradation. In that case, at least part of the observed growth in crop protection costs should not be attributed to productivity increase, but rather must be interpreted as secondary costs of resource depletion. Actual costs of crop protection Z would deviate from the path of sustainable crop protection management S (see Figure 7-1).

The ratio of pesticide costs to fertilizer costs is an indicator of possible resource degradation. In German agriculture, the ratio of expenses for pesticides to those for fertilizer in the sector, both expressed in constant prices, increased constantly (see Figure 7-2). Some of the increase in pesticide use may then be interpreted as a defensive expense against rising crop loss levels, possibly caused by resource degradation that includes resistance.

The growth rate of pesticide use is determined by technological and economic factors as well as changes in the natural resource base.[1] Currently data are too sparse to determine the status of the natural resource base and its changes over time. Therefore, the damage avoidance costs—that is, additional pesticide use in later periods as a consequence of prior intervention—is used as a proxy variable for changes in the natural resource base. Resource degradation must be separated from other factors that affect pesticide use, that is, the ratio of relative commodity and input prices, the level of fertilizer use, technological progress in terms of improved cultivars, and so forth.

To capture the effect of resource degradation on the growth rate of pesticide use, a log-linear econometric model was used. The Farm Accountancy Network of the Federal Agricultural Ministry in West Germany for the period

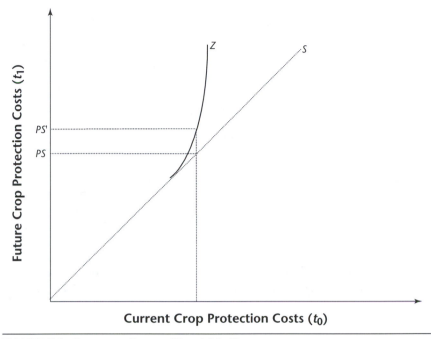

FIGURE 7-1. Resource Costs of Pesticide Use

1981–1982 to 1994–1995 comprises the averages of sample farm data in different farming systems from each of the 42 agroecological zones. On an average over the 14 years covered by the analysis, data from 4,911 farms were available for each year. The model thus pools time-series and cross-sectional data on crop yields, input use, and production costs.

A random-effect regression model is used to determine the influence of all identifiable effects on pesticide use levels, including the proxy variable for resource degradation. Data on populations of pest species and beneficial organisms are not available as part of the farm accountancy database. Therefore, an indirect approach is chosen to assess the impact of resource degradation:

$$\ln PS_t = \beta_1 + \beta_2 PS_{t-1} + \beta_3 \ln Yw_t + \beta_4 F_t + \beta_5 \ln M_t + \beta_6 P_c/P_{ps} + \beta_7 P_c/P_F + \beta_8 D_m + \beta_9 D_S + \beta_{10} D_I + \beta_{11} T + \upsilon$$

where

w = the error term
b = the coeffient on the independent variable in the regression

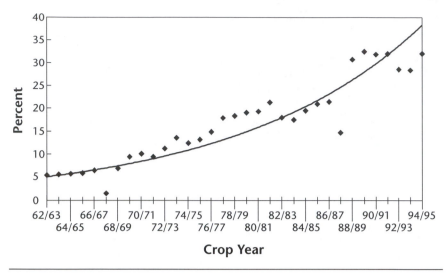

FIGURE 7-2. Development of the Ratio of Expenses for Pesticides and for Mineral Fertilizers in German Agriculture, from 1962–1963 to 1994–1995

PS_t = amount spent on pesticides in German Mark (DM) per hectare in period t
Yw_t = yield of winter wheat in t per hectare
PS_{t-1} = amount spent on pesticides in the prior year
D_m = dummy for agroecological zones in regions of medium altitude
F_t = amount of fertilizer in DM per hectare in period t
M_t = amount of organic manure per hectare in t converted into substitutive fertilizer value
P_c/P_{ps} = ratio of the index of crop prices to pesticide prices
D_S = dummy for agroecological zones in southern areas of higher average temperatures
P_c/P_F = ratio of the index of crop prices to fertilizer prices
D_I = dummy for integrated farms
T = Trend variable

For the analysis, only full-time farms of two types, namely cash crop farms (mainly cereal–sugar beet or cereal–rapeseed rotations) and integrated farms (combinations of arable farming and livestock) were selected. The preparation of the data for the analysis required some assumptions to compute the variables (see Waibel and Fleischer 1997, 1998a). For example, the amount of organic fertilizer, which plays an important role in the mixed farms, is converted into nutrient equivalents of commercial fertilizer and valued at replacement costs. Expenditures on pesticides are related to the area of field crops because pesticide use on pasture is negligible.

Technological change is captured in the increase of the yield potential of winter wheat, which is the leading crop in arable farming. Besides this embodied technological progress, other productivity-enhancing change is expected to be included in the trend variable T. Farms in medium-altitude zones in the central and southwestern part of the country generally have lower levels of input use because of less advantageous climatic and soil conditions. A considerable time lag in adopting technological progress has been observed for those areas, as opposed to lowlands in the northern part and warmer areas in the south. Therefore, a dummy variable is included in the regression.

Table 7-1 shows the results of the regression analysis for the full dataset. The lagged variable of pesticide use in prior periods is, as expected, positive and highly significant. The same is true for the trend variable. Those variables show only a small correlation, which implies that the increase in pesticide use is independent from general technological change in the sector, but rather displays a specific development in crop protection. A stepwise multiple regression demonstrated that the variable PS_{t-1} has the highest explanatory power. The economic variable P_c/P_{ps} confirms the assumption of a positive reaction of farmers to an increase in the ratio of crop prices to pesticide prices. As expected, the yield level of wheat and fertilizer use have a positive influence on pesticide use with a moderate elasticity. The dummy for agroecological zones in medium altitudes also shows the expected sign. Those farms tend to be more diversified with lower levels of pest pressure.

Variations of the model for different groups of agroecological zones did not change the direction of the results. Other variables, such as the ratio of crop to fertilizer prices and dummy variables for integrated farms and southern agroecological zones, were not significant in all model runs. Because the Durbin–Watson coefficient lies between 1.8 and 2.2 in all alternative models, it is unlikely that there is autocorrelation in the residuals.

The hypothesis of an intertemporal relationship in pesticide use cannot be rejected, which suggests that long-run resource degradation actually took place. Resource degradation has two elements: the reduction of the potential

TABLE 7-1. Parameter Estimates for German Farm Accountancy Network Data, from 1981–1982 to 1994–1995 (887 observations)

Constant	PS_{t-1}	Yw_t	F_t	M_t	P_c/P_{ps}	D_m	T	R square
–313**	0.76**	22.5*	0.13**	5.5*	178.41**	–8.6**	4.8**	0.62

Note: *significant at 5% level, ** significant at 1% level

of the agroecosystem for self-regulation (e.g., natural enemies to pests) and the buildup of resistance. The first effect is related to the substitution of chemical pesticides for natural biocontrol, whereas the second is the cost impact of additional pesticide use caused by the reduction in pest susceptibility.

However, the analysis can only serve as a first approximation because the two effects appear inseparable in the database available. The results suggest that more research on the long-term development of the natural resource base must be undertaken.

Factors in Resistance Cost Assessment—Case Study on Resistance against Atrazine

Evidence for the magnitude of adaptation costs to resistance can be derived from the case of the herbicide atrazine, which is the best-studied example of resistance in Germany. Atrazine was used as a preemergence and postemergence herbicide in maize production for more than three decades. Its availability contributed to the rapid increase of the maize area to more than 1 million hectares in the early 1990s. Atrazine was banned in the spring of 1991 with the implementation of stricter guidelines to protect groundwater resources.

Field plot-level data from a representative panel survey of the period 1987 to 1993 showed an increase of costs of maize herbicide use from less than DM 40 million in 1987 to DM 111.7 million for the area of former West Germany (Produkt und Markt 1996). Until its ban, atrazine had been the dominant herbicide in maize growing. Resistance was discovered in field trials in the late 1970s and became widespread in the 1980s. For example, in Bavaria, a major maize growing state, resistance of several weed species against atrazine increased from 5% of the surveyed area in 1983 to more than 60% in 1988 (Kees and Lutz 1991).

Crop rotation is regarded as an important factor in resistance spread because it determines the application frequency of atrazine (Kees and Lutz 1991; Zwerger and Walter 1994). This means that the impact of resistance on the costs of weed control can be isolated by categorizing the fields according to their share of maize in the crop rotation. Sustainable resource use without the development of resistance is expected to occur only with a share of maize in crop rotation of less than one-third (Kees and Lutz 1991). Therefore, maize field plots are differentiated into a group with a low maize cropping intensity (group 1 = less than 30% share of maize in crop rotation), medium maize cropping intensity (group 2 = 30 to 60%), and high maize cropping intensity (group 3 = greater than 60%).

Because the share of maize in the crop rotation in farm plots of group 1 is low, it is assumed that the observed herbicide costs represent the costs of following the path of conserving weed susceptibility to atrazine. Between 1987 and 1990, herbicide treatment costs were on average DM 43.88 per hectare in group 1. C^S in Figure 7-3 depicts the costs of sustainable weed control that remain constant if no resistance occurs. C^R shows the costs of weed control when entering the path of resistance buildup. Farmers increase the share of maize in the crop rotation to achieve short-term profit gains compared with alternative crops, for example, permanent pasture and cereals. C^T shows the costs of the alternative weed control technology.

Average herbicide treatment costs for each group are shown in Table 7-2. Farmers with a high share of maize in their crop rotation (groups 2 and 3) had higher herbicide treatment costs in the years 1987 to 1990 than those in group 1. The cost difference between the groups shows an accelerating path. Farmers used atrazine at a higher dosage, mixed it with other herbicides, or made supplementary treatments of alternative herbicides until the ban came into effect. Because changes in crop yield and prices were negligible,[2] the cost increase in real terms appears to have been caused by farmers' reaction to resistance buildup.

Farmers experienced only part of the costs of resistance buildup because the ban of atrazine in 1991 prevented further use. The available data allow us to model the further cost increase that would have happened while continuing atrazine use. The process is expected to follow a polynomial curve (Zwerger and Walter 1994), inducing an increase of herbicide costs in the same manner. The cost of a complete substitute to atrazine as observed after the ban of atrazine can be taken as the choke price K of complete resource

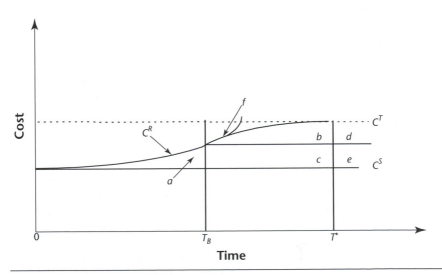

FIGURE 7-3. Costs of Resistance against Atrazine

TABLE 7-2. Average Herbicide Treatment Costs for Field Plots of Different Maize Cropping Intensity (in DM per hectare)*

Group	1987	1990	1991–1993 (average)
		Herbicide treatment costs (product + application)	
1	47.06	42.38	91.88
2	48.63	55.62	94.01
3	53.36	66.34	95.55
		Herbicide treatment frequency	
1	1.55	1.39	1.61
2	1.68	1.82	1.68
3	1.77	2.03	1.87

* Herbicide prices at wholesale level, constant prices of 1985.

Source: Author calculations on the basis of raw data from Produkt und Markt (1996).

depletion. The results demonstrate that the time span of the resistance development is influenced by the pattern of crop rotation that characterizes each group. The total duration of resistance buildup until a full substitution of atrazine is estimated as 15 years for farmers in group 3 and 32 years for group 2 farmers (Fleischer 2000).

The present value PV of the costs of resistance buildup depends on the social discount rate. Full information about the social discount rate would allow us to determine the user costs and the optimal depletion time of the resource. Society's time preference for the conservation of biological capital is not presently known. Following Cline (1992), we can hypothesize that a conservative approach should be taken when natural resource depletion is involved, especially in view of the unknown preferences of future generations. Therefore, a range of discount rates is used to estimate the PV of the costs of resistance buildup. Those costs are determined by the difference in herbicide costs between a path of sustainable resource use C^S and the resistance buildup C^R (Table 7-3). When a low discount rate of 1% as proposed by Cline (1992) is taken, the social costs of resistance exceed the private costs computed at a discount rate of 8%.

Accounting for the costs of resistance buildup also allows us to assess the residual farm-level costs of adjustment to the atrazine ban. Farmers in group 1 faced higher adjustment costs compared with those in the other groups. Farmers adopting a crop rotation with a low share of maize, and thus purposely or involuntarily delaying resistance development, were affected disproportionately by the ban. Farmers in group 1 made up 37% of the land but had to bear 69% of the adjustment costs. Early adopters of a high share of maize in crop rotation contributed more to widespread water pollution that prompted

TABLE 7-3. Present Value of Resistance Buildup Costs of Atrazine Use at Different Discount Rates (DM per hectare)

Intensity group		Discount rate (i)		
		8%	4%	1%
Group 2	Period 1[a]	157	358	713
	Period 2[b]	54	376	3,949
Group 3	Period 1[a]	218	331	463
	Period 2[b]	252	888	5,511

Notes:

a. Present value of the costs from the onset of resistance buildup until technology switch, $PV = \Sigma \, [(C^R - C^S)_t \times (1 + i)^{-t}]$, equivalent to $\Sigma(a + b + c)$ in Figure 7-3.

b. Present value of the costs after the technology switch (permanent loss of option), $PV = \Sigma \, [(C^T - C^S)_t \times (1 + i)^{-t}]$, equivalent to $\Sigma(d + e)$ in Figure 7-3.

the atrazine ban than farmers in group 1. Conversely, farmers who invested in resource conservation and gave up the short-term productivity gains that their fellow farmers in groups 2 and 3 achieved were barred from reaping the returns on their investment.

Conclusion

The theoretical considerations and the empirical studies show the importance of a number of variables for determining resistance management strategies. These are information about the magnitude and economic importance of resistance events, the expectations about the distributional effects through resistance spread, and the impact of adaptation to resistance on the competitive position of producers.

The first case study shows that although there are clear hints toward sector-wide resource degradation in modern crop protection practices, more research is needed to effectively challenge the still widely accepted paradigm that pesticide use can be assessed in a static framework. Future research needs more collaboration across parochial interests of disciplines to produce long-term representative data on changes in agroecosystem parameters that can be analytically tied to changes in the farming system.

The second case study points to the equity implications of resistance development among current and future generations of farmers. Farmers who sacrifice short-term profit maximization for long-term resource conservation have to bear a higher share of the adjustment costs caused by a regulatory decision such as banning a pesticide.

The atrazine case sheds light on the distributional consequences of the current way that pesticide use is regulated. Although the ban on atrazine was not linked to resistance but to its effects on groundwater, it is possible that the economic consequences of the current regulatory approach provide the wrong signals to farmers by making them disregard resource conservation in relation to crop protection.

Policies for better resistance management mostly concentrate on providing more information to decisionmakers to create awareness of the resistance problem. For example, present policies in Germany provide information to farmers in cooperation with the private sector using the moral suasion strategy to make farmers adopt longer-term strategies in pest control (BML 1997). However, this strategy is unlikely to be successful. It has been frequently observed that farmers adopt sustainable pest management strategies only in case of a severe crisis in crop protection although information about long-term negative effects had already been available earlier. Cowan and Gunby (1996) point to the role of network externalities and self-reinforcing mechanisms causing reliance on chemical control, path dependency, and high adjustment costs.

The decisive role of expectations about the future rate of technological progress for determining the economic importance of resistance must be stressed. On the one hand, deterministic models might be unsuitable to reveal the economic importance of the resistance threat as perceived by the farmers. On the other hand, it is likely that stakeholders in the agricultural sector share high expectations in the future availability of technological options, especially chemical pesticides, as induced by endogenous market signals.

Four factors suggest a more conservative approach toward expected benefits from technological progress. First, the ongoing process of consolidation in the agrochemical and life sciences industry, which dominate the market for pest control technologies, may provide disincentives for cooperation and resource conservation strategies. Firms with products in the early stages of the product life cycle push for conquering high market shares to stimulate diffusion in the market segment. Second, the high fixed costs of product registration lead to a narrowing of the total number of pesticides available. Third, regulatory intervention caused by externalities in other fields will trigger further restrictions on the availability of pest control technologies based on chemicals and genetic engineering. Fourth, there should be a focus on overall costs of crop protection for both farmers and society as a whole. Because externalities from resistance are in many cases not incorporated into decisionmaking, markets may provide incentives that are not in line with the social optimum.

In addition to providing information, government policies should view the resource of pest susceptibility as a public good. This would warrant a closer consideration of public investment in research, development, and extension of a broader range of technology options.

Acknowledgements

The authors thank Jan C. Zadoks and three anonymous reviewers for their helpful comments.

References

BML (Bundesministerium für Ernährung, Landwirtschaft und Forsten). 1997. *Risikominderung bei Pflanzenschutzmitteln in Deutschland.* Bonn, Germany: Federal Ministry for Food, Agriculture and Forestry.

Carlson, G. 1977. Long Run Productivity of Insecticides. *American Journal of Agricultural Economics* 59: 543–8.

Carlson, G., and M. Wetzstein. 1993. Pesticides and Pest Management. In *Agricultural and Environmental Resource Economics,* edited by G. Carlson, D. Zilberman, and J. Miranowski. New York: Oxford University Press, 268–318.

Cline, W.R. 1992. *The Economics of Global Warming.* Washington, DC: Institute of International Economics.

Cowan, R., and P. Gunby. 1996. Sprayed to Death—Path Dependence, Locked-In and Pest Control Strategies. *The Economic Journal* 106: 521–42.

Fleischer, G. 2000. Resource Costs of Pesticide Use in Germany. The Case of Atrazine. *Agrarwirtschaft* 49(11): 379–87.

GCPF (Global Crop Protection Federation). 2000. Resistance Action Committees. http://www.gcpf.org (accessed December 12, 2000).

Hueth, D., and U. Regev. 1974. Optimal Agricultural Pest Management with Increasing Pest Resistance. *American Journal of Agricultural Economics* 56: 543–53.

IVA (Industrieverband Agrar). 1999. *Annual Report.* Frankfurt, Germany: IVA.

Kees, H., and A. Lutz. 1991. Zur Problematik der Triazinresistenz bei Samenunkräutern im Mais und in gärtnerischen Kulturen. *Gesunde Pflanzen* 43(7): 216–20.

Lichtenberg, E., and D. Zilberman. 1986. The Econometrics of Damage Control: Why Specification Matters. *American Journal of Agricultural Economics* 68: 261–73.

NAS (National Academy of Sciences). 1975. *Pest Control: An Assessment of Present and Alternative Technologies.* Washington, DC: NAS.

Nevill, D., D. Cornes, and S. Howard. 1998. Weed Resistance. The Role of HRAC in the Management of Weed Resistance. http://plantprotection.org/HRAC/weedresis.htm (accessed December 12, 2000).

Oskam, A.J., R.A.N. Vijftigschild, and C. Graveland. 1997. *Additional EU Policy Instruments for Plant Protection Products—A Report within the Second Phase of the Programme: Possibilities for Future EC Environmental Policy on Plant Protection Products.* Wageningen, The Netherlands: Wageningen Agricultural University.

Pannell, D.J., and D. Zilberman. 2000. *Economic and Sociological Factors Affecting Growers' Decision Making on Herbicide Resistance.* Sustainability and Economics in Agriculture (SEA) Working Paper 00/07. Nedlands, Australia: University of Western Australia.

Pearce, D., and R. Tinch. 1998. The True Price of Pesticides. In *Bugs in the System,* edited by B. Vorley and D. Keeney. London: Earthscan.

Perman, R., Y. Ma, and J. McGilvray. 1996. *Natural Resource and Environmental Economics.* London and New York: Longman.

Pimentel, D., H. Acquay, M. Biltonen, P. Rice, M. Silva, J. Nelson, V. Lipner, S. Giordano, A. Horowitz, and M. D'Amore. 1993. The Pesticide Question—Environment, Economics, and Ethics. In *Assessment of Environmental and Economic Impacts of Pesticide Use*, edited by D. Pimentel and H. Lehman. New York and London: Kluwer, 47–84.

Produkt und Markt. 1996. Panel Data on Pesticide Use in Maize in West Germany, 1985 to 1993. Unpublished report. Wallenhorst, Germany.

Regev, U., A.P. Gutierrez, and G. Feder. 1976. Pests as a Common Property Resource: A Case Study of Alfalfa Weevil Control. *American Journal of Agricultural Economics* 58: 186–97.

Rubin, B. 1996. Herbicide-Resistant Weeds—The Inevitable Phenomenon: Mechanisms, Distribution and Significance. *Zeitschrift für Pflanzenkrankheiten und Pflanzenschutz*, Sonderheft XV: 17–32.

Steiner, R., L. McLaughlin, P. Faeth, and R. Janke. 1995. Incorporating Externality Costs into Productivity Measures. A Case Study Using U.S. Agriculture. In *Agricultural Sustainability: Environmental and Statistical Considerations*, edited by V. Barnett, R. Payne, and R. Steiner. New York: John Wiley, 209–230.

Thrupp, L.A. (ed.). 1996. *New Partnerships for Sustainable Agriculture*. Washington, DC: World Resources Institute.

van den Bosch, R. 1978. *The Pesticide Conspiracy*, Second Edition. Berkeley, CA: University of California Press.

van Schillhorn V., T., D. Forno, S. Joffe, D. Umali-Deininger, and S. Cooke. 1997. *Integrated Pest Management. Strategies and Policies for Effective Implementation*. Environmentally and Sustainable Development Studies and Monographs Series No. 13. Washington, DC: The World Bank.

Waibel, H., and G. Fleischer. 1997. Incorporating User Costs into the Assessment of Pesticide Productivity. In *Proceedings of the Wageningen Workshop on Pesticides, EU Concerted Action on Policy Measures for the Control of Environmental Impacts*, edited by A. Oskam and R. Vijftigschild. Wageningen, The Netherlands: Wageningen Agricultural University.

———. 1998a. Economic Specification for Production Ecology. Consideration of Dynamic and Intergenerational Aspects in Pest Management Research In *Active Methodology. Proceedings of a Seminar Series 1997/98*, edited by A. Stein, M.K. van Ittersum, and G.H.J. de Koning. Agricultural University: Quantitative Approaches in Systems Analysis No. 19. Wageningen, The Netherlands: Wageningen Agricultural University, DLO Research Institute for Agrobiology and Soil Fertility, and the C.T. de Wit Graduate School of Production Ecology, 41–53.

———. 1998b. *Kosten und Nutzen des chemischen Pflanzenschutzes in der deutschen Landwirtschaft aus gesamtwirtschaftlicher Sicht*. (Cost-Benefit Analysis of Pesticide Use in German Agriculture and Pesticides Produced in Germany for Major World Crops). Kiel, Germany: Vauk-Verlag.

Waibel, H., G. Fleischer, and H. Becker. 1999. The Economic Benefits of Pesticides: A Case Study from Germany. *Agrarwirtschaft* 48(6): 219–30.

Yudelman, M., A. Ratta, and D. Nygaard. 1998. *Pest Management and Food Production. Looking to the Future*. Food, Agriculture and the Environment Discussion Paper 25. Washington, DC: International Food Policy Research Institute.

Zwerger, P., and H. Walter. 1994. Modelle zum Management herbizidresistenter Unkrautpopulationen. *Zeitschrift für Pflanzenkrankheiten und Pflanzenschutz*, Sonderheft XIV: 409–20.

Notes

1. Additionally, there may be an impact of more stringent environmental regulations that increases the costs of pesticide registration for manufacturers. However, incorporating a dummy variable for the year 1986 when the plant protection law was revised and more stringent registration criteria came into effect yielded no significant results in the regression model explained later in the chapter.

2. Because of price stabilization in the Common Agricultural Policy Framework of the European Union, crop and livestock prices remained stable. A large share of the maize crop is used as on-farm fodder resource for hog, beef, and dairy farming. Results from research trials showed that other herbicides as well as mechanical weed control are equally effective as atrazine.

Commentary

Can We Justify Resistance Management Strategies for Conventional Pesticides?

Fred Gould

Fleischer and Waibel (Chapter 7) explain that the justification for regional programs aimed at decreasing the rate at which pests adapt to insecticides is uncertain. In their chapter, they mention two extreme, general situations. In the first, there is no need for regional resistance management programs "(a) when perfect information on all parameters of the biological process of resistance development is available [to farmers and others] and (b) when externalities are absent, such as in the case of the spread of resistance from one farm to other economic units." In the second general situation, these two conditions are not met and resistance in a pest results in a cropping system that becomes unprofitable. In most agricultural systems, little is known about the degree to which the properties of the system match one or more of these extreme characteristics. Without such information, there will always be debate about the utility of resistance management. Even if we had this information, more specific biological, economic, and social factors will determine the justification for a resistance management program.

Fleischer and Waibel review previous work on assessing the utility of resistance management and then take a resource economics perspective in analyzing the attributes of two case studies. I will first comment on the case studies and then make more general observations from an agricultural biologist's perspective.

In the first case study, the authors extend the logic of Carlson (1977), who pointed out that resistance can lead to decreased productivity of pesticides over time, either because of the need to increase the use of the chemical to which resistance is developing or because of the need to adopt a more expensive pesticide. Fleischer and Waibel provide a very general analysis of German agriculture from 1962 through 1995, in which they test the null hypothesis that pesticide expenses have been maintained constant relative to expenses for mineral fertilizers. Assuming that the productivity of fertilizers is not being eroded, failure to reject the null hypothesis indicates that pesticide productivity is relatively constant and has not been affected by evolution of pest resistance. The analysis does reject the null hypothesis and demonstrates that the relative expense of pesticides has increased dramatically. Fleischer and Waibel conclude that this increase in pesticide expense could be caused by resistance or decline in natural agents that control pests and that further research is needed to determine the contribution of each of these factors.

I have two concerns about this study. One is technical, and the other is more general. First, I am concerned about the data on pesticide use that were used in this study. If pesticides include herbicides, there was a great increase in the general use of herbicides between 1962 and 1995 as a substitute for mechanical cultivation (National Research Council 2000). It could be that the entire increase in pesticide expense found by Fleischer and Waibel is caused by the herbicide substitution factor. It would, therefore, be useful to analyze pesticides disaggregated into herbicides, insecticides, and fungicides.

My second concern is with the underlying assumption that if pesticide expense in a farming system remains constant as a proportion of production expenses, there is no economic impact of resistance. My general sense is the cost of insecticides (per pound of active ingredient) within a class of insecticidal chemistry (e.g., organophosphates) decreases as a function of the number of years since the class of chemistry was introduced. For example, the cost of pyrethroids in the late 1970s was approximately $15 per acre of cotton sprayed. The average cost of pyrethroids in North Carolina between 1995 and 2000 was $5.25 per acre sprayed (Bacheler 2000). In comparison, Tracer, a pesticide in a new class of chemistry, currently costs $15.82 per acre of application. Tracer is used in cotton-growing areas where the caterpillar pest, *Heliothis virescens*, has developed resistance to pyrethroids (e.g., Mississippi, Arkansas, and Alabama, but not North Carolina). Examining the general cost of insecticide use in areas that now have pyrethroid resistance, the price in 2000 is unlikely to be substantially higher than in 1977. However, if there had been no resistance in those areas, the price in 2000 might have been only one-third of the price in 1977. In this case, the assumption that a constant expenditure demonstrates a lack of a cost from resistance is faulty. Unless a study can directly estimate the expenditure for an insecticide with and without resistance, it will be difficult to determine the economic impact of resistance.

In Fleischer and Waibel's second case study, a more specific situation is assessed: the impact of atrazine resistance on three groups of corn farmers with low, moderate, and high use of atrazine. Because only a low fraction of most weeds' seeds move from farm to farm, each farmer generates most of his or her own resistance problem. Farmers with the most intense use of atrazine are expected to use up the resource of susceptible weeds on their land faster than will other farmers. In this specific case, atrazine was banned from use for environmental reasons at a time when resistance had already devalued the chemical for intense users but not for those with low use. If atrazine had not been banned, the intense users would have incurred a cost from heavy reliance on atrazine, but instead, all farmers had to switch to new chemistry at the same time because of the ban. This resulted in a net gain for the intense users compared with the low-use farmers.

This curious result emphasizes the need for any analysis to consider who bears the cost of pesticide resistance. In some cases, those who get the benefits also bear the costs; in other cases, the distribution of costs does not match the distribution of benefits. Should society intercede to make the beneficiaries pay a fair share of the cost? The current study only examines the effects on farmers, but consumers and the environment are also stakeholders.

So what are the costs and benefits of pesticide resistance to the environment? During the battle over banning DDT, resistance to the chemical already had developed in major, targeted agricultural pests and disease vectors (Brown 1971). It may be that because the benefits of DDT were declining, the case not to ban DDT failed more quickly. If we assume that the replacements for DDT were less harmful to the environment than DDT, it can be argued that DDT resistance benefited the environment. Because the U.S. Environmental Protection Agency has tightened environmental regulations for commercialization of new pesticides, it could be argued that pesticide resistance generally benefits the environment, with each replacement pesticide being more benign than the pesticide it replaces. The counterargument is that for older classes of pesticides, experience has uncovered many expected and unexpected negative effects, and we now know how to protect humans and the environment from these effects. In contrast, for new pesticides, we only know that the expected negative effects are low. We have not used these new pesticides long enough to know if there will be unanticipated effects (National Research Council 2000).

References

Bacheler, J. 2000. Cotton Notes. http://ipm.ncsu.edu/cotton/insectcorner/slideshow/sld042.htm (accessed March 8, 2002).

Brown, A.W.A. 1971. Pest Resistance to Pesticides. In *Pesticides in the Environment*, volume 1, part II, edited by R. White-Stevens. New York: Marcel-Dekker, 457–552.

Carlson, G.A. 1977. Long-Run Productivity of Insecticides. *American Journal of Agricultural Economics* 59(3): 543–48.

National Research Council. 2000. *The Future Role of Pesticides in U.S. Agriculture.* Washington, DC: National Academy Press.

Chapter 8

Pesticide Resistance, the Precautionary Principle, and the Regulation of *Bt* Corn

Real Option and Rational Option Approaches to Decisionmaking

Benoît Morel, R. Scott Farrow, Felicia Wu, and Elizabeth A. Casman

Few attempts have been made to place the recently advocated precautionary principle in an analytical framework. If successfully developed, such a framework could prove useful to decisionmakers precisely in situations such as the regulation of *Bt* corn, including concern for pest resistance, and numerous other decisions involving scientific uncertainty and large or irreversible costs. This chapter (a) summarizes how economic option theories can be used to structure regulatory decisionmaking under uncertainty and irreversibility, (b) links that structure to the precautionary principle, (c) shows how pest resistance development affects the options analysis, and (d) demonstrates the impact of pest resistance development and the option framing for *Bt* corn.

Our empirical application is the decision to allow commercialization of *Bt* corn. Building from a static model of technological change, we add the dynamic components of pest resistance modeled as a form of depreciation of the investment in *Bt* corn and of other elements of value. Using data related to *Bt* corn, we present preliminary results indicating that a standard cost–benefit analysis supports the regulatory decision to commercialize *Bt* corn, although an options analysis would likely reach the opposite conclusion because the benefits do not sufficiently exceed the costs when taking future uncertainties and irreversible costs into consideration. The impact of pest resistance, when modeled as occurring with a mean arrival rate of 12 years, has a measurable impact on the economic evaluation, but the largest impact comes from the use of the option framework.

Revolutionary technological breakthroughs can generate serious challenges to policymakers because uncertainties involving technology, health, market behavior, and the environment are frequently present. The advent of genetically modified crops is a recent, particularly acute example. When policymakers approve the commercialization of genetically modified organisms (GMOs), they are making decisions with uncertain and possibly irreversible consequences, both for better and worse. Recent events in the use of one GMO, *Bt* corn (corn that has been genetically modified to express an insecticide of bacterial origin), exemplify some of the uncertainties. These include the potential for the development of pest resistance to the *Bt* toxin, changes in economic well-being, impacts on nontarget species, public perception, and more.

There is, however, no accepted paradigm for advising decisionmakers in such a situation. Current regulatory practice evaluates what risks may exist (see, for example, EPA 2001; USDA 1997a, 1997b; FDA 1998). Some analysts may go further and seek to value those risks by generating information relevant to the cost–benefit paradigm (Hyde et al. 1999; Minor et al. 1999). However, a group of advocates supports the application of a precautionary principle to decisions with large scientific uncertainties and large or irreversible costs, including the regulation of GMOs. Although many versions of the principle exist, a succinct version states that when an activity raises threats of harm to human health or the environment, precautionary measures should be taken even if some cause-and-effect relationships are not established scientifically (Goklany 2000). A stringent and controversial version of the principle is described in the Wingspread statement: "Uncertainty about risk requires forbidding the potentially risky activity until the proponent of the activity demonstrates that it poses *no risk*" (Wiener forthcoming). In contrast, the European Union has released a communication that descriptively places the precautionary principle within the bounds of risk analysis (Commission of the European Union 2000).

To date, there have been few, if any, attempts to place the precautionary principle within an analytically tractable framework that could be used in policy and regulatory analysis. If successfully developed, such a framework could prove useful to decisionmakers precisely in situations such as the regulation of *Bt* corn, other GMOs, and numerous other decisions involving scientific uncertainty and large or irreversible costs. This chapter (a) summarizes how economic option theories can be used to structure the regulatory decision-making issues surrounding *Bt* corn (the example of *Bt* corn is used in this chapter to bring specificity to the issue of regulatory decisions in the presence of uncertainty), (b) demonstrates how that structure can be interpreted as quantifying the precautionary principle, (c) shows how pest resistance development to *Bt* corn affects the options analysis by adding a technological depreciation factor and reducing the lifetime of the technology, and (d) demonstrates with illustrative data related to *Bt* corn how the options approach might yield a different regulatory recommendation than a standard cost–benefit analysis.

Pest Resistance Development in *Bt* Corn

"If there is an assumption that the *Bt* toxins will inevitably lose their efficacy through massive expression in transformed crops, this is unacceptable to the organic community. This objection is based not just on direct self-interest but also on general grounds of sound science policy" (Lipson 1999).

Bt toxin is a naturally occurring insecticide produced by the soil bacterium *Bacillus thuringiensis* that has been commercially available primarily for the control of lepidopteran (moths and butterflies) agricultural pests for more than 40 years. Very little pest resistance development was ever observed over this time mainly because of the intermittent application patterns used and the toxin's rapid degradation in the environment, especially when exposed to light (NAS 2000). *Bt* corn is genetically modified to contain a modified transgene for *Bt* toxin along with regulatory and promoter transgenes, which allow the corn to produce *Bt* toxin on a more or less continuous basis. The toxin is produced inside the plant tissues, and the bulk of it is protected from photolysis.

With repeated use, all pesticides are expected to lose their efficacy as selective pressures favor the survival and reproductive success of resistant individuals. By increasing the duration of exposure and in some cases by delivering inadequate toxin doses to target pest populations, *Bt* corn is feared to exert greater selective pressure on insect populations to develop resistance to *Bt* compared with the transient, external applications favored before the advent of *Bt* corn.

If pests become resistant to *Bt* corn, the loss is twofold. First, society will have lost the use of a plant-incorporated protectant believed to be more ecologically friendly than conventional pesticides. Second, growers, especially organic growers, might no longer be able to use the microbial *Bt* sprays that are considered some of their few acceptable pesticides if pest resistance to *Bt* spread to those farms. Microbial *Bt* spray formulations are reported to be the single most important off-farm input of organic growers for insect pest management. For nine upper-Midwest states, recent national survey results indicated that 25% of certified organic growers in these states use *Bt* "frequently" or "occasionally." For certified organic field crop producers in this region, the number is 20%; for organic fruit crops it is 52%; and for vegetable operations in this area, 48% of the growers use *Bt* frequently or occasionally (EPA/USDA 1999).

Because of these risks, EPA has enacted insect resistance management requirements intended to delay resistance and to prolong the efficacy of *Bt* corn. In its most recent Biopesticides Registration Action Document for *Bt* corn (EPA 2001), EPA confirmed a resistant *Bt* event if experiments on pests exhibit all of the following characteristics: (a) there is less than 30% survival and less than 25% leaf area damaged in a five-day bioassay using Cry1Ab-positive or Cry1F-positive leaf tissue under controlled laboratory conditions (Cry1Ab and Cry1F are two of the hundreds of *Bt* toxin varieties), (b) standardized laboratory bioassays using diagnostic doses for European corn borer, Southwest corn borer, and corn earworm demonstrate that resistance has a genetic basis and survivorship in excess of 1% (gene frequency of population less than 0.1), and (c) a lethal concentration resulting in 50% mortality (LC_{50}) in a standard Cry1Ab or Cry1F diet bioassay exceeds the upper limit of the 95% confidence interval of the standard unselected laboratory population LC_{50} for susceptible European corn borer, Southwest corn borer, or corn earworm populations, as established by the ongoing baseline monitoring system. Currently, EPA requires a high dose and refuge strategy to slow or prevent resistance development. As implemented, this strategy requires that growers plant only cultivars expressing high concentrations of toxin and that growers plant a "refuge" of non-*Bt* corn occupying an area at least 20% of the size of the *Bt* corn planting. The refuges may be treated with insecticides. If the refuges are not treated with pesticides, they only need to be 5% the size of the *Bt* planting. The refuge planting options include separate fields, blocks within fields, or strips across the field within one-half mile of the *Bt* corn (EPA 2001). The purpose of the refuge is to provide a source of *Bt*-susceptible pests that could mate with potentially resistant pests emerging from nearby *Bt* corn. The goal is to produce an overwhelming number of susceptible pests (heterozygous and homozygous) to every resistant pest (Alstad and Andow 1995; NAS 2000). However, this strategy is based on the assumption that resistance to *Bt* corn is a recessive trait. In fact, resistance could be inherited as an incompletely dominant autosomal allele, in which case, resistance in a pest population will grow more quickly than anticipated (Huang et al. 1999). However, Huang and others (1999) observed this genetic dominance at lower *Bt* doses than are delivered by high-dose *Bt* corn.

Though infrequent, resistance to *Bt* toxins has been observed in wild lepidopteran populations. Gould and others (1997) reported the frequency of resistance alleles in *Heliothis virescens* populations at about 0.0015, and Tabashnik and others (1997) reported a frequency of 0.120 in diamondback moth populations.

Pest resistance development is one of many factors that adds uncertainty to the problem of regulating *Bt* corn. Other uncertainties may involve human health effects from consumption of the *Bt* corn or from reductions in the use of other pesticides, the degree of pest protection and the resulting cost savings, reductions in mycotoxin damage, harm to nontarget species, unintended gene transfer, and the price of corn (conventional or *Bt*), among others. Although not mandated in the current approach to registering GMOs, economic analysis provides a method to combine these disparate factors at the cost of introducing yet more uncertainty associated with the monetary value of the factors.

Recent advances in decisionmaking under conditions of uncertainty and irreversible impacts are the basis of options analysis and often take the form of when to delay taking an action compared with acting. The result can be a different decision criterion than that of standard cost–benefit analysis and one that is consistent with some of the concerns of precautionary principle advocates. In the *Bt* corn application, uncertainty is clearly prevalent, but the irreversibility is subject to debate.

Regarding irreversibility, once commercial plantings of *Bt* corn are allowed, in the short term it may be difficult to reverse either the impacts or the decision to replace traditional agriculture.[1] In the medium to longer term, there may be regulatory irreversibilities, human health impacts, other biological irreversibilities that in the extreme could include extinction, and economic irreversibilities if some inputs used for organic farming become ineffective. Alternative framings of what is irreversible may exist, such as environmental impacts (Farrow and Morel 2001).

Pest resistance has the potential to affect several of these uncertainties and irreversibilities, although its extent will depend on how quickly resistance may develop, the discount rate used to assess societal value of *Bt* corn over its technological lifetime, the rate of substitution of *Bt* events, the spread of resistance geographically, and the reversibility of the emergence of resistance.

The remaining sections of this chapter will develop these economic approaches, link them to specific issues related to *Bt* corn, and preliminarily address the question of whether an options analysis would be likely to produce a different recommendation than a standard expected net (benefit less cost) present value analysis, in which present value refers to combining a stream of net benefits into the values of a particular year.

Option Theory

Option theory was primarily developed in the context of financial decisions, but it is increasingly clear that it has wider application. This chapter applies the option theory paradigm to the regulatory decision of whether to allow *Bt* corn to be commercially grown.

Option theory is not a monolithic paradigm. It has at least two variations. Although it is very important to be aware of their differences, these two versions cannot be completely separated. One of those approaches is referred to as "real options" (e.g., Dixit and Pindyck 1994). We will refer to the other as "rational" or "financial options" (e.g., Hull 2000). Real option theory is an optimization procedure, and rational option theory leads to the Black–Scholes formula based on risk neutrality.

Real Options

The real option theory applies typically to irreversible investments under uncertainty. Assume one is making an investment that will be productive (benefit B) with a probability p and unproductive (loss L) with probability $1 - p$: if the investment is made immediately, its expected net present value is $pB - (1 - p)L$. However, if the investment is not made until it is revealed as productive or not and the uncertainty is completely resolved, the expected net present value of the same investment under that policy is pB (minus the possible cost of waiting). As long as the cost of waiting or of gathering additional information is less than the difference between the net present values of the two policies, delaying the decision to invest is beneficial. The difference is the value of the information.[2] It is also the value of the option of waiting.

There is a real options formulation of the same insight in continuous time: if I is the cost of the investment, and V the value of the investment, assume that the value of the investment follows a geometric Brownian motion stochastic process, as follows:

$$dV = \alpha V dt + \sigma V dz \tag{1}$$

where dt is a small increment of time and dz is the increment of a Wiener process. In words, this means that the value of the investment increases with time at an average rate α, but with a volatility of σ. The idea is to maximize the discounted expected value of the return of the investment and, therefore, is independent of any degree of risk aversion, that is, to maximize $F(V) = E[e^{-\rho t}(V - I)]$ where E is the expectations operator. This is a problem of optimization under uncertainty. The solution is that the best policy depends on the relative value of the average rate of growth of V, α, and the discount rate ρ:

1. If $\alpha < 0$, the decision is now or never, as the value of the investment only decreases with time.
2. If $\alpha > \rho$, the best policy is to wait forever because the value of $F(V)$ never stops growing.
3. The "interesting case" occurs when $0 < \alpha < \rho$; then the best policy is to wait for the time when the value V of the investment becomes larger than a critical value V^*, such that

$$V^* = \Gamma I \tag{2}$$

where Γ is the "precautionary" multiplier. Γ is the result of the optimization and is an increasing function of the volatility σ and the other parameters of the problem. It can be shown to be greater than or equal to one, which is its basic link to the precautionary principle (when the volatility $\sigma = 0$, $\Gamma = 1$).

Consider the properties of Γ and how it relates to concerns that motivate the precautionary principle. If there is no uncertainty ($\sigma = 0$), then Γ equals one, and the usual economic criterion (invest if the benefit exceeds the cost) applies. As uncertainty increases, the multiplier increases, and a decision-maker is less likely to take action because the observed value V is less likely to exceed V^*. Scale is also important. The larger the irreversible costs I, the larger the benefits must be as the cost is multiplied by the precautionary multiplier Γ. Therefore, we suggest that Γ can be used as an empirical measure of precaution, a measure that is associated with a missing benefit value in a standard economic analysis: the option value of waiting for more information.

Rational Options

The more dominant option paradigm for assessing the value of an option determines a risk-neutral portfolio. The typical problem is to assess the value of a buy (call) or sell (put) option on a share of a stock with exercise time T some time in the future. The one paying for the option of buying or selling at the exercise time (for the agreed price) pays for the right of exercising the option when the time comes. The one who accepts the money for the option must comply with the decision. The value of the option is given by the Black–Scholes formula:

$$H(V,T;t) = V(t)\varphi(d_1) - e^{-\rho t} I\varphi(d_2) \tag{3}$$

In that formula, $V(t)$ is the value of the share at time t, ρ is the riskless rate of return, I is the exercise price (analogous to the irreversible cost in the real options paradigm), T is the exercise time, and

$$\varphi(d) = \frac{1}{\sqrt{\pi}} \int_{-\infty}^{d} e^{-x^2} dx \tag{4}$$

$$d_1 = \frac{1}{\sigma\sqrt{(T-t)}} \left\{ Log\left[\frac{V(t)}{I}\right] + \left(\rho + \frac{\sigma^2}{2}\right)(T-t) \right\} \tag{5a}$$

$$d_2 = d_1 - \sigma\sqrt{(T-t)} \tag{5b}$$

When deriving this formula, $V(t)$ is typically assumed to follow the geometric Brownian motion of Equation 1. The average rate of growth of the share a does not appear in the Black–Scholes formula (Equation 3). This reflects a fundamental feature of the formula: it assumes risk neutrality based on a portfolio approach in which it is assumed that the value of the portfolio changes at the same rate as the riskless bond, which here is ρ. This is an important insight because it points to the fundamental difference between this approach, which is based on the assumption of risk neutrality, and the real options approach, which is an optimization.

The precautionary principle was invoked to focus interest on the precautionary multiplier Γ in the real options analysis. What about the relevance of the rational options theory to the precautionary principle? The insurance analogy is meaningful. When an individual decides to purchase an insurance policy, he or she may be viewed as proceeding from a precautionary principle, and the premium of the insurance policy is computed in a similar way as a put option. In that sense, rational option theory provides a different quantitative framing of the precautionary principle. Rational option theory is also particularly appropriate for risk management because it is based on identifying a "risk-neutral" strategy, that is, a strategy that involves a level of risk comparable with a riskless investment. In the case of *Bt* corn, some may consider the riskless approach to be growing non-*Bt* corn using conventional pesticides (i.e., not commercializing *Bt* corn).

The Static Economic Core of Analyzing *Bt* Corn

A standard cost–benefit analysis proceeds by identifying various static impacts of an action. The numerous impacts can be associated with categories of change in economic welfare (Zerbe and Dively 1994). The driving commercial purpose for the case at hand is that *Bt* corn provides protection against the European corn borer. This protection can be thought of as a technological change that reduces the cost of growing a given level of the commodity. Such impacts are well understood in static cost–benefit analysis, which we use as a starting point before proceeding to the dynamic analysis associated with real options. The areas A through G in Figure 8-1 are associated with parts of consumer and producer surplus in either the before or after commercialization state of the world. Table 8-1 identifies the welfare impacts comparing *Bt* and traditional corn, assuming in this figure that the price for each corn will be the same (an assumption relaxed in the empirical portion).

Static externality effects, such as the potential for mycotoxin reduction or for harm to nontarget species, are typically estimated independently of Figure 8-1. Taken together, these categories provide the static empirical structure for estimating the total value based on a comparison of the corn market and its associated externalities with and without a policy allowing the commercial

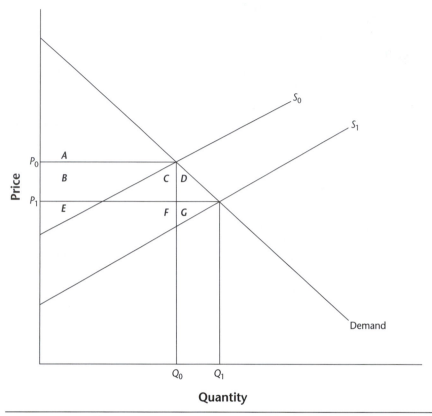

FIGURE 8-1. Welfare Effects of Cost-Saving Technological Change

TABLE 8-1. Welfare Impacts of Technological Change

Welfare measure	Traditional corn	Bt corn	Change in welfare
Consumer surplus	A	$A + B + C + D$	$B + C + D$
Producer surplus	$B + E$	$E + F + G$	$F + G - B$
Total surplus	$A + B + E$	$A + B + C + D + E + F + G$	$F + G + C + D$

production of *Bt* corn. The time-dependent aspects of the problem—pest resistance and the change in value—are discussed in the following sections.

Option Theory Applied to the Decision To Permit Commercialization of *Bt* Corn

In this section, we adapt the real and the rational option framework to a regulatory decision on whether to commercialize *Bt* corn. The algorithms of both real option theory and rational option theory depend on the dynamics of the evolution of the total value of *Bt* corn, but each algorithm is affected differently.

The Real Option Perspective

A foundation of the option value, in contrast to standard cost–benefit analysis, is the specification of the stochastic dynamics of the key variables. The first question is what general form should be given to the evolution of the value of commercialized *Bt* corn.[3] Is it legitimate to model it as a geometric Brownian motion, as was the case in our theoretical discussion of these two paradigms?

Geometric Brownian motion for the present value of *Bt* commercialization gives

$$dB = \mu B dt + \eta B dz_B \qquad (6)$$

where B represents the net present social value of *Bt* corn, the drift μ represents the average growth in value, and the volatility term η measures the uncertainty.

What do we know about the two parameters μ and η? Underlying the drift parameter μ is the evolution of the total (consumer plus producer) surplus of corn. Analogous to the size of total surplus in the well-known diamonds and water paradox in which total surplus is larger for the good with the lower price, in recent decades, we empirically observed a constant or declining price of corn, increasing production, and an increasing total surplus. What is good for the consumer is not necessarily good for the farmer. We assume that the total surplus in the corn market evolved at the same percentage rate as total production, in other words, there was a unitary elasticity between percentage changes in production and percentage changes in total surplus. Based on an analysis of corn and price production trends,[4] as U.S. production is estimated to be increasing at a rate of 2.4% per year, we assume that same value for the growth parameter of total surplus. This is strictly true only if the two production methods have the same fixed costs.

In both cases (real and rational options), the volatility η plays an important role. In the case of the real option formulation, it is a component of the precautionary multiplier determining how much the actual value of the policy should be above its cost to justify taking action.[5]

The structure of Equation 6 provides restrictions that assist in the estimation of η. Estimation of this term has been an important issue in the finance literature (Campbell et al. 1997), in which the variance of a variable such as B has sometimes been substituted incorrectly for the instantaneous variance of the diffusion process. It can be shown that dB is log normally distributed with a time-dependent variance. However, a variance-stabilizing transformation is that of $d \ln B$, which follows simple Brownian motion (Campbell, Lo, and MacKinley 1997, 362) such that the estimate of $\hat{\eta}^2$ can be based on the sample variance of $d \ln B$

$$\hat{\eta}^2 = \frac{1}{N} \sum_{n=1}^{N} (d \ln B - \overline{d \ln B})^2 \tag{7}$$

A cost–benefit model that generates a stochastic time series can then be used to construct estimates of $d \ln B$ and to estimate $\hat{\eta}^2$ from Equation 7.[6]

In general, we will compare the net present social value from planting Bt corn in comparison with current production methods (a mixture of pesticide applications and benign neglect). If P represents the value of the present way of growing corn, it too may evolve as geometric Brownian motion based on the growth in total surplus. We thus assume

$$dP = \gamma P dt + \sigma P dz_P \tag{8}$$

Correlation between the stochastic processes for B and P is also likely because many of the same elements of weather and demand affect them both. It would be anticipated that shocks in net value caused by the European corn borer would be reduced for Bt corn, although other shocks such as price processes and shocks caused by external effects may be larger for Bt corn.

Thus Equations 6 and 8 represent the dynamic evolution of both Bt and traditional corn production. In the empirical application that follows, we assume the rate of growth of both to be approximately the same, 2.5% (setting μ equal to γ, see footnote 4).

The second dynamic issue is pest resistance development. The real option framework addresses the question of when, if ever, to act when confronted with an irreversible decision under uncertainty. The rate of development and spread of insect resistance to Bt toxins may be a large source of uncertainty and some of the irreversibility. As the sublethal use of an antibiotic can select for bacteria resistant to that antibiotic, one predictable effect of growing Bt corn is the emergence of pests resistant to Bt toxin, a biological issue described earlier. Thus, growing Bt corn has the potential to decrease the amount of time during which Bt can be used as a pesticide. Increasing resistance introduces a spatial and temporal *limit* to the efficacy of Bt corn (and potentially to the use of other Bt formulations). But the time limit itself is not known and could depend on the regulatory policy adopted. However, in our simplified model, we represent the development of resistance to Bt as instantaneous, ubiquitous, and irreversible, an approach that would provide an upper bound on its importance in the decision process. For instance, resistance is more likely to develop locally and radiate through parts of the corn growing areas, achieving a patchy distribution (Park et al. 2001). Furthermore, if resistance is detected before it has become widespread (for instance by using insect resistance monitoring techniques), remedial actions are available to slow or halt the spread of resistant insects (e.g., change in pesticide regimen and crop rotation). Thus, resistance would not truly be ubiquitous or necessarily persist irreversibly.

Our approach is to model the influence of pest resistance on the lifetime of *Bt* corn as a form of "depreciation" (Dixit and Pindyck 1994, 200). That is, we assume that the stopping time when resistance is complete is random and follows a Poisson process. If the resistance has not emerged at time *T*, we assume that there is a probability λdT that this will happen during the next interval of time *dT*. The probability density function of such an event, therefore, is $\lambda e^{-\lambda T}$ with the estimated mean rate of arrival[7] of resistance (λ) equal to $1/T$. This is effectively a steady state modeling approach that ignores the transition states of partial and increasing resistance. It is as if the resistance jumps from no resistance to complete resistance. However, this form of depreciation has a mathematically equivalent effect on expected present value, as would geometrically declining productivity caused by gradually increasing resistance.

We will now characterize the real options solution to the decision of whether to commercialize *Bt* corn, including the characterization of pest resistance development. In the real option approach, the expression to maximize is the payoff between the social value of growing *Bt* corn (*B*) and of growing conventional corn (*P*):

$$F(B,P) = E\left[e^{-\rho t}(B - P)\right] \tag{9}$$

The solution to this maximization problem is outlined in Appendix A. The result is that the optimal time to allow for commercialization of *Bt* corn occurs when the social value of *Bt* corn and the value of the conventional crop exceed the threshold relationship

$$\left(\frac{B}{P}\right)^* = \frac{\beta}{\beta - 1} = \Gamma \tag{10}$$

This is a modified cost–benefit criteria, with β defined in Equation 11

$$\beta_+ = \frac{-\left(\mu - \gamma - \dfrac{\eta^2 - 2\xi\eta\sigma + \sigma^2}{2}\right)}{\left\{\eta^2 - 2\xi\eta\sigma + \sigma^2\right\}} + \frac{\sqrt{\left(\mu - \gamma - \dfrac{\eta^2 - 2\xi\eta\sigma + \sigma^2}{2}\right)^2 + 2(\rho - \gamma)\left\{\eta^2 - 2\xi\eta\sigma + \sigma^2\right\}}}{\left\{\eta^2 - 2\xi\eta\sigma + \sigma^2\right\}} \tag{11}$$

Note that the denominator is the variance of the difference of two correlated random variables with ξ denoting the correlation. If dB and dP are perfectly correlated, and their volatility is of the same size, then it is as if the uncertainty disappears in the choice between Bt and non-Bt corn and the precautionary multiplier approaches 1. As noted in Appendix A, $\beta > 1$ (and hence the precautionary multiplier $\Gamma > 1$) holds as long as $\rho > \mu$.

Where does resistance appear? If π is the instantaneous social value with Bt corn, the expected present value profit (Π) ignoring resistance is

$$E[\Pi(T)] = \int_0^T e^{-\rho t} \pi(t) dt = \pi_0 \int_0^T e^{(\mu-\rho)t} dt = \pi_0 \frac{\left[1 - e^{(\mu-\rho)T}\right]}{(\rho-\mu)} \tag{12}$$

Because we modeled the depreciation by a Poisson process, the probability density that T will be the duration of the project is $\lambda e^{-\lambda T}$. The "value" B of the project of growing Bt corn taking into account the potential for resistance is then (using Equation 12)

$$B = \int_0^\infty E[\Pi(T)] \lambda e^{-\lambda T} dT = \frac{\pi_0}{(\rho-\mu) + \lambda} \tag{13}$$

When combined with the decision threshold for action of Equation 10, the level of precaution (Γ) has not changed, although the measured cost–benefit ratio (B/P) is smaller because of incorporating resistance. The probability of passing the threshold has thus been reduced as inferred from Equation 14 where commercialization is allowed if

$$\left(\frac{\pi_0}{\{(\rho-\mu) + \lambda\}P}\right) > \left(\frac{B}{P}\right)^* = \frac{\beta}{\beta-1} = \Gamma \tag{14}$$

The Rational Option Perspective

In the alternative rational option approach, the decision to allow commercial production of Bt corn can be viewed as part of a "corn production portfolio." Another key component of that portfolio is the amount of resources invested in the current method of producing corn. In this approach, the idea is to determine the most prudent way to manage the uncertainty associated with the exploitation of Bt corn as an alternative to non-Bt corn. We assume "risk neutrality" such that the total amount of land investment in corn cultivation is constant. Consequently, we assume that some of what was invested in non-

Bt corn is transferred into *Bt* corn and "research." Research is the part subtracted from the original investment in corn that is used to provide information on *Bt* corn such as the development of pest resistance. By definition, the amount transferred into *Bt* corn (W_1) and research (W_3) balance the reduced amount of non-*Bt* corn (W_2).

We use the assumption of "risk neutrality" to generate a measure of the value of the investment in research. This is measured by the value of the option of planting *Bt* corn. The resulting land investment portfolio is assumed to include three proportions:

- W_1 of resources is invested in growing *Bt* corn, with marginal value $B(t)$
- W_2 is invested in non-*Bt* corn, with marginal value $P(t)$, and
- W_3 is invested in research reflecting the shift from each of the other categories.

By definition, $W_1 + W_2 + W_3 = 0$. We write the total corn portfolio as

$$\Pi = W_1 B(t) + W_2 P(t) + W_3 H(t) \tag{15}$$

$H(t)$ measures the marginal value of the option of using *Bt* corn (recall Equation 3). When $H(t)$ is positive, it is beneficial to commercialize *Bt* corn. The relative value of commercializing *Bt* corn is equivalent to the value of an option or contingent claim. It depends on the value of $B(t)$, $P(t)$, and T with T as the "time horizon" or planning time. Risk neutrality (the key constraint for a rational option) occurs when the corn portfolio is the same with *Bt* corn as without. It corresponds to $d\Pi = 0$.

The planning time T depends in large part on how quickly pests develop resistance to *Bt* corn. As will be seen in the equations below, as T approaches infinity, the net benefits of *Bt* corn increase relative to the net benefits of conventional (non-*Bt*) corn. That is to say, the longer we can delay pest resistance development, the greater the net present value of *Bt* corn is in comparison with conventional corn.

The solution, whose derivation can be found in Appendix B, is

$$H(B,P,T;t) = B(t)\varphi(d_2) - P(t)\varphi(d_1) \tag{16}$$

Where φ is defined as before, and

$$d_1 = \frac{1}{\sqrt{2T}}\left\{ Log\left[\frac{B(t)}{P(t)}\right] + \frac{T}{2} \right\}$$

$$d_2 = \frac{1}{\sqrt{2T}}\left\{ Log\left[\frac{B(t)}{P(t)}\right] - \frac{T}{2} \right\}$$

where T is the cumulative uncertainty over time (see also Appendix B). Namely

$$T = \int_0^\tau \left[\sigma^2 - 2\xi\sigma\eta + \eta^2\right] ds = \left[\sigma^2 - 2\xi\sigma\eta + \eta^2\right]\tau = \psi^2\tau$$

A few remarks are in order:

- If there were no uncertainty ($\psi^2 = 0$), the equation would read:[8] $H(B, P, T; t) = B(t) - P(t)$. The value of deregulating Bt corn would be directly the difference between the value of Bt corn and the value of the conventional corn.
- d_2 and d_1 are inverted with respect to the Black–Scholes formula. The mathematical origin of the difference is explained in Appendix B.
- The main reason why $H(B, P, T; t) \neq B(t) - P(t)$ is because of the uncertainties or risks associated with Bt corn. The value of Bt corn has to be significantly larger than the value of conventional corn to justify its registration for commercial use.
- To justify a regulatory action to commercialize Bt corn, the value of Bt corn must be above a certain critical value B^*, which corresponds to $H = 0$.

$$B(t) \geq B^* = P(t)[\varphi(d_2)]/[\varphi(d_1)] \tag{17}$$

- B^* depends on the stopping time T. The smaller the T or the larger the B^*, the more difficult it is to justify allowing commercialization of Bt corn. If $T \to \infty$, the condition becomes $B(t) \geq B^* = P(t)$. However, in the high stochasticity regime described as follows, if T grows, the value of Bt corn always becomes negative. This means that when the uncertainties of the risks associated with Bt corn are large in a very specific, quantitative sense, a regulatory decision to commercialize it is not a good choice.

To elaborate on this point: the value of H is strongly dependent on the value of T. When the planning horizon can be made large (i.e., in the limit where resistance can be controlled) two scenarios have to be distinguished, depending on the sign of $\gamma - (\psi^2/2)$. If $\gamma - (\psi^2/2) > 0$, in the limit $T \to \infty$, $d_1 = d_2 \to \infty$ and $H(B, P, T; t) = B(t) - P(t)$. But if $\gamma - (\psi^2/2) < 0$, in the limit $T \to \infty$, $d_1 \to +\infty$ and $d_2 \to -\infty$, meaning that eventually $H(B, P, T; t) \leq 0$ and that it is not desirable to commercialize Bt corn. The interpretation of that result points to an important meaning of option theory. The case $\gamma - (\psi^2/2) < 0$, corresponds to the case with large uncertainty. We assume that we "know" how the value of $B(t)$ and $P(t)$ will evolve with uncertainty. Within those assumptions, we compute under which conditions $H(B, P, T; t) > 0$. As long as this condition is filled, there is an expected benefit (under the assumption of risk neutrality) that deregulating *Bt* corn is advantageous. But because of the large size of the uncertainty, the time horizon is shortened. It is only to the extent that one is comfortable using a planning horizon short enough to make $H(B, P, T; t) > 0$ that allowing *Bt* corn is a prudent policy in the case of large stochasticity.

This dichotomy is illustrated in Figure 8-2, which shows a graph of the value of the option $H(T)$ as a function of T, for different levels of the stochasticity. The different curves correspond to different values of the parameter ψ^2. A small value of ψ^2 corresponds to the low stochasticity regime in which H is positive and grows slowly with T. In the high stochasticity regime, H tends to be negative.

In fact, from an economic point of view, the value of the option of *Bt* corn seems to be more sensitive to the size of the risk than to the length of the stopping time. This points to the nature of the rational option: it is a tool for risk management so it should not be a surprise if the result is more sensitive to the risk than to the stopping time.

Empirical Application: Whether To Commercialize *Bt* Corn

Does the theory of the preceding section matter in empirical application? In this section, we investigate some of the major uncertain components of the social value of *Bt* corn. From this partial analysis, we seek to infer whether it is empirically fruitful to pursue the application of options analysis in a policy setting.

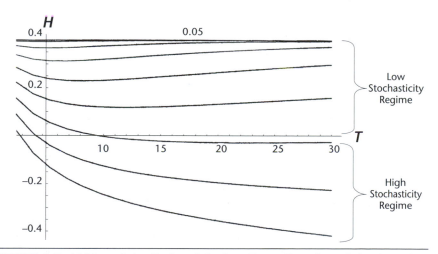

FIGURE 8-2. Values of the Rational Option *H* as a Function of the Stopping Time *T*

The policy question we investigate took place in the mid-1990s: From a social perspective, should government policymakers allow *Bt* corn to be commercially planted at all (refuge proportion of 1) or with a refuge area of 20%? The latter policy was adopted. We use information as of 2001 in this illustrative analysis so the result is not a test of the correct decision in the 1990s, which had a different information base. Nor do we quantify all impacts here. We define the "with approval" case to be the full diffusion of *Bt* corn to the limit prescribed by regulation, 80% of planted area. As a consequence of these limitations, the results are merely illustrative of the potential quantitative value in applying an options approach to policy questions.

The analysis proceeds using the real options approach to obtain an estimate of Γ, the precautionary multiplier, to determine if the economically "recommended" decision differs from that of standard cost–benefit analysis. First, key elements of the social value of *Bt* corn and traditional corn are estimated based on a literature survey and simulation methods to incorporate statistical distributions of unknown variables. The growth parameters, volatility, and correlation parameters are then incorporated or estimated and used in Equations 11 and 10 to estimate Γ.

The benefit and cost categories, their theoretical measure, and a summary of their empirical measurement are presented in Table 8-2 (added detail is in Appendix C).

The results of simulating the illustrative net social value from *Bt* and current corn growing practices (non-*Bt*) are summarized in Table 8-3. Column 1 identifies the growing method (which implicitly is the size of the refuge), column 2 reports the mean of the present value of each method (B and P). A standard cost–benefit analysis, noting the preliminary and incomplete nature of the results, would compare the expected value of the benefits from using *Bt* corn with a refuge requirement of 20% to the expected benefits from growing non-*Bt* corn.

The social expected net present value of *Bt* corn, whether with or without modeling resistance (rows two and three) is larger than the social expected value of traditional corn. Incorporating resistance has relatively little impact because the base level of producer surplus is unchanged as farmers can revert to current practice (noting that the effect on organic agriculture is not incorporated).

Based on these illustrative data and using standard expected value criteria, the commercialization of *Bt* corn should have been allowed, a conclusion that is somewhat stronger if the analyst ignores resistance. In contrast, the precautionary multiplier Γ is reported in column 3 with a value of 1.83. A decision rule that incorporates uncertainty based on real options would reject a regulatory decision to allow commercial planting of *Bt* corn because the benefits do not exceed 1.83 times those of non-*Bt* corn. Consequently, the decision for

TABLE 8-2. Summary of Benefit and Cost Categories, Measurement, and Parameters

Category	Bt or Non-Bt (N)	Theoretical measure	Empirical measure*
Benefit			
Producer surplus	N	B + E of Figure 8-1	Operating profit (revenues less cash expenses)
Change in consumer and producer (total) surplus	Bt	F + G + C + D of Figure 8-1	Cost savings because of *Bt* corn, some captured by *Bt* corn producer
Initial consumer surplus	N, *Bt*	A of Figure 8-1	Assumed proportional to social value so cancels in Equation 10
Other: pesticide exposure avoided, mycotoxin damage reduced	*Bt*	Human health and animal risk avoided	Not included
Cost			
Pest resistance	*Bt*	Depreciation	Poisson arrival rate $1/T$ where T depends on refuge size
Impact on nontarget species	*Bt*, N	Externality	Benefit transfer from English value for nonuse value
Mycotoxin damage	N	Externality	Not estimated
Human health	*Bt*, N	Externality	Allergenicity for *Bt*
Other: horizontal gene transfer from marker or other gene; substitution; cost to organic agriculture if *Bt* no longer effective; system disruption	*Bt*	Externality	Not estimated
Other parameters			
Regulatory alternative	*Bt*	Refuge proportion	0.2 as implemented
Discount rate r	*Bt*, N	Opportunity cost	7% real from the Office of Management and Budget
Growth parameters	*Bt* (μ), N (γ)	Percentage growth	2.5% from production data
Volatility	*Bt* (η), N (σ)	Equation 12	Estimated as sample variance of $d \ln X$.
Correlation	*Bt*, N	$E(dz_B dz_P)/dt$	Estimated as correlation of dBt, dN.

*See Appendix C for detail, most measured with uncertainty using statistical distributions.

Table 8-3. Real Option Precautionary Multiplier and Partial Net Present Social Value

Growing method, resistance	Mean	Precautionary multiplier Γ
Bt, λ = 0.083	$132 billion	
Bt, λ = 0 (no resistance)	$136 billion	1.83
P (non-Bt)	$127 billion	

Note: These numbers are for illustration and are not sufficiently developed for policy decisions.

action would be reversed, and the recommendation would be not to commercialize *Bt* corn. Although not reported in detail here because of the preliminary nature of the results, the relatively small precautionary multiplier is caused by a high correlation between outcomes for *Bt* and non-*Bt* corn and because the estimated size of the volatilities are similar. Had an options analysis been carried out that ignored the uncertainty in growing non-*Bt* corn, the multiplier would have been substantially higher but only as a result of omitting the uncertainty with which farmers already contend.

These illustrative results are meant merely to convey the possibility of a regulatory reversal. Known effects are omitted from the calculations, and those that are included would benefit from refinement before any actual application to policy. What we believe has been demonstrated is the usefulness of applying an option approach to regulatory decisionmaking and the potential, in this problem, for a different recommendation based on economic criteria. A quantitative measure of precaution can be computed, and decisions may change depending on its value. In this illustration, based on actual but incomplete data and analysis, it appears worthwhile to investigate further the empirical analysis of precaution.

Conclusion

Bt corn is an example of how a new technology can create a complex and uncertain situation for policymakers involving a variety of costs and benefits. Policymakers should not automatically reject the opportunities offered by such new products nor should they ignore possible costs.

Among the many questions raised by the issue of commercializing *Bt* corn, two were addressed through the framework of option theory as an extension of cost–benefit analysis. Both questions stem from the same origin: planting *Bt* corn amounts to releasing a new biological agent. It is almost certain to trigger some nontrivial reaction from the environment. One question is the likely creation of pest resistance to the toxins produced by *Bt* corn. This eventually will signal the end of the usefulness of particular varieties of *Bt* corn. The second question is a set of uncertain impacts such as those on nontarget species.

Seen from a normative point of view, the problem raised by resistance and externalities is a case of optimizing the time to commercialize the product under uncertainty and irreversibility. This strongly points to the relevance of the real option theory. We have shown that (a) real option theory can be applied empirically to regulatory problems, and (b) the results may differ from those of a standard cost–benefit analysis.

A related concern for policymakers dealing with the use of a new and revolutionary technology is balancing the benefit of the new technology with its risks. Although related to the real option optimization framework, this is a different problem. In this formulation, the economic problem is one of risk management. The rational option theory requires that the larger the uncertainty of the outcome is, the more *Bt* corn must prove superior to conventional corn to justify its use. Both real and rational option framing can be used complementarily as they emphasize different facets of the problem. Both paradigms can be interpreted as containing elements of the precautionary principle, as they answer the question, "With uncertainty and potentially large irreversible risks, how long a delay, if any, in commercializing *Bt* corn is justified based on its expected value to the economy?"

Many issues remain for further research: (a) improved spatial and temporal characterization of the development of resistance, (b) the incorporation of endogenous information and decision phases into the option application, (c) refinement of the empirical evaluation of impacts, (d) consideration of alternative framing of what is irreversible, and (e) empirical implementation of the rational option approach.

In conclusion, we believe that the options framework yields both a theoretical and an empirical approach to the precautionary principle, problems related to pest resistance, and the regulatory decisions surrounding the adoption of new and uncertain technologies.

Acknowledgements

For insightful comments, we thank Chris Gilligan, Klaas vant Velt, and seminar participants at the Resources for the Future Conference on the Economics of Antibiotic and Pest Resistance; the Association of Environmental and Resource Economists 2001 Summer workshop; and the North Carolina Benefits Transfer workshop. Support was provided by the EPA Star Fellowship Program. General funding was provided to the Centers for the Human Dimensions of Global Change and the Study and Improvement of Regulation at Carnegie Mellon University.

References

Alstad, D.N., and D.A. Andow. 1995. Managing the Evolution of Insect Resistance to Transgenic Plants. *Science* 268: 1894–6.

Bockstael, N., M. Freeman, R. Kopp, P. Portney, and V.K. Smith. 2000. On Measuring Economic Values for Nature. *Environmental Science and Technology* 34(8): 1384–9.

Campbell, J., A. Lo, and C. MacKinley. 1997. *The Econometrics of Financial Markets.* Princeton, NJ: Princeton University Press.

CDC (U.S. Centers for Disease Control and Prevention). 2001. Investigation of Human Health Effects Associated with Potential Exposure to Genetically Modified Corn. http://www.cdc.gov/nceh/ehhe/ Cry9CReport (accessed June 29, 2001).

Commission of the European Union. 2000. Communication from the Commission on the Precautionary Principle, COM(2000)–1.

Copeland, T., and V. Antikarov. 2001. *Real Options: A Practitioners' Guide.* New York: Texere.

Dixit, A.K., and R.S. Pindyck. 1994. *Investment under Uncertainty.* Princeton, NJ: Princeton University Press.

Farrow, S. 2000. Externalities, Options, and Petroleum Leasing. Discussion Paper. Pittsburgh, PA: Center for the Study and Improvement of Regulation, Carnegie Mellon University.

Farrow, S., and B. Morel. 2001. Continuation Rights, the Precautionary Principle, and Global Change. *Risk, Decision and Policy* 6: 145–55.

FDA (Food and Drug Administration). 1998. Guidance for Industry: Use of Antibiotic Resistance Marker Genes in Transgenic Plants. vm.cfsan.fda.gov/~dms/opa-armg.html (accessed February 2001).

Fisher, A. 2000. Investment under Uncertainty and Option Value in Environmental Economics. *Resource and Energy Economics* 22: 197–204.

Goklany, I.M. 2000. *Applying the Precautionary Principle to Genetically Modified Crops Policy*, Study 157. St. Louis, MO: Center for the Study of American Business, Washington University.

Gould, F., A. Anderson, D. Summerford, D. Heckel, J. Lopez, S. Micinski, R. Leonard, and M. Laster. 1997. Initial Frequency of Alleles for Resistance to *Bacillus thuringiensis* Toxins in Field Populations of *Heliothis virescens*. *Proceedings of the National Academy of Sciences USA* 94: 3519–23.

Greene, William H. 1997. *Econometric Analysis*, Third Edition. Upper Saddle River, NJ: Prentice Hall.

Huang, F., L.L. Buschman, R.A. Higgins, and W.H. McGaughey. 1999. Inheritance of Resistance to *Bacillus thuringiensis* Toxin (Dipel ES) in the European Corn Borer. *Science* 284(7): 965–7.

Hull, J. 2000. *Options, Futures, and Other Derivatives.* Upper Saddle River, NJ: Prentice Hall.

Hyde, J., M. Martin, P. Preckel, and C. Edwards. 1999. The Economics of *Bt* Corn: Valuing the Protection from European Corn Borer. *Review of Agricultural Economics* 21(2): 442–54.

Lipson, M. 1999. Remarks for the EPA/USDA Workshop on Insect Resistance Management (IRM) in Transgenic (*Bt*) Corn. http://www.ofrf.org/policy/btresistance.html (accessed November 3, 2002).

Lohr, L., T. Park, and L. Higley. 1996. *Valuing Risk Tradeoffs and Voluntary Insecticide Reduction*, Faculty Series no. 96–10. Athens, GA: Department of Agricultural and Applied Economics, University of Georgia.

Minor, H.C., C.G. Morris, H.L. Mason, D.R. Knerr, R.W. Hasty, G.K. Stafford, and T.G. Fritts. 1999. *Corn: 1999 Missouri Crop Performance*. University of Missouri-Columbia Special Report 521. Columbia, MO: University of Missouri-Columbia.

Mourato, S., E. Ozdemiroglu, and V. Soster. 2000. Evaluating Health and Environmental Impacts of Pesticide Use. *Environmental Science and Technology* 34(8): 1456–61.

NAS (National Academy of Sciences). 2000. *Genetically Modified Pest-Protected Plants: Science and Regulation*. Washington, DC: National Academy Press.

Ostlie, K., W. Hutchison, and R. Hellmich. 1997. Bt *Corn and European Corn Borer*, NCR publication 602. St. Paul, MN: University of Minnesota.

Park, A.W., S. Gubbins, and C.A. Gilligan. 2001. Invasion and Persistence of Plant Parasites in a Spatially Structured Host Population. *Oikos* 94: 1–13.

Pimentel, D., and P. Raven. 2000. *Bt* Corn Pollen Impacts on Nontarget Lepidoptera: Assessment of Effects in Nature. *Proceedings of the National Academy of Sciences of the USA* 97(15): 8198–9.

Rogers, M.D. Forthcoming. Genetically Modified Plants and the Precautionary Principle. *Journal of Risk, Decision, and Policy*.

Slade, M. 2001. Valuing Managerial Flexibility: An Application of Real Option Theory to Mining Investment. *Journal of Environmental Economics and Management* 41(2): 193–233.

Tabashnik, B., Y.B. Liu, N. Finson, L. Masson, and D.G. Heckel. 1997. One gene in Diamondback Moth Confers Resistance to Four *Bacillus thuringiensis* Toxins. *Proceedings of the National Academy of Sciences of the USA* 94: 1640–4.

Tolley, G., D. Kenkel, and R. Fabian. 1994. *Valuing Health for Public Policy*. Chicago: University of Chicago Press.

USDA (U.S. Department of Agriculture). 1997a. 96-079-2 Dekalb Genetics Corp.; Availability of Determination of Nonregulated Status for Genetically Engineered Corn http://www.aphis.usda.gov/ppd/rad/OldRules/96-079-2.f (accessed February 2001).

———. 1997b. 96-095-2 Monsanto Co.; Availability of Determination of Nonregulated Status for Genetically Engineered Corn. http://www.aphis.usda.gov/ppd/rad/OldRules/96-095-2.f (accessed February 2001).

U.S. EPA (U.S. Environmental Protection Agency). 2001. Biopesticides Registration Action Document: *Bacillus thuringiensis* Plant-Incorporated Protectants, 2001. http://www.epa.gov/pesticides/biopesticides/reds/brad_bt_pip2.htm (accessed March 13, 2002).

U.S. EPA/USDA (U.S. Department of Agriculture). 1999. Workshop on *Bt* Crop Resistance Management, held June 18, 1999. http://www.epa.gov/pesticides/biopesticides/otherdocs/btcornproceedings.htm (accessed March 13, 2002).

———. 2001. EPA Biopesticides Registration Action Document: Bacillus thuringiensis Plant-Incorporated Protectants. http://www.epa.gov/pesticides/biopesticides/reds/brad_bt_pip2.htm (accessed November 3, 2002).

Wiener, J.B. Forthcoming. Precaution in a Multi-Risk World. In *The Risk Assessment of Environmental and Human Health Hazards*, Second Edition, edited by Dennis Pausenbach. New York: John Wiley & Sons.

Zerbe, R., Jr., and D. Dively. 1994. *Benefit-Cost Analysis in Theory and Practice*. New York: Harper Collins College Publishers.

Appendix A: Real Option Approach with Two Uncertain Variables*

$$dB = \mu B dt + \eta B dz_B$$

$$dP = \gamma P dt + \sigma P dz_P$$

Let $x = B/P$.

Use Ito's Lemma and define ξ as the correlation between the two stochasticities, $E[dz_p \, dz_B] = \xi \, dt$. We are interested in $F(B, P) = E[e^{-\rho t} (B - P)]$. Let

$$Ph\left(x = \frac{B}{P}\right) = F(B,P) = PE[e^{-\rho t}\left(\frac{B}{P} - 1\right)]$$

Alternatively,

$$h\left(x = \frac{B}{P}\right) = \frac{F(B,P)}{P} = E[e^{-\rho t}(x - 1)]$$

$$F(B,P) = Ph(x) \Rightarrow \begin{cases} \dfrac{\partial F}{\partial B} = Ph'(x)\dfrac{\partial x}{\partial B} = h'(x) \\ \dfrac{\partial F}{\partial P} = Ph'(x)\dfrac{\partial x}{\partial P} = h(x) - xh'(x) \end{cases}$$

The Bellman equation for this problem, after defining dF using Ito's Lemma, is $dF = 0$,

$$(\gamma - \rho)h(x) + (\mu - \gamma)xh'(x) + \frac{1}{2}\left\{ \begin{array}{l} \eta^2 x^2 h''(x) - 2\xi \eta \sigma x^2 h''(x) \\ + \sigma^2 x^2 h''(x) \end{array} \right\} = 0 \qquad (A1)$$

This is a partial differential equation for h, with boundary conditions

$$h(x^*) = x^* - 1$$
$$h'(x^*) = 1 \qquad (A2)$$

A natural form as a solution of Equation A1 is $h(x) = Ax^{\beta}$ (A3)

Substituting in Equation A1 leads to the quadratic equation for β:

$$\gamma - \rho + \beta(\mu - \gamma) + \beta(\beta - 1)\frac{1}{2}\left\{\eta^2 - 2\xi \eta \sigma + \sigma^2\right\} = 0$$

---

* See also Dixit and Pindyck 1994, 207–11.

where the last term on the right is identifiable as the variance of the difference of two random variables with correlation ξ.

The solutions are as follows:

$$\beta_{\pm} = \frac{-\left(\mu - \gamma - \dfrac{\eta^2 - 2\xi\eta\sigma + \sigma^2}{2}\right)}{\left\{\eta^2 - 2\xi\eta\sigma + \sigma^2\right\}}$$
$$\pm \frac{\sqrt{\left(\mu - \gamma - \dfrac{\eta^2 - 2\xi\eta\sigma + \sigma^2}{2}\right)^2 + 2(\rho - \gamma)\left\{\eta^2 - 2\xi\eta\sigma + \sigma^2\right\}}}{\left\{\eta^2 - 2\xi\eta\sigma + \sigma^2\right\}}$$

The product of the two roots is negative when $\rho > \gamma$. Therefore, under that condition, one is positive, and one is negative. It can be shown that $\beta_+ > 1$ requires $\rho > \mu$.

This condition is identical to the case in which there is only one stochastic variable. Using Equation A-3, the boundary conditions become

$$\left.\begin{array}{c} A(x^*)^{\beta} = x^* - 1 \\ \beta A(x^*)^{\beta-1} = 1 \Rightarrow A(x^*)^{\beta} = \dfrac{x^*}{\beta} \end{array}\right\} \Rightarrow \frac{x^*}{\beta} = x^* - 1 \Rightarrow x^* = \frac{\beta}{\beta-1}$$

Appendix B: Rational Option Approach

As in Appendix A,

$$dB = \mu B dt + \eta B dz_B$$

$$dP = \gamma P dt + \sigma P dz_P$$

ξ is the correlation between the two stochasticities, that is, $E[dz_p\, dz_B] = \xi\, dt$.

$H(t)$, the value of the option to invest in the program, is a derivative of the value of $B(t)$ and $P(t)$. That is, using the equations above and Ito's Lemma

$$dH = \frac{\partial H}{\partial B}dB + \frac{\partial H}{\partial P}dP + \left\{\frac{1}{2}\left[\frac{\partial^2 H}{\partial B^2}\eta^2 B^2 + \frac{\partial^2 H}{\partial P^2}\sigma^2 P^2 + 2\xi\frac{\partial^2 H}{\partial B \partial P}\eta\sigma BP\right] + \frac{\partial H}{\partial t}\right\}dt \quad \text{(B1)}$$

Equation B1 can be written

$$\frac{dH}{H} = \beta dt + \delta dz_B + \varepsilon dz_P \quad \text{(B2)}$$

Implying

$$\beta H = \frac{1}{2}\left[\frac{\partial^2 H}{\partial B^2}\eta^2 B^2 + 2\xi\frac{\partial^2 H}{\partial B\partial P}\eta\sigma BP + \frac{\partial^2 H}{\partial P^2}\sigma^2 P^2\right] + \frac{\partial H}{\partial t} + \mu B\frac{\partial H}{\partial B} + \gamma P\frac{\partial H}{\partial P} \qquad \text{(B3a)}$$

$$\delta H = \frac{\partial H}{\partial B}\eta B$$
$$\varepsilon H = \frac{\partial H}{\partial P}\sigma P \qquad \text{(B3b)}$$

By definition of W_1, W_2, and W_3, $W_1 + W_2 + W_3 = 0$. \qquad (B4)

The value of this "program portfolio" Π is affected by the relative changes in the values of the expected revenue $B(t)$ and investment $P(t)$.

$$d\Pi = W_1\frac{dB}{B} + W_2\frac{dP}{P} + W_3\frac{dH}{H} \qquad \text{(B5)}$$

Risk neutrality occurs when $d\Pi = 0$. \qquad (B6)

Equations B2, B4, and B5 lead to

$$0 = dt\left[(\mu - \gamma)W_1 + (\beta - \gamma)W_3\right] + dz_B\left(\eta W_1 + \delta W_3\right) + dz_P\left[(\varepsilon - \sigma)W_3 - \sigma W_1\right]$$

which in fact translates to three equalities

$$\left[(\mu - \gamma)W_1 + (\beta - \gamma)W_3\right] = 0$$
$$\left(\eta W_1 + \delta W_3\right) = 0 \qquad \text{(B7)}$$
$$\left(\varepsilon - \sigma\right)W_3 = \sigma W_1$$

The equations in B7, in turn, lead to the relations

$$-\frac{W_1}{W_3} = \frac{(\beta - \gamma)}{(\mu - \gamma)} = \frac{\delta}{\eta} = 1 - \frac{\varepsilon}{\sigma} \qquad \text{(B8a)}$$

Equation B8a implies

$$\frac{\delta}{\eta} = 1 - \frac{\varepsilon}{\sigma} \Leftrightarrow B\frac{\partial H}{\partial B} + P\frac{\partial H}{\partial P} = H \qquad \text{(B8b)}$$

If we assume that

$$\frac{H(B,P)}{P} = h\left(x = \frac{B}{P}\right)$$ (B9)

This implies

$$\frac{\partial H}{\partial B} = P\frac{\partial h}{\partial x}\frac{\partial x}{\partial B} = \frac{\partial h}{\partial x}$$

$$\frac{\partial^2 H}{\partial B^2} = \frac{\partial}{\partial B}\frac{\partial h}{\partial x} = \frac{\partial^2 h}{\partial x^2}\frac{\partial x}{\partial B} = \frac{1}{P}\frac{\partial^2 h}{\partial x^2}$$

$$\frac{\partial H}{\partial P} = \frac{\partial}{\partial P}[Ph] = h + P\frac{\partial h}{\partial P} = h + P\frac{\partial h}{\partial x}\frac{\partial x}{\partial P} = h - x\frac{\partial h}{\partial x}$$

$$\frac{\partial^2 H}{\partial B\partial P} = -\frac{x}{P}\frac{\partial^2 h}{\partial x^2}$$

$$\frac{\partial^2 H}{\partial P^2} = \frac{\partial}{\partial P}\left[h - x\frac{\partial h}{\partial x}\right] = \frac{\partial h}{\partial P} - \frac{\partial x}{\partial P}\frac{\partial h}{\partial x} - x\frac{\partial^2 h}{\partial x^2}\frac{\partial x}{\partial P} = \frac{x^2}{P}\frac{\partial^2 h}{\partial x^2}$$

Equation B8b is automatically satisfied.

If $x = B/P$, using Ito's Lemma

$$dx = \frac{\partial x}{\partial P}dP + \frac{\partial x}{\partial B}dB + \frac{1}{2}\left[\eta^2 B^2\frac{\partial^2 x}{\partial B^2} + 2\xi\eta\sigma\,BP\frac{\partial^2 x}{\partial B\partial P} + \sigma^2 P^2\frac{\partial^2 x}{\partial P^2}\right]dt$$

$$dx = \left[\gamma P\frac{\partial x}{\partial P} + \mu B\frac{\partial x}{\partial B} + \frac{\eta^2 B^2}{2}\frac{\partial^2 x}{\partial B^2} + \xi\eta\sigma BP\frac{\partial^2 x}{\partial B\partial P} + \frac{\sigma^2 P^2}{2}\frac{\partial^2 x}{\partial P^2}\right]dt$$ (B10)

$$+ \sigma P\frac{\partial x}{\partial P}dz_P + \eta B\frac{\partial x}{\partial B}dz_B$$

$$\frac{dx}{x} = \left[-\gamma + \mu - \xi\eta\sigma + \sigma^2\right]dt - \sigma dz_p + \eta dz_B$$

Equation B3a becomes

$$\beta H = \frac{1}{2}\left[\frac{\partial^2 H}{\partial B^2}\eta^2 B^2 + 2\xi\frac{\partial^2 H}{\partial B\partial P}\eta\sigma BP + \frac{\partial^2 H}{\partial P^2}\sigma^2 P^2\right] + \frac{\partial H}{\partial t} + \mu B\frac{\partial H}{\partial B} + \gamma P\frac{\partial H}{\partial P}$$

$$\beta Ph = \frac{1}{2}\left[\eta^2 xB\frac{\partial^2 h}{\partial x^2} - 2\xi\frac{\partial^2 h}{\partial x^2}\eta\sigma Bx + \frac{\partial^2 h}{\partial x^2}\sigma^2 x^2 P\right] + P\frac{\partial h}{\partial t} + \mu B\frac{\partial h}{\partial x} + \gamma P\left[h - \frac{\partial h}{\partial x}\right]$$ (B11)

$$(\beta - \gamma)h = \frac{1}{2}\left[\eta^2 x^2\frac{\partial^2 h}{\partial x^2} - 2\xi\frac{\partial^2 h}{\partial x^2}\eta\sigma x^2 + \frac{\partial^2 h}{\partial x^2}\sigma^2 x^2\right] + \frac{\partial h}{\partial t} + (\mu - \gamma)x\frac{\partial h}{\partial x}$$

The relation $[(\beta - \gamma)/(\mu - \gamma)] = \delta/\eta$ implies $(\mu - \gamma)B(\partial H/\partial B) + \gamma H = \beta H$. This, in turn, implies

$$(\beta - \gamma)Ph = (\mu - \gamma)B\frac{\partial h}{\partial x} \Rightarrow (\beta - \gamma)h = (\mu - \gamma)x\frac{\partial h}{\partial x} \tag{B12}$$

Equation B12 substituted into Equation B11 leads to

$$0 = \frac{x^2}{2}\left[\eta^2 - 2\xi\eta\sigma + \sigma^2\right]\frac{\partial^2 h}{\partial x^2} + \frac{\partial h}{\partial t} = \frac{x^2}{2}\psi^2\frac{\partial^2 h}{\partial x^2} + \frac{\partial h}{\partial t} \tag{B13}$$

where

$$\psi^2 = \left[\eta^2 - 2\xi\eta\sigma + \sigma^2\right]$$

To integrate Equation B13, we define

$$T = \int_0^t \psi^2(s)ds \left(\Rightarrow dT = \psi^2(t)dt\right)$$

So that Equation B13 becomes the well-known equation

$$\frac{\partial h}{\partial T} = -\frac{x^2}{2}\frac{\partial^2 h}{\partial x^2}$$

whose solution is

$$h(x) = x\varphi(d_2) - \varphi(d_1)$$

$$d_1 = \frac{1}{\sqrt{2T}}\left\{Log\left[\frac{B(t)}{P(t)}\right] + \frac{T}{2}\right\}$$

$$d_2 = \frac{1}{\sqrt{2T}}\left\{Log\left[\frac{B(t)}{P(t)}\right] - \frac{T}{2}\right\}$$

or equivalently (using the assumption in Equation B9)

$$\frac{H(B,P,T;t)}{P(t)} = \frac{B(t)}{P(t)}\varphi(d_2) - \varphi(d_1) \tag{B14}$$

Equation B14 is equivalent to Equation 16 in the text.

Appendix C: Variable Explanations

Some of the items in Table 8-2 are described in more detail below. A commercially available simulation tool (Crystal Ball) was used to simulate the distribution of the net social value of *Bt* corn. That value was computed as the sum of the present value of the initial producer surplus, the change in total surplus, and the external effects that were approximately quantified for the illustration.

Producer Surplus

The mean and variance are based on U.S. Department of Agriculture reports on the "gross value of production less cash expenses per acre" for corn from 1985 to 1995, adjusted to 1998 dollars using the consumer price index: mean, $80/acre; standard error, $36. A triangular distribution with a lower bound at zero (based on exiting the industry if less than zero producer surplus) and an upper bound of two standard errors from the mean were used.

Change in Total Surplus

A regression was constructed from data in Ostlie (1997) to predict the farm benefits per acre from *Bt* corn as a function of price, yield, and severity of infestation (the vertical distance between S_0 and S_1, the original and the new supply curves). The resulting regression (available from the authors) was used as a prediction equation for benefits. The distribution of price used as a random input into the prediction equation used a lower bound of $1.20 per bushel to capture some uncertainty about the acceptability of *Bt* corn. $1.80 per bushel was used as the mean. The frequency of severe corn borer outbreaks was set at 3/8 following Ostlie. The per-acre figure was multiplied by 60 million acres based on full diffusion of *Bt* corn to 80% of the approximately 75 million acres planted to corn. This value likely overstates the benefits because the comparison is to benign neglect of the corn borer and not a mixture of treatment with pesticides and because full diffusion may involve fewer acres. Further, a significant part of the cost savings are captured by the producers of the *Bt* corn seed. Although this is a transfer and so still a benefit (assuming zero marginal cost of production of *Bt* corn compared with traditional corn), the effect would be to reduce the change in consumer surplus if the supply curve shifts less, as might also happen because of the refugia requirement.

Base Consumer Surplus (A)

Base Consumer Surplus was assumed to be equiproportional to both the traditional and *Bt* corn social values so that this multiplicative factor cancels out in the decision rule. In any event, it is doubtful that this number can be meaningfully estimated. For estimation problems of such measures of total value, see Bockstael and others (2000).

Pest Resistance

We investigate pest resistance parametrically by setting the expected terminal date of complete resistance at 12 years when a 20% refuge exists based loosely on Huang and others (1999) and Alstad and Andow (1995). If the size of the refugia is investigated as a probability distribution, this would increase the variance in the real option application and be expected to increase the degree of precaution.

Impact on Nontarget Species

The impact on nontarget species of both standard pesticides and genetically modified crops is a lively subject of debate (Pimentel and Raven 2000). In the illustration in the text, we apply the same value to both traditional and *Bt* corn. That value is based on a benefits transfer of nonuse values from a contingent valuation study in England (Mourato et al. 2000). That study investigated the additional price that consumers were willing to pay to reduce the decline of one of nine species of field birds that are believed in decline because of the use of agricultural chemicals. Using average yields, we translate a price per a one-pound loaf of bread into a value per acre and assume that the per-acre basis is independent of the crop grown on it, as between wheat or corn. For illustration purposes, we use an uncertain fraction (mean of 0.05) of the value stated for the benefit of reducing the decline in bird populations. As a sense of scale, the mean value of effect is larger than the average producer surplus at the current level of production. There is also evidence that farmers themselves are willing to pay to reduce pesticide use, although that figure was not included in our estimate (Lohr et al. 1996).

Human Allergenicity

Information submitted in support of *Bt* corn applications (NAS 2000) supports no allergenicity for several *Bt* strains whereas raising a question about the Cry9C strain (StarLink, which was withdrawn in 2001). This is a topic of scientific uncertainty, although recent work reduces the probability of such a link (CDC 2001). We assume a distribution of allergy cases with a lower bound of zero based on the potential for allergic reaction in the 35 complaints after discovery of StarLink traces in Kraft taco shells. The U.S. Food and Drug Administration initially declared that only 10 might have allergenic bases, subject to further investigation. In 2001, CDC found none of the cases to have been related to StarLink based on a particular test. We assume a reporting percentage of actual cases and a rate of exposure to generate an estimate of the number of cases. We value these events using a value of severe food poisoning per day of $130 from Tolley and others (1994). The mean number of reported cases in our illustration is 5 with a mean reporting percentage of 0.25. The value of this impact is relatively small.

Notes

1. Sequential decisionmaking can be framed as an option approach (Dixit and Pindyck 1994; Farrow 2000). Here we treat the regulatory decision as if it is a once-and-for-all decision, an assumption to be relaxed in later work.

2. Fisher (2000) analyzes the parallel between the conditional value of information in quasi-option value and the real option framework.

3. Slade (2001) has investigated the sensitivity of decisions using real options to the specification of the stochastic process.

4. A logarithmic regression of time on the U.S. production of corn yields from 1985 to 1995 resulted in an average percentage increase of corn production per year of 2.4% (t statistic = 10), which is rounded to 2.5% for empirical purposes.

5. In the case of rational options, η enters the computation of the value of the option.

6. Copeland and Antikarov (2001) also suggest an alternative estimator based on two adjacent time periods.

7. See Greene on the topic of hazard functions (1997, 738).

8. When $\psi^2 = 0$, $d_1 = d_2 = \infty$, and $\psi(\infty) = 1$.

Chapter 9

Resistance Economics of Transgenic Crops under Uncertainty
A Real Option Approach

Justus Wesseler

The development of pest resistance is one of the many concerns about the long-term success of transgenic crops. This chapter discusses resistances as additional irreversible costs related to the release of transgenic crops. These irreversible costs, their uncertainty, and the uncertainty about future direct benefits result in a real option value favoring a delay in the release of transgenic crops. This is a result well known in real option theory but ignored in most of the cost–benefit studies on transgenic crops.

In addition to irreversible costs, however, a release of transgenic crops also may provide irreversible benefits. For example, a reduction in pesticide use reduces pest resistance to pesticides and has positive impacts on human health, groundwater quality, and biodiversity. These irreversible benefits provide an incentive for an immediate release of transgenic crops in the environment.

The optimal decision to release transgenic crops depends not only on the direct costs and benefits, which we call additional net benefits, but also on the trade-off between irreversible environmental costs and benefits. Assuming uncertain additional net benefits, constant irreversible costs and benefits and applying the real options approach allows us to define the maximal tolerable irreversible costs as an important benchmark value.

The real option approach was applied by using contingent claim analysis, which allows deriving solutions that are independent of risk and time preference. Those concerned about the environmental risks of transgenic crops and those who just want to maximize their income would come to the same conclusion about the timing of release.

The effects of policies on the timing of releasing transgenic crops are analyzed by identifying the impact of marginal parameter changes on the maximum tolerable irreversible costs. The most counterintuitive result was the increase in the likelihood of an earlier release with a decrease in additional net benefits. This result was explained by the opposite impact that simultaneous changes in the growth rate and the variance rate have on the maximum tolerable irreversible costs. Mandatory refuge areas for pest resistance management and a tax on transgenic crops to compensate for possible environmental risks have this kind of effect on the timing of release.

A grobiotechnology challenges the political economy of agriculture in many countries. Never before has a new technology in the field of agriculture been so emotionally debated among different stakeholders. Developing countries' scientists are reluctant to be bypassed by the new technology (Wambugu 1999). At the same time, groups of consumers, politicians, and nongovernmental organizations, both in developed and developing countries, oppose the introduction of transgenic crops, which they see as posing a threat to biodiversity, human health, and the economy of rural communities and ultimately endangering sustainable development. Radical groups have gone as far as destroying research plots and laboratory equipment. Consumers are further disconcerted by the disagreement among scientists about the environmental and human health impact of transgenic crops. Although some highlight the potential risks, others argue that they are negligible.

Whatever people believe personally, the public debate indicates that both benefits and costs are expected from the release of transgenic crops in the environment. These benefits and costs are highly uncertain. Nobody can exactly predict the impact transgenic crops will have on the ecosystem and how successfully they can compete in the marketplace with nontransgenic crops. Nevertheless, decisions regarding the release of transgenic crops have to be made and are being made. Any such decisions include, implicitly or explicitly, a comparison of costs and benefits. Even a decision based on the assumption that the risk cannot be estimated and, therefore, that transgenic crops should not be released, implicitly assumes that the expected costs from the risks are higher than the expected benefits.

Irreversible Costs and Benefits of Transgenic Crops

The costs of agricultural biotechnology are uncertain, and some of the costs are also irreversible. From the resistance economic point of view, three areas are of special concern.

First, gene flow in plants can enable domesticated plants to become pernicious weeds or enhance the fitness of wild plants, which might turn out to be serious weeds, thus shifting the ecological balance in a natural plant community. Herbivore-resistant traits have a comparative advantage against nonresistant traits, and if the transgenic crop hybridizes with other plants, for example wild relatives, the transfer of genes will be virtually inevitable under planting at a commercial scale (Marvier 2001). Gene flows from domesticated to wild relatives of the world's 13 most important food crops are common (Ellstrand et al. 1999). These gene flows have resulted in more aggressive weeds and the extinction of wild relatives, and the same is possible for the transfer of genes from transgenic crops to wild relatives. Kendall and others (1997, 19) concluded "... it is clear that any gene that exists in a cultivated crop or plant, irrespective of how it got there, can be transferred following hybridization to its wild or semidomesticated relatives."

Second, planting pest-resistant crops increases the selection of pests resistant to the plant-produced pesticide. For example, *Bt* corn, corn that can produce toxins of *Bacillus thuringiensis*, has been developed to control the European corn borer (*Ostrinia nubilalis*). Larvae that feed on *Bt* corn are expected to be killed; however, a widespread adoption of *Bt* corn is expected to increase the chances that pest resistance will evolve (Tabashnik et al. 2000). Farmers in the United States are required to provide refuge areas where non-*Bt* crops are grown to control the chances of pest resistance (EPA 2000a).

Third, the use of marker genes in transgenic crops can increase the resistance of bacteria to antibiotics (Krimsky and Wrubel 1996). Marker genes with information about antibiotic resistance are used to identify transformed cells and are integrated in the genomes of transgenic crops. If the transgenic crops are consumed, the possibility exists that the genes carrying information about antibiotic resistance are transferred to human pathogens. The pathogens may become resistant against the specific antibiotic, and the effectiveness of antibiotics for medical treatments decreases. However, this may be very unlikely because "... most of the antibiotic resistance marker genes used in transgenic crops are of no clinical importance and are widely spread in microflora" (Malik and Saroha 1999, 3).

Other issues raised about possible irreversible effects of transgenic crops are that new viruses could develop from virus-containing transgenic crops (Kendall et al. 1997) and that they may have unknown effects on soil communities (Saxena et al. 1999).

In summary, the evidence provided in the literature cited clearly indicates that the problems of resistance to transgenic crops are inevitable if the crops are released in the environment. Because the possibility to control pests and diseases can be seen as a nonrenewable resource (Hueth and Regev 1974), a loss of this resource is irreversible.

In the United States, transgenic crops have been adopted rapidly (James 2000). Studies confirm that on average the gross margin per area from transgenic crops is about as high and sometimes higher than the gross margin from nontransgenic crops. However, there is a regional difference in the distribution of benefits, which can be explained by regional factors such as infestation level and climatic conditions. The empirical studies also indicate that the amount of pesticides used may decrease for transgenic crops but only in specific regions and specific years, depending on the same factors as mentioned earlier. In some regions, pesticide use has actually increased (Carpenter and Gianessi 1999; Fernandez-Cornejo et al. 1999; Fulton and Keyowski 1999).[1]

The rapid adoption of transgenic crops among farmers in Northern America has been explained by the greater benefits that farmers gain from planting transgenic crops. Variable production costs are reduced because of reduced pest management and labor costs. Gross revenues are increased because of an increase in yield from improved plant spacing. Additional benefits arise from improved risk management and insurance against pests and a reduction in equipment costs in zero-tillage production systems (Kalaitzandonakes 1999).

Bt cotton[2] also has been introduced successfully in China. One of the major reasons for adoption has been the savings on pesticides. Pray and others (2001) reported a decrease in pesticide costs of about 80% after adoption of *Bt* cotton in China.

The decrease in pesticide use not only reduces the expenses of farmers but also reduces the pressure on the buildup of pest resistance to pesticides. Additionally, the reduced application of pesticides has several positive impacts on the environment and human health (Antle and Pingali 1994; Waibel and Fleischer 1998; Fleischer 1998). The reduced pressure on the buildup of pest resistance and some of the other external costs of pesticide application are irreversible. If the introduced transgenic crops result in less pesticide application, the introduction provides additional benefits. Hence, the release of transgenic crops produces not only irreversible costs but also irreversible benefits,[3] a term introduced by Pindyck (2000) in the context of greenhouse gas abatement. That is, there is a trade-off from the resistance economic point of view from releasing transgenic crops between the increase in pest susceptibility because of a decrease in pesticide use and the increase in resistance to pesticides and antibiotics because of the planting of transgenic crops.

The irreversibility effects of transgenic crops and the uncertainty about their future costs and benefits will have an impact on the optimal timing of releasing them. Irreversible costs, uncertainty, and their impact on optimal investment have been widely analyzed (e.g., McDonald and Siegel 1986; Pindyck 1991; Dixit and Pindyck 1994). In the literature on real option valuations, the opportunity to invest is valued in analogy to a call option in financial markets. Investors have the right but not the obligation to exercise their investments. This right, the option to invest (real option) has a value, which is a result of the option owner's flexibility and is similar to the quasi-option value developed earlier by Arrow and Fisher (1974) and Henry (1974) (Fisher 2000). Chavas (1994) provided similar results in his application to investments in agriculture. Dixit and Pindyck (1994) also suggested an application not only to investment problems but also to all kinds of decisionmaking under temporal uncertainty and irreversibility.[4] Recently, the approach has been applied to, among others, the adoption of soil conservation measures (Winter-Nelson and Amegbeto 1998; Shively 2000), marketing (Richards and Green 2000), wilderness preservation (Conrad 2000), agriculture labor migration (Richards and Patterson 1998), and the analysis of government reforms (Leitzel and Weisman 1999). Leitzel and Weisman (1999) argued that new government policies require investments in the form of training of government officials, hiring of additional workers, and buying of equipment. Part of these costs is irreversible, but the success of the implemented policy is uncertain, which results in a positive value of the option to delay the implementation of the policy. In the case of transgenic crops, there would be additional irreversible government policy costs, for example, from the implementation of biosafety regulations and changes in patent laws.

This chapter emphasizes the economic impact of transgenic crops on pest resistance, which are either irreversible costs or irreversible benefits. The irreversible costs of regulatory policies, which may well be greater than the environmental ones, as an anonymous reviewer of this chapter indicated, also can be included in the analysis but would change the focus of analysis and are therefore left out for future research.

Recent ex ante studies on the costs and benefits of transgenic crops (Qaim and von Braun 1998; Sianesi and Ulph 1998; O'Shea and Ulph 2000) have not considered the irreversible costs and benefits of transgenic crops. Thus, one of the objectives of this chapter is to contribute to the existing literature on ex ante assessment of transgenic crops in general. Furthermore, as the real option approach used in this chapter allows us to derive solutions independent of individual preferences, this contribution may help to rationalize the debate on transgenic crops. Also, policy options for pest resistance management, like mandatory refuge areas and their impact on the decision to release transgenic crops, will be discussed. The chapter ends with conclusions for pest resistance policies and suggests areas for future research.

Methodological Approach To Assess the Benefits and Costs of Agrobiotechnology

Consider a decisionmaker or a decisionmaking body similar to the U.S. Environmental Protection Agency (U.S. EPA) that has the authority to decide whether a particular transgenic crop, for example, a toxin-producing crop like *Bt* corn,[5] should be released for commercial planting. The agency can approve an application for release or can postpone the decision. The objective of the agency is to maximize the welfare of consumers living in the economy, and it ignores positive and negative transboundary effects. The supply for all transgenic crops is perfectly elastic, and demand is perfectly inelastic per unit of time.[6] Ex ante effects of the decision to release transgenic crops on the upstream sector of the economy are ignored by the agency.

Within this setting, the welfare effect of releasing a specific transgenic crop can be described as the net present value V_T from the point of release T until infinity of the additional annual net benefits at the farm level B_t, which will be further defined below, minus the difference between irreversible costs I and irreversible benefits R.

R and I are assumed to be known and constant, which is a useful simplification for two reasons. First, not much is known about the magnitude of irreversible costs I. As will be shown later, the model can be solved for the irreversible costs and provide information about an acceptable level, which can then be compared with available information. Second, information about the irreversible damages from pesticide use on a per-hectare level, which are the irreversible benefits R of planting transgenic crops, is available and can easily be included in the model.

In analogy to financial options $-(I - R) < 0$ is equivalent to the exercise price of a call option on a stock, here with the right but not the obligation to release transgenic crops in the environment. If the option to release transgenic crops $F(V)$ is exercised, the decisionmaker acquires the additional net benefits V_T from transgenic crops equivalent to the dividend stream of a stock. The difference $V_T - (I - R)$ is the *intrinsic value* of the option to release transgenic crops. Because it is not optimal to exercise a financial option immediately if the intrinsic value becomes positive (e.g., Hull 2000), it is not optimal to exercise the option to release transgenic crops either. The option has a value of waiting, the so-called *time value*. The option should be exercised if the *time value* of the option falls to zero. The objective of the decisionmaker can be described as maximizing the value of the option to release transgenic crops:

$$\max F(V) = \max E\left\{\left[V_T - (I - R)\right]e^{-\lambda T}\right\} \tag{1}$$

where E is the expectation operator, T is the unknown future point in time when the transgenic crop is released into the environment, and λ is the discount rate.

Because the release of a transgenic crop has almost no effect on the fixed costs, the net benefits from a transgenic crop at farm level for a specific region are the total sum of gross margins over all farms. The welfare effect at farm level in year t, hence, is the difference between the sums of gross margins from transgenic crops ($BGM_t - CGM_t$), minus the total sum of gross margins from the alternative nontransgenic crop ($BCC_t - CCC_t$) (or conventional crop). From now on, this difference will be called the additional net benefit from transgenic crops B_t. Other additional benefits arising from the application of the new technology, such as through "peace of mind" (Monsanto 1999), are assumed to be balanced by concerns about the new technology on average and are therefore ignored.[7] Thus

$$B_t = \left(BGM_t - CGM_t\right) - \left(BCC_t - CCC_t\right) \tag{2}$$

The benefits and costs of Equation 2 are those that are not irreversible. Growers of transgenic crops can stop planting them if B_t turns out to be negative; they can plant conventional crops instead and move back to transgenic crops if it turns out to be positive again without bearing additional costs. When future additional net benefits B_t are discounted at $\lambda = \mu$—the risk-adjusted rate of return derived from the capital asset pricing model (CAPM)—and grow annually at a rate α, starting from the point of release T, then the present value of additional net benefits at the point of release T is:[8]

$$V\left(B_T\right) = \frac{B_T}{\left(\mu - \alpha\right)} \tag{3}$$

The difference between μ and α is the convenience yield δ. If speculative bubbles will be ruled out and as $V(0) = 0$, Equation 3 also will describe the value of releasing transgenic crops in the environment. Including constant irreversible costs I and irreversible benefits R, transgenic crops should be released in the environment if $V(B_T) > (I - R)$. This is similar to the neoclassical or Marshallian optimality condition under certainty, which states that transgenic crops should be released if the additional net benefits are greater than the irreversible costs minus the irreversible benefits. Because V is a constant multiple of B, the value of the option to release transgenic crops depends on B; therefore, writing $F(B)$ is preferred over writing $F(V)$.[9]

Following Dixit and Pindyck (1994), the maximal value of $F(B)$ under uncertainty will be derived by choosing a stochastic process that additional net benefits B_t follow, solving the model using contingent claim analysis, which results in a stochastic differential equation. Choosing appropriate functions and solving for the unknown parameters according to the boundary conditions can allow us to find a solution to the stochastic differential equation. This will provide the new optimality conditions, including the option to delay the release of transgenic crops in the environment.

To start with, a process replicating the stochastic path of the additional net benefits B_t over time is chosen. The geometric Brownian motion has been used frequently to model returns from agricultural crops (Shively 2000; Price and Wetzstein 1999) and farm investments (Khanna et al. 2000; Winter-Nelson and Amegbeto 1998; Purvis et al. 1995). The geometric Brownian motion is a nonstationary, continuous-time stochastic process in which α is the constant drift rate, σ is the constant variance rate, and dz is the Wiener process, with $E(dz) = 0$ and $E(dz)^2 = dt$

$$dB = \alpha Bdt + \sigma Bdz \qquad (4)$$

The geometric Brownian motion is the limit of a random walk (Cox and Miller 1965), hence it is consistent with the assumption of log normality of the stochastic variable with zero drift and is often chosen by economists because of its analytical tractability. The expected value of this process grows at the rate α. A positive growth rate assumes that benefits grow continuously over time. An example of a geometric Brownian motion is shown in Figure 9-1.

Richards and Green (2000) suggested decomposing returns from agricultural crops. They modeled crop prices as a geometric Brownian motion and crop yields as a geometric Brownian motion combined with a Poisson process, where the geometric Brownian motion represents "normal" years and the Poisson process years with extreme yields. If additional net benefits B_t are chosen as stochastic variable, it can be assumed that extreme yields are smoothed, and, hence, a decomposition of prices and yields would not be necessary.

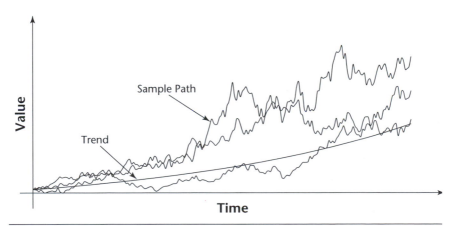

FIGURE 9-1. Sample Paths of a Geometric Brownian Motion

Additional net benefits B_t could also be modeled by a mean-reverting process, in which it is assumed that additional net benefits B_t are decreasing over time. The decrease could be explained by the observation that pests are becoming resistant to plant-produced pesticides and weeds are becoming resistant to broadband herbicides. Wesseler (forthcoming) compared the results of modeling additional net benefits with a geometric Brownian motion and a mean-reverting process and showed that the different processes could result in different decisions. This leads to the problem of identifying the relevant process. The identification of the relevant process based on time-series data is difficult, because the results are ambiguous (Pindyck and Rubinfeld 1991). Dixit and Pindyck (1994) therefore recommend identifying the process based on theoretical arguments.

In this chapter, the geometric Brownian motion is used to model additional net benefits, and hence it is assumed that research into transgenic crops results in new transgenic crops that can replace older ones continuously. The appendix shows the solution for the optimal level of additional net benefits $B*$ using contingent claim analysis following the approach of Dixit and Pindyck (1994, 147–52) with the following results:

$$B* = \frac{\beta_1}{\beta_1 - 1}\delta(I - R) \tag{A6}$$

$$\text{with } \beta_1 = \frac{1}{2} - \frac{r - \delta}{\sigma^2} + \sqrt{\left[\frac{r - \delta}{\sigma^2} - \frac{1}{2}\right]^2 + \frac{2r}{\sigma^2}} > 1 \tag{A8}$$

and $I > R$ where r is the risk-free rate of return and β_1 is the positive root of the solution to the second-order differential Equation A2 in the appendix.

The result of Equation A6 provides as a rule that it is optimal to release transgenic crops if the benefits are equal to the difference between the irreversible costs and benefits annualized by the convenience yield δ and multiplied by the factor $\beta/(\beta - 1)$. The factor $\beta/(\beta - 1)$ also is called the hurdle rate (Dixit 1989); accordingly $[\beta/(\beta - 1)]\delta$ is called here the annualized hurdle rate. In comparison with the Marshallian optimality conditions, the additional net benefits have to be higher by the factor $\beta/(\beta - 1)$. As Equation A4 indicates, the full value of releasing transgenic crops in the environment $V(B*)$ has to include not only the irreversible costs and benefits but also the real option value $F(B*)$ of the release (Dixit and Pindyck 1994, 141). This is illustrated in Figure 9-2. The horizontal axis indicates the additional net benefits B from transgenic crops. The straight line shows the present value of releasing transgenic crops immediately. The slope of the straight line is $1/(\mu - \alpha)$ and turns positive at $B = I - R$ and is called hereafter accordingly the Marshallian line. The nonlinear line shows the option value of releasing transgenic crops, in the following called the option line. The option value starts at zero and smoothly matches the Marshallian line at B^*. From B^* onward, the option value continues linearly with the Marshallian line. To the left of B^*, the option value is above the value from releasing transgenic crops immediately, and there the gains from delaying the release of transgenic crops are higher than the gains from an immediate release. The value of the option to release is equal to the value of an immediate release to the right of B^*. If the additional net benefits B_t are as high as B^* or higher, the option to release transgenic crops should be exercised.

Equation A6 also indicates that the irreversible benefits of transgenic crops offset the irreversible costs and therefore reduce the opportunity costs of the project. Including the irreversible benefits reduces the required percentage by which the additional net benefits have to be above the irreversible costs. The higher the irreversible benefits of transgenic crops are, the lower the additional benefits B^* must be to justify the release. This is similar to a parallel upward move of the Marshallian line as illustrated in Figure 9-3. The new optimal level of additional net benefits $B^{*\prime}$ moves to the left of the initial optimality level B^* with an increase in R. On the contrary, with an increase in the irreversible costs, the new optimality level moves to the right.

The irreversible benefits of releasing transgenic crops may even be higher than the irreversible costs of releasing them. In this case, a release of transgenic crops into the environment may be justified if the additional net benefits are negative. Under this scenario there is no time value, and the value of the option to release

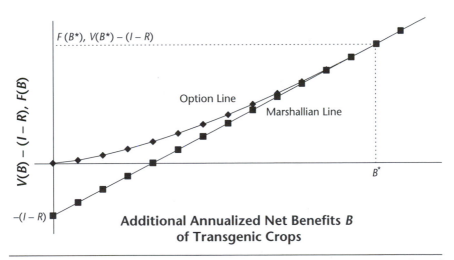

FIGURE 9-2. Value of the Option To Release Transgenic Crops as a Function of Net Benefits B

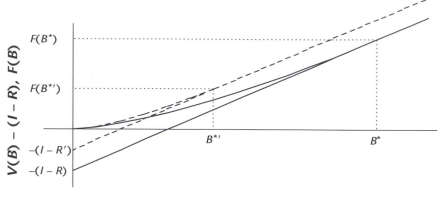

**Additional Annualized Net Benefits *B*
of Transgenic Crops**

FIGURE 9-3. Effects of a Decrease in Net Irreversible Costs $-(I - R)$ on the Optimal Minimum Level of Additional Net Benefits B^*

transgenic crops is equivalent to the value of immediately releasing transgenic crops. The Marshallian criteria can be applied, and hence transgenic crops should be released immediately if $V(B) - I + R > 0$. If there are no irreversible costs of releasing transgenic crops, they should be released if $V(B) + R > 0$. The situation in which irreversible benefits are greater than the irreversible costs is illustrated in Figure 9-4. The optimal level of B^* is to the left of the origin.

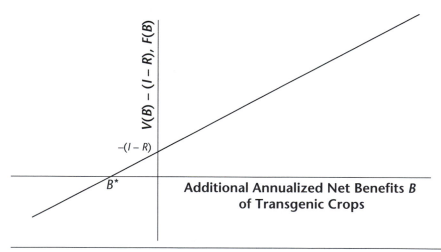

FIGURE 9-4. Optimal Minimum Level of Additional Net Benefits B^* with Irreversible Benefits Greater Than Irreversible Costs, $R > I$

Defining Maximal Tolerable Irreversible Costs

The simple model presented here provides insights into the optimal timing for releasing transgenic crops in the environment. In the model it was assumed that the irreversible costs were certain. This is a heroic assumption because most of the environmental effects of transgenic crops are not known and those that are known are not certain. Solving Equation A6 for the irreversible costs can reduce the relevance of uncertainty about irreversible costs. This provides

$$I^* = R + \frac{B_T/2}{\beta/\beta - 1} = R + \frac{B_T}{\delta} - \frac{B_T/\delta}{\beta} \tag{5a}$$

or

$$I^* = R + \gamma B_T, \text{with } \gamma = \frac{\beta - 1}{\beta \delta} \tag{5b}$$

where γ is the slope parameter.

Instead of identifying the additional net benefits required to release transgenic crops into the environment, the maximum tolerable irreversible costs under given additional net benefits B_T and irreversible benefits R are identified. If they are known, a space can be designed that shows areas of rejection and approval of releasing transgenic crops. The tolerable costs of an increase in resistance captured in I^* will be higher the higher the benefits from a reduced pressure on resistance buildup are, captured in R, and the higher the current benefits from transgenic crops are, captured in B.

Equation 5a can be formulated as a rule the agency should follow when it has to decide whether a transgenic crop should be released:

Postpone the release of a transgenic crop into the environment if the irreversible costs are higher than the irreversible benefits plus the present value of an infinite stream of instantaneous additional net benefits, using the convenience yield as the relevant discount rate, divided by the hurdle rate.

This rule has two important properties, which result from the use of the contingent claim analysis (see appendix). First, future costs and benefits have been discounted using rates provided by the market. No individual discount rates have been used. Second, uncertainty about the additional net benefits has been included by using a riskless hedge portfolio, and, hence, the evaluation of the benefits is independent of attitudes toward risk, which reduces the impact of risk preferences on decisionmaking.

The second expression of the maximum tolerable irreversible costs in Equation 5a illustrates the effect of waiting because of uncertainty and irreversibility. The first two terms, R and B/δ, illustrate the results of the orthodox approach. Without explicitly recognizing irreversibility and uncertainty, the benefits are the sum of the irreversible benefits plus the present value of infinite additional net benefits. By including irreversibility and uncertainty, a proportion of the present value of infinite additional net benefits, $(B_T/\delta)/\beta$, must be deducted. This proportion in this context can be interpreted as the economic value of uncertainty and the irreversibility of releasing transgenic crops.

Impact of Different Policies

The optimal level of B^* or I^* is not fixed. Their values will change depending on prices, interest rates, uncertainty, and other variables. This opens the window for policy impacts on the optimal level and hence on whether it is optimal to release transgenic crops immediately.

The analysis of policy impacts starts by studying the effect of changes in different model parameters on B^*. If not stated otherwise, the figures presented in this chapter are based on the following parameter values: $\alpha = 0.04$, $\sigma = 0.4$, $r = 0.04$, and $\mu = 0.08$.

The important parameters of the model are the drift rate α and the variance rate σ. An increase in the drift rate α decreases β and therefore the ratio $\beta/(\beta - 1)$ increases. This is offset by a decrease of the convenience yield δ, resulting in a net decrease of B^* for reasonable parameter values as shown in Table 9-1 and illustrated in Figure 9-5. This can be explained by two effects. First, an increase in the drift rate α makes the future more valuable and therefore increases the value of the option to release transgenic crops. The option line moves upward. Second, an increase in the drift rate reduces the convenience yield δ (see Equation 3), and the value of immediate release $V(B)$ increases as well, as indicated by the different slopes of the Marshallian line in Figure 9-5. The overall effect is a higher value of transgenic crops, lower values of B^*, and hence an earlier release. The impact on the optimal level of I^* is an increase in the slope parameter γ, which results in higher tolerable irreversible costs, as

$$\frac{\partial I^*}{\partial \alpha} = \frac{\partial \left(\dfrac{\beta}{\delta}\right)}{\partial \alpha} \frac{\beta}{\beta - 1} + \frac{B}{\partial} \frac{\partial \left(\dfrac{\beta - 1}{\beta}\right)}{\partial \alpha} = \frac{\partial \left(\dfrac{B}{\delta}\right)}{\partial \alpha} \frac{\beta}{\beta - 1} + \frac{B}{\delta} \beta^{-2} \frac{\partial \beta}{\partial \alpha} > 0 \tag{6}$$

On the contrary, an increase in the uncertainty of the additional net benefits results in a higher value of B^*. An increase in uncertainty places a higher value on the future and increases the option value of releasing transgenic crops but has no effect on the value of an immediate release if the convenience yield

TABLE 9-1. Annualized Hurdle Rates for Different Parameter Settings.[a]

Drift rate α (%)	standard deviation σ[b]				
	0.10	0.20	0.40	0.80	1.20
1.0	0.080	0.103	0.174	0.423	0.827
2.0	0.071	0.095	0.166	0.414	0.817
4.0	0.057	0.080	0.149	0.396	0.798
6.0	0.049	0.068	0.134	0.378	0.779

a. The annualized hurdle rate as defined in Equation A6. The reciprocal values are the slope for the maximal tolerable irreversible costs function.

b. The rate of return μ is set to 8%, the risk-free rate of return r is set to 4%, and the independence between convenience yield δ and standard deviation σ is assumed.

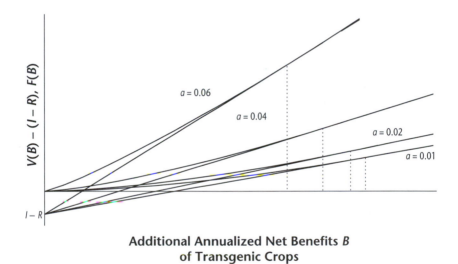

Additional Annualized Net Benefits B
of Transgenic Crops

FIGURE 9-5. Optimal Minimum Level of Additional Net Benefits B* from Transgenic Crops for Different Drift Rates a When the Risk-Adjusted Rate of Return μ Depends on the Drift Rate a

δ is independent of the variance rate σ. The slope and the intersect of the Marshallian line remain the same. This is illustrated in Figure 9-6 and Table 9-1. Figure 9-6 and Table 9-1 also demonstrate the sensitivity of B* to changes in the uncertainty of future additional net benefits. If transgenic crops reduce the uncertainty about net benefits from crops in general, the uncertainty about the additional net benefits also will be reduced, and hence the value of B* will be lower and the maximal tolerable irreversible costs will be higher, as

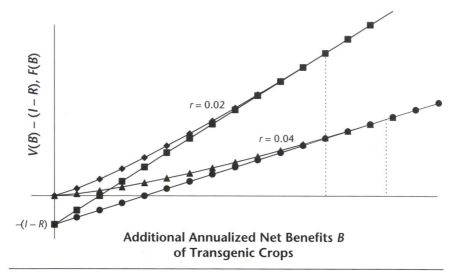

$-(I-R)$

**Additional Annualized Net Benefits B
of Transgenic Crops**

FIGURE 9-6. Optimal Minimum Level of Additional Net Benefits B^* from Transgenic Crops for Different Risk-Free Rates of Return r When the Risk-Adjusted Rate of Return μ Depends on the Risk-Free Rate of Return r

$$\frac{\partial I^*}{\partial \sigma} = \frac{B}{\delta} \frac{\partial \left(\frac{\beta - 1}{\beta} \right)}{\partial \sigma} = \frac{B}{\delta} \beta^{-2} \frac{\partial \beta}{\partial \sigma} < 0 \qquad (7)$$

Thus, if transgenic crops reduce uncertainty, they will be released earlier.[10]

Similar results are obtained by an increase of the risk-free rate of return r. An increase in the risk-free rate of return makes the future less valuable, but at the same time, decreases the value of an immediate release. The overall effect is an increase in B^* or a decrease in I^* and hence, an increase in the risk-free rate of return r results in a later release of transgenic crops, as

$$\frac{\partial I^*}{\partial r} = \frac{B}{\delta} \frac{\partial \left(\frac{\beta - 1}{\beta} \right)}{\partial r} = \frac{B}{\delta} \beta^{-2} \frac{\partial \beta}{\partial r} < 0 \qquad (8)$$

The effect is illustrated in Figure 9-7.

Table 9-1 also illustrates that a combined increase in drift rate α and variance rate σ results in a higher annualized hurdle rate over the parameter ranges considered. This can be shown by considering Young's theorem in obtaining the derivative of I^* with respect to σ and α:

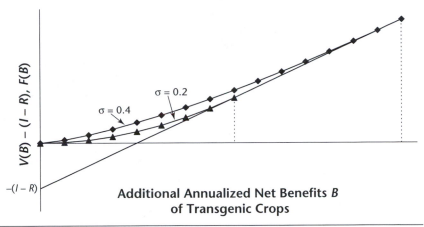

FIGURE 9-7. Optimal Minimum Level of Additional Net Benefits *B** from Transgenic Crops for Different Standard Deviations σ When the Risk-Adjusted Rate of Return μ is Independent of the Standard Deviation σ

$$\frac{\partial I^*}{\partial \sigma \partial \alpha} = \frac{\partial \left(\dfrac{B}{\delta} \right)}{\partial \alpha} \beta^{-2} \frac{\partial \beta}{\partial \sigma} + \frac{B}{\delta} \frac{\partial \left(\beta^{-2} \dfrac{\partial \beta}{\partial \sigma} \right)}{\partial \alpha} < 0 \qquad (9)$$

The first term of Equation 9 shows the change the growth rate α has on the current additional net benefits, which is positive and multiplied by the negative effect of σ on β. Hence, the total effect of the first term on *I** is negative. This negative effect is augmented by the negative second term. The overall impact of a simultaneous marginal change is a decrease in the maximal tolerable irreversible costs *I**. The positive effect of an increase in the growth rate on the likelihood of an earlier release is surpassed by the negative effect of an increase in uncertainty on the likelihood of an earlier release.

Mandatory Refuge Systems

A regulatory policy introduced in the United States to control the benefits from transgenic plants is a set-aside policy. For every acre planted to pest-resistant transgenic crops, farmers are required to cultivate *x* acres of conventional crops to provide refuge areas (EPA 1998). This policy reduces the possible total additional benefits from transgenic crops compared with a situation in which mandatory refuge areas would not be necessary. The effect can be modeled as a decrease in additional net benefits B and hence is similar to a simultaneous decrease in the drift and the risk parameter. As discussed earlier, a decrease in the drift parameter α results in an increase of B^* (see Figure 9-5). A reduction of the risk parameter σ reduces the value of the option to release transgenic crops, thus resulting in a decrease of the ratio $\beta/(\beta - 1)$. The overall simultaneous effect on both parameters results in a decrease of B^*.

Similar results are obtained by implementing a tax on the cultivation of transgenic crops to compensate for potential environmental damages. This policy will reduce the additional net benefits from transgenic crops as well. Both policies, mandatory refuge areas and taxation of additional net benefits B, result in a lower value of B^* or a higher value of I^*, and hence transgenic crops will be released earlier.[11] This is the opposite result from the orthodox framework, in which a reduction in benefits would lower the net present value and decrease the likelihood for executing the project.

Policies Affecting the Variance and the Risk-Free Rate of Return

The liberalization of agricultural markets may have different impacts on price risks. If liberalization results in an increased price risk at farm level,[12] this will result, all things being equal, in an increase of the risk parameter σ and hence of the option value of releasing transgenic crops into the environment. This increases the option value of releasing transgenic crops and hence the optimal value of additional net benefits B^*, decreases the optimal maximal tolerable irreversible costs I^*, and increases the likelihood of delaying a release in the environment.

Similar results are obtained from policies that result in an increase of the risk-free rate of return, such as an increase in the rate of return in government bonds, a common measure for the risk-free rate of return. The difference between irreversible costs and benefits are discounted at the risk-free rate of return r, whereas the additional net benefits are discounted at δ. As the risk-free rate of return increases, δ increases as well if the growth rate α is held constant. As the future becomes less important, the value of the option to release transgenic crops will be reduced, and hence B^* will decrease.

In summary, policies increasing the maximum tolerable irreversible costs I^* will lead to an earlier release of transgenic crops, although policies increasing future uncertainty and the risk-free rate of return will delay the release. The impacts of different policies on the optimal timing of releasing transgenic crops are summarized in Table 9-2.

TABLE 9-2. Effects of Policies on the Timing of Releasing Transgenic Crops

Policies	Parameter changes	Effect on release
Mandatory refuge systems tax on additional net benefits	Decrease in trend α and standard deviation σ	Earlier
Trade liberalization	Increase in standard deviation σ	Later
Increase in interest rate	Increase in risk-free rate of return r	Later

Conclusion

The release of transgenic crops into the environment is expected to have negative as well as positive impacts on the resistance of pests and bacteria against biocides and antibiotics, respectively. Because pest susceptibility may be a nonrenewable resource, a reduction in susceptibility may be irreversible. Positive impacts on resistance lead to irreversible benefits, whereas negative impacts lead to irreversible costs. In addition to being irreversible, costs and benefits of transgenic crops (both reversible and irreversible) are uncertain, and the decision to release transgenic crops can be postponed. Including uncertainty, irreversible resistance costs and benefits (and the possibility to postpone the release into the cost–benefit framework) justify a delay of the decision to release transgenic crops into the environment. This is so even if the current net present value of releasing them is positive because in the meantime, new information not only on the additional net benefits but also on the amount of irreversible costs may arrive. This is well known in the literature on real and quasi-options but has not been applied to ex ante assessments of transgenic crops. Because there is more information about reversible additional net benefits and irreversible benefits available than about the irreversible costs, we propose to use the irreversible costs as the relevant hurdle to decide about the release of transgenic crops. Applying the real options approach, the maximal tolerable irreversible costs were defined and used as the important benchmark value for decisionmaking. The decision rule was formulated as follows:

> *Postpone the release of a transgenic crop into the environment if the irreversible costs are higher than the irreversible benefits plus the present value of an infinite stream of instantaneous additional net benefits, using the convenience yield as the relevant discount rate, divided by the hurdle rate.*

The decision rule for releasing transgenic crops into the environment was derived using contingent claim analysis. This approach allows us to derive solutions independent of risk and time preference. Those concerned about the environmental risks of transgenic crops and those who just want to maximize their income would come to the same conclusion about the timing of release. The risk-adjusted rate of return μ derived from the CAPM depends on the risk-free interest rate r and the market price of risk; hence the optimal decision to release transgenic crops is not independent of changes in interest rates.

The decision rule also implies that in the extreme case, when the irreversible benefits are higher than the irreversible costs, an immediate release of transgenic crops is justified even when the net present value of the additional net benefits is negative.

The effects of policies on the timing of releasing transgenic crops were analyzed in a two-step procedure. First, the impacts on model parameters and then the effect of the parameter changes on the maximum tolerable irreversible costs were identified. The most counterintuitive result was the increase in the likelihood of an earlier release with a decrease in additional net benefits. This was explained by the opposite impact—a simultaneous change in the growth rate and the variance rate on the maximum tolerable irreversible costs. Mandatory refuge areas for pest resistance management and a tax on transgenic crops to compensate for possible environmental risks have this kind of effect on the timing of release.

In the analysis, we assumed that the irreversible benefits and costs are constant. Irreversible and uncertain regulatory costs were not included. Future research should include specification of irreversible environmental benefits and costs, their feedback on the additional net benefits, and irreversible and uncertain regulatory costs. Nevertheless, the approach presented is already an improvement compared with the *Guidelines for Preparing Economic Analyses* of the EPA (2000b), and they are easily applicable.

References

Alston, J., G. Norton, and P. Pardey. 1998. *Science under Scarcity*. New York: CAB International.

Amram, M., and N. Kulatilaka. 1999. *Real Options*. Boston: Harvard Business School Press.

Antle, J., and P. Pingali. 1994. Pesticides, Productivity and Farmers' Health: A Philippine Case Study. *American Journal of Agricultural Economics* 76(3): 418–30.

Arrow, K., and A. Fisher. 1974. Environmental Preservation, Uncertainty, and Irreversibility. *Quarterly Journal of Economics* 88: 312–19.

Carpenter, J.E., and L.P. Gianessi. 1999. Herbicide Tolerant Soybeans: Why Growers Are Adopting Roundup Ready Varieties. *AgBioForum* 2(2): 65–72.

Chavas, J.-P. 1994. Production and Investment Decisions under Sunk Costs and Temporary Uncertainty. *American Journal of Agriculture Economics* 76(1): 114–27.

Conrad, J.M. 2000. Wilderness: Options to Preserve, Extract, or Develop. *Resource and Energy Economics* 22(3): 205–19.

Cox, D.R., and H. D. Miller. 1965. *The Theory of Stochastic Processes.* London: Chapman and Hall.

Dixit, A.K. 1989. Entry and Exit Decisions under Uncertainty. *Journal of Political Economy* 97(3): 620–38.

Dixit, A.K., and R.S. Pindyck. 1994. *Investment under Uncertainty.* Princeton, NJ: Princeton University Press.

Ellstrand, N.C., H.C. Prentice, and J.F. Hancock. 1999. Gene Flow and Introgression from Domesticated Plants into Their Wild Relatives. *Annual Review of Ecology and Systematics* 30: 539–63.

Ervin, D., S. Batie, R.Welsh, C.L. Carpentier, J. Fern, N. Richman, and M. Schulz. 2000. *Transgenic Cops: An Environmental Assessment.* Arlington, VA: Henry A. Wallace Center for Agricultural & Environmental Policy at Winrock International.

Fernandez-Cornejo, J., C. Klotz-Ingram, and S. Jans. 1999. Farm-Level Effects of Adopting Genetically Engineered Crops in the U.S.A. In *Transitions in Agbiotech: Economics of Strategy and Policy,* edited by William H. Lesser. Proceedings of NE-165 Conference June 1999, Washington D.C. Including papers presented at the International Consortium on Agricultural Biotechnology Research Conference June 1999 Rome Tor Vergata, Italy.

Fisher, A. 2000. Investment under Uncertainty and Option Value in Environmental Economics. *Resource and Energy Economics* 22(3): 197–204.

Fleischer, G. 1998. *Ökonomische Bewertungskriterien in der Pflanzenschutzpolitik—Das Beispiel der Zulassungsprüfung.* Kiel, Germany: Wissenschaftsverlag Vauk.

Fulton, M., and L. Keyowski. 1999. The Producer Benefits of Herbicide-Resistant Canola. *AgBioForum* 2(2): 85–93.

Henry, C.. 1974. Investment Decision under Uncertainty: The Irreversibility Effect. *American Economic Review* 64: 1006–12.

Hueth, D., and U. Regev. 1974. Optimal Agricultural Pest Management with Increasing Pest Resistance. *American Journal of Agricultural Economics* 56: 543–53.

Hull, J.. 2000. Options, Futures, and Other Derivatives. London: Prentice-Hall International.

James, C. 2000. *Global Status of Commercialized Transgenic Crops: 2000.* ISAAA Briefs No. 21: Preview. Ithaca, NY: International Service for the Acquisition of Agri-biotech Applications.

Kalaitzandonakes, N. 1999. A Farm Level Perspective on Agrobiotechnology: How Much Value and For Whom? *AgBioForum* 2(2):61–64.

Kendall, H.W., R. Beachy, T. Eisner, F. Gould, R. Herdt, P.H. Raven, J.S. Schell, and M.S. Swaminathan. 1997. *Bioengineering of Crops.* Environmental and Socially Sustainable Development Studies and Monograph Series 23. Washington, DC: World Bank.

Khanna, M., M. Isik, and A. Winter-Nelson. 2000. Investment in Site-Specific Crop Management under Uncertainty: Implications for Nitrogen Pollution Control and Environmental Policy. *Agricultural Economics* 24(1): 9–21.

Krimsky, S., and R. Wrubel. 1996. *Agricultural Biotechnology and the Environment: Science, Policy, and Social Issues.* Urbana, IL: University of Illinois Press.

Leitzel, J., and E. Weisman. 1999. Investing in Policy Reform. *Journal of Institutional and Theoretical Economics* 155(4): 696–709.

Malik, V.S., and M.K. Saroha. 1999. Marker Gene Controversy in Transgenic Plants. *Journal of Plant Biochemistry & Biotechnology* 8: 1–13.

Maredia, M., D. Byerlee, and K. Maredia. 2000. Investment Strategies for Biotechnology in Emerging Research Systems. In *Transitions in Agbiotech: Economics of Strategy and Policy*, edited by William H. Lesser. Proceedings of NE-165 Conference June 1999, Washington D.C. Including papers presented at the International Consortium on Agricultural Biotechnology Research Conference June 1999 Rome Tor Vergata, Italy.

Marvier, M. 2001. Ecology of Transgenic Crops. *American Scientist* 89(2): 160–7.

McDonald, R., and D. Siegel. 1986. The Value of Waiting to Invest. *Quarterly Journal of Economics* 101: 707–28.

Merton, R.C. 1998. Application of Option Pricing Theory: Twenty-Five Years Later. *American Economic Review* 88(3): 323–49.

Monsanto Company. 1999. Bollgard® and Roundup Ready® Cotton Performance—1996–1997. http://www.monsanto.com/ag/articles/ bollrr.htm (accessed April 28, 1999).

O'Shea, L., and A. Ulph. 2000. Providing the Correct Incentives for Genetic Modification. Paper presented at Biotechnology, Environmental Policy, and Agriculture: A Workshop on the Management of the Impacts of Biotechnologies, May 2000, Rome, Italy.

Pindyck, R.S. 1991. Irreversibility, Uncertainty, and Investment. *Journal of Economic Literature* 29: 1340–51.

———. 2000. Irreversibilities and the Timing of Environmental Policy. *Resource and Energy Economics* 22(3): 233–59.

Pindyck, R.S., and D.L. Rubinfeld. 1991. *Econometric Models and Economic Forecasts*. New York: McGraw Hill.

Pray, C., D. Ma, J. Huang, and F. Qiao. 2001. Impact of *Bt*-Cotton in China. *World Development* 29(5): 813–25.

Price, T.J., and M. Wetzstein. 1999. Irreversible Investment in Perennial Crops with Yield and Price Uncertainty. *Journal of Agricultural and Resource Economics* 24: 173–85.

Purvis, A., W. Boggess, C. Moss, and J. Holt. 1995. Adoption of Emerging Technologies under Output Uncertainty: An Ex-Ante Approach. *American Journal of Agriculture Economics* 77(3): 541–51.

Qaim, M., and J. von Braun. 1998. *Crop Biotechnology in Developing Countries: A Conceptual Framework for Ex Ante Economic Analysis*. ZEF Discussion Papers on Development Policy No. 3. Bonn, Germany: Center for Development Research.

Richards, T.J., and G. Green. 2000. Economic Hysteresis in Variety Selection: Why Grow No Wine Before Its Time? Paper presented at the Mini-Symposium New Investment Theory in Agricultural Economics—Its Implication for Farm Management, Environmental Policy and Development. XXIV International Conference of Agricultural Economists. August 2000. Berlin, Germany.

Richards, T.J., and P.M. Patterson. 1998. Hysteresis and the Shortage of Agricultural Labour. *American Journal of Agriculture Economics* 80(4): 683–95.

Saxena, D., S. Flores, and G. Stotzky. 1999. Insecticidal Toxin in Root Exudates from *Bt*-Corn. *Nature* 402: 480.

Shively, G. 2000. Investing in Soil Conservation When Returns Are Uncertain: A Real Options Approach. Paper presented at the Mini-Symposium New Investment Theory in Agricultural Economics—Its Implication for Farm Management, Environmental Policy and Development. XXIV International Conference of Agricultural Economists. August 2000. Berlin, Germany.

Sianesi, B., and D. Ulph. 1998. Species Loss through the Genetic Modification of Crops—A Policy Framework. Paper presented at The First World Congress of Resource and Environmental Economists. June 1998. Venice, Italy.

Tabashnik, B.E., A.L. Patin, T.J. Dennehy, Y.-B. Liu, Y. Carrière, M.A. Sims, and L. Antilla. 2000. Frequency of Resistance to *Bacillus thuringiensis* in Field Populations of Pink Bollworm. *Proceedings of the National Academy of Sciences of the USA* 97(24): 12980–84.

U.S. EPA (U.S. Environmental Protection Agency). 1998. *The Environmental Protection Agency's White Paper on* Bt *Plant-Pesticide Resistance Management*. Washington, DC: Environmental Protection Agency.

———. 2000a. Bt *Plant-Pesticides Biopesticides Registration Action Document*. October 2000. http://www.epa.gov/scipoly/sap/2000/october/ brad4_irm.pdf (accessed May 21, 2001).

———. 2000b. *Guidelines for Preparing Economic Analyses*. EPA 240-R-00-003. Washington, DC: Environmental Protection Agency.

Waibel, H. and G. Fleischer. 1998. *Kosten und Nutzen des chemischen Pflanzenschutzes in der deutschen Landwirtschaft aus gesamtwirtschaftlicher Sicht*. Kiel, Germany: Wissenschaftsverlag Vauk.

Wambugu, F. 1999. Why Africa Needs Agricultural Biotech. *Nature* 400: 15–6.

Wesseler, J. Forthcoming. Assessing the Risk of Transgenic Crops—The Role of Scientific Belief Systems. In *Integrative Systems Approaches to Natural and Social Sciences—Systems Science 2000*, edited by M. Matthies, H. Malchow, and J. Kriz. Berlin, Germany: Springer-Verlag.

Winter-Nelson, A., and K. Amegbeto. 1998. Option Values to Conservation and Agricultural Price Policy: Application to Terrace Construction in Kenya. *American Journal of Agriculture Economics* 80(2): 409–18.

Appendix: Deriving the Optimal Level of Additional Net Benefits

If the option to release transgenic crops in the environment $F(B)$ is exercised, the value of the option to release transgenic crops will be exchanged against the value of additional net benefits terms from transgenic crops in present value plus the irreversible benefits R minus the irreversible costs I of releasing transgenic crops. Other reversible benefits and costs are considered in Equation A1. The objective function can be described as maximizing the value of the option to release transgenic crops. It will be assumed that V also follows a geometric Brownian motion as it is a constant multiple of B with the same parameters α and σ. As $\mu = \delta + \alpha$ it follows that $V = B/\delta$. Assuming that an asset or a portfolio of assets exists that allows us to track the risk of the additional net benefits, the arbitrage pricing principle can be applied to value the portfolio that includes the additional benefits from transgenic crops. Following Dixit and Pindyck (1994, 147–52), a portfolio can be constructed consisting of the option to release transgenic crops in the environment $F(B)$, and a short position of $n = F'(B)$ units of the additional benefits of transgenic crops. The value of this portfolio is $\Phi = F(B) - F'(B)B$. A short position will require a payment to the holder of the corresponding long position of $\partial F' (B)Bdt$. The total return from holding this portfolio over a short time interval $(t, t + dt)$ holding $F'(B)$ constant will be

$$d\Phi = dF(B) - F'(B)dB - \delta BF'(B)dt \qquad \text{(A1)}$$

Applying Ito's Lemma to $dF(B)$, equating the return of the riskless portfolio to the risk-free rate of return $r[F(B) - F'(B)B]dt$ and rearranging terms results in the following differential equation:

$$\frac{1}{2}\sigma^2 B^2 F''(B) + (r - \delta)BF'(B) - rF(B) = 0 \qquad \text{(A2)}$$

A solution to this homogenous, second-order differential equation is

$$F(B) = A_1 B^{\beta_1} + A_2 B^{\beta_2} \text{ with } \beta_1 > 1 \text{ and } \beta_2 < 0 \qquad \text{(A3)}$$

Because the value of the option to release transgenic crops in the environment is worthless if there are no additional net benefits, A_2 must be 0. The other boundary conditions are the "value matching" (Equation A4) and the "smooth pasting" (Equation A5) conditions

$$F(B^*) = V(B^*) - I + R \qquad \text{(A4)}$$

$$F'(B^*) = V'(B^*) \qquad \text{(A5)}$$

Solving Equation A3 according to the boundary conditions provides the following solutions:

$$B^* = \frac{\beta_1}{\beta_1 - 1}\delta(I - R) \qquad \text{(A6)}$$

$$A_1 = \frac{(\beta_1 - 1)^{\beta_1 - 1}}{(I - R)^{\beta_1 - 1}(\delta\beta_1)^{\beta_1}} \qquad \text{(A7)}$$

$$\text{with } \beta_1 = \frac{1}{2} - \frac{r - \delta}{\sigma^2} + \sqrt{\left[\frac{r - \delta}{\sigma^2} - \frac{1}{2}\right]^2 + \frac{2r}{\sigma^2}} > 1 \qquad \text{(A8)}$$

and $I > R$.

Notes

1. Ervin and others (2000) provide a detailed survey of the most recent empirical studies on the environmental effects of transgenic crops.

2. *Bt* cotton is genetically modified cotton that produces toxins of the soil bacterium *Bacillus thuringiensis* to control Lepidopteran pests.

3. I am thankful to Vittorio Santaniello for stressing this point.

4. Nobel laureate Robert C. Merton (1998) provided an interesting overview of the application of option pricing theory outside financial economics. The book by Amram and Kulatilaka (1999) includes several case studies of real option pricing.

5. Modified corn that produces the δ-endotoxins of the soil bacterium *Bacillus thuringiensis* to control the European corn borer.

6. This assumption is often used for this kind of analysis (e.g., Alston et al. 1998; Maredia et al. 2000).

7. Monsanto (1999) cited the positive mental effect on users because of the positive impact of transgenic crops on the environment as one positive benefit from transgenic crops. The company called this kind of benefit "peace of mind."

8. The motivation for choosing the risk-adjusted rate of return is that the risk of the additional benefits could be tracked with a dynamic portfolio of market assets. $\mu = r + \phi\sigma\rho_{bm}$, where r is the risk-free interest rate, ϕ is the market price of risk, σ is the variance parameter, and ρ_{bm} is the coefficient of correlation between the asset or portfolio of assets that track B and the whole market portfolio. See Dixit and Pindyck (1994, 147–50) for an elaboration of this assumption.

9. This follows from Equation 3, $V_T = B_T/(\mu - \alpha)$, where μ and α are constants. Hence, $dV = d[B/(\mu - \alpha)] = [1/(\mu - \alpha)]dB = \alpha V dt + \sigma V dz$.

10. The effect of an increase in uncertainty on the option value changes if the convenience yield δ is not independent of the variance rate σ anymore. Modeled this way, an increase in the variance rate σ increases the convenience yield δ. The overall effect is a lower option value, but because of changes in the value of an immediate release $V(B)$, the overall effect on B^* is positive. Under both modeling approaches, the total effect is an increase in B^*.

11. Of course, the limits to taxation or refuge area are reached by a 100% tax or 100% refuge area, which is similar to not releasing the transgenic crop.

12. A removal, for example, of the European Union minimum price policy, which exists for many products, may in the short run result in an increase in price uncertainty. In the long run, markets to hedge the risk may evolve and reduce the price uncertainty.

Commentary

Economics of Transgenic Crops and Pest Resistance: An Epidemiological Perspective

Christopher A. Gilligan

Perceptions differ: biologists and economists view the deployment of transgenic crops for pest resistance through different lenses. By focusing on uncertainty and irreversibility, the papers by Morel and others (Chapter 8, this volume) and Wesseler (Chapter 9, this volume) provide an appealing focus from which to bridge the disciplines, to challenge assumptions, and to build a coherent framework for the deployment of transgenic crops. The strategic decision about the deployment of transgenic crops common to economists and biologists, is "should we release now, should we release later, or not at all?" Caution comes from uncertainty in the benefits and costs of releasing a crop carrying genes that have never before been present in the genetic background of a widely cultivated species.

The common ground between biology and economics lies in uncertainty, although perceptions of uncertainty differ between the disciplines, and to a certain extent, within the treatments in this book by Morel and others and Wesseler. Economists focus on variability in the benefits and costs of transgenic crops and of conventional crops together with irreversible costs and benefits associated with transgenic crops that also may be subject to uncertainty. Breakdown of resistance is assumed to be inevitable and the costs estimable, although the time of breakdown is unknown. The vagaries of yield, of pest and pathogen damage, and of the growth and decline of virulent and avirulent pests are integrated into aggregate variables for economic benefits that are subject to long-term trends with year-to-year variations. This form of "top-down" analysis sits comfortably with both biologists and economists, although we shall see later that the details may differ. More important, however, is the perception of risk of resistance breakdown. Molecular biologists may contend that breakdown will not occur because the demands that novel forms of resistance, such as chitinase or major generic hypersensitive response (Stuiver and Custers 2001), impose on the pest or pathogen population are too great for them to survive. Population biologists, more familiar with the "boom-and-bust cycle" of conventionally bred crops, are likely to be less confident but still unwilling to assert that the breakdown of resistance is inevitable. An epidemiologist therefore asks

- Will a virulent form arise in the pest or pathogen population that can overcome transgenic resistance?
- Will it invade? Will it persist?
- Will it coexist with the avirulent form?
- How long will it take before the resistant form reaches a critical density?
- How does the spatial pattern of transgenic crops in the landscape affect invasion and persistence?
- If *Bt* corn fails in one state, must it be withdrawn from all states?

Variability over time and space is therefore important in both economic and epidemiological analyses. Some seasons are more conducive than others. Many nematode and insect pests and pathogenic microorganisms (mainly fungi and viruses as well as some bacteria) are capable of rapid multiplication or death. The dynamics are highly nonlinear. A small change at a critical phase in population growth can have a profound effect on subsequent dynamics; conversely a larger perturbation may have little effect as the pest rapidly recovers. Periods of growth are followed by survival between crops when the virulent form may be at a disadvantage relative to the previously endemic avirulent form. And spread occurs at the farm, regional, and continental scale in so-called spatially extended systems across a heterogeneous mosaic of fields that can themselves limit the spread of disease.

So how do we open up the dialogue between the pioneering and challenging work of Morel and others (Chapter 8, this volume) and Wesseler (Chapter 9, this volume) who analyzed deployment in the presence of uncertainty and irreversible costs and benefits with the epidemiological approaches that focus on stochasticity and nonlinearity in periodically disturbed and spatially extended systems? In this commentary, I propose to summarize an epidemiologist's perspective of the principal "take-home messages" from Morel and others and Wesseler in this book and to review the principal assumptions and implications of transgenic crops for pest resistance. Then, using examples drawn from recent work in epidemiology, I propose very briefly to review the irreversibility of resistance breakdown and to identify spatial strategies for minimizing the risks of invasion. Finally, I shall revert to consideration of stochasticity and scale in bridging the interface. The treatment is not exhaustive. It is selective and designed to advance the dialogue between economists and biologists on the release of transgenic crops for pest and disease control.

Principal Results

Conventional wisdom in the deployment of new varieties of crops focuses on cost–benefit analysis. A new variety is released immediately if the net benefits (calculated as the difference between variable benefits and variable costs) are greater than for the conventional crop. In the case of transgenic crops, variable pesticide costs are reduced, and gross revenues may increase because of enhanced yield from a new agronomically improved and pest-resistant variety. Morel and others and Wesseler convincingly argued that this reliance on cost–benefit analysis is naïve. First, they state that it fails to take into account major irreversible costs and benefits that may accompany the release of a transgenic variety. Second, it fails to take into account uncertainty in year-to-year variation in yield, pest damage, and other input variables. Decisionmaking under uncertainty—should we release the transgenic crop now, later, or never?—leads to formulation of the problem via option theory.

Put simply, this means (to a nonspecialist) that a government or other organization obtains the right to deploy a transgenic crop within a given time frame. The time at which to release the crop is obtained by optimizing a function that incorporates benefits and costs under uncertainty with a discount rate on the investment. This yields a critical value (variously represented as V^* or B^*) for net benefits of the transgenic crop necessary for release of the crop. Release is therefore delayed until net benefits match or surpass the critical value. The delay reflects the option of waiting for more information to assess whether the benefits are greater than the costs. A simplified scheme to illustrate the approaches of Morel and others and Wesseler is given in Table 1. Some of the principal variables and parameters are summarized in Tables 2 and 3, but note that parameters with the same meaning have different symbols in the two papers.

Three important results emerge. First, the critical value that must accrue for release of a transgenic crop is amplified in the presence of uncertainty [see Equation 2 in Morel and others (Chapter 8), Equation A6 in Wesseler (Chapter 9), and Table 1 in this commentary]. Second, some counterintuitive results emerge for analysis of *Bt* corn whereby mandatory refuge areas and tax incentives that might be expected to delay release actually promote earlier release (Wesseler). Third, in illustrating the application of real options analysis to the release of *Bt* corn, Morel and others show that while a simple cost–benefit analysis would favor release, preliminary allowance for uncertainty does not.

TABLE 1. Simplified Scheme To Summarize Approaches of Morel and Others (Chapter 8) and Wesseler (Chapter 9)

	Real option	Rational option
Morel and others[a]		
Generic model[a]		
Model	$dV = \alpha V dt + \sigma V dz$	$dV = \alpha V dt + \sigma V dz$
Method	$F(V) = \max E[(V - I)e^{-\rho t}$	
Inference/ decision	$\alpha < 0$ $\alpha > \rho$ $0 < \alpha < \rho$ Release Wait Release now or for- when never ever $V > V^*$	Release when $H(V,T,t) > 0$
Criterion	$V > V^* = \Gamma I$ $\Gamma = f(\alpha, \rho, \sigma)$	$H(V,T;t) = V(t)\phi(d_1) - e^{-\rho t}I\phi(d_2)$ $d_i = f(T,V,\rho,\sigma)$
Bt corn model[a]		
Model	$dB = \mu B dt + \eta B dz$ $dP = \gamma P dt + \sigma P dz$	$dB = \mu B dt + \eta B dz$ $dP = \gamma P dt + \sigma P dz$
Method	$F(B,P) = \max E[(B - P)e^{-f}$	$H(B,P,T;t) = B(t)\phi(d_1) - e^{-\rho t}P(t)\phi$
Criterion	$\left(\dfrac{B}{P}\right)^* = \dfrac{\beta}{\beta - 1} = \Gamma$ $\Gamma = f(\mu, \gamma, \eta, \sigma, \xi, \rho)$	$B(t) \geq B^* = \dfrac{\phi(d_2)}{\phi(d_1)}P(t)$ $d_i = f(B,P,T), \quad T = g(\sigma, \xi,$
Wesseler [a]		
Model	$dB = \alpha B dt + \sigma B dz$	
Method	$F(V) = \max E[(V - (I - R))e^{-\lambda T}]$	
Criterion	$B^* = \dfrac{\beta_1}{\beta_1 - 1} = \delta(I - R)$ $I^* = R + \dfrac{B(T)}{\delta}\left(\dfrac{\beta_1 - 1}{\beta_1}\right)$ $\beta_1 = f(r, \delta, \sigma)$	

a. Principal variables and parameters are summarized in Tables 2 and 3.

The detailed approaches differ between the two chapters. Morel and others distinguished in particular between real options (Dixit and Pindyck 1994) and rational option approaches (Hull 2000) (Table 1), whereas Wesseler concentrated on real options. Each approach leads to a threshold criterion for net benefit of transgenic crops. Morel and others derived the criterion $V > V^* = \Gamma I$, where Γ is an empirical measure of precaution that reflects the uncertainty in the benefits, V is the value of the net benefits of growing a transgenic crop, and I is the cost of investment. The precautionary multiplier (Γ) determines how much the actual value of the policy should be above its cost to justify releasing a novel crop [see also the annualized hurdle rate used by Wesseler (Table 9-2)]. Because Γ is greater than or equal to one (with $\Gamma = 1$ when there is no uncertainty), Morel and others argued that it can be used as a quantitative interpretation of the precautionary principle for use in regulating policy. The principle requires that precautionary measures be taken when there is a perceived threat for uncertain decisions with irreversible costs. This is an interesting and challenging approach that identifies a way forward. It demands further work, however, on several important issues. These will not be discussed further here but include:

- definition, quantification, and estimation of irreversible costs for transgenic crops;
- reconciliation of subjective and frequentist probabilities (Barnett 1999) for costs and benefits within the theoretical framework; and
- comparison of the options approach with formal decision theoretic frameworks that incorporate utilities and Bayesian analysis to update prior information (Chernoff and Moses 1959; Smith 1988).

Whatever the form of analysis, the irreversible costs of transgenic crops on the right-hand side of the threshold criterion will seldom be known. Morel and others therefore subsumed it into their later analysis as a component of variable costs and benefits associated principally with conventional crops. The arguments for this strategy are subtle, but it does allow them to incorporate uncertainty for these costs into the model. Wesseler skillfully turned the problem around to acknowledge that the irreversible costs I are not known, but it is possible to solve for I^* to define the maximum tolerable costs for given net benefits (B) and irreversible benefits (R) (see Table 2). He therefore computed the maximal tolerable irreversible costs

$$I^* = R + \frac{B(t)}{\delta} - \frac{B(t)}{\delta\beta}$$

in which the second term accounts for irreversibility and uncertainty and accordingly deflates the critical value for I for which release of the transgenic crop is delayed. This still leaves the irreversible benefits to be estimated, but the two approaches offer scope for further analysis.

Both chapters show the effects of selected policy impacts on the decision to release transgenic crops. These can be understood by analyzing the effects of changes in the growth rate (α) and the variance (σ) of B on either V^* or I^*. Some of these are succinctly summarized in Table 9-2 in Wesseler.

Whereas the real options approach employs optimization, Morel and others showed that the rational option based on the Black–Scholes formula focuses on risk neutrality. Hence, the rational option seeks to find a "risk-neutral" strategy that involves a level of risk comparable with a riskless investment such as a government bond. In the case of Bt corn, the riskless strategy may arguably be seen as growing conventional corn. The critical value for action now depends on the stopping time when resistance is considered to be complete and the transgenic crop must be withdrawn (see Tables 2 and 3). The analysis allowed Morel and others to distinguish between two regimes (one involving low stochasticity and the other high stochasticity) and their relationships with stopping time.

Variables and Parameters

It is convenient to assess the economic models in terms of the variables, parameters, assumptions, and inferences that emerge to assist the bridge with biology in order to link economic and epidemiological theory.

Variables

Several candidate variables appear. Each may be subject to uncertainty with a mean value that changes over time. In practice, some irreversible costs are considered known or fixed, while simplification of the analysis supports aggregation of variables. Here important distinctions emerge between Wesseler, who modeled the net benefits of transgenic relative to conventional crops by a single stochastic differential equation, and Morel and others, who introduced separate stochastic equations for net benefits in transgenic and in conventional crops, while dropping irreversible costs and benefits when they analyzed the release of Bt corn (see Table 1). Separation allows more control over the trend in net benefits for the two crops as well as in the year-to-year variability. It also allows for correlation in the variances when conventional and transgenic crops are subject to similar patterns of external forcing such as weather or prices. There is scope for more careful consideration of the relative importance of biologically, environmentally, and economically driven influences in the magnitude of trends, variances, and covariances in the underlying variables. We may find that for certain crops, preoccupations with biologically and environmentally driven variances may be important in influencing qualitative behavior—for example whether or not a virulent form emerges. They may be less important for the quantitative effect of the year-to-year variation in net benefit, but we do not yet know.

The temporal dynamics of the aggregated variables are modeled by stochastic differential equations for geometric Brownian motion from which two important influences emerge: variability is modeled by a Wiener process that is elegant and simple (see Figure 9-1 in Wesseler) and for which Morel and others identified a robust method for estimating the associated variance parameter. Rather more surprising for the biologist is the assumption of a simple exponential trend for the continued growth in net benefit. Limitations to growth are more familiar to biologists, for which other models are available [see, for example, Dixit and Pindyck (1994) for economics, Gardiner (1985) for physical sciences, and Nisbet and Gurney (1982) for biology]. The exponential trend is justified by Morel and others and Wesseler by reference to empirical data for corn. It seems likely, however, that future work will examine alternative models that impose some asymptotic limit. Wesseler (2001) has already explored the use of a mean-reverting process (Dixit and Pindyck 1994) to account for decreasing net benefit from transgenic crops as pests become resistant to plant-produced toxins. Not surprisingly, this can markedly change the inferences. The selection of an underlying model for net benefits needs to be considered along with the time course over which simulations are run and the range over which the stopping time for growth of the crop relative to resistance is envisaged. Parameters and other constraints may change over long periods, necessitating a stepped or gradual change in parameters and perhaps too a change in model structure.

I conclude that aggregation of net basic variables is useful. More work needs to be done in exploring alternative models for the change in net benefits over time and for the interplay between environmental, biological, and economic drivers in these variables.

Parameters

Three fundamental classes of parameters can be recognized in the models (see Table 3). These are (a) mean growth rates for net benefits (to which would be added other limiting parameters for asymptotically limited models), (b) discount rates for the return on investment (including risk-free interest rates from government bonds for comparison with investment in transgenic crops), and (c) variances (also known as volatilities) and covariances for net benefits. A fourth class consists of derived parameters that are used as precautionary multipliers to allow for uncertainty in decisions to release transgenic crops. These are strategically the most important parameters because they link uncertainty and hence environmental, biological, and economically driven variability with criteria for decisions about whether it is economically justified to release transgenic crops. In the following section, I will discuss the relationship between economic and biological variances.

TABLE 2. Summary of the Principal Variables Used in Economic Analyses

Description	Components	M^a	W^a
Variable benefits of transgenic crop	Yield, pest, and pathogen damage driven by environmental and demographic stochasticity		
	Commodity prices		
Variable costs of transgenic crops	Fertilizer, pesticide input for nontarget pests, harvesting		
	Input prices		
	Imposition of quotas or environmental taxes		
	Management constraints (e.g., refugia)		
	Responses to manage emergence of virulent pests		
Variable benefits of conventional crop	Same as for transgenic crop		
Variable costs of conventional crop	Same as for transgenic crop with additional pesticide inputs		
Irreversible benefits of transgenic crop	Lower pesticide use leading to Reduced residues in soil, water, and crops Reduced risk of resistance to these pesticides		R
Irreversible costs of transgenic crop	Pest or pathogen overcomes resistance in transgenic crop[b]		I
	Gene transfer to other species especially weeds		
	Harm to nontarget species such as other invertebrates		
	Squandering of resistance or toxin genes by promoting premature buildup of counter measures in pest population		
	Loss of *Bt* toxin as a pesticide		

Aggregated variables			
Net benefit of transgenic crop	= benefits − costs	B	
Net benefits of conventional crop	= benefits − costs	P	
Net benefits of transgenic over conventional crops	= (benefits − costs) transgenic − (benefits − costs) conventional		B

Critical times			
Time of release of transgenic crop			T
Stopping time for removal of transgenic crop			T

a. *M,W* symbols used by Morel and others (Chapter 8) and Wesseler (Chapter 9).

b. Pest resistance is commonly regarded as irreversible but may be a variable cost if it is manageable.

TABLE 3. Principal Parameters Used in the Economic Analyses

Parameter	Morel and others			Wesseler
	Generic model	*Bt corn model*		
		GM^a	CC^b	
Mean growth rates				
Drift rates for net benefits/value	α	μ	γ	α
Discount rates				
Discount rate on investment	ρ	ρ		λ, μ
Risk-free interest rate		ρ		r
Variances				
Variance/volatility in net benefits/value	σ	η	σ	σ
Covariance between uncertainty in transgenic and conventional crops		ξ		
Derived parameters				
Precautionary multiplier	$\Gamma = \beta/(\beta - 1)$			
Hurdle rate				$\beta/(\beta - 1)$
Convenience yield				$\delta = \mu - \alpha$

a. Genetically modified, transgenic crop.

b. Conventional crop

Assumptions and Biological Implications

Assumptions

The analyses are based on three important assumptions about the growth of transgenic crops concerning space and the way that resistance arises. Most important, from an epidemiological perspective, is the assumption of mean-field responses, whereby the growth of a transgenic crop in a state or even a country is treated as though it occurs in a spatially uniform environment. The second assumption is that resistance is inevitable. The third assumption is that resistance is instantaneous (albeit at some unknown time), ubiquitous, and irreversible. These assumptions can be challenged, but they are still a necessary and valuable starting point. The assumption of spatial homogeneity in particular is discussed below. Irreversibility of resistance is implicitly relaxed in the way that Morel and others analyzed the dynamics of *Bt* corn by optimizing with respect to net benefits for transgenic and conventional crops each subject to uncertainty (see Table 1) but without allowance for irreversible costs. This implies that the irreversible costs are subsumed into the net benefits for the conventional crop, thereby allowing for some uncertainty in the irreversible costs (Farrow 2001). The distinction, quantification, and interpretation of irreversible costs and their relationship to pest resistance deserve further detailed study.

Biological Implications

Put simply, the principal biological implication of the analyses is that the greater the uncertainty in net benefits and irreversible costs of transgenic crops, the more cautious we should be in releasing these novel crops. Morel and others showed this elegantly in their illustrative analyses of *Bt* corn given in their Table 8-3 in which they compared standard cost–benefit analysis that fails to take uncertainty into account with the real option approach. They concluded that whereas a standard analysis leads to a conclusion to release *Bt* corn, the precautionary multiplier for the real option approach is such that allowance for uncertainty militates against immediate release. Moreover, analysis with and without a breakdown of resistance surprisingly appears to make little difference, implying that variability in year-to-year yield of crops is dominant over the risk of *Bt* resistance. This requires further sensitivity analysis of the model to the parameters as well as to the assumptions and functional forms. Morel and others stressed that their analysis is preliminary and not prescriptive.

One of the decisions is to delay release of a transgenic variety. This is explored in Wesseler's chapter and clearly illustrated in his Figures 9-3 through 9-7. Whether later release is recommended depends on

- continued growth in net benefits such that the net benefits eventually exceed the critical value,
- reduction in uncertainty as more information becomes available so that the precautionary multiplier is reduced, and
- reliable estimates for irreversible costs associated with environmental risk damage associated with the transfer of *Bt* or other toxins to weed species.

The assumption of continued growth in yield is reasonable only so long as agriculture remains free of major changes, such as the imposition of severe penalties for the use of pesticides and a move toward lower input, lower output crops. Notwithstanding developments in pest forecasting and improved efficiency in fertilizer use, significant reductions in the uncertainties associated with crop growth are unlikely to occur, but it may well be profitable to analyze the components of variability and the degrees of correlation.

Further work on sensitivity analysis initiated by Wesseler and Morel and others is imperative together with continued dialogue with biologists to explore the sensitivity and dynamics of the systems.

Reversible and Irreversible Costs and the Invasion and Persistence of Pest Resistance

Whether the occurrence of a resistant pest or pathogen is a reversible or irreversible cost depends from a biological perspective on the population dynamics of invasion, persistence, scale, and heterogeneity. Theoretical and experimental work in this area is spread through a diverse but related range of disciplines. A coherent theoretical framework, however, is slowly emerging that links the invasion of weeds, pests, and pathogenic microorganisms, including pesticide and fungicide resistance and the spread of antibiotic and antiviral drug resistance in bacterial and viral populations. The fundamental questions supporting the framework are essentially the same. Will a resistant, aggressive, or virulent strain invade the parasite population or will it be eliminated? Will it persist? If it does invade, will it completely replace the susceptible or avirulent strain, or can the two strains coexist? How long will it take before the resistant form reaches a critical density? Coexistence matters. It reflects a balance of selection forces and fitness costs and affects the stability of equilibria obtained by genetic strategies for the control of pests and disease.

Here I want to make the following points.

- Theoretical progress can be made in predicting the risk of invasion and persistence of resistant pests and parasites.
- Deterministic models are useful in identifying crude criteria for invasion.
- Stochastic models are essential for understanding the risks of invasion and for identifying criteria for persistence.
- Invasion is not inevitable, even when a resistant form arises.
- The spatial structure of the transgenic and conventional crops in the landscape are critical in determining the chances of invasion and persistence.
- Failure to allow for spatial structure may seriously bias estimates of invasion and assessments of the risk of breakdown of resistance.

Two important methodological and dynamic features emerge from work on invasion and persistence. These are heterogeneity in space and time. Temporal heterogeneity occurs as periodic and stochastically driven changes in driving variables such as temperature. It also arises as discontinuities between crop and intercrop periods. This, in turn, affects the ability of the virulent or counterresistant strains to compete with wild-type strains. Spatial heterogeneity reflects the distribution of crop plants. Large tracts of a single crop, such as corn, with a uniform mode of resistance to a pest or disease are notoriously susceptible to invasion by a virulent or counterresistant strain. This was devastatingly shown by the huge losses caused by Southern corn leaf blight in the United States in 1970. Losses amounting to 15% of the total U.S. crop (2.5×10^7 hectares) occurred when race T of the fungus *Bipolaris maydis* spread rapidly through the previously resistant crop (Zadoks and Schein 1979). Although corn varieties at the time carried several different genes for resistance to *B. maydis*, 85% of the U.S. acreage was planted to a relatively small number of varieties of hybrid maize that carried the same cytoplasmic male sterility gene. This rendered 85% of the crop genetically uniform and susceptible to race T of the pathogen, with devastating consequences that led to complete loss in many places because of the efficient and rapid aerial dispersal of the fungus. The work of Peck and others (1999; 2000) and Tabashnik (1994) has focused on *Bt* cotton and corn, where considerable attention is given to high-dose strategies together with the role of refugia, in which populations of susceptible pests are sustained to delay the buildup of resistance to the toxin in pest populations. Many crops in Europe are grown in heterogeneous mosaics within the landscape. An example is given in Figure 1 for growth of sugar beet in East Anglia and the United Kingdom.[1] The figure shows stochastic realizations of the spread of an introduced disease, Rhizomania, in East Anglia (Figure 1a and b). This virus disease is carried by a fungal vector and is spread by movement of soil on machinery between farms. The spread is localized around a few initial foci. Figure 1d, e, and f shows the result of two simulations for the spread of disease into other sugar-beet growing areas in the United Kingdom. From Figure 1 it may be seen that markedly different scenarios may be obtained for identical parameters for intensification, crop susceptibility, and transmission when allowance is made for stochastic variability.

Invasion and persistence of resistant and susceptible strains play an important part in assessing uncertainty and in the spatial and temporal deployment of transgenic crops. Each of these processes impinge on the reversible and irreversible costs and benefits listed in Table 2 as well as on the critical times for release and removal of transgenic crops in ways that have yet to be rigorously explored. The threats to transgenic crops are clear if a resistant pest arises. But persistence and coexistence of competing strains that can grow on conventional crops affect the mean performance and uncertainty of these in quite subtle but, arguably, predictable ways. Considerable progress may be made by estimating the magnitude of these effects on the uncertainties relative to economically driven externalities. Only if the biologically and environmentally driven components are small can they be safely ignored. In the following section, I show briefly how thresholds for invasion can be derived from simple epidemiological assumptions and how these can be elaborated to allow for stochasticity and spatially extended populations of fields of transgenic crops.

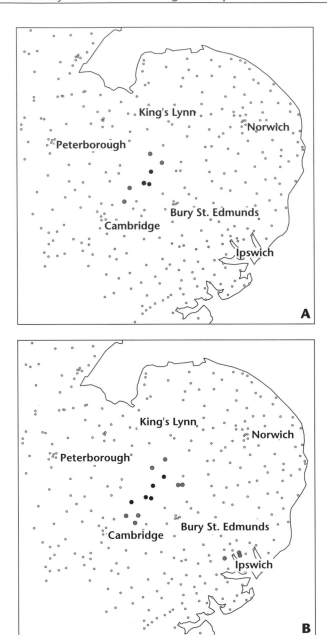

FIGURE 1. Spatial Heterogeneity of Disease Spread through a Heterogeneous Mosaic within the Landscape

(Figure continues on the following page.)

Note: Please see note 1 at the end of the chapter.

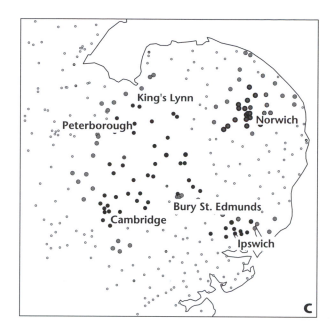

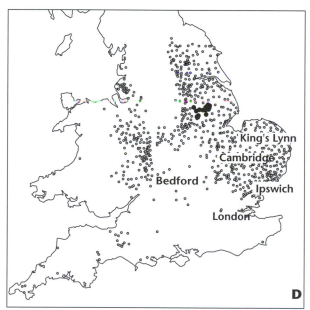

FIGURE 1. Spatial Heterogeneity of Disease Spread through a Heterogeneous Mosaic within the Landscape (*continued*)

(*Figure continues on the following page.*)

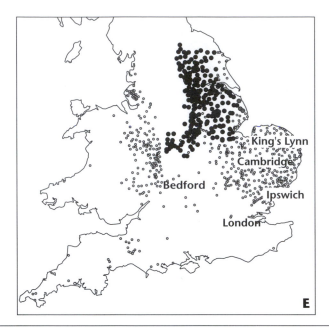

FIGURE 1. Spatial Heterogeneity of Disease Spread through a Heterogeneous Mosaic within the Landscape (*continued*)

Invasion and Persistence

Invasion involves the mutation of an endemic strain or the immigration of a resistant strain followed by spread within the susceptible population. The study of invasion naturally gives rise to the concept of thresholds. This means that *invasion is not inevitable*. Certain criteria must be satisfied for invasion to occur. Hence the resistant strain may be eliminated; it may increase rapidly, exhaust the supply of susceptible hosts, and be eliminated; or it may switch to a new equilibrium state and coexist with the host and previously endemic (susceptible) strains of the parasite.

Invasion thresholds often are related to the basic reproductive number of a parasite R_0, usually defined as the average number of new infections produced when a single infective individual is introduced into a wholly susceptible host population (Heesterbeek and Roberts 1995). This concept is central to the analysis of the population dynamics of host–parasite interactions and, clearly, for a parasite to invade requires $R_0 > 1$. Invasion criteria also can be defined in terms of a threshold host density above which invasion can occur. The relationships between these two criteria are analyzed in Gubbins and others (2000).

Invasion criteria reflect the parameters of the underlying model. Thus for a simple epidemiological model defining the flows of susceptibles (S) to infecteds (I)

$$\frac{dS}{dt} = (b_0 - b_1 N)S - (d_0 + d_1 N)S - \beta IS \qquad \frac{dI}{dt} = \beta IS - (\mu + d_0 + d_1 N)I$$

where $N = S + I$ is the total host density. The crop population has density-dependent birth ($b_0 - b_1 N$) and death ($d_0 + d_1 N$) rates, which imply that, in the absence of infection, the host population in each patch grows logistically with net rate $r = (b_0 - d_0)$ to carrying capacity $\kappa = (b_0 - d_0)/(b_1 + d_1)$. The parameter μ is the disease-induced death rate of infected hosts. The corresponding value for R_0 is given by

$$R_0 = \frac{\beta\kappa}{\mu + d_0 + d_1\kappa}$$

If $R_0 < 1$, the infection is eliminated, and the susceptible population grows to its carrying capacity κ. Conversely, if $R_0 > 1$, the infection can establish itself, and the susceptible and infected hosts coexist at stable levels. The invasion criterion can be rewritten in terms of a critical patch size that must be exceeded for an invasion to occur (Gubbins et al. 2000). In this case, the parasite can only invade the host population provided that

$$\kappa > \frac{\mu + d_0}{\beta - d_1}$$

where κ is now the critical patch size. If the patch size is below the threshold level, the parasite cannot produce sufficient new infections to establish itself.

Although most models like these were designed with plants as the units and fields defining population size, the models can be scaled up to consider populations of fields in which whole fields are classified as susceptible or infected and the critical patch size now defines aggregations of fields. Exploration of the parameter space then allows some crude insight into how changes in the parameters associated with transmission rates and cropping frequencies can be used to inhibit invasion. The models can be extended to consider fields as occupiable points, and the spread of resistant forms is modeled as a probabilistic cellular automaton (Keeling and Gilligan 2000) or as a percolation process on a lattice (see for example, Bailey et al. 2000) from which it is possible to compute the probability of the spread of a resistant form.

More usually, space is explicitly included by the use of dispersal kernels or as metapopulation (Park et al. 2001) in which fields or regions are regarded as aggregations of loosely coupled subpopulations on a lattice or random graph. Careful analysis of the resulting metapopulation model identifies three key parameters that can be used to characterize invasion dynamics (Park et al. 2001). These are the within-field basic reproductive number [now more strictly denoted by R_p to distinguish the local or patch from the global reproductive number (Park et al. 2001)], the strength of coupling between fields (ε), and the size of the neighborhood of interaction (ρ), which determines the distance over which inoculum is dispersed (see Figure 2).[2]

Deterministic versus Stochastic Models

Although deterministic models are useful in identifying invasion thresholds and the key parameters that control invasion, they ignore crucial aspects of the population dynamics and, in particular, often fail to capture the patterns of persistence. Three thresholds are identified for a stochastic metapopulation in Figure 2, taken from Park and others (2001). Above the threshold, the parasite is always able to invade the host population in the deterministic model. However, in the stochastic model, there is a finite probability of invasion above the threshold that increases from zero to one. Moreover, comparison of the deterministic and stochastic thresholds shows that the stochastic threshold is effectively higher than the deterministic analogue.

Parasite persistence depends critically on the dynamics of infection in postepidemic troughs that usually develop between crops when the populations drop to very low levels (Diekmann et al. 1995). In a deterministic model, numerical simulations imply that if the parasite can invade, it also can maintain itself in a host population in the long term. Consequently, the invasion threshold (see Figure 2a) is also the persistence threshold. This is not correct, however, because it fails to take into account elimination when population levels are low. In marked contrast, there are distinct invasion and persistence thresholds in the stochastic model (see Figure 2c). So in stochastic, spatially explicit populations typical of agricultural crops (Park et al. 2001), three scenarios may be identified (see Figure 3): (a) the resistant parasite fails to invade, (b) the parasite invades and persists, or (c) the parasite invades but cannot persist.[3] It is a relatively simple matter to extend analyses to derive estimates for times to achieve critical densities or the corollary of times to extinction for different spatial deployments of susceptible crops. An example for an animal disease is given in Swinton and others (1998). These analyses can be used to inform decisions about the risk of resistance, and much has already been done with insects and *Bt* resistance and the nature and structure of refugia (Rausher 2001). Some analytical work is possible in computing the so-called critical community size for the persistence of pests and disease, but more is needed.

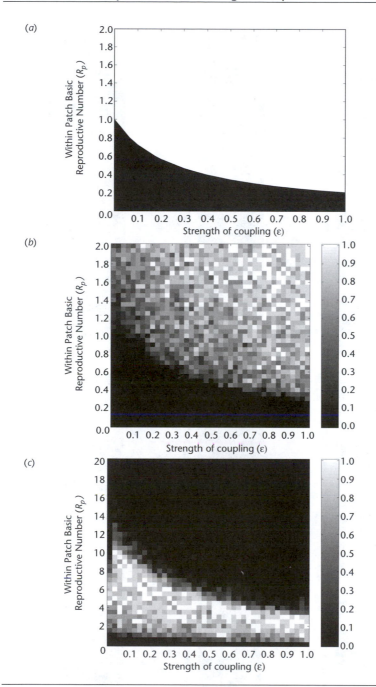

FIGURE 2. Invasion Thresholds for Metapopulations

Note: Please see note 2 at the end of the chapter.

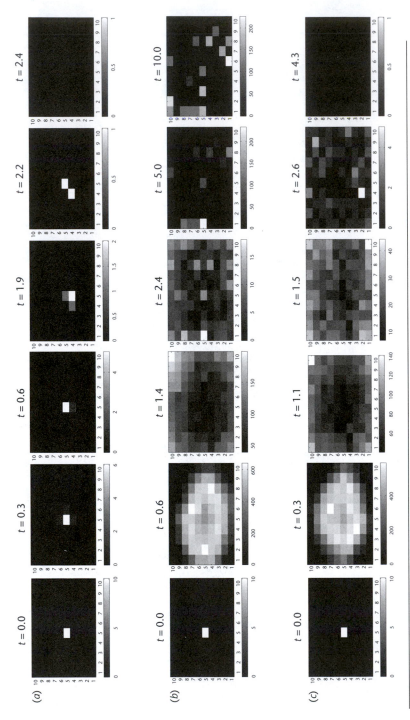

FIGURE 3. Examples of Infection Dynamics in the Stochastic Model for Invasion

Note: Please see note 3 at the end of the chapter.

Conclusion: Linking Epidemiological with Economic Theory

Much still remains to be done in linking epidemiological theory and population dynamics of pest and disease with economic theory proposed by Morel and others and Wesseler, but some approaches are evident. These are listed below:

- reanalyze and redefine variables for benefits and costs, especially reversible and irreversible costs and the relationships with pest and disease dynamics;
- realize that breakdown of resistance in transgenic crops is not inevitable even if the counterresistant strain arises in the population;
- compare the relative magnitudes of economically driven with environmentally and biologically driven sources of variability;
- analyze invasion and persistence in stochastic, spatially extended settings to simulate the risk of breakdown of resistance in the landscape;
- define the spatial scale for analyses of risk of resistance breakdown for different crops, pests, and pathogens;
- provide a similar definition of temporal scales within which parameters can be reasonably assumed to be constant; and
- analyze strategies to allow spatially and temporally buffered introductions of transgenic crops rather than blanket coverage and rapid saturation of the landscape.

More detailed technical considerations concerned with nonlinearities and stochasticities should follow, for example, identifying the feedbacks in the system and how these affect the probability of invasion and persistence. More important is the challenge of stochasticity and how it can be estimated, modeled, and used to shed light rather than darkness.

Acknowledgements

I am grateful to Justus Wesseler at Wageningen University and Research Centre and to Scott Farrow and his colleagues at Carnegie Mellon University for generous discussion of their work with a noneconomist. Uncertainties in economic theory in this commentary are, of course, of my own making. Some of the work referred to from the Epidemiology and Modelling Group at Cambridge was funded by the Biological and Biotechnological Research Council, the Natural Environment Research Council, the Royal Society and Leverhulme Trust in the United Kingdom, which I gratefully acknowledge.

References

Bailey, D.J., W.O. Otten, and C.A. Gilligan. 2000. Percolation, Heterogeneity and the Saprotrophic Invasion of Soil by the Fungal Plant Pathogen *Rhizoctonia solani*. *New Phytologist* 146: 535–44.

Barnett, V. 1999. *Comparative Statistical Inference*. New York: John Wiley.

Chernoff, H., and L.E. Moses. 1959. *Elementary Decision Theory*. New York: Dover Publications, Inc.

Diekmann, O., J.A.P. Heesterbeek, and J.A.J. Metz. 1995. The Legacy of Kermack and McKendrick. In *Epidemic Models: Their Structure and Relation to Data,* edited by D. Mollison. Cambridge, U.K.: Cambridge University Press, 95–115.

Dixit, A.K., and R.S. Pindyck. 1994. *Investment under Uncertainty*. Princeton, NJ: Princeton University Press.

Farrow, Scott. 2001. Communication with the author, December 17, 2001.

Gardiner, C.W. 1985. *Handbook of Stochastic Methods for Physics, Chemistry and the Natural Sciences*. Berlin, Germany: Springer–Verlag.

Gubbins, S., C.A. Gilligan, and A. Kleczkowski. 2000. Population Dynamics of Plant-Parasite Interactions: Thresholds for Invasion. *Theoretical Population Biology* 57: 219–33.

Heesterbeek, J.A.P., and M.G. Roberts. 1995. Mathematical Models for Microparasites of Wildlife. In *Ecology of Infectious Diseases in Natural Populations*, edited by B.T. Grenfell and A.P. Dobson. Cambridge, U.K.: Cambridge University Press, 90–122.

Hull, J. 2000. *Options, Futures, and Other Derivatives*. Upper Saddle River, NJ: Prentice Hall.

Keeling, M.J., and C.A. Gilligan. 2000. Bubonic Plague: A Metapopulation Model of a Zoonosis. *Proceedings of the Royal Society of London Series B-Biological Sciences* 267: 2219–30.

Nisbet, R.M., and W.S.C. Gurney. 1982. *Modelling Fluctuating Populations*. Chichester, U.K.: Wiley.

Park, A.W., S. Gubbins, and C.A. Gilligan. 2001. Invasion and Persistence of Disease in a Spatially Structured Metapopulation. *Oikos* 94: 162–74.

Peck, S.L., S.P. Ellner, and F. Gould. 1999. Spread of Resistance in Spatially Extended Regions of Transgenic Cotton: Implications for Management of *Heliothis virescens* (Lepidoptera: Noctuidae). *Journal of Economic Entomology* 92: 1–16.

———. 2000. Varying Migration and Deme Size and the Feasibility of the Shifting Balance. *Evolution* 54: 324–7.

Rausher, M.D. 2001. Co-Evolution and Plant Resistance to Natural Enemies. *Nature* 411: 857–64.

Smith, J.Q. 1988. *Decision Analysis: A Bayesian Approach*. London: Chapman and Hall.

Stuiver, M.H., and J.H.H.V. Custers. 2001. Engineering Disease Resistance in Plants. *Nature* 411: 865–8.

Swinton, J., J. Harwood, B.T. Grenfell, and C.A. Gilligan. 1998. Persistence Thresholds for Phocine Distemper Virus Infection in Harbour Seal *Phoca vitulina* Metapopulations. *Journal of Animal Ecology* 67: 54–68.

Tabashnik, B.E. 1994. Delaying Insect Adaptation to Transgenic Plants: Seed Mixtures and Refugia Reconsidered. *Proceedings of the Royal Society of London Series B-Biological Sciences* 255: 7–12.

Wesseler, J. 2001. Assessing the Risk of Transgenic Crops—The Role of Scientific Belief Systems. In *Integrative Systems Approaches to Natural and Social Sciences—Systems Sci-*

ence 2000, edited by M. Matthies, H. Malchow, and J. Kriz. Berlin, Germany: Springer–Verlag, 319–29.

Zadoks, J.C., and R.D. Schein. 1979. *Epidemiology and Plant Disease Management.* New York: Oxford University Press.

Notes

1. Figure 1a, b, and c shows the spread at successive times of an introduced disease Rhizomania (large dark dots) of sugar beet through farms (small light dots) in East Anglia. Large pale dots represent infested but not yet symptomatic farms. The outbreaks are predicted by a stochastic spatial model. The spread is localized around three initial foci. Figure 1d and e shows the result of two simulations for the spread of disease into other sugar-beet growing areas in the United Kingdom (light dots represent susceptible farms, and dark dots represent infested farms). The disease dynamics are highly nonlinear and stochastic. Markedly different scenarios may be obtained from identical parameters for intensification, crop susceptibility, and transmission when allowance is made for stochastic variability. (Reproduced with permission from Dr. A. Stacey, Epidemiology and Modelling Group, Cambridge, U.K.)

2. (a) Invasion thresholds for a deterministic model of disease introduced into a metapopulation (i.e., a population comprising 100 subpopulations with loose coupling between contiguous subpopulations). The figure shows how the invasion threshold varies with the strength of coupling between subpopulations and the ability to multiply within subpopulations (here denoted as R_p; equivalent to R_0 for a single subpopulation used in the text). The deterministic model implies that the parasite cannot invade in the black region and always invades in the white region. Invasion thresholds also correspond to persistence thresholds: Once it invades, a deterministic model predicts that it will persist. (b) Invasion thresholds for the stochastic version of the model. Invasion is now shown as a stochastic process denoted by the gray scale for the probability of invasion, ranging from zero probability (black) to a probability of one (white). (c) Comparison of invasion and persistence thresholds for the stochastic model. Increasing one of the parameters (R_p) reveals three regimes in the behavior of a parasite: no invasion (lower black region), invasion *and* persistence (midregion), and invasion followed by elimination (upper black region). The model is a spatially extended generalization of the simple *SI* model in the text with the introduction of a small amount of parasite near the center of a 10×10 array of subpopulations and allowance for dispersal within and between subpopulations. Details are given in Park et al. (2001).

3. (a) Parasite cannot invade ($R_p = 0.5$); (b) parasite invades and persists ($R_p = 8.0$); and (c) parasite invades but cannot persist ($R_p = 16.0$). The plots show the infection level in each subpopulation at various times. The radius of the neighborhood of interaction is $\rho = 1$, the strength of coupling is $\varepsilon = 0.1$, and the remaining default parameters and initial populations are given in Park et al. (2001). Similar results can be derived for systems with more distant dispersal across subpopulations.

PART III

The Behavior of Firms

Chapter 10

An Economic Model of a Genetic Resistance Commons:

Effects of Market Structure Applied to Biotechnology in Agriculture

Douglas Noonan

Genetic resistance resources represent an emerging class of environmental resources. These resources are the subject of increasing public interest, especially for resistance in agriculture and antibiotic use. This chapter models genetic resistance resources as common-pool resources. The static model applies directly to the case of *Bt* corn, whose seeds are bioengineered to contain a pesticide. Firms produce an agricultural output (corn) using two inputs: *Bt* corn seeds and refuge areas. Production also depends on the common stock of environmental resistance. Seed use contributes to greater resistance, whereas refuge areas abate resistance. This costly form of abatement represents another (positive) externality, which allows for the optimal seed use to be greater than the competitive level. The use of seeds and refuge areas by other firms can be shown to be substitutes and complements in production, respectively, for each firm. This simple model of externalities is complicated by introducing another important feature common to genetic resistance resources: monopoly supply in the biotechnology factor market. Monopoly provision of seeds, with imperfect price discrimination, leads the monopoly to act as a gatekeeper of the commons, which tries to maximize its own rents rather than the rents from the resource. This divergence in interests leads to a deadweight loss because seed use is curtailed through higher monopoly prices. This equilibrium is compared with the competitive and the optimal cases. The way in which the resistance externality operates—through damaging others' output or through affecting their marginal productivities—suggests whether the monopoly improves the efficiency of the seed market. Further consideration is given to the possibility that the monopoly determines the firms' level of abatement. Assuming some enforcement mechanism, the monopoly chooses higher abatement levels to increase factor demand for seeds and increase its rents. Under some plausible conditions, a monopoly supplier of the input that accesses the genetic resistance commons can be shown to actually improve welfare by mandating a higher level of care that also maximizes its profits. The distributional consequences of the different market structures are shown, noting how gains for the monopoly come at the expense of firms. In 2000, EPA and Monsanto required purchasers of *Bt* corn to plant specific refuge areas to forestall resistance. This approach is readily extended to other cases, such as pesticides more generally or antibiotic use in the production of health services by households.

At the nexus of several burgeoning fields of research and public interest is genetic resistance. The rapid growth and application of biological science in the past century has ushered in dramatic advances in health care and high-yield agriculture. Health care and agriculture share important characteristics besides their biological roots and political prominence. They often evoke very passionate responses from environmentalists and international development policy analysts. Both fields have come under increasing scrutiny in areas concerning microbiological interactions between humans, food, bacteria, and other organisms. Tensions are mounting as antibiotics and pesticides fail, viral outbreaks and crop infestations occur, and a threat to the food supply looms. Perhaps their most important, and most overlooked, common link is their pervasive reliance on environmental genetic susceptibility in production. Whether it is a patient using antibiotics or a farmer spraying pesticides, both fields rely on the biological organism's inability to resist the treatment. Given that these stocks of genetic resistance are typically common-pool resources, it is little wonder that many people call for nonmarket responses to recent developments.

Background

Histories of human civilization would not be complete without prominent discussion of linkages between genetic resistance, agriculture, and health care. Jared Diamond's Pulitzer Prize-winning *Guns, Germs, and Steel* (1999) gives the ultimate influence of germs and agriculture its due. Throughout the course of human history, the relationship between gene pools and production has affected the way in which economies develop and ultimately which groups prosper. Although such a vantage is perhaps too broad for conventional economic analysis, human history is replete with examples of genetic resistance affecting welfare. Economies and gene pools are mutually adapting to each other and have been doing so for many millennia. In modern times, this relationship becomes even more pronounced with scientific and economic progress. Just as animal domestication led to enhanced Eurasian resistance to disease (and the lack of such resistance in the Americas), the use of biotechnology enhances resistance at a much faster pace. The consequences of the lack of certain resistance in the Americas after the rapid introduction of new organisms during colonization was catastrophic. At the root of this story, and countless smaller-scale examples, are fundamental issues of genetic resistance and spillovers within and between communities.

Stories of genetic resistance fill the popular press, recanting the familiar story: a farmer uses a new weapon against crop-damaging pests, and sooner or later the pests adapt a resistance to the weapon. The "superpests" then continue to plague farms. Many times this process is likened to an "arms race" against nature in which science's best technology is ultimately countered by natural adaptive forces, leaving society back where it started or worse. In agriculture, this race against nature's adaptation is being run on numerous fronts and has been run for ages. Perhaps today the only difference is that we can run faster. Numerous farming techniques, from breeding selectively to spraying insecticides to bioengineering crops, capitalize on nature's vulnerabilities to increase production. The effectiveness of these innovations, whether they are stronger plants or more lethal pesticides, is often observed to decline rapidly, becoming useless within a few years. The required dosages for pesticides increase over time as pests turn into superpests, and even insect-resistant crop strains lose effectiveness.

Other technologies, especially in health care, also must grapple with genetic resistance. Increased antibiotic use has led to growing resistance among bacteria. Resistance to antibiotics has been observed both at large in communities and within particular hospitals. Resistance has been observed for antibiotics like azithromycin, ciprofloxacin, methicillin, metronidazole, penicillin, streptomycin, and vancomycin. This resistance challenges effective treatments for infections caused by *Escherichia coli*, *Streptococcus pneumoniae*, *Salmonella typhimurium*, *Mycobacterium tuberculosis*, and *Neisseria gonorrhoeae* bacteria. Resistance has been found in diseases ranging from malaria to pneumonia. The use of antibiotics on livestock has produced similar resistance effects. The use of antiseptics and disinfectants also may cause resistance. The costs of resistance climb with its incidence because secondary treatments are frequently more costly or less effective (GAO 1999). Costs from antimicrobial resistance in U.S. hospitals alone approach $10 billion each year (WHO 2000).

With heightened concern has come a widespread perception, especially in the health care field, that "overuse" or "misuse" of the biological tools (antibiotics, insecticides, biotech crops, and so forth) is largely responsible for their decline in effectiveness. One-third of all antibiotic prescriptions may be unneeded, and most doctors have apparently prescribed them against their better judgment (Levy 1998). Similar refrains sound out in agriculture: "wasteful" or "excessive" use of certain tools has accelerated natural adaptation. In the race to keep up, researchers have spent considerable time investigating the relationship between the use of these technologies and the eventual onset of superbugs and superpests. Practitioners are experimenting with techniques to slow the onset of resistance in the environment. These include rotating antibiotic use, developing hybrid insect-resistant crops, using multiple-antibiotic drugs ("cocktails"), establishing refuge areas, and applying more concentrated treatments of antibiotics and pesticides. Early results suggest that some techniques hold promise, while others do not.

An Economic Approach

What is the efficient level of antibiotic use? Under what conditions will biotechnology crops improve welfare? An economic approach to these genetic resistance problems provides a powerful analytical tool. Ultimately, this chapter attempts to indicate *where* the "problem" lies and to suggest *how* efficiency might be improved when optimal solutions are unavailable.

At issue is a common-pool of resources (namely, the susceptibility of "bugs" to certain technologies) that is depletable as more users tap into it. Like a common pasture or fishery, producers will overexploit the pool's resources because they do not bear the full social cost for their actions. The costs of their appropriation of the pool's resources are borne in part by all users of the resource. With others footing the bill for their use of the common-pool, users can be expected to rationally overexploit the resource.

The genetic resistance in the environment is a common-pool resource. The level of resistance, although a "bad," fits the two primary criteria for a common-pool resource: depletability and open access. First, as more producers use the resource, it becomes less valuable to everyone. Second, there is no (direct) price for access to this resource—nobody owns it (Baden and Noonan 1998). Genetic commons pose particularly intractable problems. Usual solutions to commons problems include privatization, mergers, and taxation or regulation. Each conventional policy solution seems infeasible in the foreseeable future because of one or more of the following: moral and ethical problems, large group coordination and transaction costs, and information costs. Private ownership of gene pools appears as politically palatable as "merging" all corn farmers or as technically possible as picking the perfect tax. The lack of availability of first-best solutions warrants this inquiry into unconventional approaches to managing the genetic commons.

The level of genetic resistance can be thought of as a stock of natural capital G. The use of some inputs by producers can cause an increase in G. Technologies that rely on genetic susceptibilities in the environment (such as insecticides or some biotech crops) will become less effective as G increases. Although the inputs themselves may have a price (e.g., the price of bioengineered seeds), the externality caused by their use is not priced by the market. Because a producer's use of the input can reduce the effectiveness of all other producers' technologies, producers will generally overuse the input, and a socially suboptimal level of G (too much resistance) prevails in equilibrium. The model that follows formalizes this story after discussing some earlier literature on the subject. It is then extended to include mitigating behavior by producers and a monopoly supplier of the technology.

Brief Literature Review

Formal inquiries into the theoretical nature of environmental externalities and common pools are numerous. Beginning with H. Scott Gordon (1954) through most intermediate microeconomic textbooks today, common-property resources or impure public goods have received considerable attention. A lengthy discussion of various externality models like this can be found in Baumol and Oates (1988).

The bulk of the environmental economics literature addresses this fundamental issue of externalities in one of two ways. Pigovian taxes and Coasian property rights occupy a central place in environmental economics and policy. Although both approaches to solving the externality problem face considerable practical problems—owing predominantly to information and transaction costs, respectively—researchers have analyzed the implications of numerous different assumptions. One prominent strain in the literature examines the effect of market structure on externalities and optimal taxation policy. Buchanan (1969) opened the door for externalities in noncompetitive market structures. The monopoly's desire to set $MR = MC$ (where MR is marginal revenues and MC is marginal costs) creates the possibility that a Pigovian tax actually reduces welfare when the final products market remains distorted. Barnett (1980) showed how taxing a monopoly equal to its marginal damages (a Pigovian approach) might exacerbate the deadweight loss because of the monopoly's restricted output. Ideally, a two-part tax would correct both the undersupply of the output by the monopolist and the oversupply of the externality separately and simultaneously.

In addition to their role in generating externalities, monopolies can play a role in managing externalities. A common intuition, expressed by Knight (1924) with regard to road congestion, holds that granting ownership of a common-pool resource is akin to internalizing an externality. The owner could theoretically charge firms their full marginal costs (including spillovers) and thereby optimize production. In practice, however, the owner possesses monopoly power. A monopoly would choose to limit access to the commons, above and beyond correcting any externality, to equate marginal revenue and marginal cost for the final output. A price-discriminating monopoly would profit most by charging users equal to their marginal external damages (to equate the value of their marginal products to their social costs). They would then extract a franchise fee equal to users' rents. A monopoly owner of a commons could achieve the socially optimal outcome in this way. A monopoly capable of only a single price would partially account for the spillover among its customers with respect to their interdependent demands for the monopoly's resource. Nonetheless, it would still restrict output based on marginal revenue rather than price at social marginal cost. Mills (1981) demonstrated this for congestion-prone facilities.

The Formal Model

Competitive Allocation of g

Begin with a simple model in which competitive firms produce q. They use g as an input in production, with factor price w. Firms also use a common, environmental resource G as an input, where the level of G is jointly determined by the firm's own use of g and other firms' use of g, denoted by $\tilde{g}$. Thus, their production function is $q = f[g, G(g, \tilde{g})]$. Each firm takes $\tilde{g}$ as exogenous. G is a "bad" input (e.g., genetic resistance) that impairs production. The marginal product of G is negative ($\partial f/\partial G < 0$) and decreasing ($\partial^2 f/\partial G^2 < 0$). Assume that the marginal product of g is nonincreasing in G ($\partial^2 f/\partial g \partial G \leq 0$). The use of g contributes to G at a rate increasing in g (i.e., $\partial G/\partial g > 0$, $\partial G/\partial \tilde{g} > 0$, $\partial^2 G/\partial g^2 > 0$, $\partial^2 G/\partial \tilde{g}^2 > 0$, $\partial^2 G/\partial g \partial \tilde{g} > 0$). Firms sell q for a fixed price p. A typical firm's profit function is as follows:

$$\Pi = pf\left[g, G(g, \tilde{g})\right] - wg$$

The firm maximizes its profits Π by choosing g. Assume throughout this chapter that profit functions are negative semidefinite at the optimum choice to satisfy the second-order conditions. The first-order condition for the representative firm using $g > 0$ is

$$p\frac{df}{dg} = p\left[\frac{\partial f(g,G)}{\partial g} + \frac{\partial f(g,G)}{\partial G}\frac{\partial G(g,\tilde{g})}{\partial g}\right] = w \tag{1}$$

The marginal revenue product has a positive component from g's direct use and a negative component indirectly from g's contribution to G. The firm's choice depends jointly on all users of g's choices.

An aside on the existence of well-behaved factor demand functions is in order. Equation 1 implicitly defines a factor demand function $g^*(p, w, \tilde{g})$.

Cornes and Sandler (1986) discussed the nature of Nash equilibria among firms, selecting their g given their expectation of other firms' choices ($\tilde{g}$). This chapter assumes (for this and every other extension wherein a factor demand function is used for an externality-causing input) that equilibria exist to support a continuous inverse factor demand function $w^*(p, g, \tilde{g})$. Changes in p or in $\tilde{g}$ will cause the $w^*(g)$ curve to shift. The effect on g^* of increasing output price is positive. The effect of $\tilde{g}$ on g^* can be seen from the implicit function theorem

$$\frac{\partial g^*}{\partial \tilde{g}} = -\frac{\dfrac{\partial^2 \Pi}{\partial g \partial \tilde{g}}}{\dfrac{\partial^2 \Pi}{\partial g^2}} = -\frac{\dfrac{\partial^2 f}{\partial g \partial G}\dfrac{\partial G}{\partial \tilde{g}} + \dfrac{\partial^2 f}{\partial G^2}\dfrac{\partial G}{\partial \tilde{g}}\dfrac{\partial G}{\partial g} + \dfrac{\partial f}{\partial G}\dfrac{\partial^2 G}{\partial g \partial \tilde{g}}}{\dfrac{d^2 f}{dg^2}} < 0 \qquad (2)$$

That $\partial g^*/\partial \tilde{g} < 0$ amounts to a negatively sloped "reaction curve." This feature of factor demands throughout this chapter provides some stability to solutions involving a representative firm. As firms use more g, their collective increase in use tempers each firm's increase in demand. Finally, the aggregate factor demand for g is sensitive to the number of firms using g. Increases in $\tilde{g}$ reduce profit, which conceivably leads to large drops in Σg^* as some firms shut down, even though all remaining firms' use more g.

In the long run, entry will occur until $p = AC$ or average cost for the marginal firm. Equivalently, each firm's marginal product will equal its average product. This basic model is well discussed in the literature. This chapter allows for heterogeneous firms and maintains a $p = AC$ long-run equilibrium condition only for marginal firms.

Optimum Allocation of g

Compare the competitive equilibrium with the socially optimal allocation of resources. A social planner chooses each firm's quantity of g, denoted as g_i, to maximize the sum of firms' profits where each firm's production and profits still depend on other firms' use of g. The ith first-order condition for the optimal choice of g_i, denoted as $g_i{}^o$, captures the external effects of each firm:

$$p\left[\frac{\partial f(g_i, G)}{\partial g_i} + \frac{\partial f(g_i, G)}{\partial G}\frac{\partial G(g_i, \tilde{g})}{\partial g_i}\right] + \sum_{j \neq i} p\frac{\partial f_j(g_j, G)}{\partial G}\frac{\partial G(g_i, \tilde{g})}{\partial g_i} \leq w \qquad (3)$$

This holds with equality for $g_i{}^o > 0$. The first part of Equation 3 is the usual marginal revenue product (MRP) term, and it is followed by the marginal social damage (MD) of g_i. Naturally, MD is negative. In the MD term, the choice of g_i affects the marginal revenue product of G for all other firms ($j \neq i$) through its contribution to G. The obvious difference between the optimum necessary condition in Equation 3 and the competitive condition in Equation 1 is that the competitive firms do not include the marginal social damage term MD in their calculus. A Pigovian tax equal to MD would correct this, aligning private and social marginal costs. Entry still occurs until $p = AC$ for the marginal firm, but firms optimally pay for the added costs they inflict on others. When g is supplied at its marginal cost, $MC(g)$, the optimal equilibrium is characterized by

$$MC = w = MRP + MD \tag{4}$$

Allowing competitive firms to use g up to the point where $MC = MRP$ leads to overuse of g. In this simple model, G is also too large ($G^* > G^0$ and $g^* > g^0$).

Monopoly

An interesting extension of the model involves monopoly provision of g. The monopoly provides g for a price w; "the firm" or "firms" always refer to actors who use g to produce q. The downstream market for q remains competitive while the upstream market for g has a single seller and an externality among users of g.

The current investigation begins with two different ways to frame monopoly control of g that yield different results. First, the monopoly might merge with the firms, operating them by giving them g and selling their output. The "merger" monopoly has revenues of $p\Sigma q$ and costs of $C(\Sigma g)$. Maximizing the difference by choosing each g_i, the ith first-order condition is

$$p\left(\frac{\partial f_i}{\partial g_i} + \frac{\partial f_i}{\partial G}\frac{\partial G}{\partial g_i}\right) + \sum_{j \neq i} p \frac{\partial f_j}{\partial G}\frac{\partial G}{\partial g_i} = MC(g) \tag{5}$$

for all $g_i^* > 0$. Comparing Equation 5 to Equation 4 reveals that the "merger" monopoly achieves the efficient allocation of resources (assuming throughout that p is fixed).

A second approach has a "gatekeeper" monopoly selling access rights to g to each firm at a price w_i for the ith firm. This problem is fundamentally different for the monopoly owner of g and yields quite different results. As shown earlier, the monopoly could achieve the optimal equilibrium and maximize total rents by charging $w = MC - MD$. This price, however, leaves profits for the firms. The monopoly captures these rents in the merger approach earlier but cannot do so as a gatekeeper. Instead, the monopoly has the incentive to set

$MR = MC$ and to claim some of those profits for its own. Consider the monopoly's profit function, $\Pi_M = \Sigma w_i^* g_i - C(\Sigma g)$ (where M denotes the monopolist). If the monopoly maximizes this profit by choosing g_i^M, with w_i^*, an inverse factor demand function, the ith first-order condition is as follows:

$$w_i + g_i \frac{\partial w_i}{\partial g_i} + \sum_{j \neq i} g_j \frac{\partial w_j}{\partial g_i} = MC(g) \tag{6}$$

The left-hand side of this equation represents the marginal revenue of g_i, which is the familiar MR terms plus the (negative) marginal revenue effect of g_i on other firms' demand for g. The monopoly equates the MR of g_i to its marginal cost plus the marginal revenue lost from the spillover. This condition differs significantly from Equation 5 in how the spillover is treated. Equation 5 explicitly accounts for the marginal damage of g and raises the effective price accordingly. Equation 6 takes it into account partially by raising the price according to how much additional g reduces its value to other firms. The optimal solution compensates for damages regardless of how responsive others' demands are.[1]

Firms' profits need not be zero with a gatekeeper, unlike in the "merger" model in which the monopoly captures all profits. The downward sloping demand curves of firms, while not inconsistent with the efficient equilibrium, will distract the limited monopoly away from the optimum. Even a gatekeeper monopoly capable of charging a different price to each firm would deviate from the efficient outcome. Maximizing its own rents is not the same as maximizing the total rents from the resource when the monopoly cannot capture them all. A monopoly able to supplement its choice of w by charging a fixed franchise fee to the firms could achieve the efficient outcome where $w = MC - MD$ and the franchise fee captures firm profits. In practice, more limited monopolies should not be expected to manage the resource optimally.

Monopoly Contracting over α

As another extension, consider the model in which the production function is $q = f[g, \alpha, G(g, \tilde{g})]$. Let α be some other input into the production of q. To make this change interesting, consider the possibility that the monopoly is able to costlessly require a particular level of α use by firms. The monopoly will use this as a tool to extract more rent from firms by choosing α and g for each firm. Raising α_i above what is optimal for the firm lowers its profits.[2] The higher α_i, denoted α_i^c, also entails a higher g_i (or else why would the monopoly regulate α?). Firms' factor demands for g will depend on w_i, p, other firms' use of g, and the level of α_i^c set for them. Hence, inverse factor demand will be w_i^* (p, g, $\tilde{g}$, α_i^c), and at some level of α_i^c, the firm will shut down. Whether $\partial w_i^* / \partial \alpha_i^c > 0$

depends on the complementarity in production of inputs g and α. For a monopoly-set level of α_i, denoted α_i^f, firms' profits will decline.[3] Firms' factor demands for g will depend on w_i, p, other firms' use of g, and the level of α_i^f set for them. Hence, inverse factor demand will be w_i^* $(p, g, \tilde{g}, \alpha_i^f)$, and at some level of α_i^f, the firm will shut down. Whether $\partial w_i^* / \partial \alpha_i^f > 0$ depends on the complementarity in production of inputs g and α.

The monopoly ideally sets each firms' g and α to maximize its profit function: $\Pi_M = \sum w_i^* g_i - C(\sum g)$. The first-order conditions for its choice of g_i^f and α_i^f are

$$w_i^* + \sum_j g_j \frac{\partial w_j^*}{\partial g_i} \leq MC(g)$$

$$\sum_j g_j \frac{\partial w_j^*}{\partial \alpha_i} = g_i \frac{\partial w_i^*}{\partial \alpha_i} \leq 0$$

with equality when $g_i^f > 0$ and $\alpha_i^f > 0$. The first condition is unchanged from the one-input case. The second condition, however, suggests that the monopoly will raise α until the marginal revenue from doing so has been exhausted. Because the factor demand for g does not depend on other firms' use of α, the second condition requires $\partial w_i^* / \partial \alpha_i = 0$ or $g_i = 0$. If g and α are complements, the monopoly will raise $\alpha_i^f > \alpha_i^*$ until the inputs cease to be complements or the firm becomes unprofitable and stops using g altogether, perhaps because α is costly to the firm. If g and α are substitutes, the monopoly lowers $\alpha_i^f < \alpha_i^*$ until the inputs cease to be substitutes or $g_i^f = 0$. The monopoly's choice of α^c effectively shifts the factor demand curves for g outward (relative to allowing α to be chosen competitively), leading to higher w_i, g_i, and Π_M. When the inputs are substitutes, G is larger than in the competitive case. The effect on G is ambiguous for complementary inputs.

A comparison of these different scenarios is presented in Figure 10-1. The market for g is shown with three different factor demand curves. The middle one, $w^*(g)$, represents the competitive demand for g, where $w = MRP$. Imposing a Pigovian tax on firms shifts the factor demand curve by MD to $w^o(g)$. The third demand curve, $w^c(g)$, represents factor demand when $\alpha^c \neq \alpha^*$, where α^* is the competitively chosen level of α. The marginal revenue curves for w^* and w^c are shown as MR^* and MR^c respectively. The effect of monopoly provision of g can be seen in reducing the quantity of g and raising w. Whether g^* is more or less than g^o, however, depends on the magnitude of the marginal damage and the elasticity of demand. Figure 10-1 (arbitrarily) shows $g^* < g^o$. The effect of contracting over α is to shift demand and marginal revenue outward. This necessarily leads to $g^M > g^*$. This might be a movement toward the optimal allocation of g^o, although this is not a necessary result.

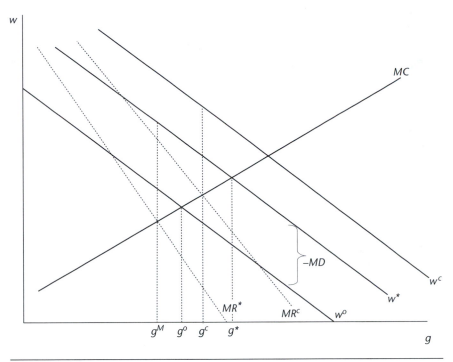

FIGURE 10-1. Comparison of Market Structures for *g* in the Basic Model

The Extended Model

This section extends the basic model by including abatement and applies it to bioengineered seeds in agriculture. These models incorporate abatement by allowing for another factor to affect G. Specifically, the input α abates the harmful effects of G. Let $\tilde{\alpha}$ denote other firms' use of α. Assume the following technological relations hold for $G(g, \alpha, \tilde{g}, \tilde{\alpha})$, for any firms' use of g or α:

$$\frac{\partial G}{\partial g} > 0 \qquad \frac{\partial^2 G}{\partial g^2} > 0$$

$$\frac{\partial G}{\partial \alpha} < 0 \qquad \frac{\partial^2 G}{\partial \alpha^2} > 0 \qquad \frac{\partial^2 G}{\partial g \partial \alpha} < 0$$

The stock of G is increased at an increasing rate by g and decreased at decreasing rate by α. There is also a negative interaction between g and α such that the marginal effect of g on G decreases as α increases.[3]

The firm has the production function $q = f(g, \alpha, G)$. The inputs to the production function are biotech seeds used (g), "care" in the form of refuge zones (α), and the total stock of environmental resistance (G, a detrimental input). Market prices for g and α are w and r, respectively. The price of the output, q, remains p. This model can apply to any firm using a technology that exploits the genetic susceptibility of some pests in the environment and has the opportunity to undertake costly "care" to reduce their impact on the environmental resistance.

Production technology exhibits these relationships for all firms:

$$\frac{\partial f(g,\alpha,G)}{\partial g} = \frac{\partial f}{\partial g} > 0 \qquad\qquad \frac{\partial^2 f(g,\alpha,G)}{\partial g^2} = \frac{\partial^2 f}{\partial g^2} < 0$$

$$\frac{\partial f(g,\alpha,G)}{\partial \alpha} = \frac{\partial f}{\partial \alpha} > 0 \qquad\qquad \frac{\partial^2 f(g,\alpha,G)}{\partial \alpha^2} = \frac{\partial^2 f}{\partial \alpha^2} < 0$$

$$\frac{\partial f(g,\alpha,G)}{\partial G} = \frac{\partial f}{\partial G} < 0 \qquad\qquad \frac{\partial^2 f(g,\alpha,G)}{\partial G^2} = \frac{\partial^2 f}{\partial G^2} < 0$$

$$\frac{df(g,\alpha,G)}{dg} = \frac{\partial f}{\partial g} + \frac{\partial f}{\partial G}\frac{\partial G}{\partial g} > 0 \qquad\qquad \frac{\partial^2 f(g,\alpha,G)}{\partial g \partial G} \le 0$$

$$\frac{df(g,\alpha,G)}{d\alpha} = \frac{\partial f}{\partial \alpha} + \frac{\partial f}{\partial G}\frac{\partial G}{\partial \alpha} > 0 \qquad\qquad \frac{\partial^2 f(g,\alpha,G)}{\partial \alpha \partial G} \ge 0$$

The marginal product of biotech seed use is declining in g. The marginal product of refuge zones is also declining. Increasing genetic resistance reduces output at an increasingly harmful rate. The total effects of raising g and α include these direct effects plus their effects through G.[4] Though conceivable that $df/dg < 0$, df/dg will be assumed to be positive throughout this analysis. Individual farms' use of seeds does more good than harm to that farm's productivity. Increasing resistance makes seeds no more marginally productive, and it makes refuge areas no less marginally productive.[5]

Producer Optimization (α Endogenous)

The firm's optimization problem is to choose g^* and α^* to maximize profit $\Pi = pf(g, \alpha, G) - C(g, \alpha)$, where $C(g, \alpha) = wg + r\alpha$. Firms choosing $g^* > 0$ and $\alpha^* \ge 0$ satisfy the first-order conditions

$$\frac{\partial \Pi}{\partial g} = p\left[\frac{\partial f}{\partial g} + \frac{\partial f}{\partial G}\frac{\partial G}{\partial g}\right] - w = 0 \tag{7}$$

$$\frac{\partial \Pi}{\partial \alpha} = p\left[\frac{\partial f}{\partial \alpha} + \frac{\partial f}{\partial G}\frac{\partial G}{\partial \alpha}\right] - r \le 0 \tag{8}$$

Equation 8 holds with equality for $\alpha^* > 0$. Farmers who select $\alpha^* = 0$ imply that the total marginal revenue product for α is less than r.

Competitive firms equate their marginal revenue product to factor price for each input.

Producer Optimization (α Exogenous)

Now consider firms that face a floor for α. Although they could opt for a higher α^*, they continue to assume that at least locally the marginal profit of α is nonpositive. The firm's choice essentially becomes over g with α as a parameter. The profit function can be rewritten as

$$\Pi = pf(g,G; \alpha) - wg - r\alpha$$

The first-order condition in choosing g^c where $\alpha = \alpha^c$ is

$$\frac{\partial \Pi}{\partial g} = p\left[\frac{\partial f}{\partial g} + \frac{\partial f}{\partial G}\frac{\partial G}{\partial g}\right] - w \le 0 \tag{9}$$

with equality for $g^c > 0$. The firm continues to choose g^c such that its marginal revenue product equals its price, given that α^c is unprofitably high.[6]

When one input is fixed, firms still producing equate marginal revenue product to factor price for the other input.

Comparative Statics for the Firm

Before proceeding, recall the functional assumptions made to this point. Production is concave in inputs g and α. The input G is detrimental to production, and G is a function of g and α. G rises increasingly in g and falls decreasingly in α. The second-order conditions for maximizing a profit function where α is endogenously determined are

$$\frac{\partial^2 \Pi}{\partial g^2} = < 0, \frac{\partial^2 \Pi}{\partial \alpha^2} < 0$$

and

$$\frac{\partial^2 \Pi}{\partial g^2}\frac{\partial^2 \Pi}{\partial \alpha^2} - \left(\frac{\partial^2 \Pi}{\partial g \partial \alpha}\right)^2 > 0$$

where

$$\frac{\partial^2 \Pi}{\partial g \partial \alpha} = p \left[\frac{\partial^2 f}{\partial g \partial \alpha} + \frac{\partial^2 f}{\partial g \partial G} \frac{\partial G}{\partial \alpha} + \frac{\partial^2 f}{\partial \alpha \partial G} \frac{\partial G}{\partial g} + \frac{\partial^2 f}{\partial G^2} \frac{\partial G}{\partial \alpha} \frac{\partial G}{\partial g} + \frac{\partial f}{\partial G} \frac{\partial^2 G}{\partial g \partial \alpha} \right] \qquad (10)$$

The first term in Equation 10 could be positive or negative. The remaining terms are all positive. It seems likely that $\partial^2 \Pi / \partial g \partial \alpha > 0$, and it is necessarily true when $\partial^2 f / \partial g \partial \alpha \geq 0$.

Let $g^* = g^*(w, p, r, \tilde{g}, \tilde{\alpha})$ and $\alpha^* = \alpha^*(r, p, w, \tilde{g}, \tilde{\alpha})$ be factor demand functions fulfilling the first-order conditions in Equations 7 and 8. The effects of price changes are

$$\frac{\partial g^*}{\partial w} = \frac{\dfrac{\partial^2 \Pi}{\partial g \partial \alpha} \dfrac{\partial^2 \Pi}{\partial \alpha \partial w} - \dfrac{\partial^2 \Pi}{\partial \alpha^2} \dfrac{\partial^2 \Pi}{\partial g \partial w}}{\dfrac{\partial^2 \Pi}{\partial g^2} \dfrac{\partial^2 \Pi}{\partial \alpha^2} - \left(\dfrac{\partial^2 \Pi}{\partial g \partial \alpha} \right)^2} = \frac{\dfrac{\partial^2 \Pi}{\partial \alpha^2}}{\dfrac{\partial^2 \Pi}{\partial g^2} \dfrac{\partial^2 \Pi}{\partial \alpha^2} - \left(\dfrac{\partial^2 \Pi}{\partial g \partial \alpha} \right)^2} < 0 \qquad (11)$$

$$\frac{\partial \alpha^*}{\partial w} = \frac{\dfrac{\partial^2 \Pi}{\partial g \partial \alpha} \dfrac{\partial^2 \Pi}{\partial g \partial w} - \dfrac{\partial^2 \Pi}{\partial g^2} \dfrac{\partial^2 \Pi}{\partial \alpha \partial w}}{\dfrac{\partial^2 \Pi}{\partial g^2} \dfrac{\partial^2 \Pi}{\partial \alpha^2} - \left(\dfrac{\partial^2 \Pi}{\partial g \partial \alpha} \right)^2} = \frac{-\dfrac{\partial^2 \Pi}{\partial g \partial \alpha}}{\dfrac{\partial^2 \Pi}{\partial g^2} \dfrac{\partial^2 \Pi}{\partial \alpha^2} - \left(\dfrac{\partial^2 \Pi}{\partial g \partial \alpha} \right)^2} \qquad (12)$$

By the negative definiteness of the profit function, the denominators are positive and the numerators determine the sign of each price change. The own-price effects are necessarily negative. When inputs are complements and $\partial^2 \Pi / \partial g \partial \alpha > 0$, the cross-price effects are negative.

The effects of price changes for the case in which α is exogenous can be found more easily. The concavity of the profit function in g determines the responsiveness of the firm to changes in w. The effect of α on the choice of g^* can be found as

$$\frac{\partial g^*}{\partial \alpha} = - \frac{\dfrac{\partial^2 \Pi}{\partial g \partial \alpha}}{\dfrac{\partial^2 \Pi}{\partial g^2}} \qquad (13)$$

The sign of $\partial g^* / \partial \alpha$ depends on the complementarity of inputs. When α negatively affects the total marginal product of g, the firm will decrease its use of g when α is raised. Factor demand for g also depends on parameters $\tilde{g}$ and $\tilde{\alpha}$. In a fashion similar to Equation 13, the sign of $\partial g^* / \partial \tilde{\alpha}$ is determined by

$$\frac{\partial^2 \Pi}{\partial g \partial \tilde{\alpha}} = p \left[\frac{\partial^2 f}{\partial g \partial G} \frac{\partial G}{\partial \tilde{\alpha}} + \frac{\partial^2 f}{\partial G^2} \frac{\partial G}{\partial \tilde{\alpha}} \frac{\partial G}{\partial g} + \frac{\partial f}{\partial G} \frac{\partial^2 G}{\partial g \partial \tilde{\alpha}} \right] > 0 \tag{14}$$

As expected, Equation 14 shows g and $\tilde{\alpha}$ are complements, regardless of whether g and α are complements. An approach similar to Equation 2 shows that g and $\tilde{g}$ are substitutes.

When g and α are complementary inputs, raising the floor on α leads to higher seed use. Others' use of care complements seed use, and their use of seeds is a substitute.

Externality

The model presents externalities in the use of both g and α. With superscripts identifying the source of the externality, the marginal damages caused by a representative firm are as follows:

$$MD^g = p \sum \frac{\partial f}{\partial G} \frac{\partial G}{\partial g} < 0$$

$$MD^\alpha = p \sum \frac{\partial f}{\partial G} \frac{\partial G}{\partial \alpha} > 0$$

where summations range over all other firms. The MD^g term, as before in Equation 4, reflects the damage caused by the choice of g. The MD^α term reflects the benefit to other firms caused by the choice of α. A two-part Pigovian tax corrects this externality. One part taxes g according to MD^g, and another part subsidizes α based on MD^α. Marginal damages of g and α are proportional to $\partial G/\partial g$ and $\partial G/\partial \alpha$, respectively. Conditions characterizing optimal use of g and α (denoted g^o and α^o) for the representative firm are as follows:

$$p \left[\frac{\partial f}{\partial g} + \frac{\partial f}{\partial G} \frac{\partial G}{\partial g} \right] = w - MD^g \tag{15}$$

$$p \left[\frac{\partial f}{\partial \alpha} + \frac{\partial f}{\partial G} \frac{\partial G}{\partial \alpha} \right] = r - MD^\alpha \tag{16}$$

These conditions resemble the competitive equilibrium except for the inclusion of the MD terms. With these taxes, firms internalize their marginal damages. They effectively raise the price of g and lower the price of α. Comparing the optimal equilibrium to the competitive one requires tracing the effects of simultaneous price changes. The presence of externalities encourages firms to use too much g and too little α and create too much G when inputs are substitutes ($\partial^2 \Pi / \partial g \partial \alpha < 0$). When they are complements, the difference between the optimum and competitive equilibria depends on magnitude of marginal damages and price elasticities.

The marginal damage, or Pigovian tax, is the sum of marginal losses to other firms' revenue.

Supply of g

Consider an upstream factor supply market for biotech seeds. Let the total market supply of biotech seeds be Σg. Furthermore, assume that $w_i^*(g, p, r, \tilde{g}, \tilde{\alpha})$ is the inverse factor demand for the ith firm. From Equation 11, the factor demand curves for g slope downward. Suppose that a representative supplier in the factor market for g has the cost function $C = C(g)$ and marginal costs equal to $MC = MC(g)$, which are nondecreasing in g. The representative supplier chooses g to maximize $\Pi = wg - C(g)$. For a competitive, price-taking supplier of $g > 0$, given factor price w^*, the first-order condition is $w^* = MC(g)$. The market price is determined by the intersection of the supplier's MC and the inverse aggregate factor demand w^*.

Suppose instead that a monopoly supplies the seed market. It provides a quantity g_i to each firm for price w_i to maximize $\Pi_M = \Sigma wg - C(\Sigma g)$. In the case where $g_i > 0$, the ith first-order conditions is

$$w_i^*\left(g, \tilde{g}, \tilde{\alpha}\right) + \sum_j g_j \frac{\partial w_j^*\left(g, \tilde{g}, \tilde{\alpha}\right)}{\partial g_i} = MC(g)$$

This condition for monopoly pricing parallels that of Equation 6. The monopoly prices g to extract the most rent possible from the resource. From Equation 2, the effect of g on the marginal revenue from sales to all firms is negative, so the monopoly raises w over its marginal cost. Equations 11 and 12 show the effects of increasing w on g^* and α^*. Monopoly markup of w causes g^* to decrease. For complementary inputs, the monopoly equilibrium exhibits less α than the competitive equilibrium. For substitutes, α will increase and G will unambiguously decrease.

How this compares with the optimal outcome, however, depends on comparing Equations 15 and 16 where $w = MC(g)$ with Equations 7 and 8 where w includes the monopoly markup. Whether the monopoly markup inflates α and the effective price of g more than the Pigovian taxes will determine how g^* and α^* compare with g^o to α^o. As noted earlier, this depends on whether the margins g causes more damage to firms than it elicits in substitution away from g. The crux of the difference between the monopoly and competition, to put it another way, is the difference between the externality's effect on others' output and its effect on others' marginal productivity. If the former effect is larger, the marginal damage will be larger. If resistance predominantly makes seeds less productive, then the monopoly markup will be larger.

A monopoly raises w based on each firm's impact on others' marginal productivity, not their damage to others' output.

Monopoly Contracting over α

The monopoly might be able to extract more rent by requiring each firm to use α at a certain level, α_i^c. For a fixed α_i^c, the firm's factor demand function for g is g_i^c $(p, w, r, \alpha_i^c, \tilde{g}, \tilde{\alpha})$ implicitly defined by Equation 9. Using the inverse factor demand function for g_i^c, w_i^c $(g_i, \alpha_i^c, \cdot)$, the monopoly maximizes profits $\Pi_M = \Sigma(w^c g) - C(\Sigma g)$ by choosing g and α^c for each firm. The first-order conditions arise for the ith firm in the g market:

$$w_i^c\left(g_i, \alpha_i^c, \cdot\right) + \sum_j g_j \frac{\partial w_j^c\left(g_i, \alpha_i^c, \cdot\right)}{\partial g_i} = MC(g)$$

$$\sum_j g_j \frac{\partial w_j^c\left(g_i, \alpha_i^c, \cdot\right)}{\partial \alpha_i} \leq 0$$

with equality when $\alpha^c > 0$. The first condition represents the $MR = MC$ condition for the monopoly, where each firm's w is inflated over MC by the amount of g_i's effect on the marginal revenue from all firms. The second condition, $MR = MC$ for α, shows how the monopoly will raise α until doing so no longer increases its (net) revenues from sales of g to *all* firms. Raising α_i^c alters that firm's demand for g according to Equation 13. Raising α_i^c increases demand for g by other firms because g and $\tilde{\alpha}$ are always complements. As α_i^c climbs higher, firms will approach their shutdown point and some may exit, until the necessary condition that the net MR of raising α_i^c be zero is satisfied. More g and more α lead to ambiguous effects on G. Resistance under monopoly could be above or below the optimum.

Finally, briefly consider the case in which the monopoly is unable to discriminate between its consumers. Assume w^* $(\Sigma g, p, r, \tilde{\alpha})$ is the inverse aggregate factor demand. If it can only charge a single $w = w^*$ for all users, then its first-order conditions become the following:

Where α is competitively determined and $\Pi_M = w^* \Sigma g - C(\Sigma g)$, we have

$$w^*\left(\sum g\right) + \frac{\partial w^*\left(\sum g\right)}{\partial g} \sum g = MC(g)$$

Where the monopoly sets one $\alpha = \alpha^c$ for all firms and $\Pi_M = w^*(\alpha^c, \cdot)\sum g - C(\sum g)$, we have

$$w^c\left(\sum g, \alpha^c, \cdot\right) + \frac{\partial w^c\left(\sum g, \alpha^c, \cdot\right)}{\partial g}\sum g = MC(g)$$

$$\frac{\partial w^c\left(\sum g, \alpha^c, \cdot\right)}{\partial \alpha}\sum g = 0$$

Contracting over care allows the monopoly to shift out the demand for seeds, extract more rents from firms, and increase seed use and care.

Efficiency

Consider the effects on efficiency in the factor market of removing Pigovian taxes, providing g via a monopoly, and then having that monopoly contract over α. Let superscripts $\{o, *, M, c\}$ represent the optimal, competitive, simple monopoly, and monopoly-contracting-over-α cases, respectively. Removing the Pigovian taxes where $\partial^2\Pi/\partial g\partial\alpha > 0$ leads to increased g and decreased α by all firms: $g^* > g^o$ and $\alpha^* \leq \alpha^o$. Therefore, $G^* > G^o$. Where $\partial^2\Pi/\partial g\partial\alpha < 0$, however, the total changes in g and α depend on their substitutability and the magnitudes of MD^g and MD^α.

The case of $\partial^2\Pi/\partial g\partial\alpha > 0$ has important efficiency implications for monopoly factor supply. The monopoly exerts its power, and seed use and care will decline ($w^M > w^*$, $g^M < g^*$, $\alpha^M < \alpha^*$). The effect of monopoly on G is ambiguous. If $\alpha^* = \alpha^M = 0$, then $G^M < G^*$. Though the externality encourages overuse of g and monopoly pricing reduces this, it is possible that the monopoly overcorrects for the externality. Also, the monopoly captures more of the resource rents at the expense of the firms. If possible, the monopoly might require increased abatement to boost sales of g. This leads to $\alpha^c > \alpha^M$, $g^c > g^M$, and $w^c > w^M$.

Figure 10-2 illustrates one possible series of these changes for the factor market. Following the same approach as Figure 10-1, let w^o, w^*, and w^c be the inverse factor demands for g under Pigovian taxes, under no taxes, and under a $\alpha^c > \alpha^M$ set by the monopoly. Marginal revenue curves are given for the two monopoly cases (MR^M and MR^c). If the effect of the Pigovian taxes is to move the demand for g down to w^o, the market will clear at $g^o < g^*$. Instead, if the monopoly controls g, the use of g will decline, possibly to a point below g^o as shown in Figure 10-2. The monopoly gains considerable rents, while the firms lose surplus. Moreover, a monopoly that achieves g^o will still not be optimal if α remains suboptimal. When demand for g and $\tilde{\alpha}$ are positively related, the monopoly that raises α^c shifts the demand for g outward and increases output (and w and profits). The increase in g might move the equilibrium closer to g^o,

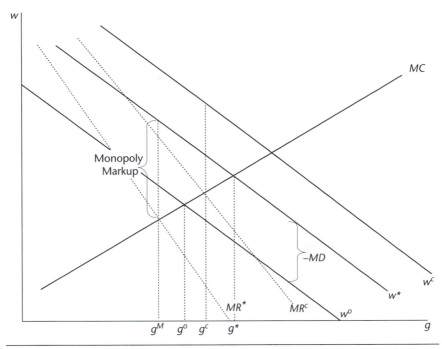

FIGURE 10-2. Comparison of Market Structures for *g* in the Extended Model

although this outcome is not necessary. The possibility of raising α leaves the monopoly with still more profits, possibly at the expense of firms.

This model provides a framework than can be applied easily to genetic resistance resources. When a genetically engineered crop becomes available, farmers often implement it with $\alpha = 0$. If the externalities were corrected, the equilibrium would shift to $\alpha > 0$. Under monopoly provision of g, expect w to rise and g and G to fall. The amount of care remains bounded at zero. Whether resistance predominantly affects seeds' marginal productivity or yields should serve as a qualitative indicator of whether the monopoly markup exceeds the marginal damages. Allowing the monopoly to require a higher α should bring windfall gains to the monopoly, higher w and g, and possibly some exit from the industry. In some cases (especially those with large monopoly markups and large "damages" from underusing α), efficiency gains can be made. This story should be subjected to empirical tests.

The downstream market for q also may figure prominently in welfare analysis, especially when the final product (e.g., cotton, corn) provides substantial consumer surplus. The effects of upstream market structure on the marginal costs for q are not investigated formally in this chapter. Nonetheless, Figure 10-3 can illustrate the downstream implications of market structure. Suppose that correcting the externalities lowers the marginal costs of q from the competitive case $MC^* > MC^o$. Suppose that monopoly pricing of w raises the marginal costs of q, despite any cost savings of lower G. Finally, suppose that mandating a higher α leads to lower marginal costs as the input mix approaches the optimum.[7] Figure 10-3 depicts $MC^M > MC^* > MC^o$ and $MC^M > MC^c$. An arrow is included for MC^c because although it is to the right of the MC^M curve, this case might not have lower marginal costs than the competitive one. If it does, then the welfare gains in the downstream market from having a monopoly contract over α are evident. As a policy matter, a monopoly contracting over α might be preferred to requiring the factor market to price at marginal cost. It is also worth noting that the downward sloping demand curve in Figure 10-3 has not been incorporated into the preceding analyses that fixed p. Such a demand curve would entice the monopoly to further restrict g and raise the price of q.

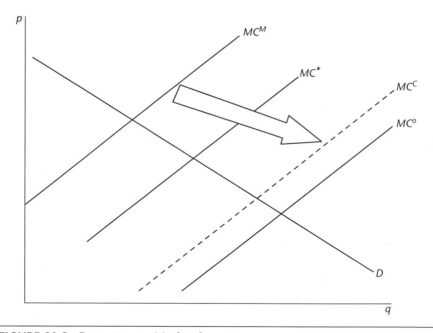

FIGURE 10-3. Downstream Market for q

Household Production

A similar model, building off of Grossman's (1972) model of household production of health services, can be applied to the health care side of the genetic pool commons. The appeal of the preceding analysis is its applicability to a broad family of genetic resistance problems in which production involves an impure public good and costly abatement options are available. Whereas in Grossman's model, the household produces healthy days using inputs such as medical services and healthy time, additional inputs are specified: g and G. As earlier, g represents the use of antibiotics and G is a measure of antimicrobial resistance. Optimization of the household production would follow in a similar way as the firms optimized their output of q. Market structure may similarly play an important role to the extent that a monopoly controls the supply of antibiotics to the household. This could be the case when a dominant pharmaceutical firm supplies the medicine protected by patents. Alternatively, a large-scale health maintenance organization may possess sufficient market power to affect abatement behavior by dictating prescription guidelines to its physicians or requiring more diagnostic tests. A health maintenance organization may internalize the effects of the resistance spillover much like hospitals may be expected to do likewise. Further work is needed to fully elaborate this model.

Conclusion

Many aspects of a simple model of production externalities have been explored. The basic externalities model is applied to a stock of genetic resistance that is contributed to by users of a particular input, such as biotech seeds. The model also investigates the implication of another costly input, a form of abatement affecting the stock of resistance. Abatement behavior represents an important, and often overlooked, aspect of resistance management.[8] Other firms' abatement levels are complements in production to a firm's use of seeds, just as others' use of seeds makes each firm's own use of seeds less valuable. This relationship across firms can make higher levels of abatement consistent with greater factor demand for seeds, irrespective of abatement and the fact that seeds are substitutes within a firm. With prices not reflecting the social cost of seed use (or the social benefit of abatement), too much resistance can be expected in equilibrium.

This chapter extends this model to discuss monopoly ownership of the critical input (e.g., seeds). Despite essentially controlling access to the common-pool resistance resource, a monopoly lacking perfect price discriminating ability will inefficiently steward the resource. A monopoly incapable of capturing all of the resource rents raises the seed price above its marginal cost of production. In doing so, seed use declines relative to the competitive equilibrium. If the optimal use of seeds is less than the competitive level, then monopoly pricing may shift the equilibrium closer to the optimal quantity of seeds. For a fixed level of abatement, the comparison between the optimal and the monopoly prices of seeds is straightforward. Comparing the monopoly markup to the Pigovian tax involves comparing

$$\sum_j g_j \frac{\partial w_j^*(g, \tilde{g}, \tilde{\alpha})}{\partial g_i} \quad \text{and} \quad p \sum_{j \neq i} \frac{\partial f_j}{\partial G} \frac{\partial G}{\partial g_i}$$

The monopoly markup depends on the price elasticity of factor demand for all firms with respect to a firm's use of seeds, whereas the Pigovian tax depends on the firm's marginal damage to other firm's output. This result suggests that the efficiency gains to monopoly pricing depend in part on how the resistance spillover affects other firms' marginal productivity and their output. The monopoly deviates from optimal pricing because the resistance externality operates predominantly through the marginal productivity of seeds and not through output or vice versa.

Incorporating abatement complicates matters but also reflects an important feature of resistance externalities. Users of the resistance resource can undertake costly abatement, whereas the monopoly supplier typically cannot. Given the opportunity (including some enforcement mechanism), the monopoly will choose to require a level of abatement above the competitive level to spur demand for its revenue-generating product, the seeds. This higher level of abatement, however, depends only on the cost of enforcement and the complementarity of abatement and seed use. It does not necessarily relate to optimal resource use. The deadweight loss from the monopoly pricing of seeds may, in fact, be exacerbated when the firm can require inefficiently costly levels of abatement. If the monopoly markup exceeds the marginal damage caused by seed use, however, the possibility remains that allowing the monopoly to contract over the level abatement can lead to welfare gains in the seed market. The different market structures examined here also have an effect on the downstream market (for corn or medical services), where considerable consumer surplus may be at stake.

This analysis applies readily to the behavior of a dominant biotechnology supplier to farms. Monopoly suppliers may conserve resistance resources better than a competitive market, especially when the marginal resistance externality is large. In addition, abatement is an important aspect of resistance management. If the marginal resistance damage is small relative to the monopoly's markup, requiring more abatement may reduce the deadweight losses. Moreover, the monopoly has an interest, albeit limited, in supporting such a requirement. Monsanto, Inc., for example, regularly contracts over "refuge areas" in farms using their seeds, so as to mitigate the development of genetic resistance. In 2000, EPA and Monsanto required all users of *Bt* corn seeds to plant 20% of their acreage with non-*Bt* corn in an attempt to provide refuges for nonresistant insects to dilute any genetic advantage that resistance may confer. This model suggests how such a policy ($\alpha^c = 0.25g$) might be in the interests of Monsanto and also represent efficiency gains.

Several important elements have been neglected in the present treatment, most especially the dynamic nature of the problem. Future research may integrate the temporal nature of decisionmaking. Preliminary indications suggest that this static model sufficiently captures the important elements of the actors' choice of the use of seeds and abatement. Yet managing genetic resources requires more than merely optimally using the current stock. Changing technologies and improving the stock are crucial tasks. Historically, genetic resistance often has been more effectively addressed by inventing new inputs to keep one step ahead of advancing adaptation than by using existing inputs more efficiently. Research and development into new technologies such as biotech crops and antibiotics yield welfare gains not considered here. One obvious connection between developing new technologies and managing them once they are implemented is monopolies. Monopoly control over new technologies may do more than allow for some regulation of externalities—it provides the rents that encourage research and development investment in the first place (Aledort et al. 2000).

The model is ripe for extensions into other areas with genetic common-pool resources. This basic framework points to policies likely to remedy the overuse of certain resources. Changing incentives via property rights and regulation of abatement behavior hold some promise. Research in antibiotic use suggests that "better educated" producers and consumers are unlikely to provide much help (Gonzales et al. 1999). Given the enormity and complexity of resistance externalities, first-best policy solutions do not appear feasible. Changes in institutional design (e.g., monopolizing certain inputs, encouraging producer-regulated abatement) may offer the best avenue for resource conservation. The next step is to find and assess empirical evidence in light of this framework.

This chapter attempts to lay the groundwork for a rigorous economic treatment of one aspect of production in agriculture that is growing in salience. This appears due in part to genetic commons' immunity to technical solutions and conventional economic solutions (privatization, merger, or state control). Formal analysis of different management possibilities merits attention. This chapter begins that process.

References

Aledort, J., R. Laxminarayan, D. Howard, and E. Seiguer. 2000. *Final Conference Report. International Workshop on Antibiotic Resistance: Global Policies and Options.* Cambridge, MA: Center for International Development at Harvard University, http://www.cid.harvard.edu/cidabx/final_conf_report.htm (accessed June 19, 2001).

Baden, J., and D. Noonan. 1998. *Managing the Commons.* Bloomington, IN: Indiana University Press.

Barnett, A.H. 1980. The Pigouvian Tax Rule under Monopoly. *American Economic Review* 70 (5): 1037–41.

Baumol, W.J., and W.E. Oates. 1988. *The Theory of Environmental Policy.* Cambridge, U.K.: Cambridge University Press.

Buchanan, J.M. 1969. External Diseconomies, Corrective Taxes, and Market Structure. *American Economic Review* 59(1): 174–7.

Cornes, R., and T. Sandler. 1986. *The Theory of Externalities, Public Goods, and Club Goods.* Cambridge, U.K.: Cambridge University Press.

Diamond, Jared. 1999. *Guns, Germs, and Steel: The Fates of Human Societies.* New York: W. W. Norton & Co.

GAO (U.S. General Accounting Office). 1999. *Antimicrobial Resistance: Data To Assess Public Health Threat from Resistant Bacteria Limited.* Report to Congressional Requesters. GAO/HEHS/NSIAD/RCED-99-132. Washington, DC: GAO.

Gonzales, R., J.F. Steiner, A. Lum, and P.H. Barrett, Jr. 1999. Decreasing Antibiotic Use in Ambulatory Practice: Impact of a Multidimensional Intervention on the Treatment of Uncomplicated Acute Bronchitis in Adults. *Journal of the American Medical Association* 281(16): 1512–9.

Gordon, H.S. 1954. The Economic Theory of a Common-Property Resource: The Fishery. *Journal of Political Economy* 62(2): 124–42.

Grossman, M. 1972. On the Concept of Health Capital and the Demand for Health. *Journal of Political Economy* 80 (2): 223–55.

Knight, F.H. 1924. Some Fallacies in the Interpretation of Social Cost. *Quarterly Journal of Economics* 38: 582–606.

Levy, S.B. 1998. The Challenge of Antibiotic Resistance. *Scientific American* 278(3): 46–53.

Mills, D.E. 1981. Ownership Arrangements and Congestion-Prone Facilities. *American Economic Review* 71(3): 493–502.

WHO (World Health Organization). 2000. *Overcoming Antimicrobial Resistance: World Health Organization Report on Infectious Diseases 2000.* Geneva, Switzerland: WHO.

Notes

1. Consider a simple system in which production is concave in g and decreasing linearly in G (e.g., $q = g^{0.1} - G$). Also, suppose $G = \Sigma g$. Then $\partial g^* / \partial \bar{g} = 0$, and the gatekeeper monopoly ignores the externality and acts as a traditional monopoly with $MR = MC$. The merger monopoly sets $w = MC + Np$, for N firms.

2. When the monopoly is constrained to dictate a single α for the entire industry, some marginal firms may exit as the monopoly equates the MR of α (across all firms) to zero.

3. Only the negative effect of g or the negative interaction between g and α are needed in this model if the other is zero or small. The former condition is one in which a actually reduces resistance, which may not be consistent with some biological dynamics. The latter suggests that α mitigates g's contribution to G.

4. These include the net present value of a firm's own impact on G.

5. This assumption can be motivated from an ecological viewpoint. Suppose a certain number of pests invade a farm with biotech-seeded land and refuges. As more pests become resistant, the productivity of an additional biotech seed decreases because the pests that land on it are more likely to resist its biological defenses. The productivity of an additional refuge area, however, is unlikely to decrease with resistance, because resistant pests have no advantage in the refuge. If anything, more pests might spill over from the refuges when resistance increases because the resistant pests do not compete with the vulnerable pests on the rest of the farm.

6. A comparable analysis could be made for α being set below the competitive value. $\alpha^c > \alpha^*$ is used here to highlight the difference from the competitive equilibrium where often $\alpha^* = 0$.

7. Future research will investigate these conjectures. The monopoly seeking to maximize demand for g has incentives to expand the downstream market for q by their selection of α^c. Choosing α^c closer to the optimal might accomplish this by lowering MC.

8. In different contexts, this abatement behavior can take many different forms like refuge areas, careful pesticide application, diagnostic screening for bacterial infections, "finishing off" a prescription, and the like.

Commentary

Does the Monopolist Care about Resistance?

Carolyn Fischer

Inputs to agriculture often have effects external to the particular farmer using them. Some, like fertilizer runoff or habitat creation or destruction, do not affect agricultural productivity. Others, like resistance to pesticides or to genetically engineered crops, do affect that productivity, creating situations akin to common-pool resources. In these types of problems, with unclear property rights or diffuse ownership, individual users do not take into account the effect their impact on the resource stock has on all other users. Two classic examples are overfishing, with more resources spent to catch fewer fish overall, or traffic congestion, with more drivers and longer commute times than optimal. In the case of Noonan's chapter (Chapter 10), the implication is increased pest resistance, with overuse of the biotech product and reduced effectiveness.

For biotech products, however, ownership of the resource (effectiveness) is often concentrated in the hands of the single producer with the patent. A single owner does recognize the impact of the externality because using more of the product reduces the value of the units already in use. In the classic resource models, single ownership can lead to the socially efficient outcome—if the owner derives the full value of the use of the resource. For a monopolist to "own" all the rents from its biotech corn, it would have to be able to charge each farmer a fixed licensing fee equal to the farmer's surplus from using the corn. Then the monopolist would choose the price of the corn that maximizes the collective surplus, which is the socially efficient allocation of the factor input, but all the rents would be transferred from the farmers to the monopolist.

However, the monopolist may not be able to charge a fixed fee; rather, it may offer the farmer a per-unit price for the corn. The monopolist still recognizes the effect of the externality but through its effects on the producer's revenues rather than on the farmers' rents.

This commentary combines two traditions of economic analysis, that of imperfect market structure and that of common-property resources, to investigate the impact of monopolistic provision of the biotech input on the level and efficiency of its use. An important innovation—and complication—is the effect of another input, characterized as "care," that is costly to provide but that generates a positive externality by mitigating resistance. As with the negative externality, individual farmers on their own would not reap the benefits of their care on other farmers, and they would use too little, such as planting too few refuge areas. A single owner reaping all the rents from the use of the biotech corn would subsidize or require the use of the efficient levels of care. However, a revenue-maximizing monopolist would require care to the extent it increases the value of its sales. The distinction is important not only for the profits of the biotech producer but also for its strategy of setting the price of its product.

Although the analysis is of a factor market, the intuition is identical to that of a traditional market of consumers and suppliers. In this case, the consumer is the farmer, whose willingness to pay for the monopolist's biotech product is derived from the value of the corresponding production. The productivity of an additional unit of seed corn to one farmer is a function not only of the extent of his own use and the extent of his own care but also of the use and care of all the other farmers. The value of that additional production also depends on the price received by farmers for their corn harvest. These variables together determine each farmer's demand curve. The producer's willingness to supply to a farmer then reflects the marginal costs of producing the biotech corn, as well as the impact of the externality on its rents. Because the externality is resistance, which causes a productivity change, the costs are transmitted through shifts in the demand curves of all the farmers.

A social planner would maximize total surplus, that is, the areas under the demand curves less the production costs of biotech corn and care. At the optimum for use of the factor, the price equals marginal costs plus a tax reflecting the external cost of marginal damages. A monopolist, however, maximizes total revenue less costs. For traditional pollution problems where the damages are external to the firms, the monopolist sets marginal revenue equal to marginal production costs, and the monopolist can price above or below the optimum, depending on whether the markup overcompensates or undercompensates for the externality. However, when the monopolist internalizes the externality, as with any production cost, the monopolist equates marginal revenue with total marginal costs, including marginal damages. The resulting monopoly price is greater than the socially efficient price, as in the traditional case of imperfect competition without externalities.

The decision for care presents a more complex innovation in the monopoly problem. Although one may often think of care in proportions, like the share of land planted for refuge areas, the model in Noonan's chapter uses levels of care. A point not elaborated is that this distinction allows one to consider the farmer's demand for the monopolist's product separate from the level of care, up to a point. Given any mandated level of care, the cost of care is fixed for the farmer, and, as long as it is less than the farmer's surplus, small changes in the cost of care do not affect the farmer's demand. However, although traditional models have used fixed fees as a form of rent extraction, this model has two important differences: the monopolist does not itself charge for and profit from care; rather, care induces a positive externality that enables it to capture more rent from its product sales.

As a result, the monopolist's decision with respect to mandating care is different from a social planner's. While a planner would seek to maximize *total* productivity of the biotech input, less the costs of care, the monopolist seeks to maximize *marginal* productivity. Furthermore, the monopolist does not incorporate the cost of care into its decisions as long as the farmer's profits are positive. This latter point represents an important caveat recognized but not explicitly modeled in Noonan's chapter. The monopolist is constrained in choosing levels of sales and care by the profits of the farmer: the factor costs it imposes on the farmer cannot exceed the surplus, or else the farmer would not use the product.

Given any level of biotech corn use, the monopolist should demand more care than the planner, as long as care is costly. Because a farmer would have positive surplus at the social optimum,[1] the monopolist would not perceive a cost to itself from raising the level of care, and it would do so until marginal productivity is maximized or until the farmer's profits are zero.[2] The profit constraints are therefore important: they determine how much the monopolist *can* charge for its biotech product and how much care it *can* require distinct from what it would *want* to do if concerned with productivity changes alone.

Revisiting the sales decision, the constrained monopolist would not only set marginal revenue equal to marginal costs plus marginal damages but also take into account how one price change affects every farmer's profits because the externality may change what price and care it can ask of the others.[3] The main effect of the constraint would be to temper the revenue effects of increasing price or care levels because both reduce individual profits. However, they also lower the externality, which tends to raise the profits (and loosen the constraints) of the other farmers.

Given the level of biotech sales offered by the monopolist, the level of care is generally higher than would be desired by a social planner. As a result, the monopolist is able to sell more of the input at a higher price than it would at the socially efficient level of care. This effect mitigates the monopolist's contraction of biotech sales relative to the efficient level, although the price remains unambiguously higher. Still, in equilibrium, the overall level of care required by the monopolist might be more or less care than that required by the planner. Although the monopolist might only perceive a share of the marginal cost of extra care through the farmer's profits constraint, if it sells less of the biotech product, the marginal impact of extra care is also smaller.

In summary, Noonan's work considers a common-pool resource, sold by a monopolist that cannot capture all the corresponding rents, but it can charge each buyer a per-unit price for the product and also require a certain level of care. The resulting equilibrium is generally characterized by

- a higher price of the resource compared with the optimum, which is itself higher than the competitive (no-policy) price;
- a monopoly markup constrained by the profits remaining to the farmers after the care requirement;
- greater care than would be efficient, given sales, but fewer sales than would be efficient, given care; and
- greater sales and a higher price than if the monopolist could not contract over care.

The actual equilibrium levels of care and biotech sales would depend on the complex interactions between the farmers' production functions, individual and overall use, and care. For example, if resistance of a certain pest is a local problem, the farmer may internalize a large part of the resistance costs of additional use. If it is widespread, the monopolist must incorporate more of the external effects. The type of care also may differ widely. Larger refuge areas may reduce the productivity of an individual farmer's stock of biotech corn because less land remains to plant it in, although the areas may enhance productivity overall by reducing resistance buildup. Careful techniques in the application of pesticides, however, might have beneficial results for crops as well as resistance prevention. Understanding these interactions is important because how exactly the externalities shift factor productivity is critical to determining the difference between marginal surplus and marginal revenue.

Regardless, the third result is provocative in its implications for policy. In discussions over refuge guidelines, the assumption is that too little care is afforded. This assumption would be correct for a competitively provided input or for a case in which the monopolist could not require care itself. In this latter case, one needs to consider the second-best policy alternative: what would be the appropriate refuge policy, given a monopolist's pricing strategy? If the monopolist can require care, could welfare be much improved by a refuge policy, and would that take the form of a mandatory ceiling, a system of subsidies, or both?

Noonan's work represents a first step toward understanding the important interactions between market structure and the provision of a common-pool resource with a secondary common pool of mitigation activities. It has the potential for several other interesting extensions, including the case in which the monopolist also sells the input with the second externality. Related applications would be a monopolist selling complementary goods with an externality. Such double-externality and double-monopoly models, though challenging, will bear fruit in understanding many resource and resistance problems, the management of not only pest-resistant plants but also "Roundup ready" corn or antibiotic "cocktails" that involve two or more drugs.

Notes

1. Noonan's chapter makes this assumption implicitly to have an interior solution.

2. If productivity always increases with care, absent the profit constraint, the monopolist would always demand more care until every farmer's profits are zero. This condition is that of Equation 10 in Noonan's chapter. If marginal profits are strictly increasing in care, then the constraints must always bind: the monopolist will require as much care as possible, given the total profit constraint, and the shadow value of that constraint will matter both for the level of care and sales of the input. To ignore the profit constraint, one must assume either that care is costless or that it ultimately has a negative impact on productivity.

3. Note that if the profit constraint binds for any farmer, all the other equilibrium prices are affected. Changing the use of inputs or care by one farmer generates an externality for the others, including the one facing the binding constraint. The change in revenues that can be appropriated from the constrained farmer follows not only the change in marginal productivity but also the change in the constraint.

Chapter 11

The Interaction of Dynamic Problems and Dynamic Policies
Some Economics of Biotechnology

Timo Goeschl and Timothy Swanson

In this chapter, we describe biotechnology as the sector that addresses recurring problems of resistance such as those that occur in the pharmaceutical and agricultural industries. The sector may be conceived of as the research and development layer of a three-tiered industry that makes the fundamental determination regarding the allocation of biological resources between stabilization and production objectives. We examine the capacity for decentralized, patent-based incentive mechanisms to result in socially optimal outcomes in the biotechnology industry. We demonstrate a fundamental incompatibility between the dynamics of the patent system and the dynamics of the resistance problem. The patent-based incentive mechanisms are incapable of sustaining society against a background of increasing resistance problems. In addition, the externalities within a patent-based system indicate that decentralized mechanisms will result in systematic underinvestment in the stabilization objective.

Human interventions within the biological world produce natural responses that automatically erode the effectiveness of the initial intervention. This effect is seen in the phenomenon of antibiotic resistance in the health context and in the phenomenon of pest resistance in the agricultural context. These responses from nature are predictable and automatic because when we choose to make a biological resource more prevalent than it would otherwise be we are simultaneously selecting higher rates of prevalence for the pests and pathogens that prey on that resource. These pests and pathogens will prosper from our choices and erode any gains from the initial intervention unless we can intervene again to restore the original gain. Thus, by intervening within the biological world, we are committing ourselves to a continuing race of innovation against nature. Sustaining production in the face of these contests of biological innovation is the essence of the task that society assigns to the biotechnological industries.

Weitzman (2000) recently analyzed the potentially unsustainable impacts of human intervention within biological systems. He proposed that a sustainability constraint on human intervention in the biological world could be equated with the optimal allocation of biological resources between an "unstable" production objective and the more inherently stable "diversity" objective. Concern about sustainability within biological systems will lead to the imposition of constraints on the extent of human intervention within the biosphere. We expand on this intuition by developing the evolutionary dynamics that cause the production sector to tend toward instability and by incorporating the dynamics that cause the reserve or diversity sector to promote stability. This focus enables us to define more clearly the role of a biotechnology sector in managing the race of biological innovation and allocating biological resources between production and sustainability objectives.

We depart from Weitzman's framework by focusing on the industrial dimensions to this problem. Our emphasis is on the use of patent-based incentive mechanisms for motivating the biotechnology industry. The analytical framework that we use is the model of "creative destruction" devised by Aghion and Howitt (1992). Their model considers the dynamics occurring within an industry motivated by the pursuit of patent-based rents from innovation. This is a second, parallel race of innovation between industrial competitors, in which success is measured by the displacement of a rival's innovation with one's own.

Thus our chapter examines the intersection between two distinct races of innovation—one biological and one industrial. We examine the interaction between the dynamics of the problems of biological resistance and the dynamics of the policies based on patent-based incentive mechanisms. We have three fundamental enquiries concerning biotechnology.

Our initial enquiry concerns the nature of the social value of the biotechnology sector. How should a sector that provides only sustainability be balanced against those that provide production within the economy? What share (or weighting) of investment should be allocated to each objective? Our first task is to set out what society's objectives should be when managing a biotechnology sector (see generally Goeschl and Swanson 2002).

The second enquiry concerns the use of decentralized incentive systems to motivate the pursuit of these objectives. The Aghion and Howitt framework enables us to investigate the impact of patent-based incentive systems on the biotechnology industry. Under patent-based research and development (R&D) systems, firms compete for patents that provide revenue streams until another innovation renders that patent obsolete. In the biotechnology industry, these patents will be displaced by a competitive firm's creation or a competitive pathogen's adaptation. How will firms operating under a patent system respond to the challenge implied by these biological contests? Are patents adequate to achieve the gains sought by society? The distinction between the social objectives regarding biotechnology and the patent-based incentives to pursue them is the second focus of this enquiry.

Finally, a crucial determination to be made by the biotechnology industries is the allocation of biological resources between the R&D and production sectors. This question has been intimated in the earlier work by Weitzman (2000). Just as society must give a relative weighting to production and sustainability, the biological world also must be allocated between the two objectives. Thus the biological world ultimately must be allocated between two sectors—one used for specialized production (such as agriculture) and the other used to maintain the stability of the first. These are the production and reserve sectors, respectively.[1] The biological resources within the reserve sector act as inputs into the biotechnology industry to generate solutions to problems developing within the production sector. Will the biotechnology industry capture sufficient value under a decentralized system? Will the biotechnology industry channel this value toward the maintenance of reserves? The capacity of the industry to affect the socially optimal allocation of natural resources to this stability function is the third enquiry of this chapter.

Resistance Problems and R&D Policies: The Intersection of Dynamic Systems

We will use biotechnology to refer to the use of biological resources as inputs into the research and development for the development of solutions to biological problems within the context of evolutionary processes. Biological problems are perceived by evolutionary biologists as zero-sum games between competing predators. Thus an infestation or infection simply represents the appropriation of a larger share of the available surplus by a competing organism. The evolutionary process is the combined result of the processes of selection, adaptation, and reproduction. Thus the application of a particular pesticide or pharmaceutical to a pest population simply selects disproportionately those in the population that are resistant to it, which results in disproportionate reproduction by resistant pests and the observed adaptation of resistance over time. Table 11-1 presents empirical examples of these kinds of processes.

The biotechnology industries engage in an ongoing contest to solve these biological problems against the background of these evolutionary processes. For example, the pharmaceutical industry deals with such problems in its research into antibiotics; it attempts to halt the progress of pathogens successfully reproducing themselves within the human population. After application of an antibiotic, the industry must then deal with the consequences of selection and adaptation when the pathogen population begins to demonstrate resistance to the antibiotic (Laxminarayan and Brown 2001). The agricultural industry deals with such problems in its research into new plant varieties when it attempts to produce new varieties to replace those with declining yields. The commercially obsolete plant variety, as host to an increasingly successful pest population, demonstrates the same problem preying on the human population in the pharmaceutical context. Again, the introduction of the new plant variety induces the responses of the pest population by selection and adaptation, and the new variety begins its decline (Evans 1993; Scheffer 1997).

One unusual characteristic of these sorts of problems is their refusal to go away (Munro 1997). When a solution has been found and applied within the biological world, the nature of the biological world is such that it will commence immediately to erode the usefulness of that application (Goeschl and Swanson 2000).

Adaptation of biota (pests and pathogens) to widely used pharmaceuticals and plants is a fact of life, and it suggests that the widespread use of any biotechnology must necessarily imply its own eventual demise (Anderson and May 1991). Even more perversely, the pace at which technological innovation proceeds will simply increase the number of responses by the pathogen population because innovation implies selection. Widespread and rapid rates of innovation by biotechnologists, therefore, lead to widespread and rapid rates of innovation by the pathogens as well. Biologists refer to these as "Red Queen" contests, in which it is necessary to innovate more and more rapidly merely to maintain parity within the contest (Maynard Smith 1976).[2]

Within this context, the meaning of technological progress is much less straightforward. If the widespread use of a technological advance must necessarily imply the increasing rate of the arrival of problems, then what is to be the measure of success? Think of the biotechnology sector as engaged in a race by the innovator running up the "down" escalator. Then success in the race must be measured relative to actual progress up the escalator, not just steps taken by the innovator. Imagine as well that the escalator belt runs freely, so that quicker or larger steps by the innovator simply result in bringing the stairs down more quickly. Given that individual attempts at progress result in both discrete moves forward and an increasing pace of the background contest, the full impact of an innovation must be discerned by its aggregate impact across time. Small initial advances might ultimately aggregate into large net losses.

Interestingly, the presence of a biological contest of innovation implies a dual function for the set of biological resources set aside for "reserve use" (or nonproduction). Weitzman noted one function of the reserve sector is that of an epidemiological buffer that helps limit the pressure on pathogens to evolve in a specific direction and provides a form of static insurance against a sudden suc-

TABLE 11-1. Characteristic Time for the Appearance of Resistance in Some Specific Biological Systems

Species	Control agent	Time to resistance Generations[a]	Years
Avian coccidia			
Eimeria tenella	Buquinolate	6 (<6)	1
	Glycarbylamide	11 (9)	<1
	Nitrofurazone	12 (5)	7
	Clopidol	20 (9)	6
	Robenicline	22 (16)	10
	Amprolium	65 (20)	14
	Zoalene	11 (7)	22
	Nicarbazin	35 (17)	27
Gut nematodes in sheep			
Haemonchus contortus	Thiabendazole	3	<1
	Cambendazole	(4)	<1
Ticks on sheep			
Boophilus microplus	DDT	32	4
	HCH-Dieldrin	2	<1
	Sodium Arsenite		40
Black flies (Japan)			
Simulium aokii	DDT+Lindane		6
Simulium damnosum	DDT		5
Anopheline mosquitoes			
(different localities)			
Anopheles sacharovi	DDT		4–6
	Dieldrin		8
An. maculipennis	DDT		5
An. stephansi	DDT		7
	Dieldrin		5
An. culicifacies	DDT		8–12
An. annuaris	DDT		3–4
An. sundaicus	DDT		3
	Dieldrin		1–3
An. quadrimaculatus	DDT		2–7
	Dieldrin		2–7
An. pseudopunctipennis	DDT		>20
	Dieldrin		18 weeks

a. The figures give the number of generations before a majority (>50%) of the individuals in the population are resistant to the control agent. The number of generations before resistance is first observed (usually >5% of individuals resistant) is shown in parentheses.

Source: Anderson and May 1991.

cessful adaptation by pathogens to the human intervention (2000). The other function of the reserve sector arises from the coevolved history of hosts and their pathogens over millions of years and from the continued exposure of this diverse set to new forms of pathogens. For evolutionary biologists, it is no surprise that the genetic makeup of biological hosts contains the solutions to many problems posed by pathogens. Previous stages of Red Queen races have left behind traces of these episodes in the genes of parts of the population (Myers 1997; Frank 1994; May and Anderson 1983). This accumulated history of previously successful biological innovations is often useful as a starting point in the search for industrial innovations to address current problems. Biological reserves are the subject of commercial exploitation in the R&D processes of the plant-breeding industry (Brown 1989; Gollin et al. 1998; Evenson 1998) and of the pharmaceutical industry (Rausser and Small 2000; Swanson 1993). Thus one important additional feature of our model is that the nonproduction sector of biological resources provides *both* epidemiological and informational services.

The biotechnology sector is presented here as that area of human enterprise dedicated to maintaining the stability of the biological production sector against this background of competing organisms that is continually evolving to introduce new biological problems. It pursues this objective by making investments that (a) slow the rate of arrival of biological problems, (b) increase the rate of arrival of solutions to such problems, or (c) accomplish both. One of the primary functions of the biotechnology sector is to determine the optimal amount of the diverse biological resources necessary to achieve these objects and then to reserve them as inputs. The biotechnology sector is the manager of society's R&D efforts to make progress in the contest of biological innovation through the appropriate management of biological resources.

Having described the role of the biotechnology sector as that of generating innovations within the biological contest, we turn briefly to the role of the industrial contest that motivates the biotechnology industry to generate these innovations. The biotechnology sector is motivated by the pursuit of limited-term monopolies created by the conferment of patents on its innovations. In accordance with patent law, monopolies of a specified duration are allowed for useful innovations of a specified magnitude, that is, representing a certain minimum level of advance. In focusing on patent-based mechanisms for motivating decentralized R&D, this chapter is related to the literature on contests of innovation well known from the theory of industrial organization (Tirole 1988). The specific framework we adopted is the model of a sector engaged within a process of creative destruction (Aghion and Howitt 1992). Creative destruction is of course Schumpeter's (1942) term for the process by which firms innovate against a background of competitive innovation within the industry. In this scenario, an innovation secures an advance for the firm but only until a second firm within the industry secures an innovation that destroys the usefulness of the first. Hence a patent-based incentive mechanism provides the capacity to capture a stream of rents from an innovation, but it also provides the prospect that the stream of rents may be truncated because of a competitor's innovation.

The one significant modification we apply within this framework is that we incorporate the possibility of another overlaid process of ongoing obsolescence deriving from forces within the biological, as opposed to the industrial, world. The stream of rents from an innovation may be truncated because of a competitive innovation originating in either contest, biological or industrial. We term the impacts of the biological contest on the industrial innovation contest a process of *adaptive destruction*.

Against this background of creative and adaptive destruction, the biotechnology firm must compete to innovate to remain within the industry. Hence, the intersection of the dynamic systems represented by biological problems and patent-based policies generates the ultimate incentives that motivate the biotechnology industry. How these unusual dynamics produce outcomes and how these outcomes relate to the ultimate objectives society holds for the sector are the subjects of this chapter.

A Model of a Biotechnology Sector

In our model of a biotechnology sector, we examine the role of the underlying R&D sector that sustains the production sector. The biotechnology sector conducts R&D to provide a flow of necessary innovations to sustain society in the contest of biological innovation. Implicitly, it determines the level of investment in R&D, including the level of investment of biological resources, and, consequently, the relative sizes of the production and reserve sectors. In between the research and production sector is an intermediate goods sector whose sole role is to embody the information developed in the research sector for application within the production sector.

To render the discussion concrete, we fix it within the agricultural sector. Within this context, the base R&D sector is the plant-breeding sector of the agricultural industry, and the intermediate goods are the registered seeds and high-yielding plant varieties (HYVs) within which innovations are embodied.[3] The only consumer good resulting from this industry is the agricultural output ultimately produced by the application of the intermediate good (HYVs) to the lands retained within the production sector.

Plant breeders' R&D efforts increasingly focus on the ongoing problems of pest adaptation and resistance.[4] Pests and disease now account for average annual crop losses of 28.9%, increasing with each year of the use of a given plant variety (Oerke et al. 1994; Evans 1993; Scheffer 1997). Plant breeders also engage individually in a contest of innovation against one another.

Together these contests limit the commercially useful life of any newly introduced HYV to between three and seven years.[5] Hence the biotechnology sector underlying agriculture must continually innovate to address the problem of depreciation occurring within the production sector.

Two important inputs into plant breeders' R&D address this biological contest: the diversity of plant genetic resources on which they rely and the (nonproduction) lands on which they are grown. Such reserve lands of course provide the epidemiological function noted by Weitzman (2000). They also provide the flow of genetic resources required to produce innovative plant varieties. Thus, the plant-breeding sector must make the fundamental determination on the level of reserves created to maintain the agricultural sector.

In sum, agricultural production takes place within an ongoing biological contest against continually adapting pests and pathogens. In this contest, the plant-breeding sector acts as society's innovator and thus determines society's ability to sustain production within this biological contest. As adaptation to existing HYVs occurs, the plant-breeding sector must develop new varieties of plants that are sufficiently innovative to thwart the advance of the prevailing population of pests and pathogens. Of course, if it succeeds, its success merely selects another strain of pests and pathogens for disproportionate evolutionary success, and the contest begins anew.

Modeling the Role of a Biotechnology Sector

Assume a single consumption good is generated by a three-tiered production system. The final goods sector consists of only production, but it is sustained and stabilized by decisions made in the underlying R&D sector. The R&D sector generates innovations, which are embodied in intermediate goods that are then inputs into the production of the final consumption goods. Think of the plant-breeding sector at the base (the R&D sector) of the crop production industry, the seed producers in the middle (the intermediate good sector), and agricultural production in the third tier (the final good sector). All value within the system derives from consumption of the final good, but that level of consumption is sustained by advances within the R&D sector.

Final Goods Sector
Final good production relies on only two inputs: the intermediate good (seeds) and the natural resource (land). Production of the final good occurs under the conditions of a fixed proportions production function, such that a fixed amount β of the intermediate input x is combined with each unit of the natural resources input L. The proportion of the natural resources factor L allocated to final good production is termed d.[6]

The final goods sector produces a final good y_t based on a production function of the form

$$y_t = A_t \times F(x_t) \tag{1}$$

with $F(0) = 0$, $F' > 0$ and $F'' < 0$ defining a concave production function in C^3. The productivity parameter A_t is determined by the level of technology being employed in the final goods sector at time t, and x is the amount of the intermediate good being used in that sector. This function is well defined. Because of the fixed proportions in production, a choice of x uniquely determines the optimal allocation of L to this sector, d.

Intermediate Goods Sector

The intermediate good sector provides the link between the production sector and the underlying R&D sector. It does so through the production of an intermediate good that embodies the information produced within the latter while being an essential input into the former. The actual production of the intermediate good exhibits the same type of production function as before. Here a unit increase in the amount of L allocated to intermediate good production will generate an increase in the production of the intermediate good x proportional to the factor z. The proportion of L allocated to intermediate good production will be termed g. Given these assumptions about the two production functions, the following identity will hold:

$$x_t = \frac{d_t}{\beta} = \frac{g_t}{z} \tag{2}$$

Therefore, a given level of production of the intermediate input x is always associated with a specific allocation of the essential input L to production, as well as its allocation between intermediate and final good production.[7] The Leontievian structure of production in both the intermediate and the final sector can be justified by reference to the actual practice in the agricultural industry in which there is an optimal fixed input of seed per hectare. It also helps abstract from the substitutability between production factors that would otherwise cloud the analysis.

This sector is important in this model only in that it affords the biotechnologist the capacity to capture the value of its innovations. Intermediate goods (here seeds) are patented products that encapsulate the information generated within the underlying R&D process. Without the intermediate good, the production of information in the R&D sector would go unrewarded. We will return later to the role of the intermediate market good as an incentive mechanism in the section on optimal allocation of resources to the biotechnology sector.

The R&D Sector

The R&D sector of the biotechnology industry produces disembodied technological innovations through the combination of human and natural resources. These innovations are then fed into the intermediate good sector for embodiment and ultimate use in the production sector.

The biotechnology industry must attract investment to this stabilization function. Within this model, we examine a single factor of production used within both R&D and production sectors, namely, the supply of biological resources. A supply of biological resources is necessary for R&D to generate innovations. Likewise, biological resources are also required for production to occur in the production sector. The biotechnology sector's ability to attract investment will determine the relative allocation of these essential resources between the two functions, production or R&D.

Figure 11-1 depicts the biotechnology sector and its role in this production system. Here the biotechnology sector performs R&D and uses the essential natural resource as an input into its research activities. Innovations result in new technology that is embodied within patented products in the intermediate sector; the intermediate good also requires a small allocation of the essential input for production. Finally, the intermediate good is then used in the final goods production sector in combination with the essential natural resource to produce the goods that are marketed to consumers.

Here we define "land" as the underlying factor that determines how biological resources will be allocated between production and R&D (see note 1). Land provides agricultural production when allocated to the production sector and diverse plant genetic resources when dedicated to nonproduction (the "reserve sector"). The problem is the manner in which the biotechnology sector determines the optimal allocation of the natural resource (land) between production and R&D. A part of this problem concerns the capacity of patent-based systems for providing optimal incentives to attract investments into the biotechnology sector. Before we turn to these issues, we will define the dynamic structure of the model.

Dynamics—Innovation and Adaptation

Within the step-climbing context we used to describe the biological contest in which innovations induce adaptations, an innovation is a step upward, and an adaptation is a step backward. The current stage of technology is then a single parameter that captures the history of the competition to date as the net of the number of such steps, forward and backward.

Innovation and Creative Destruction

The timing of innovations flowing from the biotechnology sector is assumed to follow a Poisson process denoted by ϕ. The frequency of innovations

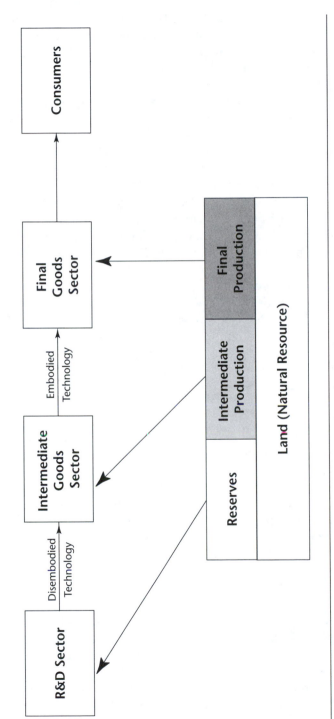

FIGURE 11-1. The Biotech Sector within a Three-Tiered Production System

within this process is determined in part by the level of investment in R&D. A distinguishing characteristic of biotechnology industries is that they depend in part on supplies of biological resources for undertaking the R&D process. This is the factor of production on which we focus. Specifically, we assume that the frequency of innovation increases with the proportion v of the essential input L allocated to R&D. Innovations hence arrive at a rate $\phi\, i(v)$ per time period where $i(v)$, $i' > 0$ is an innovation production function.

The impact of an innovation consists of a discrete shift in the level of productivity in the final sector, which we denoted in Equation 1 by A_t. This shift is of magnitude $\gamma > 1$ such that $A_{I+1} = A_I \times \gamma$.[8] The index I denotes the current level of technology in use in final goods production.

Innovations also have a destructive facet to their characters within the industrial context. The occurrence of a "technological innovation" is an event that renders the currently prevailing technology within the industry obsolete, that is, innovations in this model are "drastic."[9] Hence each act of creation is an act of destruction with regard to the usefulness of all previous innovations. Under a patent system, this is equivalent to stating that an "innovation" is defined to be only that amount of technological change sufficient to warrant patent protection. We will standardize innovation at this magnitude to provide a standard measure of innovation with which to compare technological progress across various systems of organization. Hence we will measure aggregate technological change as the sum of the number of discrete "steps" of innovation of the minimum length required to acquire a patent.

Innovation and Adaptive Destruction

The biotechnology sector has the unusual characteristic that the application of its innovations within the production sector results in an induced response in the form of "biological innovations" by pathogens. This happens because of the widespread use of the innovation in the production sector and the consequent adaptation of the pests and pathogens to the particular characteristics of that innovation. Their adaptation then renders the innovation obsolete, a process we termed "adaptive destruction." Biological innovation reduces the economic productivity of the final goods sector by eliminating the gains generated by the adoption of the current technology.

Analytically, we model this dynamic process of biological innovations forced by selection pressure as a Poisson process represented by λ.[10] The frequency of innovation increases with the use of the intermediate input that embodies the current technology in accordance with an induced evolution function $a(x)$, $a(0) = 0$, $a' > 0$.[11] Hence, pathogens adapt to and overcome current technologies at a rate of $\lambda\, a(x)$.[12]

As indicated earlier, the rate and extent of adaptation depends on the rate and extent of uniform adoption of the innovation. Because we have assumed that innovations are "drastic," a technological innovation displaces all other competitors from use throughout the final goods sector.[13] Then the extent of use of the innovation will depend only on the relative size of the production sector (relative to the reserve sector). Thus, the only limitation on the use of the intermediate good x will be the extent of the reserve sector v, and we can equivalently express the function determining the rate of biological innovation as a function of the size of the reserve sector. Thus the induced evolution function will henceforth be expressed in the form $a(v)$.

A biological innovation is normalized so that a single innovation eliminates the relative advantage of the current technology.[14] This results in a shift of γ^{-1} in productivity.[15] Thus, with D denoting the stage of biological innovations (i.e., depreciation), $A_{D+1} = A_D \times \gamma^{-1}$. This implies that after a biological innovation has occurred, the economy reverts to a technology of the previous productivity level.[16]

The Net State of Technology

These two processes of innovation and adaptation jointly determine the current state of productivity (A) within the final goods sector. Each technological innovation that occurs represents a positive shift in sector productivity, whereas each biological innovation represents a negative shift. With s denoting the current technological stage given a history of innovations and adaptations, the productivity at stage s is then[17]

$$A_s = A_0\gamma^S = A_0\gamma^{I-D} \qquad (3)$$

Equation 3 therefore describes the current state of technology in use in the final goods sector as a single parameter expressing the history or aggregate impact of the contests of creative and adaptive destruction. Progress in the production sector in the sense of absolute improvements in productivity occurs only to the extent that the number of technological innovations exceeds the number of biological ones.

The Social Objective for Biotechnology

We assume society consists of a continuum of individuals of mass 1, each with an intertemporal utility function $u(y)$ linear in the consumption of final good y, of the type

$$u(y) = \int_{\tau=0}^{\infty} e^{-r\tau} y \, d\tau \qquad (4)$$

where r is the social rate of time preference and τ is time.

In this representation of the problem, the individuals concerned are giving no direct consideration to the costs of instability, uncertainty, or risk. The individuals in this society value only the flow of consumption goods from the final production sector, giving no inherent value to the products of the R&D sector. This social objective creates a role for an intermediate goods sector in which R&D outputs are embodied, and it makes clear that any increase in production will be considered equally valuable.[18] Hence the decision problem we are concerned with is the optimal allocation of natural resources (land) in the pursuit of the objective of maximum production. The importance of sustainability within this objective will be inferred from the need to maintain production against the background of pathogen adaptation.

Noting that the total amount of land will be allocated between the various sectors of this industry, this implies the existence of the constraint (for $L = 1$)

$$1 = v + d + g \tag{5}$$

We now need to incorporate the concepts of creative and adaptive destruction within the model. We use the probability distributions $\Pi(I,t)$ (the probability of I technological innovations by the time t) and $\Pi(D,t)$ (the probability of D biological innovations by the time t) defined as

$$\Pi(I,t) = \frac{1}{I!}\left[\phi i(v)t\right]^{I} e^{-\left[\phi i(v)\right]t} \tag{6}$$

and

$$\Pi(D,t) = \frac{1}{D!}\left[\lambda a(v)t\right]^{D} e^{-\left[\lambda a(v)\right]t} \tag{7}$$

We are now in a position to set out the social objective for a biotechnology sector. As shown in the appendix, we can combine Expressions 1 through 7 and aggregate over all individual utilities u to restate the social objective for the biotechnology sector of maximum social utility U as follows:

$$\underset{v}{Max} U = \int_{t=0}^{\infty} e^{-rt} \sum_{I=0}^{\infty} \sum_{D=0}^{\infty} \left[\Pi(I,t) \times \Pi(D,t)\right] A_s F(x) dt \tag{8}$$

The social objective is to maximize Equation 8 by choosing the proportion v of the essential input L to be allocated to R&D, subject to Equation 5. This objective contains the race of innovation. A_S represents the current state of technology, which is generated by the history of past innovations. The probability distributions indicate the current period's contest, that is, the number of innovations and adaptations occurring within that period. Production is the outcome of both the net state of technology generated by the race (represented by A_S) and the amount of land dedicated to production. Thus the restated objective intimates the trade-off between investing biological resources into production or into innovation.

We are able to see the explicit nature of the trade-offs involved by integrating Equation 8 over real time and making use of Equation 4. The appendix shows how to arrive at the following expression for the present value of social welfare from the allocation of this input between these sectors.

The Role of the Biotechnology Sector:

$$U = \frac{A_0 F(\bullet)}{r - \left[\phi i(v) - \lambda a(v)\gamma^{-1}\right](\gamma - 1)} \tag{9}$$

where $F(\bullet)$ is $F[\beta^{-1}(1 - v - g)]$ and $a'(v) < 0$ from Equation 5.

Equation 9 captures the differentiated roles of the production and R&D sectors in generating social welfare over time. The impact on output from the allocation of lands to the production sector is denoted in the numerator, whereas the impact from allocation of lands toward the R&D sector is captured in the denominator. In simplest terms, the choice of the size of the production sector determines the initial level of production, whereas allocation of resources to the R&D sector determines the growth path of production. The role of the biotechnology sector is then the determination of the trajectory of welfare generated within the production sector by sustaining the sector in the biological contest.

The numerator exhibits a straightforward impact of increased land in production because reducing v benefits the output in the final sector. The denominator gives a sort of "own discount rate of biodiversity" that must be applied to determine the value of the perpetuity that is the flow of final sector output over the infinite time horizon. It is a composite of the social rate of time preference r reduced[19] by the rate of technological innovation $\phi i(v)$ and increased[20] by the rate of biological innovation $\lambda a(v)$.

This own discount rate captures the expected impact of the contest of innovation between the biotechnology sector and the biological world. There are really three cases. If the sector is successful in maintaining innovation rates significantly in excess of adaptations, then the own discount rate may approach zero, implying a substantial multiplier on initial production levels. In this case, the growth trajectory is very steep. Conversely, if the biotechnology sector is very unsuccessful, the number of adaptations will significantly exceed the number of innovations, and the growth trajectory will be downward. Then the production system is unsustainable, the time horizon is short, and the multiplier is very low. This is essentially the case of potential collapse investigated by Weitzman (2000). Then there is the situation in which the biotechnology sector is in a closely contested Red Queen race in which it attempts to make advances against the background of a system always responding to depreciate those gains. We believe that, in the long run, this is the correct way to view the role of the biotechnology sector. It is the sector responsible for attaining and maintaining small amounts of relative advantage within a contest of biological adaptation.

The Optimal Allocation of Resources to the Biotechnology Sector

Solving Equation 9 and making use of Equation 2 for the optimal level of v, we get the following expression for the socially optimal level of investment in the biotechnology sector.

Socially Optimal Allocation of Resources to Biotechnology Sector:

$$\frac{F'(\bullet)}{\beta + z} = \frac{\left[\phi i'(v) - \lambda a'(v)\gamma^{-1}\right]F(\bullet)}{r - \left[\phi i(v) - \lambda a(v)\gamma^{-1}\right]} \tag{10}$$

at the optimum with $F(\bullet) = F[\beta^{-1}(1 - v - g)]$.[21]

The left-hand side of Equation 10 is the marginal cost of increased allocations to R&D (i.e., in terms of lost production). The right-hand side of Equation 10 is the marginal benefit from increasing such allocations. This is equal to the net present value of the net increase in productivity (in the final goods sector F) from the marginal increase in the rate of arrival of innovations and the marginal reduction in the rate of biological innovation.[22] The own discount rate applied is, as discussed later, the composite rate used by the social planner, which takes into account the rates of technological and biological innovation.[23] In short, the trade-off is between an initially increased level of production and a perpetual increase in the rate of growth.

To demonstrate, consider Equation 9. This expression defines an expected expansion path for final output in the economy along the path $[\phi i(v^*) - \lambda a(v^*)\gamma^{-1}]$ ln γ. This path is unambiguously increasing in R&D investments v. Any small advantage acquired in the current period's contest of innovation may be warranted by the change in path that it implies.

Equation 10 may be seen as another rendition of Weitzman's Equation 12 (Weitzman 2000), which explicitly determines the relative weights that society will give to the goals of production versus stabilization within the biological sector. In our chapter, these weights are determined implicitly by the biotechnology industry determining the relative allocations of resources to the "production" and "diversity" sectors required to implement those goals. As in Weitzman's model, the threat of unsustainability may be viewed as the choice of any path that might lead ultimately toward zero production, but more generally the problem of optimal biotechnology investment may be any decision that places the sector on a path with inadequate rates of innovation.

Firm Decisionmaking and Investments in R&D for Resistance Problems

A decentralized R&D industry requires substantial policy intervention to be operable. The benefits generated from investments in R&D are usually inappropriable or very inexactly appropriable, and this situation leads to suboptimal levels of investment in R&D (Arrow 1962). One policy response to this problem is the creation of monopoly rights in the marketing of intermediate goods that embody some of this information, for example, patent rights. We will initially explore how an individual firm in pursuit of a patent in the intermediate goods sector will approach the same decision faced by the social planner, that is, the allocation of an essential input between the R&D and production sectors.

Patent-Based Profits in the Intermediate Good Market

The initial question concerns the magnitude of the rewards to be obtained through innovation. Firms in possession of a patent have the capacity to choose the optimal level of output for the intermediate good embodying the patented technology. Because we are assuming a perfectly competitive final goods sector, the optimal amount of good x produced is the level of output that maximizes revenues minus the cost of producing the intermediate good on land $g(x)$, where land commands the price p per unit.

$$x_s^* = \arg\max\left[A_s \times F'(x)x - p(x)gx\right] \tag{11}$$

In the context of an industry with an effective monopsony over the use of the essential input, the price of that factor may be endogenized.[24] Then the monopolist would consider the effect of its intermediate output decision on the demand for land generated by the final and intermediate goods sectors and thus on the price of land. With the price of land p a function of x, then

$$x^* = -\frac{F'(x)}{F''(x)} \tag{12}$$

This means that monopolistic profits p_s in the technological state s would be

$$\pi_s = -A_s \times \frac{\left[F'(x_s^*)\right]^2}{F''(x_s^*)} \times \left(1 - \frac{z}{\beta}\right) \tag{13}$$

Private Firm's Investment in R&D

Assume there are n firms in this sector of the economy, one of which will hold a patent for the current technology. The balancing condition for investment is that at the margin the expected profits generated by investment in R&D must equal the opportunity cost of capital (Kamien and Schwartz 1982). Hence, taking into account the expected obsolescence of technological innovations (because of the processes of both creative and adaptive destruction), each firm that is not currently producing the intermediate good faces the R&D balancing condition that

$$rV_{I+1} = \pi_{I+1} - (n-1)\phi i(v_{I+1})V_{I+1} - \lambda\alpha(x_{I+1})V_{I+1} \tag{14}$$

This condition states that the expected return on the next innovation (the right-hand side) must equal the opportunity cost of capital on the left-hand side. The expected return consists of the monopolistic profits from selling the intermediate good embodying the innovation to the final goods sector in the future technological stage minus the expected impact from obsolescence of the technology because of technological innovations made by one of the $(n - 1)$ competitors minus the expected impact from obsolescence of the technology because of biological innovation. Note we assume that technologies of the previous technological stage are supplied competitively, implying a zero-profit condition on technologies of earlier vintage.[25] Rearranging Equation 14 and making use of Equation 3, we get the net present value of a single technological innovation:

$$V_{I+1} = \frac{\pi_{I+1}}{r + (n-1)\phi i(v_{I+1}) + \lambda a(d_{I+1})} \tag{15}$$

In this expression, the numerator represents the monopolistic profits generated by the innovation and the denominator represents the own rate of discount for private investments in innovative activities. This is a composite rate made up of the opportunity cost of capital, the rate of obsolescence because of (others') technological innovation, and the rate of obsolescence because of biological innovation. In sum, the private firm values only the monopoly rents that may be acquired from a technological innovation, and it discounts any future stream of such rents with regard to the expectation of any future technological and biological innovation.

Firm Decisionmaking Regarding Investment in R&D

The private firm analog to Equation 10 is the private incentive for investment in reserves for R&D. Land is allocated by the patent holder to equalize returns in both the final goods sector and in R&D.

$$p = A_s \frac{F'(\bullet)}{\beta} = \phi i'(v_s)V_{I+1} \tag{16}$$

where p is the price of land and $F(\bullet)$ is $F[\beta^{-1}(1 - (n - 1)v - g)]$. Condition 16 provides the intertemporal link between technological stages.[26]

Combining Equation 4 with Equations 15 and 16, solving for the steady state, and using Equation 5 to simplify, we derive the optimality condition for the private firm's allocation of land to the reserve sector in the steady state of a decentralized economy.

$$\frac{F'(\bullet)}{\beta} = \phi i'(v) \frac{\gamma \frac{[F'(\bullet)]^2}{-F''(\bullet)}}{r + (n-1)\phi i(v) + \lambda a((n-1)v, g)} \tag{17}$$

As in Equation 10, the left-hand side of Equation 17 shows the marginal value of land allocated to production and the right-hand side of the marginal value of land allocated to reserve status.[27] The marginal value of lands as reserves is equal to the expected value of monopoly rents accruing to the successful innovator because of the allocation of an additional unit of land to R&D, discounted at the private firm rate that includes not only the opportunity cost of capital but also the anticipated effects of patent obsolescence (deriving from either the processes of creative or adaptive destruction). In the following sections, we will contrast the private incentives for investments in biotechnology with the social optimum.

The Capacity for Patent-Based Incentives for R&D To Address Resistance Problems

Now that we have derived the alternative decisionmaking rules for social and patent-based decisionmaking regarding resistance problems, it is possible to compare how these alternative decisionmaking systems respond to the fundamental determinants of resistance problems. The following propositions establish the comparative statics of social and decentralized decisionmaking processes.

PROPOSITION 1: *The socially optimal amount of investment in biotechnology increases with (a) a decrease in the discount rate* r*, (b) an increase in the magnitude of the impact of an innovation* γ*, (c) an increase in the arrival rate of technological innovations* ϕ*, and (d) an increase in the arrival rate of biological innovations* λ*.*[28]

PROOF: Take the partial derivatives of Equation 10 with respect to the variables specified. Proposition 1 states that a higher discount rate leads to a lower present value of the benefits of innovation and hence of the inputs that generate these innovations. Likewise, if the magnitude of the impact of a technological innovation increases, innovation becomes relatively more profitable, which leads to increased investment in reserves. This is correspondingly the case when an increase in the arrival rate of innovations improves the profitability of the R&D sector. This shifts allocation of reserves toward the R&D sector as the sacrifice in current consumption is outweighed by the gains from a higher growth trajectory. Finally, and perhaps most importantly, investment in R&D is society's instrument for responding to biological innovations, and so the marginal benefits from R&D will increase as the rate of biological innovation increases.[29]

As in the case of the social planner, we can make the following statements about Equation 17 to describe the response of the individual firm's investment in R&D in response to changes in the basic parameters.

PROPOSITION 2: *The optimal level of investment by the individual biotechnology firm responding to patent-based incentives increases with (a) a decrease in the discount rate* r, *(b) an increase in the magnitude of the impact of an innovation* γ, *(c) an increase in the arrival rate of technological innovations* ϕ, *and (d) a decrease in the arrival rate of biological innovations* λ.

PROOF: Take the partial derivatives of Equation 17 with respect to the variables specified. The intuition behind the various assertions within Proposition 2 is straightforward. The net present value of any investment in R&D increases with a lower discount rate, making investments more profitable at the margin. The same is true for an increase in the magnitude of the impact of innovations. If technological innovations are less frequent, then monopoly rents are likely to accrue over longer periods, thus raising the benefits associated with R&D, although the impact is less straightforward because competitors also gain from this increase, which affects expected monopoly rents in an adverse manner.[30] Finally, when biological innovations are more frequent, then patents become obsolete more quickly, thus reducing incentives for investments.

The development of the basic character of the respective incentive systems allows us to develop our main result, stated in Proposition 3.

PROPOSITION 3: *A patent-based system of incentives is incapable of addressing the fundamental problem of biological adaptation because the incentives to invest in solutions are weakened as the problems become more serious.*

PROOF: Compare (d) of Propositions 1 and 2.

Proposition 3 states the obvious implication from the comparison of Propositions 1 and 2. As the rate of biological adaptation increases, the socially optimal response is to allocate more resources to the solution of an increasingly threatening problem. Proposition 2 demonstrates, however, that the industry motivated by a patent-based system of incentives will in fact respond in a perverse manner. Increasing rates of adaptation imply reduced time horizons for product usefulness and hence a truncated flow of future benefits. The industry will see reduced incentives to investing in the solution of problems if the expected life of that solution is reduced, and so a patent-based system is ill suited to the problems of biotechnology.

How serious is this problem? That is, what would cause the rates of biological innovation to increase? The fundamental nature of adaptation problems is such that an increasing rate of biological innovation is a given because it results from any attempts by society to make progress. Society pursues growth in production through either increased allocations of biological resources to the production sector or increased rates of innovation. Either approach results in increased rates of biological innovation. Increased areas of land dedicated to production result in increased prospects for any given biological innovation taking hold. Increasing numbers of technological innovations increase the number of different pathogens that are implicitly selected by society for possible trial. For this reason, biotechnological processes are usually modeled as a form of "arms race": an increasing rate of response from the competitor is induced by any attempt to gain an advantage.

Intellectual property rights systems are very poor mechanisms for providing incentives in such contests of innovation. The induced response from nature implies an expectation that any innovation's life span will be short, and this reduces the incentives to invest in innovation from the outset. If, for some reason, society does make an initial attempt to achieve growth in production in the biological sphere, the intellectual property rights system provides an increasingly diminishing incentive to attempt to remain within the contest of innovation that results. Just as society becomes reliant on the biotechnology sector to address the resulting problems, the biotechnology sector becomes increasingly less motivated to pursue those problems.

Comparing Private and Social Investment in the Biotechnology Sector

We now have the basic results necessary to address the third fundamental question raised in the introduction of this chapter: how well does the patent-based system perform the role of allocating biological resources between the production and reserve sectors? Weitzman (2000) identified this as a fundamental problem to be addressed with regard to the instabilities in the biological world, and we wish to know how well a decentralized industry will resolve this issue.[31]

This is equivalent in our framework to the general question of how well a patent-based system will motivate investments in the biotechnology sector. Because we are varying only a single factor of production in our biotechnology industry (the essential input—land), the incentives to invest in biotechnology generally will be represented by the level of investment in this factor of production. We wish to know how patent-based incentives motivate investment in biotechnology's stability-enhancing function and how this will ultimately determine the level of reserves retained for this function.

The Externalities within the Patent-Based Management System

The optimal allocations of land to R&D by the private firm and the social planner are captured in Equations 17 and 10, respectively. A comparison of these allocations shows six distinct factors that will determine the relative size of the reserve sectors under these different regimes: the business-stealing effect, the single supplier effect, the appropriability effect, the differential internalization of externalities, the own discount rate effect, and the collateral cost effect.

The first factor is what Aghion and Howitt (1992) termed the "business-stealing" effect. This effect captures that the social planner will accrue only the net benefits from its innovations. This is because new types of technology supersede those developed previously by the social planner, denoted by ($\gamma -$ 1). In contrast, private incentives for innovation are greater because innovating firms tend not to compete against their own patents (see also Tirole 1988) and thus receive the total impact of innovation (γ). In this respect, the incentives to invest in biotechnology are greater for private industry than for the social planner.

This is counterbalanced by the "single supplier" effect that results because the social planner faces only the net impact of biological innovations ($\lambda a(v)/\gamma$), whereas the private firm faces the full effect ($\lambda a(v)$). The social planner is the sole supplier of technology, whereas in the private industry case of obsolescence through biological innovation, technology (of a previous productivity stage) will be supplied by a competitive market with zero profits. The social planner—in the same circumstance—will supply its own technology from an earlier stage.

The third effect is the "appropriability" effect, which reflects that the social planner takes into account the full social welfare benefits denoted by $F(\bullet)$, that is, all of the social value resulting from production and consumption.

The private firm instead will consider only the monopoly rents $-[F'(\bullet)]^2/F''(\bullet)$ that it will appropriate from its own output.[32] This shortfall in rent appropriation decreases the private incentives for R&D activities and has a negative effect on private investment into reserve lands.[33]

The fourth effect is the "differential internalization" of externalities: The social planner fully internalizes both of the benefits from holding the marginal unit of land as a reserve—the direct benefits from increased rates of technological innovation $\phi i'(v)$ and also the indirect benefits from reduced rates of biological innovation (i.e., $-\lambda\, a'(v)$). The firm considers the direct benefit $\phi i'(v)$ as the indirect benefit externality diffuses over all market participants. This is another reason that the incentives for investment in reserve lands are reduced under a decentralized regime.

The fifth difference is the *"own discount rate"* effect: The denominator in Equation 10 shows that the social planner's discount rate has the rate of technological innovation subtracted from it, whereas in Equation 17 these two rates are summed. This is attributable to an increased rate of innovation that generates growth that is valuable from the social perspective but that the same renders private investment in R&D less profitable by increasing the expected rate of technological obsolescence.

The last effect that differentiates the private firm from the social planner is the "collateral cost" effect. This effect appears in the denominator of the left-hand side of Equations 10 and 17: The social planner takes into account that the expansion of intensive agriculture requires an allocation of land to produce the intermediate good, that is the aggregate cost (in terms of land) is $\beta + z$. This implies that the loss of reserves from expanding intensive agriculture is less than the gain in intensive lands. The private firm does not consider this externality, as the left-hand side denominator featuring only β shows.

Three of these effects have been noted in the existing industrial organization literature. The "business-stealing effect" has previously been explored in Aghion and Howitt (1992). The problem of imperfect appropriation of rents from R&D is a well-known source of suboptimal provision of R&D when Ramsey pricing of innovations is not feasible (see, for example, Tirole 1988). The differences in the impact of technological progress on the discount rate of social planner and private firms have been studied by Reinganum (1989).[34] The remaining three effects are peculiar to the problem at hand. Of these, the fact that there is a difference in internalization of externalities between social planner and private industry must be the most significant one. This is because it highlights the failure of private industry to take into account the negative relationship between intensive use of the essential resource and the rate of obsolescence of the technologies employed intensively. This means that in all economic settings in which such a class of relationships exists, additional deviations of the private industry allocation of resources can be expected.[35]

The "single supplier" effect is important in settings in which imitation costs are low such that gains from innovation diffuse quickly across the industry. In these cases, the value of shelving innovations is low, which contributes to underinvestment into R&D relative to the social optimum. The last source of difference between the social planner and the private industry case is the problem of "collateral cost." This is very specific to the agricultural setting of this model and therefore likely to have little application beyond the context of conserving biodiversity as an R&D input. However, it points to the more general problem that private decisionmaking does not account for collateral effects if they are not conveyed through market prices.

In total, therefore, we find six reasons to believe that the incentives under a patent-based system vary from the social optimum. Five of these effects indicate that a private firm will underinvest in the reserve sector. The only effect that runs counter is the "business-stealing effect," which allows one firm's innovation to replace another's *before* its useful life has been fully served. Of course, this is the essence of the patent race as an incentive mechanism, and its precise effect varies significantly on the basis of assumptions and expectations (Kamien and Schwartz 1982). In the biotechnology sector, the incentives to overinvest built into a patent race (if any such exist) must be sufficient to compensate for the many clear benefits that the private decision-making externalizes.[36]

In any event, the patent-based system performs poorly in generating the optimal level of investments in the biotechnology sector. It contains six clear externality problems, five of which indicate that the patent-based system will tend toward underinvestment in biotechnology.

Comparing Social and Industrial Investments—A Simulation

The results of a simulation exercise of difference between centralized and decentralized decisionmaking with regard to the allocation of lands to R&D display how the underestimation of the value of reserves for these purposes is not only systematic but also substantial over a wide range of parameter values. To illustrate, we must first move from the individual firm level of analysis to that of the aggregate industry. The industry equilibrium concept that determines the optimal allocation of land depicted in Equation 17 is that of a patent race involving $n - 1$ firms.[37] Because innovations are drastic by definition, the patent race generates a sequence of monopolies that replace one another. In this sense, individual monopolies do not persist, but the market structure will remain monopolistic.

To assess n, we examine the conditions under which firms enter the race. Entry is profitable so long as positive rents are associated with being engaged in R&D. We restrict our attention to the case in which the costs of R&D are only the cost of holding land as a reserve.[38] Then firms will continue to enter into R&D as long as the expected present value of R&D is not less than the cost of holding the optimal amount of land given by Equation 17; that is

$$\phi i(v^*)V_{I+1} - A_s \frac{F'(\bullet)}{\beta} v^* \geq 0 \tag{18}$$

Making use of Equations 17 and 18 and simplifying, this means that the total number of firms in the market is determined by the condition

$$i'(v^*) = \frac{i(v^*)}{v^*} \tag{19}$$

In the absence of any barriers to entry, the optimal level of reserves v^* will be chosen so that the marginal productivity of reserves equals average productivity. This means that entry is occurring until the monopoly rents are dissipated across the industry by virtue of firms entering R&D until average profits equal zero. This zero profit entry condition will then determine the aggregate level of investment within the industry.

To address the issues raised at the beginning of this chapter, we make a direct comparison of the optimal reserve decisions made by a social planner, by a private industry, and by an individual firm within that industry. This requires us to look for ways to evaluate Equations 10 and 17 explicitly, and this will require the selection of specific functional forms. Table 11-2 lists the explicit functional forms chosen for the various analytical functions contained in the model.

We assume that $\delta < 1$. This means we are assuming decreasing returns to scale in the production sector for both the intermediate input and—by virtue of fixed proportions in production—land. In the R&D sector, we assume that both technological and biological innovation functions are linear in land inputs.[39] This allows us to solve explicitly for land allocation decisionmaking under the circumstances of the social planner and the private industry. However, because the number of firms is indeterminate in the case of a linear innovation function, we will access market data to depict the level of land demanded by an individual firm.

TABLE 11-2. Assumed Functional Forms

	Analytical	Explicit
Agricultural production function	$F(x)$	x^δ
Technological innovation function	$\phi i(v)$	ϕiv
Biological adaptation function	$\lambda a(v)$	$\lambda a(1 - v)\beta/(\beta + z)$

Solving Equation 10 for the optimal level of reserves chosen by the social planner *RS*, we get

$$RS = 1 - \frac{\delta\left(\dfrac{r}{\gamma-1} - \phi i\right)}{\dfrac{\lambda}{\gamma} a \dfrac{\beta}{\beta+z}\left(\beta^2 - \delta\right) + \beta^2 \phi i - \delta \phi i} \tag{20}$$

Equation 20 conforms to the tenets of Proposition 1, and it exhibits other characteristics we would expect, such as the conditions under which it provides values less than one.[40] Solving Equation 17 for the level of reserves chosen by the industry as a whole *RI*, we get

$$RI = 1 - \frac{r + \phi i}{\dfrac{(\beta - z)\phi i \gamma \beta^2}{(1-\delta)(\beta+z)} - \dfrac{\lambda \beta a}{\beta+z} + \phi i} \tag{21}$$

Again, Equation 21 conforms to the tenets of Proposition 2 and exhibits the characteristics required for our simulations.[41]

We are now able to provide some simulations of the chosen levels of reserves under varying assumptions about innovation, adaptation, and discount rates. Table 11-3 summarizes the choices for the baseline parameters that generate these plots and the literature from which they derive.

The results from these simulations are depicted in Figures 11-2 to 11-4. They underline the basic point set forth earlier. The private valuation of reserve lands for R&D is a very poor estimator of the social value of these lands for these purposes. The simulations demonstrate this point over a wide range of plausible parameter values. They further illustrate the direction and the magnitude of the bias. Over almost the entire range of parameter values, the private metric systematically underestimates the social value of reserves for purposes of R&D. The magnitude of the underestimate depends on the specific parameter values, but it can vary from a small amount to a difference of several orders of magnitude.

Several further important differences between social decisionmaking and private decisionmaking are illustrated in these figures. Figure 11-2 shows how variations in the rate of technological innovation affect the optimal reserve levels. Private industry allocates consistently less to reserves, and its optimum declines more pronouncedly than that of the social planner. At very low rates of technological innovation, R&D becomes unprofitable. In contrast, the social planner is willing to preserve land even if the innovation rate is zero. The reason for this lies in the fact that reserves not only serve as an R&D input but also act as an epidemiological buffer. This difference in investment levels reflects the differential rate of internalization of this externality.

TABLE 11-3. Baseline Simulation Parameters and Sources

Parameter Description	Symbol	Value	Source
Discount rate	r	0.01	
Productivity in agriculture of intermediate good	δ	0.35	Evenson 1998 Contribution of genetic resources to global rice production
Innovation rate	$\phi\, i$	0.0019	Cartier and Ruitenbeek 1999 "Hitrate" of 10^{-6} times three samples per species times species richness per hectare[42]
Adaptation rate	$\lambda\, a$	0.0025	Heisey and Brennan 1991
Intermediate good per land ratio in final goods sector	β	3	Relative productivity of final and intermediate goods sector. In agriculture between 1:0.003 to 1:0.2. Here 1:0.06 (Smith 1998).
Intermediate good per land ratio in intermediate sector	z	0.2	
Magnitude of innovations	γ	1.5	Legal requirement of "significance"
Number of firms in industry	N	25	Market data (RAFI 1997)

The simulation in Figure 11-3 illustrates how the general incentives for investment in reserves diminish as the discount rate increases. Of course the private incentives to invest lie everywhere beneath the social incentives and, to such an extent that the discount rate at which it becomes unprofitable for industry to conduct R&D, lies below that at which the social planner ceases to innovate by a factor of 5. However, it is also worth noting the difference here that the rate of discount will vary for industry and social planner, with the industry operating under a rate that is greater than or equal to that of the planner. This standard difference would aggravate the already existing tendency of private industry to underinvest in reserves.

Finally, the response to changes in the rate of biological innovation depicted in Figure 11-4 demonstrates the most pronounced difference in the two decisionmaking processes, as discussed earlier. In the context of rapid rates of biological innovation, the social planner responds with increased levels of investments in reserves for R&D. This is indicative of the fundamental role of such reserves as the generators of the information required to respond to these recurring problems. In contrast, the private industry responds to

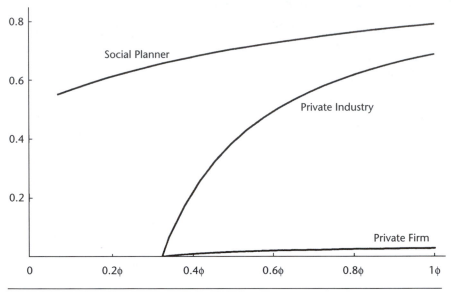

FIGURE 11-2. Share of Reserves for Varying Rate of Technological Innovation

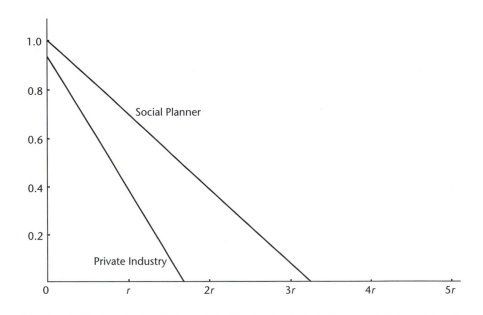

FIGURE 11-3. Share of Reserves for Varying Discount Rate

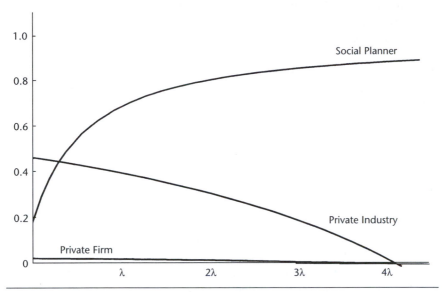

FIGURE 11-4. Investments in R&D for Varying Rate of Biological Innovation

increasing rates of biological innovation in a perverse manner. The private industry actually reduces its R&D activity in response to increased pathogen activity. This response sharpens as the adaptation rate increases which, in turn, widens the gap between the social optimum and the industry response.

Conclusion

The dynamics of the biological world generate certain predictable and destabilizing responses to attempts to make progress within that world. Attempts to expand the production sector are met automatically with biological adaptations that neutralize those efforts. Increasing the rates of intervention also increases the rates of arrival of such adaptations. And, once intervention has occurred, the option of retaining the status quo is no longer available. Society is then engaged forever within a contest of innovation and adaptation.

The biotechnology sector is the branch of R&D that undertakes society's cause within this contest. As described in Weitzman (2000), we view the fundamental determination to be made by this sector as the optimal relative size and extent of the biological resources dedicated to productive as opposed to "reserve" uses. Because these reserves serve an important role within the R&D process, the decision is also related to the decision concerning the amount of investment to allocate to the stabilizing role of biotechnology. Investments in biotechnology may be seen as investments in maintaining sustainable growth within these parts of the economy.

The novel question we have addressed here is whether a decentralized industry motivated by a patent-based incentive mechanism is able to approximate the socially optimal outcome in this contest of innovation. We have demonstrated that in the most fundamental sense, the incentives facing private firms motivated by patents simply do not accord with the objectives of society. The basic societal objective in this arena is to manage the growth capacity of the economy by investing in the capacity to respond to biological innovations. Our analysis of the patent-based incentives facing private firms indicates that these firms are wholly indifferent to the growth capacity of the economy (as opposed to the cyclical pursuit of technological innovation),[43] and that the incentives for investments in response mechanisms are positively perverse. Hence, at the most fundamental level, the decentralized biotechnology industry is not pursuing the objectives society would set out for it.

In addition, the incentives that do exist under the patent system contain numerous externalities that generally cut in the direction of underinvestment. To the extent that the biotechnology industry does invest, it invests demonstrably less than that which is socially efficient. This results in a biological world that is insufficiently invested in the reserve function or, equivalently, too heavily invested into the production function.

The problem here is the institutional one caused by the intersection of two dynamic phenomena: the patent-based incentive system and the biology-based adaptation system. Patent systems require widely demanded innovations with reasonable life spans to be effective. Biological systems contain inherent adaptations that automatically respond to and shorten the life span of any innovation that is applied extensively. The dynamics of the two systems are incompatible. This is because patent-based incentive mechanisms are based on a single view of technological progress, that is, the view that progress consists of a continuing climb up a one-way ladder. In this view, the coincidence between the patent-based incentives and the social objective are perfect. This is because the patent-based reward is awarded for any step up the ladder, and each step represents a permanent achievement. In the case of biotechnology, however, progress is more of the nature of the race up the escalator. Each step in this contest is necessarily impermanent, and it may achieve nothing in the long run. In this instance, awarding patents for "steps" provides incentives for firms without pointing in the direction of real "progress." This may be seen by the fact that firms responding to such systems would be able to achieve maximum rents simply by timing their steps to coincide with the expiration of their patents. In general, a patent system provides the biotechnology sector with incentives to take steps rather than to make real progress.

Acknowledgements

We thank our discussant David Simpson, and three anonymous reviewers for helpful comments and suggestions on the chapter. The authors thank Philippe Aghion and Gardner Brown for comments and discussions. We have benefited from the comments of seminar participants at the School of Public Policy and the Department of Economics, University College London, at the Institute of Advanced Studies, Vienna, and at the European Economic Association Meeting in Santiago. Timo Goeschl acknowledges support from the European Commission, DG XII, under its Fellowship Scheme.

References

Aghion, P., and Howitt, P. 1992. A Model of Growth through Creative Destruction. *Econometrica* 60: 323–51.

Anderson, R.M., and R.M. May. 1991. *Infectious Diseases of Humans. Dynamics and Control.* Oxford, U.K.: Oxford University Press.

Arrow, K. 1962. Economic Welfare and the Allocation of Resources for Invention. In *The Rate and Direction of Inventive Activity*, edited by R. Nelson. Cambridge, MA: Harvard University Press.

Barrett, S. 1992. Economic Growth and Environmental Preservation. *Journal of Environmental Economics and Management* 23: 289–300.

Brown, A.D.H. 1989. *The Use of Plant Genetic Resources.* Cambridge, U.K.: Cambridge University Press.

Cartier, C.M., and H.J. Ruitenbeek. 1999. Review of the Biodiversity Valuation Literature. In *Issues in Applied Coral Reef Biodiversity Valuation: Results for Montego Bay, Jamaica*, edited by H.J. Ruitenbeek and C.M. Cartier. World Bank Research Committee Project RPO#682-22 Final Report. Washington, DC: World Bank

Evans, L.T. 1993. *Crop Evolution, Adaptation, and Yield.* Cambridge, U.K.: Cambridge University Press.

Evenson, R. 1998. Plant Breeding: A Case of Induced Innovation. In *Agricultural Values of Genetic Resources*, edited by R. Evenson, D. Gollin, and V. Santaniello. London: CABI.

Frank, S. 1994. Recognition and Polymorphism in Host–Parasite Genetics. *Philosophical Transactions of the Royal Society, London, Series B* 346: 191–7.

Goeschl, T., and T. Swanson. 2000. *Lost Horizons: IPR and Antibiotic Resistance.* Paper presented at the annual meeting of the American Economics Association. January 2001, New Orleans, LA.

———. 2002. *Pests, Plagues, and Patents.* Paper prepared for the European Economics Association. August, 2002, Venice, Italy.

———. Forthcoming. The Social Value of Biodiversity for R&D, *Environmental and Resource Economics.*

Gollin, D., M. Smale, and B. Skovmand. 1998. *Optimal Search in Ex Situ Collections of Wheat Genetic Resources.* Economics Working Paper No. 98-03. Mexico City: CIMMYT.

Heisey, P.W. 1990. *Accelerating the Transfer of Wheat-Breeding Gains to Farmers: A Study of the Dynamics of Varietal Replacement in Pakistan.* CIMMYT Research Report No. 1. Mexico City: CIMMYT.

Heisey, P.W., and J.P. Brennan. 1991. An Analytical Model of Farmers' Demand for Replacement Seed. *American Journal of Agricultural Economics* 73(4): 1044–52.

Kamien, M., and N. Schwartz. 1982. *Market Structure and Innovation.* Cambridge, U.K.: Cambridge University Press.

Kiyosawa, S. 1989. Breakdown of Blast Resistance in Rice in Relation to General Strategies of Resistance Gene Deployment to Prolong Effectiveness of Disease Resistance in Plants. In *Plant Disease Epidemiology, Volume 2: Genetics, Resistance, and Management,* edited by K. Leonard and W. Fry. New York: McGraw-Hill, 251–83.

Laxminarayan, R., and G. Brown. 2001. Economics of Antibiotic Resistance: A Theory of Optimal Use. *Journal of Environmental Economics and Management* 42(2): 183–206.

Mason, R., and T. Swanson. 2002. The Costs of Uncoordinated Regulation. *European Economic Review* 46(1): 143–67.

May, R.M., and R. Anderson. 1983. Epidemiology and Genetics in the Coevolution of Parasites and Hosts. *Proceedings of the Royal Society London B* 219: 281–313.

Maynard Smith, J. 1976. A Comment on the Red Queen. *The American Naturalist* 110: 325–30.

Munro, A. 1997. Economics and Evolution. *Environmental and Resource Economics* 9: 429–49.

Myers, N. 1997. Biodiversity's Genetic Library. In *Nature's Services: Societal Dependence on Natural Ecosystem,* edited by G.C. Daily. Washington, DC: Island Press.

Oerke, E.C., H.W. Dehne, F. Schönbeck, and A. Weber. 1994. *Crop Production and Crop Protection: Estimated Losses in Major Food and Cash Crops.* Amsterdam, The Netherlands: Elsevier.

RAFI (Rural Advancement Foundation International). 1997. *The World's Top 10 Seed Corporations.* RAFI Communiqué 28, November 1997.

Rausser, G., and A. Small. 2000. Valuing Research Leads: Bioprospecting and the Conservation of Genetic Resources. *Journal of Political Economy* 108(1): 173–206.

Reinganum. 1989. The Timing of Innovation: Research, Development, and Diffusion. In *Handbook of Industrial Organization, Volume 1,* edited by R. Schmalensee and R. Willig. Amsterdam, Oxford, and Tokyo: North-Holland, 849–908.

Scheffer, R. 1997. *The Nature of Disease in Plants.* Cambridge, U.K.: Cambridge University Press.

Schumpeter, J.A. 1942. *Capitalism, Socialism and Democracy.* New York: Harper and Bros.

Simpson, R.D., R.A. Sedjo, and J.W. Reid. 1996. Valuing Biodiversity for Use in Pharmaceutical Research. *Journal of Political Economy* 104(1): 163–85.

Smith, S. 1998. Personal communication with the authors, October 12, 1998.

Swanson, T. 1995. *The International Regulation of Extinction.* London: MacMillan.

——— (ed.). 2002. *The Economics of Managing Biotechnologies.* Dordrecht, The Netherlands: Kluwer.

Swanson, T., and T. Goeschl. Forthcoming. Searching for Solutions: Renewable Resources, IPR and Problems Resistant to Resolution. *Research in Law and Economics.*

Swanson, T., and R. Luxmoore. 1998. *Industrial Reliance on Biodiversity.* Cambridge, U.K.: WCMC.

Tirole, J. 1988. *The Theory of Industrial Organization.* Cambridge, MA: MIT Press.

Weitzman, M. 2000. Economic Profitability versus Ecological Entropy. *Quarterly Journal of Economics* 115(1): 237–63.

Zadoks, J., and R. Schein. 1979. *Epidemiology and Plant Disease Management.* Oxford, U.K.: Oxford University Press.

Appendix: Derivation of Equation 9

From Equation 1 and setting $A_0 F(x) = 1$, we can rewrite the utility function as

$$U = \int\limits_{t=0}^{\infty} e^{-rt} \sum_{s=-\infty}^{+\infty} \Pi(s,t)\gamma^s dt \tag{A1}$$

$$\text{with } s = I - D \tag{A2}$$

and with the histories of I and D generated by the processes described in Equations 6 and 7,

$$\Pi(I,t) = \frac{1}{I!}\left[\phi i(v)t\right]^I e^{-[\phi i(v)]t} \tag{6}$$

$$\Pi(D,t) = \frac{1}{D!}\left[\lambda a(v)t\right]^D e^{-[\lambda a(v)]t} \tag{7}$$

such that

$$\Pi(s,t) = \Pr\left(\begin{array}{l} I \text{ innov. have occurred by time } t \mid D \text{ adapt.} \\ \text{have occured by time } t \end{array}\right) \tag{A3}$$

Then,

$$U = \int\limits_{t=0}^{\infty} e^{-rt} \sum_{I=0}^{\infty} \sum_{D=0}^{\infty} \frac{1}{I!}(\phi it)^I e^{-\phi it} \times \frac{1}{D!}(\lambda at)^D e^{-\lambda at} \times \gamma^{I-D} dt \tag{A4}$$

$$\text{which is } U = \int\limits_{t=0}^{\infty} e^{-rt} \sum_{I=0}^{\infty} \sum_{D=0}^{\infty} \frac{(\gamma\phi it)^I}{I!} e^{-\phi it} \times \frac{\left(\frac{1}{\gamma}\lambda at\right)^D}{D!} e^{-\lambda at} dt \tag{A5}$$

Making use of the infinite series of the factorial and the exponential function, we can rewrite Equation A5 as

$$U = \int_{t=0}^{\infty} e^{-rt-\phi it-\lambda at} \times e^{\gamma\phi it} \times e^{\frac{\lambda a}{\gamma}t} \, dt = \frac{1}{r - \phi i(\gamma - 1) + \lambda a \frac{\gamma - 1}{\gamma}} \tag{A6}$$

The denominator of Equation A6 gives then the effective discount rate applied to the output function. Reformulating A6 for some arbitrary $A_0 F(x)$, we arrive at Equation 9.

Notes

1. In the remainder of this chapter we will use "land" as the base, limiting factor that must be allocated between the production and sustainability functions. Land then represents the instrument by which all biological resources can be allocated between these two competing functions. The more general question would of course devolve to the allocation of the sum of society's resources between the objectives of production versus sustainability.

2. The term originates from Lewis Carroll's *Alice in Wonderland* in which the Red Queen proclaims to Alice that "around here, we must run faster and faster, merely to stand still ...."

3. It is possible to claim "plant breeders rights" in new plant varieties under the so-called Convention of the International Union for the Protection of New Varieties of Plants or patent rights in genetically modified seeds and animal varieties.

4. A 1998 survey found that plant breeders cited pest resistance as the primary focus of their activities (Swanson and Luxmoore 1998).

5. The literature on seed replacement cycles in agriculture documents a cycle of three to seven years between introductions of new pest-resistant plant varieties on commercially meaningful scales (Heisey 1990; Heisey and Brennan 1991).

6. In the context of agriculture, this only implies a proportional increase in the amount of high-yielding seed x required with an increase in the amount of intensively cultivated land d.

7. This is a close approximation to reality within the seed industry, in which there is a crop-specific, but nevertheless linear, relationship between the land used in seed production and the land sown using this seed. The relative size of β and z is on the order of 100:0.1 to 100:5 depending on the crop (Smith 1998).

8. The "significance" of a technological innovation is a legal requirement for the acquisition of property rights in the innovation. Because this is an issue that we will introduce in the section on the social objective of biotechnology, we will normalize the magnitude of any technological innovation to be equivalent to the magnitude (γ) required for the acquisition of a private property right in that innovation.

9. The industrial organization literature defines innovations as "drastic" if the technological advantage conferred by the innovation is of such a magnitude that the innovating firm captures the entire market when setting the monopoly price (Tirole 1988). This is simply the "substantial improvement" required under patent law to qualify for the issuance of a patent and hence the establishment of a new monopoly right. We

standardize the concept of a relevant innovation in this manner to compare the system (for generating such innovations) that would exist under a patent system with other systems.

10. This assumption follows the standard literature in crop epidemiology in which the emergence of virulence is assumed to follow a Poisson process (see also Zadoks and Schein 1979; Kiyosawa 1989).

11. This assumption is consistent with both the theory of selection (because those pests with a matching gene for x have a relative advantage that increases with the use of x) and the empirical observation that the widespread use of HYVs is associated with reduced periods of commercial viability.

12. We can rewrite this as $\lambda\,a(d)$ making use of Equation 3 where λ is a parameter that measures successful mutation or recombination of the pathogen population and a, $a' < 0$ measures the adaptive response rate of biological competitors relative to size of intensive agriculture once a successful mutation has occurred.

13. For an analysis of the situation in which adaptation may be dampened by the simultaneous use of many different production methods, see Goeschl and Swanson (2000).

14. Modelers of the dynamics of evolutionary games view resistance as the accumulation of "matching genes" within the pest population, where such matches enable the pest to prey on the host. A biological innovation in this context would consist of a change from a paucity to the relative prevalence of such a matching gene throughout the current pest population.

15. This assumption represents a uniform metric of a continuous process of depreciation. The unit of analysis is fixed within the technological sector (by the requirement that a patentable innovation be a significant improvement. See Note 9.).

16. In this chapter we assume that the responsiveness of pests is "stage independent"; that is, the pests do not react differently to different levels of technological intervention. Of course, it might be that systems respond very differently to different levels of technological intervention. Another assumption might be that natural systems attempt to return to previous states of equilibrium, and hence greater levels of intervention generate more drastic reactions from the natural system (i.e., more innovations by the pests and pathogens). It also might be possible that greater levels of intervention have the capacity to take the system outside of the area of attraction to its previous equilibrium, and then there is no responsive innovation from pests and pathogens (i.e., the hypothesis of winnability). These various assumptions and their implications for the model are investigated in a separate work (Goeschl and Swanson 2002).

17. It is important to notice a subtlety here in that the discrete nature of the Poisson process introduces two "time scales" into the system. One is natural time, denoted by t, whereas s denotes the productivity stage of the economy.

18. One benefit of choosing this functional form for this problem is that it implies no bias in favor of intergenerational transfers of utility (see Barrett 1992 for a discussion in the context of biodiversity).

19. This reduces the own discount rate because new technologies shift the production set outward and relax the budget constraint.

20. In this instance, the innate growth capacity of the biological resource—pests and pathogens—detracts from available consumption and so increases the own discount rate.

21. A stationary solution to the problem is to be expected because of the linearity of the objective function.

22. Recall that $a' < 0$.

23. The result is discussed in more detail in comparison to the private market solution in the section on comparing private and social investment in the biotechnology sector.

24. This assumption is not essential to the argument, but it simplifies the analysis. It is also not an unrealistic assumption in the context of agricultural lands when it is highly likely that there is a single most productive use of most arable lands and a single monopolist of the intermediate goods (HYVs) requisite for that use.

25. Other papers cover the issue of strategic shelving of patents in situations where technologies degrade over time (Goeschl and Swanson 2000, Mason and Swanson 2002).

26. There is a subtlety in Equations 14, 15, and 16: Because $s = I - D$, the payoff from delivering the next innovation depends on the history of biological adaptations that have occurred since the last technological innovation. Strictly speaking, the net present value of the next technological innovation, V_{I+1}, is the expected value of monopoly rents based on a probability distribution over s. This is because the flow of profits p is directly affected by the current level of productivity A_s, which is a joint outcome of both technological and biological processes. The present value thus decreases if pathogen adaptations have occurred. But if the price of land is allowed to change within technological stages, then the fact that marginal productivity will decrease at exactly the same moment at which a biological adaptation occurs means that the relationship between land prices and private R&D is unaffected by pathogen adaptation because the real cost of R&D (measured in terms of the cost of land) does not change.

27. Because the left-hand side is increasing in v and the right-hand side is decreasing in v for $F' \leq 0$ (sufficient condition), the equilibrium will be unique assuming this restriction on F'''.

28. The effect of the rate of biological innovation requires a qualification in that it holds only as long as the discount rate exceeds the net marginal productivity of land for innovations, that is, for

$$r > (\gamma - 1)\left[\phi\left(i(v) - \frac{i'(v)}{a'(v)} \right) + \lambda(1 - a(v))\gamma^{-1} \right]$$

If this condition does not hold, it would mean that land in R&D is the most competitive opportunity to generate welfare available in the economy. We would therefore generally expect this condition to hold.

29. The only qualification on this result is that if the reserve sector has a higher intrinsic growth rate than all other sectors in the economy that have impact on consumption, then a higher arrival rate of biological innovations frees up resources to be put to final goods production.

30. In fact, there are two effects at work, one as mentioned earlier, the other decreasing the expected value of innovations. But the latter is only a second-order effect, which is dominated by the first as the partial derivatives show.

31. Tangentially we note that the private valuation of reserve lands for purposes of R&D systematically underestimates the social value of these lands for those purposes. This is an important problem in theory as well as practice. The private valuation of reserve lands has been used as a suggestive measure for the valuation of reserves for R&D purposes (Goeschl and Swanson forthcoming; Simpson et al. 1996).

32. Of course this result holds only if the monopolist is not able to Ramsey price its output.

33. The fact that the monopolist at any point will only be concerned with the optimal output severs the link between output and conservation decisions. We would therefore not expect the monopolist to exhibit the conservationist effects in terms of resource extraction observed in mining models of the Hotelling type.

34. The specific manifestation of biological obsolescence in this model adds a novel perspective to the analysis of the different discount rates, however.

35. Such settings can arise generally where there is a scale-related risk to technological breakdown. Such situations may be quite common. We are grateful to Philippe Aghion for stressing this point.

36. We can therefore conclude that the use of the private firm's valuation of reserve lands is a highly problematic estimator of the societal interest in such lands. Specifically, it is very likely that this estimator will underestimate the social value of reserves significantly. The reason lies in the fundamental difference between the valuation of reserves as an input into a patent race between private firms whose patents are threatened both by economic and biological competitors, and the valuation of reserves as an input into a race of continuous innovation (technological and biological) between society and adapting pathogens.

37. Because one out of n firms will hold the patent of the preferred technology at any point in time and because this firm has no incentive to invest in R&D (as it would replace its own patent), $n - 1$ firms will be engaged in a race to produce the next patentable innovation.

38. This eliminates issues of sunk and fixed costs and creates conditions in which there are no barriers to entry into the R&D sector.

39. Other specifications are possible and have been attempted. The fundamental results are robust over many plausible specifications.

40. Equation 20 shows that the level of reserve lands chosen by the social planner will generally be less than one so long as the discount rate is greater than net productivity increases in the final sector at the margin. This means that as long as there are other competitive opportunities available in the economy to generate welfare, not all land will be used for R&D. We would generally expect this condition to hold.

41. It is apparent that the private industry level of reserves will be less than one independent of the discount rate.

42. We assume that the exponent has the standard value of 0.25 and the species richness parameter the (comparatively low) value of 200.

43. See Swanson and Goeschl forthcoming and Mason and Swanson 2002 for related analyses.

Chapter 12

Industrial Organization and Institutional Considerations in Agricultural Pest Resistance Management

Jennifer Alix and David Zilberman

This chapter demonstrates the complexity of the relationship among incentives, pesticide applications, and resistance buildup.

First, analysis of the impacts of pesticide use must consider both the dynamics of the overall pest and the resistance buildup. Farmers may *overapply* chemicals if they ignore resistance dynamics but may *underapply* chemicals if they ignore population dynamics. Furthermore, other factors (e.g., including alternative chemicals, integrated pest management, crop rotation) must be considered in assessing the impact of pesticide use on resistance.

Second, pest resistance is significantly affected by the structure of the industry, property rights, and patent considerations. Manufacturers will likely have a monopoly on the production of new pesticides during the life of the patent, which will provide the incentive to *underapply* them relative to the optimal solution. Furthermore, manufacturers are concerned with the negative side-effects of resistance buildup because of the impact on future sales and their reputation. Thus, they may be actively involved in activities to reduce resistance buildup. Indeed, we present evidence of manufacturer involvement in resistance management and resistance prevention. We also show that manufacturers' incentives to control resistance may be weaker than what is socially desirable because of the limitation of a patent's life.

Third, manufacturers' incentives and choices will likely lead to overapplication of pesticides by myopic farmers as the chemicals get older and the supply network becomes more competitive. There are several old pesticides (mostly organophosphates or carbonates) that have long been used because of a lack of significant resistance buildup potential or the existence of effective resistance management schemes. Pest management agencies should be especially aware of potential problems with fairly new chemicals once the initial patent period lapses, if the provision of the chemicals increases, or if the initial manufacturer does not get very involved in the product stewardship.

Finally, in addition to the manufacturers and users of the pesticides, other economic agents, in particular pesticide advisors and extension specialists, are involved in pest control decisions. Extension and especially individual consultants have the incentive to reduce resistance buildup and improve the performance of pest control agents. Our analysis suggests that the network of economic agents concerned about and involved in decisions regarding pest management and control of resistance buildup is quite complex. Even if individual growers may not be concerned with resistance and population dynamics issues when applying pesticides, other agents affecting their decisions may have these issues in mind.

Pesticide use is the result of a web of decisions connecting the farmer to the researchers, manufacturers, regulators, and consumers. Given its wide range of impacts and its importance in the sequence of events that determine agricultural supply, it is no surprise that pesticides have inspired a large literature in the field of economics. Of growing importance within this literature is the topic of pest resistance to pesticides.

According to the Food and Agriculture Organization, the number of pest species with resistance to pesticides has increased from almost none 50 years ago to more than 700 today (FAO 2001). As the number of resistant species increases, so do losses incurred by farmers. The Insecticide Resistance Action Committee states that "insecticide resistance in the United States adds $40 million to the total insecticide bill in additional treatments" (2001). It also cites the case of Michigan potato producers who in 1991 suffered a $16 million crop loss caused by resistance in the Colorado potato beetle. In the case of pyrethroids, in which serious resistance has been encountered among cotton pests, a 50% replacement of it by alternatives would approximately double the control costs and reduce yield by 11% (Riley 1990).

There is a rich body of literature on pest resistance spawned by Regev and Hueth's (1974) seminal work (see surveys by Carlson and Wetzstein 1993; Pannell and Zilberman 2000). The majority of the literature views resistance in the context of renewable or nonrenewable resources. A main result of this vein of research is that common-pool problems, myopic behavior, or both lead to the overuse of pesticides. The logical policy response to this prognosis was a call for collective action or government intervention to reduce pesticide application and buildup of resistance.

Clearly, adapting the framework of renewable and nonrenewable resources to existing problems has generated valuable insight. Moreover, a new wave of studies on resistance emerged recently in response to concern about resistance buildup to pest control agents embodied in genetically modified crops (Secchi and Babcock, Chapter 4; Laxminarayan and Simpson, 2002; and Hurley et al., forthcoming) and has been applied for policy choices, for example, the design of refuge. Perfect competition, however, is a central assumption of this literature, which potentially obscures features essential to understanding the dynamics of resistance in a more complex reality. In this chapter, we attempt to point out some of these features, and we introduce empirical evidence on the cost and magnitude of resistance problems in agriculture.

In the first section, we will set up a conceptual framework to analyze resistance that includes two dynamic phenomena—the buildup of resistance and the dynamics of the pest population. This framework will be used to derive some of the major results about resistance management. We will then adapt it to consider the emerging issues of integrated pest management (IPM) and crop rotation, among other technologies important to pest management, and analyze their impact on resistance buildup. The final two sections of this chapter will address environmental regulation and institutional problems that have been absent from the literature; in particular, the fourth section will address the role manufacturers play in dealing with resistance problems through product development and stewardship. We consider how individual farmer incentives interact with manufacturer concerns and present evidence regarding manufacturer participation in resistance management.

Factors Affecting the Management of Resistance

We now sketch out a framework for modeling the impact of resistance on farmers' pesticide decisionmaking processes over time. For interested readers, the mathematical details can be found in Alix and Zilberman (2001). The farmer solves his or her problem by maximizing discounted expected profit, which includes revenue minus application costs and declines with pest damage. Damage, in turn, is controlled by the effectiveness of pesticide applications, and resistance is the key factor in controlling the impact of pesticide application. We model resistance as a stock variable, which is measured by the fraction of the pest population not vulnerable to chemical treatments. However, we also explicitly introduce another stock variable, pest population. With our specifications, we distinguish between two pest populations: pests that are vulnerable to the pesticide and pests that are *resistant*. This framework is consistent with the work of Regev and Hueth (1974) and Laxminarayan and Simpson (2002).

Our farmer undertakes his or her optimization problem subject to two constraints:

- *Growth of resistance*: Resistance growth is affected by the growth rates of vulnerable and resistant populations and the pesticide kill function. Pesticide applications increase resistance, although the marginal effect of spraying on resistance increases for some resistance range and then decreases.
- *Pest population growth*: The second constraint, pest population growth, is affected by three factors: the kill function (which depends on pesticide application), the growth of the resistant population, and the growth of the vulnerable population. We expect pest population growth to decrease with chemical applications.

The solution to this problem leads to the conclusion that the optimal pesticide application at any given time is at a level at which the farmer equates immediate marginal and future marginal benefits from reduced pest populations to the price of pesticides plus marginal resistance cost. The equation is

$$VMPx_t + VMF_t = W + VR_t$$

where the left-hand side of the equation represents the marginal benefits that come from reducing pesticide damage. $VMPx_t$ is the private marginal benefit of reduced pest damage associated with pesticide applications in period t, and VMF_t is the marginal value of reducing the pest population by application, thus reducing future damage. The right-hand side is the private cost of purchasing pesticides plus the marginal social cost of resistance from the pesticide application. W is the pesticide cost, and VR_t is the marginal cost of resistance from pesticide application. Farmers may not behave according to the socially optimal behavior for two main reasons: (a) they may be myopic, and (b) the pest population pool is a common-property resource.

Myopic decisionmakers ignore the future implications of their decisions. As in the basic modeling case, the farmer will choose a profit-maximizing level of pesticides; the difference is that he considers only the short term. At the myopic optimum, the value of marginal product of pesticide applications is equal to the cost, where $VMPx_t^m$ represents the value of marginal product of using x amount of pesticide and w is the price. The equation describing the equilibrium is as follows:

$$VMPx_t^m = W$$

This condition ignores the impact of pesticide use on resistance and on future levels of the pest population. We assume that the resistance effect dominates the population's growth suppression effect of pesticide use. The situation is depicted in Figure 12-1. If the concern about resistance dominates the gain from suppression of pest population buildup, myopic behavior will lead to overuse of pesticide. This is exactly the conclusion that results from comparing points A and B. If, however, the gains from suppression of population growth overcome the gains from slowing resistance buildup, myopic behavior results in underapplication. Figure 12-2 describes this case.

Common resource pool problems in pest management occur because pest populations are mobile, and farmers' plots may be small relative to the pests' range. Under these circumstances, farmers may believe that their activity has little impact on resistance buildup of the pest population, and that may lead to the tragedy of the commons.

One implication of the common-resource problem is that farms large enough to contain much of the pest movement are likely to be superior pest managers. In other words, "big is beautiful" from a pest management perspective. Alternatively, in regions where plots are fragmented, collective action and government intervention are required to coordinate pest management activities. Indeed, in many regions, major extension activities have imple-

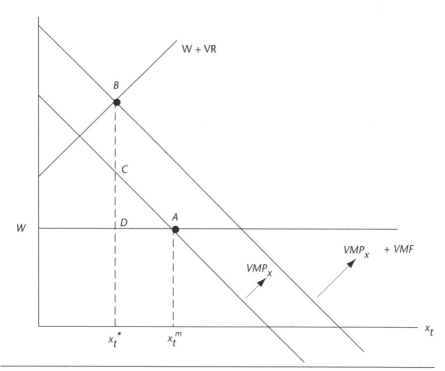

FIGURE 12-1. Resistance Effect Dominates Population Growth

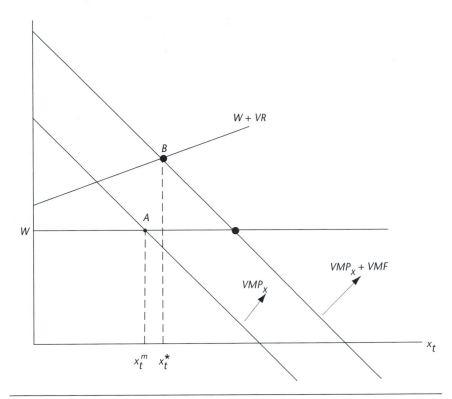

FIGURE 12-2. Population Growth Dominates Resistance Effect

mented integrated strategies to address pesticide problems. The importance of neighbors' activities in the suppression of pest populations is frequently mentioned in the pest control literature. With some effort, activities may help to educate farmers to underuse chemicals to slow the buildup of pest resistance. However, in other cases, most notably in some southern states plagued by the cotton boll weevil, collective action includes extra application aimed to eradicate that pest.

To summarize, although much of the economic literature recognizes that either myopic behavior or common resource problems may lead to overapplication of pesticides by farmers who ignore the dynamics of resistance, other studies suggest that similar situations may actually lead to underapplication of pesticides. Several other factors that may affect resistance management and that have not gained much attention are addressed in the remainder of this chapter.

Farm-Level Factors Influencing Resistance

Ignorance about Resistance

Another plausible cause of suboptimal pesticide application is ignorance about resistance. Resistance problems vary among and within pesticide categories. Narrowly targeted chemicals, which attack one system in the body that are controlled by a small number of genes, are more likely to develop resistance problems than broad-use chemicals that have several modes of operation. John Damicone, an extensionist for the University of Oklahoma, argues that multisite fungicides, which interfere with many metabolic processes of fungus, are much less likely to result in buildup of resistance than fungicides with a site-specific mode of action (2001). Benomil, a fungicide that was able to both prevent and cure plant diseases caused by fungi, is a site-specific fungicide that has encountered significant resistance problems since its introduction in the 1970s. Damicone suggests laboratory experiments can identify fungicides that will more likely encounter resistance and thus lead to the design of strategies to avoid these problems.

To complicate the matter further, it takes time before the existence of such problems is discovered, a phenomenon exacerbated by the fact that information is not always transferred very quickly across regions. Let us consider a situation in which a farm may be large enough that common resource pool is not a problem, and thus farmers take into account the dynamic pest population suppression effect of pesticide use but not resistance buildup. Pesticide use in this case is therefore determined by solving

$$VMPx_t + VMF_t = W$$

In this case, there will be overuse of pesticides. Note, however, that owners of large farms are likely to hire pest control professionals. Pest control specialists have developed the capacity to identify the circumstances under which introduction of a new pest control agent is likely to result in the buildup of resistance. Indeed, guidelines by DuPont and others for the application of herbicides suggest that frequent application of any herbicide will likely lead to the buildup of resistance, and they suggest herbicide management strategies that will overcome or minimize these problems.

Fixed Cost of Application

Features of crop systems affect applications of pesticide and, hence, resistance. One of them is fixed application costs. Application of chemicals in a field may be rather costly. Running a tractor through one acre of land can cost between

$10 and $20. In most cases, the application cost may be more expensive than the cost of the chemical. Furthermore, the frequent running of machinery on a field leads to compaction of the soil, which, in turn, reduces yield. Application cost considerations are crucial to developing the economic threshold. Carlson and Wetzstein (1993), in particular, suggest that farmers should monitor pest populations to determine the timing of applications when the population is sufficient, so that the gain from reducing the pest exceeds the cost of application. Of course, the threshold level also can be adjusted to take into account the cost of resistance buildup and population growth.

Application cost considerations may lead to reduced pesticide use only in certain situations. They will also likely reduce resistance buildup. This is because the vulnerable portion of the population grows faster, and, with reduced pesticide levels, its share will increase.

Integrated Pest Management

As the name suggests, IPM is a broad concept that integrates different tools and a variety of available information to manage pest problems and reduce the reliance on and use of chemical pesticides. A key component of IPM is the monitoring of pest populations, followed by responsive rather than preventive chemical applications. Pest appearance is random, depending on weather situations, the relationship between the populations of various species and pest control activities by neighboring farmers, and other variables. Frequent preventive applications that release a large volume of chemicals at a time when the arriving pest population is small or when it is too early for the chemical to be effective may actually increase the resistance. In addition, preventive applications may have a negative environmental effect. The responsive application, however, may be expensive in the sense that it requires a high monitoring cost and that the pest may destroy crops if the response is slow; however, it may save both materials and application costs.

Some studies actually argue that IPM may be cost-effective in a wide variety of situations (see Carlson and Wetzstein 1993). Responsive applications in most cases will lead to a reduction in pesticide use and better timing of chemical applications, which together may decrease resistance buildup. Empirical results regarding the effects of IPM on pesticide use have been mixed. In one paper, however, Fernandez-Cornejo and others (1998) reported an unweighted average of 44 studies, which showed that pesticide use declined 15% with the adoption of IPM techniques.

Several biologists have noted that responsive applications may not always be preferable to preventive ones. In the case of fungicides, for example, research by extension agents at Oklahoma State University (Damicone 2001) suggests that application in the early season when infection levels are low may be more effective than waiting for a buildup of fungus. The same may be true for the application of herbicides. In those situations, uncertainty about the emergence of pest problems is low, and applying relatively small levels of chemicals may prevent the need to apply larger volumes of materials later in the season.

Agricultural Practices

Applying chemicals is only one way that farmers have to treat pest problems. Additionally, farmers rely quite extensively on mechanical means such as weeding, plowing, and physically killing pests by other methods. Although some of these techniques are components of an IPM strategy, the fact that many non-IPM farmers use them suggests that their impacts should be considered separately. Mechanical means provide a very good substitute for chemical strategies. For example, to address these problems pruning trees, especially during the postseason, may significantly reduce pesticide use, disease incidences, and buildup of resistance.

When mechanical alternatives for pest control exist, the farmer may view them as backstop technologies that can overcome future problems of resistance as well as population buildup over time. That may lead to myopic behavior closer to the social optimum. This may actually cause lower pesticide use in some cases and increase application when resistance buildup is otherwise a major concern.

Crop Rotation

Farmers throughout the world engage in crop rotation for several reasons: soil fertility buildup, risk diversification, productivity management, and population control. The practice of crop rotation may lead to underemphasis of dynamic considerations, especially relative to crop-specific pests. Many decisions about pests are taken within the context of a field, and, if the crop is not grown in the same field season after season, then some of the dynamic implications of pesticide management become much less relevant. The effect renders the optimal pesticide-use decisions to be closer to the myopic ones.

Careful consideration of the impact of crop rotation on pest management suggests some basic flaws in the modeling of the dynamics of pest populations. To make computation cleaner, we tend to assume the existence of regional stocks of pest populations and pest resistance. This assumption, however, is overly simplistic. In reality, the movement of some pests, for example, weeds or fungi, is limited, especially for some species. Progenies of a particular pest are more likely to reside close to its original location than farther away. More realistic modeling may require having a large number of locational stocks of both pest population and pest resistance described in a way that recognizes their interdependencies. A farmer engaging in crop rotation drastically affects the pest population in his own field, which may affect neighboring populations.

The overall impact of crop rotation on global pest population and resistance is quite complex. On the one hand, crop rotation may lead to a drastic reduction of pest population in the fields where it occurs. On the other hand, the myopia suggested earlier may encourage larger applications of chemicals that could increase resistance in other fields. Although the answer is unclear, the fact that crop rotation is being promoted as an antiresistance strategy suggests that the overall effect is positive. For example, "According to Nebraska extension offices, University of Nebraska, Lincoln, more than 35% of Nebraska's corn acreage was rotated to soybeans in [19]96, reducing the need for insecticides to control corn rootworms. Use of crop rotation has resulted in a reduction of over one million lbs. of active ingredient per year, and an annual savings in production costs of at least $10 million" (Pure Foods Campaign 2001).

Precision Technologies

Loosely defined, precision technologies monitor the state of relevant variables over space and time, be it pest population, temperature, or soil condition. They also contain a decisionmaking element that determines an appropriate response and an application component to implement it. To a certain extent, IPM can be viewed as a precision technology, as can modern irrigation technology combined with an irrigation scheduling system. The term "precision technology," for most commercial agriculture, is a more narrowly defined set of technologies that takes advantage of developments in remote sensing, communication, and computers. These tools have the potential to play important roles in alerting farmers, who may not enter a field for months at a time, to important changes in pest populations.

Precision technologies are still in their infancy, even though the evolution of data gathering has improved over time. There is a need to develop both software to interpret data and inexpensive intervention mechanisms. Precision technologies provide the means to collect the data needed for large-scale statistical analysis. These analyses are essential to improving current econometric studies that attempt to quantify the relationships between environmental conditions and productivity. The technologies remain in the early stages of their evolution, although equipment is now being introduced to monitor environmental variables. Eventually, decisionmaking will be done using tools that closely resemble the conceptual model that we presented earlier.

There is evidence, however, that the availability of more precise information modifies pest control strategies, reduces applications, and minimizes pest damage and buildup of resistance. For example, the impact of the California

Irrigation Management Information System detailed by Osgood and others (1997) suggested that one of the most important applications (valued at $10 million annually) was to provide weather information to pest control advisors who use them to time pesticide applications. Improved information will enable transition away from generalized preventive applications. The advantage of moving away from this traditional strategy is more precise and less frequent applications and possibly in larger dosages. This reduces their immediate impacts and the likelihood of resistance buildup.

The integration of monitoring technologies, like remote sensing with geographic information systems, are especially important in tracing the evolution of diseases and pest problems over space. They may be used to identify weed infestation and trigger intervention. Eventually, special sensors may identify insect infestation. Geographic information system technology is used to trace the spread of pest problems.

New Pesticides

When resistance is modeled as a renewable or nonrenewable resource, then the development of alternative or new chemicals can be treated as a backstop technology. As the literature on renewable resources suggests, the availability of backstop technology reduces the shadow cost of the stock. The prospect of having an alternative is likely to reduce the incentive for farmers to develop resistance control strategies. The discovery, development, and introduction of alternative chemicals are affected both by specific knowledge and by institutional and economic conditions, some of which we will discuss in the section on chemical companies and consultants.

The Value of Maintaining Pest Control Alternatives

As was mentioned earlier, resistance problems are omnipresent. Recent statistics suggest that more than 700 pest species have developed resistance to one product or another. That, in spite of all the constraints, new chemicals are being introduced and that many problematic pesticides have substitutes may raise the question, why worry about pesticide resistance or ability to maintain chemicals and pest control agents? The answer may not be found in resistance per se but in a broader view of pest control. Although most chemicals have substitutes that are useful, there is some evidence that some agents are difficult to replace.

One obvious example is the use of *Bacillus thuringiensis* (*Bt*) in organic farming. In this case, the set of "natural" pest controls is small, and losing any crucial element may be very costly. Even with chemical pesticides, many pesticides have survived despite regulatory pressure and expensive attempts to find substitutes. One example is methyl bromide, a fumigant used to address soilborne diseases. Methyl bromide applications are relatively expensive ($100 to $300 per acre) and cause severe environmental problems (depletion of the ozone layer). Yet, farmers fight to maintain their use, even in a limited capacity. U.S. farmers in California and elsewhere have used a wide variety of means to delay phase-outs of chemicals until an appropriate alternative is found. However, finding alternatives is still not easy. A significant body of research on the importance of methyl bromide to U.S. agriculture finds its annual value to be several hundred million dollars (Yarkin et al. 1994; Carpenter et al. 2000).

Diseases that cannot be treated are very costly to agriculture. For example, Pierce's disease is now wreaking havoc in California agriculture, the number of strategies available to combat it is limited, and their vulnerability to resistance may prove to be costly. Therefore, when analyzing the cost of resistance and efforts to combat it, emphasis should be on cases in which there are few alternatives and in which damage, once pest problems are controlled, is substantial.

Institutional Factors Influencing Resistance: Environmental Regulation

Concern about environmental side-effects from pesticide use—including problems of worker safety, food safety, and environmental health—has led to the development of a wide array of pesticide policy prescriptions, each of which has impacts on resistance buildup. Economists have suggested solutions such as pesticide taxes as policy tools to reduce externalities (see Zilberman et al. 1991). Some western European countries, notably Norway and Sweden, have relied on pesticide taxes. Practical realities often intercede, however, and implementation of optimal taxes may be difficult because of variability of externalities over space (Zilberman and Millock 1997).

Optimality problems that determine pesticide use have to be modified to include the externality cost whenever pesticides cause externality problems including harm to farm workers, food consumers, nontarget species, and water and air quality. Some externality costs have a dynamic dimension; for example, accumulation of pesticide residues in a body of water over time may reach saturation levels that are harmful to fish. Other pesticides are a source of chronic risks and may cause cancer after long, frequent exposure. Because of space limitations, we will not cover optimal resource management problems of externalities in great detail. However, let $MECx_t$ denote the marginal externality cost associated with application of x_t, and then the optimal pesticide allocation rule at time t will be determined by solving

$$VMPx_t + VMF_t = W + VR_t + MECx_t$$

If all other factors are taken into consideration (resistance, pest dynamics) and a tax equal to $MECx_t$ is introduced, it will lead to optimal resource allocation. Introduction of a tax will lead to a reduction in pesticide use and, in some cases, adoption of more precise pesticide application technologies, thus leading to reduction of resistance buildup. When the value of the implicit benefits from a tax that reduces resistance problems becomes larger or when farmers are myopic or ignorant about resistance problems, pesticide taxation thus may provide an extra dividend in reducing resistance damage.

In the United States, however, the major tool for combating pesticide externality problems is banning their use and canceling their registration. In this case, the impact on resistance is more complex. The 1996 Food Quality Protection Act aimed to phase out the older categories of pesticides such as organophosphates. Some of these chemicals, for example, parathion and malathion, used a broad range of applications and had been effective for a long time without encountering much resistance. They were replaced by more narrowly focused chemicals that addressed specific problems but that were more vulnerable to resistance buildup. In addition, one of the most effective ways of reducing resistance is to use multiple chemicals with different modes of operation or to rotate chemicals. Banning chemicals, replacing them with more targeted chemicals, and reducing options, as done by the Food Quality Protection Act, may reduce the strategies available to control pests and thus increase resistance.

Government policies also include restrictions on production activities for the sake of safety. One example is reentry regulation which sets a restriction on the minimum amount of time workers can begin working in a field after spraying. Lichtenberg and others (1993) argued that reentry regulation may lead farmers to switch from responsive to preventive applications. This is true especially before harvesting; instead of waiting to spray until the first appearance of pest population, farmers may spray ahead of time to ensure that harvesting will be feasible at the right time. Thus, in many cases, spraying occurs even though the pest population is very small, and in other cases, early application of the pesticides reduces their effectiveness when the pest actually arrives.

The impact of a strict regime of registration and testing on chemical companies' efforts to produce new chemicals should not be underestimated. One study found that increased regulation led to a 7–9% decline in pesticide registration (Fernandez-Cornejo et al. 1998). The testing aims to reduce the likelihood of environmental side-effects and unintended consequences. Financial and institutional capacity to introduce and market chemicals is an edge that chemical companies have over new entrants. Several authors suggested that the oligopolistic structure of the chemical industry is caused by registration requirements and marketing costs rather than production consideration per se (see Carlson and Wetzstein 1993).

If the regulatory requirements are effective and generally reduce environmental side-effects, another serious problem associated with pesticide use, then the price paid in terms of resistance buildup and control is worthwhile. If, however, as some suggest, many of the regulatory requirements are aimed at maintaining the oligopolistic structure, then they may impose an extra cost in terms of resistance. Research that will lead to more realistic assessment of the regulatory framework and its improvement is one of the most challenging aspects of research and pest control.

Chemical Companies' Choices and Resistance

In examining the choices that lead to pesticide use, one can hardly ignore the influence of agrochemical producers and distributors on the process. Most analyses of resistance have been microeconomic in nature and, as such, have ignored industrywide considerations. However, the dynamics of pesticide use is determined by manufacturers. Manufacturers control product development, pricing, promotion, and most informational use guidance; thus, their self-interest affects the evolution of resistance. The appendix contains the details of a mathematical model of chemical producers' choices, taking into account the effects of resistance. Here we sketch out the assumptions and main conclusions.

Consider a case in which the pest population is renewed every season, and resistance is the only dynamic variable that changes over time. We also assume that the farming industry consists of many small farms so that resistance control does not affect farmer behavior. The inverse demand function for pesticides increases in the price of output and decreases with aggregate pesticide use and resistance.

When pesticides are relatively new, the manufacturer's patent gives it monopoly power, which also depends on availability of substitutes (chemical, biological, or agronomical). Chemicals more than 20 years old are produced by competitive (or semicompetitive) industries. The presence of patents allows us to model a monopolistic manufacturer who maximizes expected profits subject to a resistance constraint that depends on both resistance buildup and the recovery rate of the vulnerable population. The constraint increases with chemical use.

At the optimal pesticide production level of the manufacturer, marginal revenue (MR_t) is equal to marginal cost of production (MC_t) plus resistance cost (MRC_t)

$$MR_t = MC_t + MRC_t$$

This situation is depicted in Figure 12-3. The manufacturers' optimum occurs at A and results in use price W_A and quantity X_A. If the manufacturers ignore

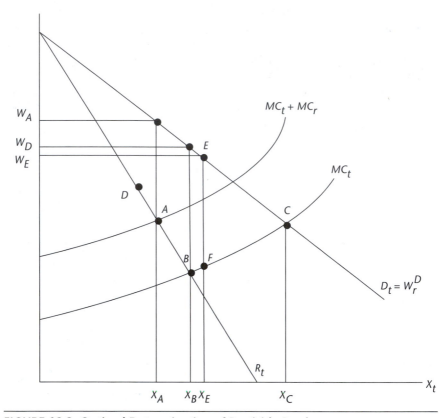

FIGURE 12-3. Optimal Determination of Pesticide Products

resistance, the optimal outcome could be $X_B > X_A$. If they are competitive and ignore resistance, the outcome is at C.

The dynamics of the shadow price of resistance μ_t changes the value of MRC_t over time. The details of the derivation are covered in the appendix. When the value of this shadow price declines over time, we expect MRC_t to decrease, and the reduction in pesticide production by the monopolist because of resistance considerations also will decline over time. This suggests that the monopolistic resistance control effort in general will decline as the product matures.

To compare this case with the social optimum, consider the social welfare optimization problem, in which a welfare function describing the gross benefit to farmers from chemical use is maximized subject to the resistance constraint. The optimality condition for this problem is

$$W_t^D = MC_t + MSR_t$$

where W_t^D is the demand price, MC_t is the marginal cost of production, and MSR_t is the marginal social shadow cost of resistance, which is distinct from the monopolist's MRC_t. Thus, it follows that the optimal social quantity is smaller than X_C but may be greater than X_A unless at X_A society's marginal resistance cost is much higher than the monopoly's, and the social optimum is at D. This is described by the following equation:

$$W^D + MRS_t < W^D - \frac{\partial W^D}{\partial X_t} X_t + MRC_t$$

This equation shows that the monopoly will likely produce less pesticide and farmers will likely use less pesticide than is *socially optimal*.

We suggest that if resistance is the only dynamic biological process that affects pesticide productivity, production of chemicals under monopoly may be below the social optimal level; furthermore, the chemical company will take resistance into account in both the production and pricing of chemicals. The mathematical model only sketches some of the key features of real-life behavior, but its main insight is that chemical companies care about resistance reduction, especially when they own the patents of a product. However, even after the patent lapses, the chemical company still has its brand name, and that gives them an edge. Other companies will produce an alternative generic product, but the original company with the commercial brand name may charge a premium. Furthermore, the company may charge generic producers for registration data. In sum, a product that has less resistance and a better reputation will be easier to market, and manufacturers will be willing to pay for the rights to produce the product and to obtain information related to it.

Our analysis ignores issues of product marketing and introduction to various user groups. As the survey article by Sunding and Zilberman (2001) suggests, it may take several years before agricultural products reach a full range of users. Adoption processes are long and require significant investment for chemical companies to generate awareness of the product, demonstrate its potential, and educate individuals about its value and use. This theoretical argument suggests that manufacturers (a) will invest in research about resistance, (b) may help efforts in collective action to contain it, and (c) may be active in the efforts to deal with it. We will introduce some evidence that justifies our argument.

Our argument also indicates that manufacturers' concern about resistance varies throughout the different stages of a product's life. From the manufacturer's perspective, the value of resistance buildup declines throughout the life of a product. The original manufacturer may be less interested in combating resistance as the product ages, especially when it does not expect a large market share after patents expire or in markets where it does not benefit from protection of IPM. Generic producers in more competitive markets do not enjoy monopolistic power and are less likely to worry about resistance. When patent rights are not respected, the original manufacturer is less committed to reducing resistance problems. It follows that manufacturers in developing countries are less likely to fight resistance than those in developed ones.

The results of our analysis are supported by the behavior of several large chemical manufacturers. For example, pesticide companies are liable when pesticide use results in crop damage. Indeed, Dupont recently paid $750 million to users of Benomyl in compensation for damage resulting from resistance buildup (www.pan-uk.org/actives/benomyl.htm). As mentioned earlier, even in the absence of legal repercussions, manufacturers are in the business of selling their product, and if their product is found to be ineffective, profits plummet. This alone provides a strong incentive to manage resistance.

It is often argued that chemical companies ignore the resistance issue, particularly because they have scores of increasingly expensive and toxic substitutes available when one of their products proves not to be viable. Our discussion suggests that producing a series of faulty products is no way to attract more customers. Indeed, one industry spokesperson claimed that a single nonperformance complaint can cost 10 to 1,000 individual sales (Thompson 1997). Furthermore, the enormous research and development costs to produce just one pesticide, in addition to the 7 to 10 years spent undergoing the federal regulatory approval process, are sufficient disincentives to creating a wide gamut of substitutable pesticides. According to the American Crop Protection Association (ACPA), on average, only one in 20,000 chemicals emerges from the chemist's laboratory and is applied on the farmer's field. This development costs manufacturers between $35 million and $50 million for each product (ACPA 2001). Other estimates of these costs run between $15 million and $30 million.

In addition, as was pointed out by Gary Thompson, a representative from Dow AgriServices, "While it is true that the failure of existing technology due to resistance or other reasons can increase research efforts and allow more selective products to compete, it is also true that selective products have smaller markets, need longer market life, and consequently, protection from resistance development to be financially viable" (Thompson 2001). Interestingly, however, the cases in which farmers entirely cease to demand a product because of resistance have been rare. Even in the extreme case of pyrethroids in the United States, their market value dropped by only 50%, and they remain on the shelves of agricultural supply stores. In fact, pyrethroids have remained in high demand; Fernandez-Cornejo and others (2001) estimated that the impact of its loss on corn producers would be in excess of $172 million per year.

There is considerable evidence that the chemical industry invests heavily in developing strategies for resistance management. As Bayer-Pflanzenschutz

(2001) put it, "If resistance is likely to arise, further development of the product can be practically excluded." Individual companies finance scientists both within and outside of their corporations. Monsanto, a major producer of *Bt* crops, collaborates directly with the NC-205 research committee on research regarding the European corn borer, an important pest for *Bt* corn. Monsanto also has extensive projects among entomologists working on resistance among cotton pests (Sachs 2001). Bayer Corporation employs 68 scientists in its Institute for Insect Control, whose major focus is the study of insect biology. Among the projects listed on their website are studies of aphids, beetles, spider mites, the codling moth, and nematodes and their various interactions with maize, rice, cotton, soy, and vegetables. Overall, spending on resistance management by companies is substantial and increasing, particularly since 1995, with larger amounts spent by companies offering transgenic projects (Thompson 2001).

During the late 1970s, a host of international organizations were created by agrochemical companies to help coordinate research and to generate information exchange regarding resistance. Initially, efforts were crop- or product-specific, such as the Australian Wheat Broad Working Party on Grain Protectants and the Pyrethroid Efficacy Group. The early 1980s saw the creation, under the umbrella of the Global Crop Protection Federation (GCPF), a series of interindustry committees addressing herbicide, insecticide, fungicide, and rodenticide resistance.

The Insecticide Resistance Action Committee (IRAC), formed in 1984, states its mission as follows: "to provide a coordinated crop protection industry response to the development of resistance in insect and mite pests. The mission of IRAC is to develop resistance management strategies to enable growers to use crop protection products in a way to maintain the efficacy. The organization is implementing comprehensive strategies to confront" (see IRAC 2001). The IRAC organizes several conferences a year regarding the management of insecticide resistance and publishes extensive guidelines regarding insecticide use. It funds specific resistance projects and coordinates country groups in the United States, Brazil, India, Pakistan, Australia, South Africa, Spain, and China. Current projects include monitoring resistance to pyrethroids of cotton pests in West Africa and Asia (an incipient project to understand the reaction of the codling moth), a variety of pesticides, and an ongoing effort to develop resistance management strategies for the Colorado potato beetle in Poland.

The Herbicide Resistance Action Committee (HRAC), founded in 1989, has a mission similar to that of the IRAC, and its membership includes representatives from 13 major agrochemical companies: AgrEvo, BASF, Bayer, American-Cyanamid, Dow AgriServices, DuPont, FMC, Monsanto, Novartis, Rhone-Poulenc, Rohm & Haas, Tomen, and Zeneca (Nevill et al. 1998). A major component of the HRAC's responsibilities is the dissemination of information among farmers and researchers. Like IRAC, HRAC funds an ongoing global resistance survey study. In addition, it has supported specific projects in the monitoring wild oats in the United Kingdom, gene flow in Russian thistle in the United States, management of urea-resistant *Pharalis* in India, and the economics of herbicide-resistant blackgrass. Its most recent focus has been determining the financial impacts of herbicide resistance in the agricultural industry. During the 1990s, HRAC spent more than $300,000 funding scientific studies on herbicide resistance (Jutsum and Graham 1995).

The Fungicide Resistance Action Committee (FRAC), developed from an industry seminar in 1980, has since formed a variety of working groups focused on particular fungicides. The current groups include scientists researching anilinopyrimidines, benzimidazoles, dicarboximides, phenylamides, sterol biosynthesis inhibitors, and strobilurin type action and resistance (see FRAC 2001).

The GCPF, the umbrella over the action committees (formerly the International Group of National Associations of Manufacturers of Agrochemical Products), has a strong regional focus. It is composed of six regional crop protection associations: Africa and the Middle East, Latin America, Asia and the Pacific, Japan, North America, and Europe. Many of the regional organizations have a long history; the North American branch, for example, was founded in 1933 and boasts a membership of firms ranging from Aventis to Zeneca (see ACPA 2001). Although the regional organizations are responsible for a much broader range of issues than just pesticide resistance, their participation in the resistance management process is crucial because they allow for the collection and dissemination of information across regions. Their major effort in this area includes the coordination of the action committees. Information regarding total spending by the GCPF and its committees on research and contributions of industry to the organizations is, unfortunately, not available.

Despite this informational barrier, the evidence suggests that our model describes an important and understudied piece of the pesticide resistance puzzle.

Pesticide Use Advisors

Another area of research that has been almost completely ignored by the traditional analysis of resistance management is the role of pesticide consultants, particularly in the United States. Such consultants play a role analogous to a doctor, identifying the culprit disease and prescribing a treatment. Although independent consultants have provided services to farmers for more than 40 years, their participation was previously limited to fruit and vegetable production. Presence in other food and feed grain production is a more recent phenomenon (Wolf 1998). In 1993, consultants were found to have played a role in the production of 53% of cotton acres, 53% of vegetable acres, 21% of corn acres, and 13% of soybean acres. The same study estimated that, overall, diagnostic services were provided by consultants on 16% of U.S. farmland (Nowlin 1993).

The past 10 years have seen a burst of activity in this field. The National Alliance of Independent Crop Consultants, a professional society representing independent consultants and researchers, was founded in 1978. In 1985, the organization had more than 150 members, a number that has since increased to more than 500. It was not until 1991 that it founded the Certified Professional Crop Consultant Program, which competes with the American Society of Agronomy's Certified Crop Advisor Program. Both are intended to raise the standards of the industry, although the Certified Professional Crop Consultant Program is seen as more rigorous, requiring a bachelor's degree in agriculture, pest management, or biology; extensive experience; and continued education (Wolf 1998). The growing importance of consultant certification is illustrated by the fact that between February 1993 and February 1995, the American Society of Agronomy administered almost 12,000 Certified Crop Advisor national examinations.

Work by Wiebers (1992) suggests that reputation is the key element that determines the success of consultants. If they switch from private practice to working for a company, often they take their clients with them. Given that consultants may work for a large number of firms in a region, they play a potentially important role in affecting regional resistance. The fact that large farms are more likely to hire consultants provides further explanation as to why large farms are more likely to use lower levels of pesticides.

However, Wiebers's study (1992) also shows that consultants may adjust chemical use instruction according to farmers' perception of effectiveness in using a chemical. Farmers who are less effective may be prescribed more chemical applications to reduce the likelihood of pest damage. This practice provides further support for the doctor–patient analogy. One might also suspect that, like many patients, farmers may either ignore the advice of their consultants and "self-medicate," a process similar to that of the rampant and unnecessary use of antibiotics for many diseases in the United States. The opposite effect might also hold true—farmers may not finish their cycle of pesticide applications (similar to two year olds who will not take their last dose of amoxicillin)—thus contributing to resistance buildup caused by chemical underuse, an effect that may be exacerbated by both environmental and price concerns.

In either case, agricultural consultants have an important role to play in the management of pesticide resistance, and one could easily imagine beneficial coordination efforts taken across farms and regions that might significantly lower the resistance buildup.

Conclusion

Our chapter suggests that the main line of research on the economics of pesticide resistance has been rather narrow and too heavily dependent on the logic and main analysis of the economics of nonrenewable and renewable resources. It challenges the main result of this literature, namely, that resistance provides incentive to overapply pesticides, which creates resistance buildup. Thus, the policy implication of the traditional analysis is that intervention is needed to reduce application levels to slow pesticide resistance buildup.

We introduce a new conceptual framework and institutional evidence from the field to demonstrate the complexity of the relationship among incentives, pesticide applications, and resistance buildup. Furthermore, we indicate that in many situations, there may be an underapplication of pesticides. It is important for policymakers to be able to distinguish between circumstances and to focus their effort against resistance buildup that occurs when there are incentives to overapply pesticides.

We introduce new considerations in evaluating resistance buildup at three levels. First, at the field level, we argue that the dynamics of pesticide use must take into account both the dynamics of the overall pest populations and the dynamics of resistance buildup. The existing literature considers only the dynamics of resistance buildup, which tends to bias the results toward the traditional conclusion of overapplication of pesticides. Plausible situations can exist in which ignoring the dynamics of population buildup may actually lead to underapplication of chemicals. Thus, to assess the overall effect of growers who may ignore dynamic implications of pesticide application, the impact of their choices on resistance and overall populations must be incorporated.

Furthermore, we argue that farmers' pesticide choices are affected by other factors beside resistance considerations. When examining the impact of individual behavior on pesticide resistance and pest population dynamics, other factors, including alternative chemicals, IPM, crop rotation, and the like, must be taken into account

Our chapter further suggests that a correct analysis of pest resistance problems must consider aggregate decisions regarding pesticide pricing and overall supply and that these decisions are affected by the structure of the industry, property rights, and patent considerations. Manufacturers will likely have a monopoly on the production of new pesticides during the life of the patent, which will provide the incentive to underapply them relative to the optimal solution. Furthermore, manufacturers are concerned with the negative side-effects of resistance buildup because of its impact on future sales and their reputation. Thus, they may be actively involved in activities to reduce resistance buildup. Indeed, we present evidence of manufacturer involvement in resistance management and resistance prevention. We also show that manufacturers' incentive to control resistance may be weaker than is socially desirable because of the limitation of a patent's life and because manufacturers consider only the impact on their sales rather than on social welfare.

In addition, we suggest that manufacturer's incentives that result in pesticide supply and pricing, as well as actual involvement in resistance control, will likely lead to overapplication of pesticides by myopic farmers as the chemicals get older and the supply network becomes more competitive. There are several old pesticides (mostly organophosphates or carbonates) that have long been used because of a lack of significant resistance buildup potential or the existence of effective resistance management schemes. Pest management agencies should be especially aware of potential problems with fairly new chemicals once the initial patent period lapses, the provision of the chemicals increases, or the initial manufacturer does not get very involved in the product stewardship.

We also argue that, in addition to the manufacturers and users of the pesticides, other economic agents, in particular pesticide advisors and extension specialists, also are involved in pest control decisions. Extension and especially individual consultants have the incentive to reduce resistance buildup and improve the performance of pest control agents. Our analysis suggests that the network of economic agents concerned about and involved in decisions regarding pest management and control of resistance buildup is quite complex. Even if individual growers may not be concerned with resistance and population dynamics issues when applying pesticides, other agents affecting their decisions may have these issues in mind.

In addition to conceptual models and simple econometric analysis of pesticide use levels, more empirical studies are needed. These studies should be based on understanding the basic structural and institutional relationships, the attitudes of various agents to pest control choices, and the extent to which they have inference on these choices. Furthermore, policy analyses affecting resistance should be integrated and combined with policy analyses addressing other side-effects of pesticides, in particular, human and environmental health.

References

ACPA (American Crop Protection Association). 2001. From Lab to Label: The Research, Testing and Registration of Agricultural Chemicals. http://www.acpa.org/public/pubs (accessed January 12, 2001).

Alix, J., and D. Zilberman. 2001. *Industrial Organization and Pest Dynamic Considerations in Agricultural Pest Resistance Management*. Working Paper, Department of Agricultural and Resource Economics, University of California at Berkeley. Berkeley, CA: University of California at Berkeley.

Bayer–Pflanzenschutz. 2001. http://www.agrobayer.com (accessed January 27, 2001).

Carlson, G.A., and M.E. Wetzstein. 1993. Pesticides and Pest Management. In *Agricultural and Environmental Resource Economics*, edited by G.A. Carlson, D. Zilberman, and J.A. Miranowski. New York: Oxford University Press, 268–318.

Carpenter, J., L. Gianessi, and L. Lynch. 2000. *The Economic Impact of the Scheduled U.S. Phaseout of Methyl Bromide*. Report of the National Center for Food and Agricultural Policy. Washington, DC: National Center for Food and Agricultural Policy.

Damicone, J. 2001. Fungicide Resistance Management. OSU Extension Facts, Oklahoma Cooperative Extension Service. http://www.agweb.okstate.edu /pearl/plantdiseases/ f7663.htm (accessed March 2001).

FAO (Food and Agriculture Organization of the United Nations). 2001. Controlling pests. http://www.fao.org/focus/e/SpeclPr/SPro12-e.htm (accessed January 22, 2002).

Fernandez-Cornejo, J., S. Jans, and M. Smith. 1998. Issues in the Economics of Pesticide Use in Agriculture: A Review of the Empirical Evidence. *Review of Agricultural Economics* 20: 462–88.

FRAC. 2001. Fungicide Action Committee. http://www.gcpf.org/frac/frac.html (accessed March 17, 2001).

Hurley, T.M., B.A. Babcock, and R.L. Hellmich. Forthcoming. Biotechnology and Pest Resistance: An Economic Assessment of Refuges. *Journal of Agricultural and Resource Economics*.

IRAC (Insecticide Resistance Action Committee). 2001. http://www. plantprotection.org/ IRAC/general_resources/facts.html (accessed March 17, 2002).

Jutsum, A.R., and J.C. Graham. 1995. *Managing Weed Resistance, the Role of the Agrochemical Industry*. http://www.plantprotection.org/HRAC/brighton.html (accessed January 17, 2001).

Laxminarayan, R., and R.D. Simpson. 2002. An Economic Analysis of Refuge Strategies in Transgenic Agriculture. *Environmental and Resource Economics* 22: 521-36.

Lichtenberg, E., R.C. Spear, and D. Zilberman. 1993. The Economics of Reentry Regulation of Pesticides. *American Journal of Agricultural Economics* 75: 946–58.

Nevill, D., D. Cornes, and S. Howard. 1998. The Role of HRAC in the Management of Weed Resistance. http://www.plantprotection.org/HRAC/weedresis.htm (accessed July 19, 2002).

Nowlin, B. 1993. National Alliance of Independent Crop Consultants Report. *Ag Consultant* Fall: 13.

Osgood, D., D. Cohen, D. Parker, and D. Zilberman. 1997. Forecasting the Production Benefits and Incidence of a Public Program: An Integrated Survey and Estimation Procedure Applied to Study the California Irrigation Management Information System. *Advances in Econometrics* 12: 303–17.

Pannell, D.J., and Zilberman, D. 2000. Economic and Sociological Factors Affecting Growers' Decision Making on Herbicide Resistance. In *Herbicide Resistance and Management in World Grain Crops*, edited by D. Shaner and S. Powles. Sidney, Australia: CRC Press.

The Pure Foods Campaign. 2001. http://www.purefoods.org (accessed January 17, 2001).

Regev, U., and D. Hueth. 1974. Optimal Agricultural Pest Management with Increasing Pest Resistance. *American Journal of Agricultural Economics* 56: 543–52.

Riley, S.L. 1990. Pyrethroid Resistance in *Heliothis spp.*: Current Monitoring and Management Programs. In *Managing Resistance to Agrochemicals: From Fundamental*

Research to Practical Strategies, edited by M.B. Green. ACS Symposium Series, 421. Washington, DC: American Chemical Society, 134–48.

Sachs, E.S. Director, Scientific Outreach, Monsanto Company. 2001. Personal communication with the authors, February 19, 2001.

Sunding, D., and D. Zilberman. 2001. The Agricultural Innovation Process: Research and Technology Adoption in a Changing Agricultural Industry. In *Handbook of Agricultural Economics*, edited by B. Gardner and G.C. Rausser. Amsterdam, The Netherlands: Elsevier.

Thompson, G.D. 1997. Industry and Individual Company's Perspective on Resistance Management. *Resistant Pest Management* 9: 5–8.

———. Global Insect Management, Dow AgriServices. 2001. Personal communication with the authors, February 15, 2001.

Wiebers, U.C. 1992. *Economic and Environmental Effects of Pest Management Information and Pesticides: The Case of Processing Tomatoes in California*. Ph.D. dissertation. University of Berlin, Department of Agricultural Sciences.

Wolf, S. 1998. Privatization of Crop Production Information Service Markets. In *Privatization of Information and Agricultural Industrialization*, edited by S.A Wolf. Boca Raton, FL: CRC Press, 151–82.

Yarkin, C., D. Sunding, D. Zilberman, and J. Siebert. 1994. Methyl Bromide Regulation … All Crops Should Not Be Treated Equally. *California Agriculture* 48: 10–15.

Zilberman, D., and K. Millock. 1997. Pesticide Use and Regulation: Making Economic Sense Out of an Externality and Regulation Nightmare. *Journal of Agricultural and Resource Economics* 22: 321–32.

Zilberman, D., A. Schmitz, G. Casterline, E. Lichtenberg, and J.B. Siebert. 1991. The Economics of Pesticide Use and Regulation. *Science* 253: 518–22.

Appendix: Chemical Companies' Choices and Resistance

This appendix provides the mathematical detail of the model described in the second half of the chapter. We consider a case in which the pest population is renewed every season and resistance is the only dynamic variable that changes over time. We also assume that the industry consists of many smaller farms and thus resistance control does not affect farmer behavior. At period t, the inverse demand function for pesticides is

$$W_t = W_t^D(P_t, X_t, R_t) \tag{A1}$$

where P_t is the price of the crop to be grown, X_t is pesticide use, and R_t is resistance in period t. W_t is demand at time t. This demand curve increases in output price, $\partial W^D/\partial P_t > 0$; decreases with aggregate pesticide use, $\partial W_t^D/\partial X_t < 0$; and decreases with resistance, $\partial W^D/\partial R_t < 0$.

When pesticides are relatively new, the manufacturer's patent gives it monopoly power, which also depends on the availability of substitutes. Chemicals more than 20 years old are produced by competitive (or semicompetitive) industries.

We will consider the behavior of a monopolistic manufacturer. It will maximize expected profits subject to resistance constraint,

$$R_{t+1} - R_t = g(X_t, R_t) - \psi(R_t) \tag{A2}$$

where $g(X_t, R_t)$ is the resistance buildup function that increases in chemical use $\partial g/\partial X > 0$ and the pest vulnerability recovery is $\psi(R_t)$. For simplicity, we assume linearity, but population genetics may require a more complex structure (see, for example, Laxminarayan and Simpson, 2002). However, this specification will not affect the results here.

The cost function of the manufacturer is given by $C(X_t)$, and marginal cost $C'(X_t)$ is positive and increases,

$$C'(X_t) > 0, C''(X_t) > 0$$

Thus, the optimal production choice problem is

$$\max_{X_t} \sum_{t=0}^{T} \beta^t \left[W_t^D(P_t, X_t, R_t) X_t - C(X_t) \right] \tag{A3a}$$

where the time horizon T denotes the end of the patent's life, subject to

$$R_{t+1} - R_t = g(X_t, R_t) - \psi(R_t), t = 0, 1 \dots T \tag{A3b}$$

The Lagrangian for this problem is

$$\begin{aligned} L = \max_{X_t, \mu_t} \sum_{t=0}^{T} &\beta^t \left[W_t^D(P_t, X_t, R_t) X_t - C(X_t) \right] \\ &+ \mu_t \left[R_{t+1} - R_t - g(X_t, R_t) + \psi(R_t) \right] \end{aligned} \tag{A4}$$

where μ_t is the temporal shadow cost of resistance. The first-order conditions to this optimization problem are

$$\frac{\partial L}{\partial X_t} = \frac{\partial W_t^D}{\partial X_t} X_t + W_t^D - \frac{\partial C}{\partial X_t} - \mu_t \frac{\partial g}{\partial X_t} = 0, t = 0, T \tag{A5}$$

$$\frac{\partial L}{\partial R_t} = \beta^t \left[\frac{\partial W_t^D}{\partial R_t} X_t - \mu_t \left[1 + \frac{\partial g}{\partial R_t} - \frac{\partial \psi}{\partial R_t} \right] \right] + \mu_{t-1} \beta^{t-1} = 0, \text{ for } t = 0, T \tag{A6}$$

and $R_0 = 0$. We also assume $\mu_T = 0$ because, after period T, the patent has lapsed and monopoly power and extra profit disappear.

Condition A5 suggests that at the optimal pesticide production level, marginal revenue,

$$MR_t = \frac{\partial W_t^D}{\partial X_t} X_t + W_t^D$$

is equal to the marginal cost of production plus resistance cost, $MRC_t = \mu_t[\partial g(X_t, R_t)/\partial X_t]$, that is,

$$MR_t = MC_t + MRC_t \tag{A7}$$

Figure 12-3 depicts optimal determination of pesticide production by the manufacturers as well as other outcomes. The manufacturers' optimum occurs at A and results in user price W_A and quantity X_A. If the manufacturers ignore resistance, the optimal outcome could be $X_B > X_A$. If the manufacturers are competitive and ignore resistance, the outcome is at C. The equation of motion of the shadow price μ_t is derived from Equation A6 to shed light on the behavior of MRC_t. From Equation A-6 and $\beta = 1/(1 + r)$, one obtains

$$\mu_t - \mu_{t-1} = \frac{\partial W_t^D}{\partial R_t} X_t - \mu_t\left[\frac{\partial g}{\partial R_t} - \frac{\partial \psi}{\partial R_t}\right] + r\mu_{t-1} \tag{A8}$$

The difference in $\mu_t - \mu_{t-1}$ is the change in cost from delaying the marginal expansion of resistance from period $t - 1$ to period t. The delay has several effects:

- $\partial W/\partial R_t$ represents reduction in cost because of lower resistance damage in period t.
- $-\mu_t[(\partial g/\partial R_t) - (\partial \psi/\partial R_t)]$ represents the effect of delay from expanding resistance or resistance growth. It is negative if the marginal growth of resistance $\partial g/\partial R_t$ is greater than the marginal growth in pest vulnerability $\partial \psi/\partial R_t$.
- $r\mu_{t-1}$ represents the adjustment from using temporal shadow prices. It is an interest gain associated with delay cost. When resistance buildup is fast and the first effect is dominant, the shadow cost of resistance stock declines. This is reasonable because $\mu_T = 0$, which reflects our assumption that no extra profits are earned once the patent expires.

As the value of μ_t declines over time, and assuming that $\partial g/\partial R_t$ does not drastically increase, we expect MRC_t to decline over time, and the reduction in pesticide production by the monopolist (relative to X_B) because of resistance considerations will also decline over time. That suggests that the monopolist resistance control effort in general will decline as the product matures.

To assess the monopolist's choice against the social optimum, let us derive the social optimality consideration. If there are other externality considerations, the social welfare optimization problem is

$$\max_{X_t} \sum_{t=0}^{\infty} \beta^t \left[\int_0^{X_t} W_t^D(P_t, x_t, R_t)\,dx - C(X_t) \right] \tag{A9}$$

subject to Equation A3b and given R_0, where

$$\int_0^{X_t} W_t^D(\cdot)\,dx$$

is the gross benefit of farmers from using the chemical. If the optimization problem can be solved by a Lagrangian technique, let the shadow price of the equation of motion be denoted by μ_t^0.

The optimality condition determining output under the optimal solution is

$$W_t^D - \frac{\partial C}{\partial X_t} - \mu_t^0 \frac{\partial g}{\partial X_t} = 0 \tag{A10}$$

which can be rewritten as

$$W_t^D = MC_t + MSR_t \tag{A11}$$

where MSR_t is the marginal social shadow cost of resistance, which is different than MRC_t, the monopolist's shadow cost of pollution. Thus, at the social optimum, the demand price is equal to the marginal cost of production plus resistance cost. It follows that the optimal social quantity is smaller than X_C but may be greater than X_A if at X_A

$$W^D + MRS_t < W^D - \frac{\partial W^D}{\partial X_t} X_t + MRC_t \tag{A12}$$

As Equation A12 suggests, unless society's marginal resistance cost is much higher than a monopoly's and social optimum is at D, the monopoly will likely produce less pesticide than is *socially optimal*.

Commentary

Strategic Issues in Agricultural Pest Resistance Management

R. David Simpson

Both "The Interaction of Dynamic Problems and Dynamic Policies: Some Economics of Biotechnology" by Timo Goeschl and Timothy Swanson (Chapter 11) and "Industrial Organization and Institutional Considerations in Agricultural Pest Resistance Management" by Jennifer Alix and David Zilberman (Chapter 12) deal with what one might call "strategic" aspects of pest resistance management. They consider how the actions of firms providing new products and the interactions between firms seeking to develop new products affect the nature of products developed, their use, and the role for public regulation of such products. The two contributions take different expositional approaches, however. Goeschl and Swanson structure their chapter around a mathematical model of new biotechnology product development. Although Alix and Zilberman present some formal modeling in a technical appendix, the main thrust of their exposition is more discursive. They present an extensive discussion of a number of scientific, institutional, and economic factors that affect the use of pesticides and the consequent evolution of pest resistance. In this respect, the chapters are complementary. Goeschl and Swanson delve deeply into the specifics of a specialized, but nonetheless illuminating, model. Alix and Zilberman present a wealth of "on-the-ground" detail.

The Goeschl and Swanson contribution might best be summarized by reference to its terminology of "creative" and "adaptive" destruction. The former refers to the tendency of one innovation to displace another as rivals in the technology sector seek to introduce new products and profit from the monopoly rents the possession of a superior product provides. This phenomenon has been much studied in economics, from the seminal contributions of Joseph Schumpeter (1943), who coined the term "creative destruction," through the more recent advances of Philippe Aghion and Peter Howitt (1992). Goeschl and Swanson layer a concern with "adaptive destruction" wrought by biological adaptation on top of the "creative destruction" occasioned by industrial competition.

Adaptive destruction arises from selection. The introduction of a new pesticide, for example, places selection pressure on the organisms against which it is targeted. Those few that are genetically favored survive in disproportionate numbers, causing resistant organisms to become increasingly common in the general population. The rents the supplier of a new pesticide earns are eroded as the product's effectiveness declines and incentives rise for other researchers to supply more effective products. The authors, borrowing a phrase from the biological literature, characterize the situation as a "Red Queen" game. As in *Alice in Wonderland*, one must run faster and faster to remain still because the biological landscape is itself racing by.

Two important implications can be drawn from Goeschl and Swanson's analysis. The first is that the patent system may be ineffective in providing incentives for advances in biotechnology. The protection of a 17-year patent is of little value for a product whose effective life span may be considerably shorter. The inadequacies of the patent system have long been the subject of economic investigation (Schumpeter 1943). It is not surprising the authors conclude that it is inadequate in this context—although they do identify in "adaptive destruction" a novel mechanism.

While the authors emphasize the shortcomings of patents in their analysis and conclusions, I find a point over which they gloss rather quickly more compelling. The supply of innovations is not fixed. It depends on the resources allocated to the research sector. These resources may include things such as manufactured capital and trained researchers, but they also include natural prototypes. The products of biotechnology are, almost by definition, derived from natural biota. It stands to reason, then, that the more natural biota are maintained, the more options there are for new product development. This subject has been the topic of some prior investigation (Simpson et al. 1996; Rausser and Small 2000), but Goeschl and Swanson offer a new and important perspective on the matter. Previous investigations have presumed that the demand for new products arises exogenously. As Goeschl and Swanson showed, however, the demand for new products may depend importantly on the management of existing ones. (In this respect, the authors' reference to recent work by Martin Weitzman [2000] is also germane. Weitzman relates the likelihood of catastrophic failure to the diversity of the agricultural base).

The Alix and Zilberman chapter contributes a number of interesting insights. Let me begin with a few that complement the Goeschl and Swanson analysis nicely. First, Alix and Zilberman present an extensive and enlightening discussion of several strategies available for resistance management. Although Goeschl and Swanson focus on the development of products de novo, and much of the existing literature concentrates on refuge areas (largely because this is the strategy adopted by the U.S. Environmental Protection Agency (EPA) in its management of bioengineered *Bt* crops (see Hurley et al. 1997; Laxminarayan and Simpson 2000, 2002), Alix and Zilberman also discuss practices such as integrated pest management, crop rotation, and precision technologies that can accomplish the same goal. This reviewer feels considerable sympathy[1] with Goeschl and Swanson in the need to strip an analytical model down to its bare essentials to obtain tractable results. Even Alix and Zilberman have faced this necessity in constructing the model presented in their appendix. Having said this, however, one would surely want to consider the broader management strategies Alix and Zilberman discussed in making policy choices. Their chapter provides an excellent overview of these options.

A second common theme in the two chapters concerns the role of patents. Goeschl and Swanson focus on the limitations of patent protection in providing incentives for new biotechnology product development. Alix and Zilberman consider the role of patents in the more general context of resistance management. They point to a straightforward but very important insight: a manufacturer's incentive to manage resistance to its product depends on its maintenance of a monopoly position in that product. Naturally enough, then, the purveyor of a brand-new pesticide would have a strong incentive to maintain its franchise by preventing the evolution of resistance. Conversely, as patent expiration looms, the manufacturer may care little for maintaining the long-term efficacy of its product. As Alix and Zilberman noted, however, patent expiration does not necessarily imply the abandonment of all investments in continued efficacy. Even the manufacturer of a product whose chemical composition will soon pass into the public domain may have some incentive to maintain the value of its brand and, more generally, the reputation of its company, by maintaining the efficacy of the product.

Alix and Zilberman ask the right questions concerning the basis for public policy intervention regarding resistance. In a world in which the adoption of *Bt* crops remains far from universal, critics might take exception to the refuge requirements that EPA has announced. Alix and Zilberman raise crucial issues of timing and mobility (on the latter question, see also Secchi and Babcock, Chapter 4). If farmers can change crops when resistance develops, or largely "reap what they sow" from pests that remain close to home, the externality argument that presumably motivates regulation is at least reduced.

Perhaps the most compelling argument that the costs of resistance will be internalized within the private sector is, as Alix and Zilberman consider in some detail, that a monopolist in a pesticide has an incentive to preserve the value of its monopoly. The monopolist can, then, by setting the price of the product or the conditions of its use, determine its adoption and hence, the rate at which resistance develops. As the authors note, these motives may be attenuated by the impending expiration of the patent. As they also note, however, the monopolist has a sort of "built-in" conservationist tendency. Because a monopolist charges a price in excess of marginal cost (however the marginal cost may be constituted between current production and distribution and discounted resistance costs), it will supply less to the market than would a competitor. This is the essence of Buchanan's classic (1969) argument, although work done on exhaustible resources demonstrates that one must be careful in its application to dynamic settings (Stiglitz 1976).

Alix and Zilberman have done a wonderful job of laying out the issues, and in the process, they have sketched a rich agenda for further research. Any or, one might hope, all of the topics they have introduced may be the subject of more intensive exploration. There are clear and important policy implications of such research. The central issue remains the role of public regulation of biotechnology and resistance, but subjects such as innovative activity, market power, firms' ability to determine the use of the products they sell, mobility among pest populations, refuges, and the role of integrated pest management and precision technologies are central to the resolution of that issue.

References

Aghion, P., and P. Howitt. 1992. A Model of Growth through Creative Destruction. *Econometrica* 60(2): 323–51.

Buchanan, J.M. 1969. External Diseconomies, Corrective Taxes, and Market Structure. *American Economic Review* 59: 174–77.

Hurley, T.M., B.A. Babcock, and R.L. Hellmich. 1997. *Biotechnology and Pest Resistance: An Economic Assessment of Refuges.* Ames, IA: Center for Agricultural and Rural Development, Iowa State University.

Laxminarayan, R. and R.D. Simpson. 2000. Biological Limits on Agricultural Intensification: An Example from Resistance Management. Discussion Paper 00-43. Washington, DC: Resources for the Future.

———. 2002. Refuge Strategies for Managing Pest Resistance in Transgenic Agriculture. *Environmental and Resource Economics* 22: 521–36.

Rausser, G.C., and A.A. Small. 2000. Valuing Research Leads: Bioprospecting and the Conservation of Genetic Resources. *Journal of Political Economy* 108(1): 173–206.

Schumpeter, J. 1943. *Capitalism, Socialism, Democracy.* London: Unwin University Books.

Simpson, R.D., R.A. Sedjo, and J.W. Reid. 1996. Valuing Biodiversity for Use in Pharmaceutical Research. *Journal of Political Economy* 104: 163–85.

Stiglitz, J. 1976. Monopoly and the Rate of Extraction of Natural Resources. *American Economics Review* 66(4): 655–61.

Weitzman, M.L. 2000. Economic Profitability vs. Ecological Entropy. *Quarterly Journal of Economics* 115(1): 237–63.

Note

1. This commentator also should acknowledge that he has motivated the highly schematic models he and his colleague have produced (Laxminarayan and Simpson, 2000, 2002) with this argument.

Index

Abatement
 functions, damage control agents,
  139–40, 142
 refuge zones as "care" in model,
  263–64, 273–82, 283–85, 289–92
 See also Refuges
Adaptation (biological), 295–99, 302,
  304–8, 312–13, 321–22
 See also Biological innovation
Adaptive destruction, 299, 306, 357–58
Additional net benefits, 214–15, 219–21,
  231–32
 optimal levels, 222, 224*f*, 226–30,
  235–36
Agricultural consultants, 331, 348–49
Agricultural innovation. *See*
  Biotechnology innovation
Agriculture. *See* Farming; Pesticides;
  Productivity
Agrobiotechnology. *See* Biotechnology
  innovation
Alleles, susceptible vs. resistant pests,
  105–8, 187
Allergic reactions, *Bt* crops, 212–13
Allocation of resources
 competitive vs. optimal, 268–70,
  288–92
 impact of pesticide taxation, 341–42
 for private vs. social investments,
  311–22

for production vs. reserves, 293–95,
  300–301, 307–14, 358
Amoxicillin, 64, 126–27, 128*t*
Animal feed, use of antibiotics, 11
Antibiotics
 in animal feed, 11, 135
 for ear infections, 125–31
 effectiveness, as a natural resource,
  4–5, 34–35, 43–44
 heterogeneity of treatment, 65–68,
  69–74
 mathematical analysis of use, 45–61
 resistance, 9, 295–96
  benefit–cost analysis, 3–4, 6, 44–46,
   48–50, 76–82, 90–92
  caused by transgenic crops, 216, 217
  fitness costs of, 17–19, 20, 23–25,
   26, 29, 77
  impact of market structure, 283
  impact on demand, 119–25,
   127–31
  measuring costs, 134–36
  model of endogenous resistance,
   67–69
  See also Genetic resistance;
   Resistance
"Appropriability" effect (biotechnology
  innovation), 314–15
Assumptions about pest resistance
  variables, 113–15, 244, 246–47

Atrazine, xv, 172–75

Bacillus thuringiensis (Bt). See Bt crops
Bacteria, 21–25, 28–29, 78–79
Banning pesticides, 172, 174–75, 342
Bayer Corporation, 346–47
Bellman's Principle of Optimality, 30–31
Beneficial organisms, depletion from
     pesticide use, 142–43, 145, 212
Benefit–cost analysis, 182, 308
     commercialization of *Bt* corn, 201*t*,
          211–13
     estimating antibiotic benefits, 135–36
     GMOs, 146, 149, 150–54
     infection control, xiii, 6
     irreversible costs and benefits,
          215–29, 231–32
     policy impact, 226–30, 232
     of option theory, 184–86, 195–96,
          200–203, 214
     resistance management strategies,
          162–63
     transgenic crops, 214–32, 238–47
     treatment and antibiotic resistance,
          3–4, 6, 44–46, 48–50, 76–82,
          90–92
     See also Costs; Treatment (antibiotics),
          costs
Benomil (fungicide), 336
Bias, 123–24, 150
Bioengineered *Bt* corn seeds, as
     production inputs, 263–64, 273–82,
          283–85, 288–92
Biological innovation, resistance as,
          293–300, 304–5, 308–9, 311–14,
          317–19, 321–22
     See also Adaptation (biological);
          Biotechnology innovation;
          Technological innovation
Biologists and economists, 113, 115,
          238–40, 247, 257
Biotechnology innovation
     impact assessment of, 145–54
     intermediate goods sector in,
          299–303, 309–10
     market model limitations, 145–47
     market structure effects, 263–85,
          357–60

production (final goods) sector in,
          299–304, 306–8
surplus, 145, 147, 191–93, 201*t*
utility functions, 305–6
welfare effects, 294–95, 305–9, 311–22
     See also Biological innovation; *Bt*
          crops; Firms; Genetically
          modified organisms (GMOs);
          Technological innovation;
          Technology; Transgenic crops
Bipolaris maydis (fungus) invasion (U.S.,
          1970), 248–49
Birds, impact of pesticides, 212
Black–Scholes formula, 190–91, 198
Bonhoeffer model, 20–21
Broad-spectrum antibiotics, 120, 126,
          128*t*, 129
Brownian motion, 189, 190, 193–94,
          221–22
Bt crops
     bioengineered *Bt* corn seeds, 263–64
     control alternatives, 340
     corn commercialization decisions,
          184–86, 191–203
     economic studies, 147–48, 191–203,
          211–13
     pest refuges, xiv–xv, xvi, 11–12,
          94–110
     resistance to *Bt*, 151, 186–88
     U.S. distribution of *Bt* corn, 98*f*, 99*f*
     See also Biotechnology; Corn;
          Genetically modified organisms
          (GMOs); Transgenic crops
"Business-stealing" effect (biotechnology
     innovation), 314, 315

Care. *See* Abatement
Certification of agricultural consultants,
          349
Children, ear infections, 119–20, 125–29
Choice models, antibiotic demand,
          122–23
Choice of antibiotics. *See* Demand, for
     antibiotics
Choke prices, resource depletion,
     atrazine, 173–74
Civil society, concerns about GMO risks,
          138–39, 148–49, 215

Clinical treatment guidelines, 64–67
Cobb–Douglas (C–D) functions,
    productivity measurement, 139–40
"Collateral cost" effect (biotechnology
    innovation), 315, 316
Collective action. *See* Regulation
Commercialization of *Bt* corn, economic
    analysis, 184–86, 191–203, 211–13
Common property
    antibiotics, 7
    genetic resistance, 263–85, 288–92
    pest susceptibility, 143, 145, 166,
        333–35
Communication among disciplines
    economists and biologists, 113, 115,
        238–40, 247, 257
    simulation models as aid to, 88–89
Comparative statics
    for decisionmaking processes, 311–13
    for firms, 275–77
    See also Static analysis
Competition
    between industries, 294–95, 298–99,
        330–31, 343–46
    See also Contests
Competition, imperfect, 289–90
Competitive allocation, 268–69
Competitive equilibrium. *See*
    Equilibrium
Complementarity of inputs, 276–77
Compliance, as factor in resistance
    management, 110
Computer simulation models for
    interdisciplinary communication,
    88–89
Confidence intervals, antibiotic market
    share, 130
Congestion analogy, 85–87
Conservation of resources and
    decisionmaking, 163–67, 175–76
    See also Reserves (biological)
Constant variance rate, 221
Consultants, agricultural, 331, 348–49
Consumer surplus. *See* Surplus
Contests
    biological vs. technological
        innovation, 293–99, 302, 304–8,
        311–13, 318–22

See also Competition; Innovation,
    rates
Contingent claim analysis, release of
    transgenic crops, 231–32
Contracting over, monopoly, 271–72,
    279–80, 282
Control agents, Darwinian selection,
    1–2
Controls (treatment regimes), 26–29,
    32–36
Convenience yield, as discount rate,
    225–27
Corn
    Bt vs. conventional production,
        193–203
    pest management, 94–110, 172–75,
        187
    Southern corn leaf blight (U.S., 1970),
        248–49
    See also Bt crops
Cost–benefit analysis. *See* Benefit–cost
    analysis
Cost-effectiveness
    antibiotics, 64–67, 72–73
    See also Effectiveness, of antibiotics
        and pesticides
Costate variables. *See* Shadow prices
Costs
    of crop protection, 4, 158–60, 165,
        167–75, 181
    of introducing new products, 3–4, 9
    irreversible, 248–49
        in benefit–cost analysis, 214–32,
            242
        in regulatory decisionmaking,
            184–85, 188–90
    pesticide application, 336–37
    See also Benefit–cost analysis;
        Externalities; Incentives;
        Marginal costs (MC); Prices;
        Treatment (antibiotics), costs;
        Welfare effects
Creative destruction model, 294,
    298–99, 302, 304, 306, 357–58
Critical values, release of transgenic
    crops, 240, 243
Crop advisory certification programs,
    349

Crop protection costs. *See* Costs, of crop
protection
Crop rotation, 113–15, 172–75, 338–39
Cumulative probability distribution,
GMO benefits, 152–54

Damage control factors, 139–40, 143,
145, 148, 153–54
Damage functions, European corn borer,
101–2
Darwinian selection, 1–2
Data collection
GMO study guidelines, 150–51
precision technologies for pest
control, 339–40
DDT, resistance as added incentive to
ban, 182
Decisionmaking
commercialization of *Bt* corn, 184–86,
192–203
option theory, 188–91, 192–203
pesticide production, 354–56
pesticide use, 163–67, 331–40, 350–51
R&D investments, 309–13, 316–19,
321–22
release of transgenic crops, 218–25,
231–32
Degradation of natural resources. *See*
Natural resources, depletion from
pesticide use
Demand
for antibiotics, impact of resistance,
119–25, 127–31
elasticity, agricultural innovation, 145
See also Factor demand
Depreciation of *Bt* corn effectiveness,
195–96
"Differential internalization" of
externalities, 315, 318
Diminishing returns, treatment benefits,
32
Discounted present value. *See* Present
value (PV)
Discounting
atrazine resistance, 174, 175*t*
convenience yield, 225–27
cure vs. increased resistance, 50–51
disease incidence, 33–34

own discount rate, 307–8, 310, 315
private vs. social investments, 319–20
risk-free rate of return, 230
Disease ecology, 77–81, 248–52
Distributional effects. *See* Welfare effects
Doctors. *See* Optimal treatment;
Physicians; Treatment (antibiotics)
Drift rate, 221, 226–28
Drug prices, 120, 124, 126–29
Drug treatment regime schematic, 22*f*
Dynamic analysis
of antibiotic treatment, 30–32, 87–90
farm production models, 100–105

Ear infections (otitis media), xv, 119–20,
125–31
Economic models vs. epidemiological
models, 6–7
antibiotics, 32–33, 44, 79–80
transgenic crops, 238–40, 253–54,
257
Economics
application to GMOs, 145–54
application to policy design,
xvii–xviii, 1–12
natural resources and pesticides,
142–45
productivity measurement, 137,
139–40, 149–51
risk reduction in pest control, 141–42
thresholds for using GMOs, 160
thresholds for using pesticides, 101,
337
See also Resource economics
Economists and biologists, 113, 115,
238–40, 247, 257
Ecosystem complexity, and GMOs,
158–60
Effectiveness
of antibiotics and pesticides, 2, 7–9,
65, 216, 217, 265–66
See also Cost-effectiveness
of pesticides
in *Bt* corn, 194–96
and firm incentives, 343–46
influenced by usage, 349
refuges, 94–110
Efficiency of factor markets, 280–82

Elasticity of demand, agricultural innovation, 145
Empirical models
antibiotic demand, 123–25
commercialization of *Bt* corn, 199–202
Endogenous antibiotic resistance, 65–69, 72, 74
Environmental externalities. *See* Externalities
EPA. *See* U.S. Environmental Protection Agency (EPA)
Epidemiological models
Bonhoeffer model, 20–21
"ecological" vs. interventionist strategies, 21–25
vs. economic models, 6–7
antibiotics, 32–33, 44, 79–80
transgenic crops, 238–40, 253–54, 257
SIS (susceptible→infected→ susceptible) model, 42–43, 77–81
Equilibrium
of bacteria populations, 23–25, 29, 35
competitive vs. optimal, 269–70, 277–82, 291–92
value of treatment rate, 38–41
Escalator analogy (technological progress), 296, 322
European corn borer, 94–110, 113, 115, 147, 187, 191
Expectations
of decisionmakers, 166
of technology, 176
Expense ratios, fertilizer vs. pesticides, 168–71
Expensive treatments as social benefit, 65–67
Export market, genetically modified organisms (GMOs), 97
Externalities
depletion of beneficial organisms, 142–43, 145
drug resistance costs, 43–44, 70–72
genetic resistance, 267–68, 277–79, 283–85, 289–92
of GMOs, 149, 151–53
and patent systems, 314–16

of pest management, 5, 96–97, 100, 138, 162–64, 341–43
treatment homogeneity, 63–67, 73–74
See also Costs; Private vs. social costs; Risk; Welfare effects

Factor demand, 268–72, 276, 279, 282, 284
Factor productivity, bioengineered *Bt* corn, 291–92
Factor supply market, for bioengineered seeds, 278–82
Farm accountancy network database (Germany), 167–72
Farm size, 334, 336, 349
See also Field size; Patch size
Farming
Bt crops and resistance management, 94–110
organic, impact of *Bt* crops on, xvi, 95, 186
pesticide use and resistance, 5, 11–12, 172–76, 289–91, 330–43, 348–49
productivity of transgenic crops, 217, 219–20
sustainable agriculture, 162
Fertilizer, use tax, 160
Fertilizer, vs. pesticides, expense ratios, 168–71
Field size, 166–67
See also Farm size; Patch size
Final goods (production) sector, 299–304, 306–8
Firms
comparative statics for, 275–77
marginal revenues (MR) of, 271–72, 275
optimization for, 274–75
Pigovian taxation of, 270, 272, 277–79, 280, 284
profit functions of, 268, 271, 274–76
resistance management incentives for, 343–48, 350–51, 353–56
See also Biotechnology innovation; Industrial organization; Technological innovation
Fitness costs
of antibiotic resistance, 17–19, 20, 23–25, 26, 29, 77

optimal paths with and without, 30*f*, 31*f*
Functional forms
  induced evolution function, 304–5
  innovation, 317–18
  productivity measurement of pesticide use, 140
Fungicide Resistance Action Committee (FRAC), 348
Fungicides, 336, 337–38
Fungus invasion by *Bipolaris maydis* (U.S., 1970), 248–49

Game theory. *See* Contests; "Red Queen" contests (technological progress)
Gene flows, transgenic crops, 215–16
Genetic resistance
  as common property, 263–64, 266–67, 288–92
  externalities, 267–68
  history, 264–66
  model with abatement, 273–82
  monopoly effects, 279
  See also Resistance
Genetically modified organisms (GMOs)
  and ecosystem complexity, 158–60
  export market, 97
  lessons of pesticide economics, 137–39, 145–54
  resistance, 151–52, 184–86
  risk, 141–42, 145, 153–54, 158–60, 184–88, 191–203
  risk perception, 138–39, 148–49, 215
  See also Biotechnology; *Bt* crops; Resistance; Transgenic crops
Geographic information systems (GIS), 340
Geometric Brownian motion, 189, 190, 193–94, 221–22
Germany, case studies in economic pesticide resistance, 161–76
Global Crop Protection Federation (GCPF), 347, 348
GMOs. *See* Genetically modified organisms (GMOs)
Government intervention. *See* Regulation

Grids, *Bt* and non-*Bt* crops, 104–5
Gross margins, transgenic crops, 216–17, 219–20

Hamiltonian, 26, 36–37, 47–50, 51
Hand-washing by medical staff, as infection control, xiii, 6, 35
Hardy–Weinberg principle, 96, 100
Health services. *See* Antibiotics; Optimal treatment; Treatment (antibiotics)
Herbicide Resistance Action Committee (HRAC), 347–48
Herbicides vs. insecticides, cost increases, 181
Hessian fly, pest mobility, 114
Heterogeneity
  in pest resistance, 248–54
  of treatment (antibiotics), 65–68, 69–74
High dose strategies, pest control, 95–96, 187, 340
Highway congestion analogy, 85–87
Homogeneity, treatment (antibiotics), 9, 63–67, 73–74
Hospital-acquired infections, costs, 3–4
Human allergenicity, *Bt* crops, 212–13
Hurdle rates, release of transgenic crops, 225, 226–27

Imperfect competition, 289–90
Incentives, 176
  for developing new products, 2, 7–10
  for doctors and patients, 10, 65–66
  for farmers to minimize resistance, 11–12, 175–76, 330–43, 350–51
  to maximize value of existing products, 2, 4–7
  of patent systems, 293–95, 309–22, 330–31, 343–46, 350–51, 354–56
  for technological innovation, 293–95, 301, 311–16, 322
  See also Costs; Rents
Induced evolution function, 304–5
Industrial innovation. *See* Biotechnology innovation; Technological innovation
Industrial organization
  impact on antibiotic resistance management, 283

impact on genetic resistance
management, 263–64, 273–82,
288–92
impact on pest resistance
management, 330, 342–51,
353–60
market structure comparison, 273f,
281
theory, 298–99
See also Firms; Monopoly
Inequity. See Welfare effects
Infection control, xiii, 6, 35
Infection dynamics, 44–45
economic models, 26–30, 45–54,
55–61
epidemiological models, 21–25,
252–54, 256f
singular and optimal paths, 51–53
SIS model, 42–43
Information gathering. See Data
collection
Innovation, 244
and adaptive destruction, 304–5
and creative destruction, 302, 304
rates, 311–13, 318–22
See also Biological innovation;
Biotechnology innovation;
Contests; Technological
innovation
Insect release and recapture studies,
109–10, 115
Insecticide Resistance Action
Committee (IRAC), 347
Insecticides, vs. herbicides, cost
increases, 181
Institutions. See Regulation
Integrated pest management (IPM),
337–38
Intellectual property rights. See Patent
systems
Interdisciplinary communication
economists and biologists, 113, 115,
238–40, 247, 257
simulation models as aid to, 88–89
Interior solutions, optimal drug
combinations, 69–70
Intermediate goods sector, 299–303,
309–10

Internalization of externalities, 315,
318, 359–60
International Group of National
Associations of Manufacturers of
Agrochemical Products. See Global
Crop Protection Federation (GCPF)
Intrinsic value of option to release
transgenic crops, 219
Invasion, by pests, 248–56
Investments. See Allocation of resources;
Decisionmaking
Iowa, fertilizer use tax, 160
IPM. See Integrated pest management
(IPM)
Irreversibility
in benefit–cost analysis, 214–32, 242
pest resistance not inevitable, 248–49
in regulatory decisionmaking,
184–85, 188–90

Liberalization of markets and farm price
risk, 230
Life cycle of products, 345–46
Limitations of market models, 145–47
Linear control problems, 26–27, 36–41
Log-linear econometric models, growth
rate of pesticide use, 168–69
Logit models, 120–25, 127–29

Maize. See Bt crops; Corn
Manufacturers. See Firms
Marginal costs (MC), 343–45, 354–55
allocation to R&D, 308
in monopoly pricing, 278–79, 282,
283–85, 289–92
of pesticide resistance, 333
See also Costs
Marginal productivity, 274, 276–77,
279, 281, 290–92
Marginal revenues (MR), 271–72, 275,
279, 280, 343–45
Marginal social damage (MD). See
Welfare effects
Marker genes, in transgenic crops, 216
Market models, limitations, 145–47
Market penetration. See Market share
Market share
of antibiotics, 120–25, 129–30

of *Bt* crops, 94–110
Market structure. *See* Industrial
  organization; Monopoly
Markup, monopoly pricing, 278–79,
  281, 284
Marshallian optimality, 222–24
Mathematical disease models. *See*
  Epidemiological models
Mathematical methods applied to
  antibiotic use, 45–61
Maximal tolerable irreversible costs,
  225–29, 230–32, 242
Maximization strategies in crop
  protection, welfare effects, 167–72,
  175–76
Maximum likelihood estimation,
  antibiotic demand, 125, 129
Mean-reverting process, for modeling
  additional net benefits, 222, 244
Measurement
  of antibiotic resistance costs, 134–36
  of crop protection costs, 167–72
  of productivity with pesticide use,
    137, 139–40, 149–51, 167–68
Mechanical pest control practices, 338
Medical treatment. *See* Optimal
  treatment; Treatment (antibiotics)
Metapopulation. *See* Population
  dynamics
Methyl bromide, 341
Mixed multinomial estimates, 127–29
Mixed-policy of antibiotic use. *See*
  Antibiotics, heterogeneity of
  treatment
Mobility, European corn borer, 94–110
Models. *See specific types of models*
Monitoring pest populations, 337, 339–40
Monoculture and pest invasion, 248–49
Monopoly, 357–60
  bioengineered seeds, 263–64, 278–82,
    283–85, 288–92
  contracting over, 271–72, 279–80,
    282, 285
  control of inputs, 270–72
  externalities, 267–68
  health care, 283
  patent rights, 309–12, 316, 343–46,
    354–56

pricing, 288–92
  marginal costs (MC), 278–79, 282,
    283–85, 289–92
  markup, 278–79, 281, 284
  See also Industrial organization
Monsanto, 285, 347
Multinomial models, antibiotic
  demand, 122–23, 124–25, 127–29
Multipliers, precautionary. *See*
  Precautionary principle
Multipliers, user costs of drugs, 70
Myopic behavior. *See* Private vs. social
  costs

National Alliance of Independent Crop
  Consultants, 349
National Ambulatory Medical Care
  Survey (NAMCS), 125–27
Natural resources
  depletion from pesticide use, 142–45,
    158–60, 165, 168–76
  See also Resource economics
Net benefits (release of transgenic
  crops). *See* Additional net benefits
Net present value. *See* Present value (PV)
Nonrenewable resources. *See* Natural
  resources; Resource economics

Optimal allocation, 269–70
Optimal equilibrium. *See* Equilibrium
Optimal levels
  additional net benefits, 222, 224*f*,
    226–30, 235–36
  refuges, 107, 109
Optimal treatment
  antibiotic heterogeneity, 65–67,
    69–74
  benefit–cost analysis, 44–45, 80–82
  epidemiological vs. economic models,
    44, 79–80
  for managing antibiotic resistance,
    25, 26–30, 32–36, 39–41
  mathematical analysis, 45–61
  policy vs. implementation, 84–87
  See also Physicians; Treatment
    (antibiotics)
Optimality conditions, 220, 222–24,
  343–45, 356

See also Marshallian optimality
Optimization
    of antibiotic and pesticide use, 19–21
    for farmers, 332–35
    for firms, 274–75, 343–45, 354–56
    real options, 189–91
    software, 88–89
    of treatment cost parameters, 34
    of treatment regimes, 35–36
Option theory, 184–86, 188–91,
        192–203
    See also Rational options; Real options
Option value
    defined, xvi
    in release of transgenic crops, 217–24,
        230, 235–36, 240–43
Organic farming, impact of *Bt* crops on,
        xvi, 95, 186
Otitis media (ear infections), xv, 119–20,
        125–31
Own discount rate, 307–8, 310, 315

Parameters, benefit–cost analysis,
        transgenic crops, 244, 246*t*
Patch size and pest invasion, 253
    See also Farm size; Field size
Patent systems, xvii, 7–9, 288, 354–56,
        358–60
    incentives of, 293–95, 309–22,
        330–31, 343–46, 350–51
    See also Industrial organization;
        Resistance management
Path dependence, chemical pesticides,
        142–43
Pathogens. *See* Bacteria; Pests
Patients. *See* Children; Optimal
        treatment; Treatment (antibiotics)
Penicillin resistance, 120
Perception of GMO risk, 138–39,
        148–49, 215
Persistence (pest invasion), 248–49, 254
Pest control costs. *See* Costs, of crop
        protection
Pest refuges. *See* Refuges
Pest susceptibility to pesticides. *See*
        Susceptible vs. resistant pests
Pesticides, 184–86
    efficacy, 101, 105–8

vs. fertilizer, expense ratios, 168–71
interaction with natural resources,
        142–45, 158–60, 165, 168–76
measurement of productivity with
        pesticide use, 137, 139–40,
        149–51, 167–68
regulation, 95, 159–60, 174–76,
        341–43
and risk reduction, 141–42
Pests
    alleles, 105–8, 187
    control alternatives, 337–41
    mobility, 94–110, 113–15, 338–39
        simulation models, 100–105
    resistance
        as biological innovation, 293,
            295–300
        in *Bt* corn, 186–88, 194–99
        economic studies, transgenic crops,
            240–47
        epidemiological perspective,
            238–40, 247–57
        farm-level factors, 336–41
        as irreversible cost, 215–18
        regulatory factors, 341–43, 359–60
        resource economics applied to,
            161–76, 331–32, 340
        as stock variable, 332–35, 338–39
        See also Genetic resistance;
            Resistance
Pharmaceutical industry, 295–96, 298
Phase space diagrams, 23–25, 28*f*, 29,
        33*f*
Physicians
    choice of treatment, 63–67, 73–74,
        119–31
    enforcing policy, 87
    See also Treatment (antibiotics)
Pierce's disease, 341
Pigovian taxation, 270, 272, 277–79,
        280, 284
Planning, time horizons, 197–99
Plant breeding, 296, 298, 299–300
Poisson processes
    frequency of innovation, 302, 304
    pest resistance, 195–96
    selection pressure, 304–5
Policy design, 225–27, 242–43

application of economic principles to, xvii–xviii, 1–12
and benefit–cost analysis of transgenic crops, 226–30, 242–43
and optimal treatment, 84–87, 91–92
and resource conservation, 175–76
See also Decisionmaking; Regulation
Pontryagin optimality, 26, 37–38, 88
Population dynamics of pests, 100–108, 239, 248–49, 252–57, 332–35, 336–39
Precautionary principle, 150–54, 190–91, 242
defined, 185
multipliers, 193–96, 202
Precision technologies for pest control, 339–40
Preference for antibiotics. *See* Demand, for antibiotics
Prescriptions. *See* Physicians
Prescriptive use of GMOs, 159
Present value (PV), 79–80
in allocation of resources, 307
equation derivation, 325–26
benefit–cost analysis, 188–90
Bt and non-*Bt* crops, 105, 193–96, 200–203
of costs of resistance, 174
"Crystal Ball" simulations, 211–13
option theory, 193–96, 197–99
Prices, antibiotics, 120, 124, 126–29
Pricing, monopoly. *See* Monopoly, pricing
Private vs. social costs
incentives, 2, 309–19, 321–22, 333–35, 343–48, 350–51
of medical treatment, 66–67, 68–69, 73–74, 87, 88
pesticide resistance, 162–64, 167–72, 174–75, 288–92, 331
See also Externalities; Welfare effects
Probability density, pest resistance, 195–96
Probability distribution, innovation and adaptation, 306
Producer optimization, 274–75
Producer surplus. *See* Surplus

Product life cycle and firm incentives, 345–46
Production (final goods) sector, 299–304, 306–8
Production functions, 139–40, 142–44, 300–301
Production inputs, 268–73
bioengineered *Bt* corn seeds, 273–82
Production vs. reserves, allocation of resources, 293–95, 307–11
Productivity
and technological progress, 305
See also Factor productivity; Marginal productivity; Welfare effects
Productivity measurement
and GMOs, 147–48, 149–51
modeling of crop yields and prices, 221
with pesticide use, 137, 139–40, 142–45, 167–68
Profit functions, 268, 271, 274–76
Prospect theory, 141
PV. *See* Present value (PV)
Pyrethroids, 331, 346

R&D (research and development), 295–96, 298–304, 306–7, 309–19, 346–48
Random-effect regression models, determinants of pesticide use, 169–72
Random numbers, pesticide resistance, 100–101
Random-parameters multinomial logit models, 124–25
Rate of innovation. *See* Contests; Innovation
Rate of return, release of transgenic crops, 227f, 228, 229f
Rational options, 189, 190–91
and transgenic crop policy, 196–99, 241f
with uncertainty variables, equations, 207–10
See also Option theory
Real options, 188–90
and transgenic crop policy, 193–96, 217–18, 222–23, 231–32, 241f

with uncertainty variables, equations, 206–7
See also Option theory
"Red Queen" contests (technological progress), 296, 298, 307, 358
Reference systems, for GMO benefits, 138, 147, 148, 149, 154
Refuges, 94–110, 187, 212
optimal levels, 107, 109
as production input in model, 274–82
regulatory policy, xiv–xv, xvi, 11–12, 94–97, 110, 229–30
See also Abatement; Reserves (biological)
Regression analysis, determinants of pesticide use, 169–72
Regulation
GMOs, 184–86, 191–203
pest control, 95, 174–76, 334–35, 359–60
See also Policy design
Renewable resources. *See* Natural resources; Resource economics
Rents
impact of market structure, 270–71, 280, 283–85, 288–92
innovation incentives, 299, 310–12, 316–17
See also Incentives
Research and development. *See* R&D (research and development)
Reserves (biological), 295–96, 298, 302–3, 311–14, 316–21
See also Conservation of resources and decisionmaking; Refuges; Sustainability
Resistance
as biological innovation, 293–300, 304–5, 308–9, 311–13, 317–19, 321–22
as depreciation, 195–96
time for the appearance of, 297*t*
See also Adaptation (biological); Antibiotics, resistance; Genetic resistance; Genetically modified organisms (GMOs), resistance; Pests, resistance; Resistance management

Resistance management, 175–76, 244
Bt crops, 94–110
Crop rotation, 113–15, 172–75, 338–39
economic strategies, 152–53, 161–76, 180–82
farmer optimization, 332–35
impact of industrial organization, 263–64, 273–82, 288–92, 330, 342–51, 353–60
antibiotic resistance, 283
incentives in biotechnology, 293–95, 311–14, 343–48, 350–51, 353–56
pest control alternatives, 337–41
time horizons, in planning, 197–99
See also Patent systems
Resource economics
applied to antibiotic resistance, 18–19, 21, 29, 30–32, 43–44
applied to pest resistance, 161–76, 266–85, 331–32, 340
See also Economics; Natural resources
Resources, conservation, and decisionmaking, 163–67, 175–76
Resources, degradation. *See* Natural resources, depletion from pesticide use
Revenue curves, fertilizer and pesticide use, 143–44
Rhizomania (disease) spread (U.K.), 249–52
Risk, 186
and decentralized decisionmaking, 66
of GMOs, 141–42, 145, 153–54, 158–60, 184–88, 191–203
See also Externalities; Welfare effects
Risk-free rate of return, release of transgenic crops, 228, 230
Risk neutrality, 190–91, 197–99, 243
Risk perception of GMOs, 138–39, 148–49, 215
Risk reduction in pest control, 141–42
Rotation of crops, 113–15, 172–75, 338–39

Saddle point, social value of reducing infection, 50–51
Selection bias. *See* Bias

Selection, pest resistance, 1–2, 295–96, 304–5
Sensitivity analysis, limitations for GMO benefit calculations, 154
Set-aside policies. *See* Refuges
Shadow prices, 26, 48–49, 53–54, 150, 344–45, 354–56
Shocks, European corn borer, 100–101, 193–96
Showers experiment, pest mobility, 109–10, 115
Side-effects. *See* Externalities
Simulation models
 for interdisciplinary communication, 88–89
 of pest mobility, 100–105
 of treatment policy changes, 90
"Single supplier" effect (biotechnology innovation), 314, 316
Singular path, infection, 51, 52–53
SIS (susceptibleÆinfectedÆsusceptible) model, 21, 42–43, 77–81
Size
 of farms, 334, 336, 349
 of fields, 166–67
 patch size, 253
Social costs. *See* Externalities; Present value (PV); Private vs. social costs; Welfare effects
Social discount rate. *See* Discounting
Software for optimization, 88–89
Southern corn leaf blight (U.S., 1970), 248–49
Spatial grids, *Bt* and non-*Bt* crops, 104–5
Spatial heterogeneity in pest resistance, 248–54
Stabilization (biological resources). *See* Reserves (biological); Sustainability
StarLink (*Bt* strain), 212–13
State equations, for optimal treatment rate, 38–41
Static analysis, 84–87, 191–92
 See also Comparative statics
Steady state
 antibiotic use, 46–47
 level of infection, 50–53
 pest resistance, 195–96
 stock of antibiotic resistance, 29

stock of infected individuals, 23–25
Stochastic processes
 Bt corn, 194–95, 198–99
 deterministic vs. stochastic models, 254–57
 European corn borer populations, 100–101
 net benefits of transgenic crops, 220–21
 pest invasion and persistence, 248–49
 simulation models, 138, 152–54
Structure (industrial). *See* Industrial organization
Substitution of inputs, 277, 278–79
Surplus, 280
 biotechnology innovation, 145, 147, 191–93, 201*t*
 U.S. corn production, 211
Surveys, ear infection diagnosis and treatment, 125–27
Susceptible bacteria. *See* Bacteria; SIS (susceptibleÆinfectedÆsusceptible) model
Susceptible vs. resistant pests, 95–96, 216
 corn pests, 187
 Hessian fly, 114
 as a natural resource, 4–5, 100, 137, 142–45, 151
 German case studies, 161–76
 transgenic crops, 216, 230–32
 population dynamics, 100–108, 164–65, 248–49, 332–35, 336–39
Sustainability, 162, 293–95, 306–9, 321–22
 See also Reserves (biological)
Switching functions, 26–27, 37–41

Taxation
 of fertilizer, 160
 of pesticide use, 159–60, 341–42
 of transgenic crops, 230
Technological innovation
 and biological adaptation, 302, 304–8
 competition between industries, 294–95, 298–99
 GMOs and pesticides, 138–39
 incentives for, 293–95, 301, 311–16, 322

in R&D, 295–96, 298–300, 302, 304,
  307–19
See also Biological innovation;
  Biotechnology innovation; Firms
Technology, 319–20
  in crop protection, 165, 176, 191–92
  and productivity, 171, 305, 306–8
Temporal heterogeneity in pest
  resistance, 248
Time-attribute interactions, in antibiotic
  demand models, 124
Time horizons, in planning, 197–99
Timing
  of innovation, 302, 304
  of pesticide application, 337–38, 340
  release of transgenic crops, 214–15,
    219–22, 224–32
Tragedy of the commons. See Common
  property
Transgenic crops, 191–92, 214–15
  irreversible costs and benefits,
    215–29, 231–32
  methodological approach to
    benefit–cost analysis, 218–24,
    238–47
  policy impact on decision to release,
    226–30, 232, 242–43
  and uncertainty, 225–29, 240,
    242–44, 247, 249
See also Biotechnology; Bt crops;
  Genetically modified organisms
  (GMOs)
Treatment (antibiotics)
  costs, 34, 48–51, 69–72, 79–80,
    119–25, 130–31
    measurement, 134–36
    with multiple drug resistance, 43
    private vs. social optimum, 65–67
  See also Costs; Optimal treatment
  homogeneity, 9, 63–67, 73–74
  strategies, 21–25, 32–36

Uncertainty
  about benefits of resistance strategies,
    162

about GMOs, 138–39, 225–29, 240,
  242–44, 247, 249
  with options, equations, 206–7
  in regulation, 184–85, 187–203
U.S. Environmental Protection Agency
  (EPA), refuges, xiv–xv, xvi, 11–12,
  94–97, 110
User costs, resistance and treatment,
  70–71
Utility, antibiotic demand models,
  123–24, 129
Utility functions
  biotechnology innovation, 305–6
  gains vs. losses, 141

Valuation, public health, 79–80
Value. See Present value (PV)
Variables, benefit–cost analysis,
  transgenic crops, 243–44, 245t
Variance rate, release of transgenic
  crops, 226–28
Volatility, option theory, 193–96

Water pollution, from atrazine, 172,
  174–75
Weeds, 215–16
Welfare effects
  of biotechnology innovation, 294–95,
    305–9, 311–22
  marginal social damage (MD),
    269–70, 277–79, 281
  of market structure, 281–82, 283–85
  of maximization strategies in crop
    protection, 167–72, 175–76
  of pesticide resistance management,
    174–76, 182
  of transgenic crops, 191–92, 211–13,
    219–20
See also Externalities; Marginal social
  damage (MD); Present value
  (PV); Private vs. social costs; Risk
Wiener process, 221, 244

About the Editor

Ramanan Laxminarayan is a fellow at Resources for the Future. His research on resistance economics focuses on using economic analysis to develop policy responses to such problems as bacterial resistance to antibiotics and pest resistance to pesticides. He is currently a member of the National Academy of Sciences/Institute of Medicine Committee on The Economics of Antimalarial Drugs. He has worked with the World Health Organization on evaluating malaria treatment policy in Africa and was a member of the World Health Organization Task Force on Drug Resistance and Policies in 2000 and 2001.

His other research interests integrate environmental quality and public health. Current studies include an analysis of the household economic impact of tobacco use in Vietnam, and an examination of social and environmental factors that influence the spread of infectious diseases within households and villages in Cambodia.

Trained in both economics and public health, his research on the economics of resistance has appeared in the *Annals of Pharmacotherapy*, *Journal of Environmental Economics and Management*, *American Journal of Agricultural Economics*, and *Journal of Health Economics*.